D1595232

GROWING PAINS: TENSIONS AND OPPORTUNITY IN CHINA'S TRANSFORMATION

Edited by
Jean C. Oi, Scott Rozelle, and
Xueguang Zhou

THE WALTER H. SHORENSTEIN
ASIA-PACIFIC RESEARCH CENTER

THE WALTER H. SHORENSTEIN ASIA-PACIFIC RESEARCH CENTER (Shorenstein APARC) is a unique Stanford University institution focused on the interdisciplinary study of contemporary Asia. Shorenstein APARC's mission is to produce and publish outstanding interdisciplinary, Asia-Pacific–focused research; to educate students, scholars, and corporate and governmental affiliates; to promote constructive interaction to influence U.S. policy toward the Asia-Pacific; and to guide Asian nations on key issues of societal transition, development, U.S.-Asia relations, and regional cooperation.

The Walter H. Shorenstein Asia-Pacific Research Center
Freeman Spogli Institute for International Studies
Stanford University
Encina Hall
Stanford, CA 94305-6055
tel. 650-723-9741
fax 650-723-6530
http://APARC.stanford.edu

Growing Pains: Tensions and Opportunity in China's Transformation may be ordered from:
The Brookings Institution
c/o DFS, P.O. Box 50370, Baltimore, MD, USA
tel. 1-800-537-5487 or 410-516-6956
fax 410-516-6998
http://www.brookings.edu/press

First printing, 2010.
13-digit ISBN 978-1-931368-18-6

GROWING PAINS: TENSIONS AND OPPORTUNITY IN CHINA'S TRANSFORMATION

THE WALTER H. SHORENSTEIN
ASIA-PACIFIC RESEARCH CENTER

CONTENTS

PREFACE

B y now it is well recognized that China's great transformation in the past three decades is one of the epic episodes in contemporary world history, with far-reaching impacts that will be felt for years to come. The changes are widespread and profound, reshaping the country's socioeconomic and political landscapes. But they are also multifaceted, transient, and—often—conflicting. How do we interpret the state of reform in China? What challenges does China face? How might changes in China—both those that are underway and those that are on the horizon—play out in the months and years ahead?

To address these and related issues, the Stanford China Program (SCP) at the Walter H. Shorenstein Asia-Pacific Research Center (Shorenstein APARC) invited leading scholars from the United States, China, and Great Britain to a conference held at Stanford University, November 1–3, 2008. We used this occasion to celebrate the SCP's launch and to provide a public venue to discuss some of the key challenges to China's reforms. The SCP also held a well-attended public session on November 1 at Stanford's Bechtel Conference Center, which included a panel discussion by Scott Rozelle, Leonard Ortolano, and Melanie Manion, moderated by Andrew Walder. Detailed discussion of the papers took place at the workshop during the ensuing two days. This volume is the result of that conference and the papers, now considerably revised, presented there.

As we planned for the conference and subsequently prepared this book for publication, we repeatedly returned to the theme of a China in transition. Along with spectacular economic growth and societal changes, China has been experiencing extensive tensions, dislocations, and multifarious changes that are not always in sync with one another. We sensed that these are part of the "growing pains" that Chinese society must confront as it gradually transforms itself. Thus, "Growing Pains: Changes and Challenges in China's Transformation" became the theme of the conference and of the volume that resulted.

In addition to those who contributed to this book, several scholars—Jennifer Adams, Hongbin Li, Ching Kkwan Lee, Liu Yaling, and Melanie Manion—participated in the conference and presented their work. We thank them for their contributions to the event and for their commentary during the proceedings. We also acknowledge our doctoral student rapporteurs, Chris Chan and Xiaojun Li, for a masterful job taking notes on the conference.

The SCP at Shorenstein APARC and the Center for East Asian Studies cosponsored the conference. We thank Shorenstein APARC for hosting the event, providing both facilities and staffing. Professor Gi-Wook Shin, the Center director, supported our efforts fully and gave opening remarks at the gathering. Daniel Sneider, the associate director for research at Shorenstein APARC, was a driving force in initiating the conference and the ensuing book, and helped us at many stages of the process. The staff members of the Center, especially Neeley Main and Denise Chu, ably assisted in handling conference logistics. Michael Armacost, our colleague at Shorenstein APARC and the editor of the Brookings Institution Press series of which this book is a part, kindly handled review of the manuscript. Victoria Tomkinson, Shorenstein APARC's publications manager, did a superb editorial job on the chapters to create this volume, with additional copyediting and indexing help from Fayre Makeig and Diane Brenner.

Xueguang Zhou, Jean C. Oi, and Scott Rozelle

INTRODUCTION

Irresolvable Contradictions or Growing Pains? Perspectives on China's Challenges

Andrew G. Walder

There is often a metaphysical quality to contemporary discussions of China's reforms. Such commentaries usually boil down to generalizations, which allegedly reflect either established theories or the conclusions of past research. Analysis then proceeds with certain abstract claims about the essential nature of a planned economy and a Leninist political system, which contrast with similarly abstract claims about the essential nature of a competitive market economy or a multiparty political system. These abstract features, each with its own separate "logic," are seen to be in conflict, and they generate contradictions that are inherently irresolvable. Accordingly, problems that arise in the course of China's economic transformation are interpreted as expressions of these logical contradictions; they are "tensions" inevitably created by the task of holding together a single-party dictatorship, even as its traditional foundations in a planned economy are washed away.

When serious policy challenges confront China's leaders in the course of their reforms, this kind of abstract analysis tends to interpret problems as potential crises. Because the problems embody logical contradictions in the Chinese Communist Party's (CCP's) strategy of gradual market reform under a single party dictatorship, they threaten the entire reform strategy. And because they express contradictions that are fundamental, there is no easy way out. Even short-term fixes, if they can be found, only delay the inevitable showdown. China's leaders are trapped within the political limits that they place on the reform process, making it much more difficult to move forward than would otherwise be the case.

Analysts of China's reforms have offered several different versions of this type of thinking over the past three decades. At first, there was deep skepticism about the ability of a Leninist dictatorship to even embark on fundamental market reform. The past history of limited reform in Hungary and the Soviet Union was a case in point. When China began its own reforms, many commentators were certain that its leaders would balk at implementing the changes needed to free the economy from the shackles of central planning. To do so was impossible, the thinking went, because such change would threaten the leaders' political power. However, as it became obvious that China's leaders did indeed possess the political will to proceed with reforms far beyond what was ever observed under other Communist regimes, the argument shifted. Now, analysts claimed, a Leninist political system could try to reform, but the reforms could not be successful. A Leninist system must, by nature, control economic decisions and resources; officials would therefore intervene excessively, and the economy would languish. Simply put, it was widely assumed that gradual reform under Communist-party rule was bound to stall. And if it did not, a single-party dictatorship in an emerging market economy would be unable to constrain its officials from becoming corrupt predators, choking off economic growth.[1]

As China's economy took off in the late 1980s and early 1990s, yet another version of this argument appeared. It was now conceded that China's reforms had reaped early successes by beginning with the easy tasks: shifting to household agriculture and permitting family businesses and small village enterprises to flourish. But such a strategy only postponed the far more difficult task of reforming the grossly inefficient state sector, which required laying off tens of millions of urban workers who expected lifetime employment. Surely the CCP, mindful of the role Solidarity played in the downfall of Polish Communism, would not dare to touch this sacred cow. If it did so, the inevitable wave of protests would surely imperil the regime.[2]

After the mid-1990s, China's leaders once again defied predictions by restructuring and downsizing the country's urban state firms with a vengeance, radically reducing state employment, and either closing or privatizing most small- and medium-sized enterprises. This much smaller state sector—after restructuring, downsizing, partial privatization, and other policy changes—was transformed from an unprofitable and backward mass of enterprises to a smaller group of more competitive and increasingly profitable corporations that began to make an impact on world markets.[3]

Today, outdated modes of analyzing China's reforms are still with us, even though, for several decades, the country has overcome reputedly insurmountable contradictions and avoided the inevitable crises that these steps were supposed to create. Now, we are sometimes told, China's reforms have *finally* reached a cul-de-sac. They cannot move forward any further. Is this really the case?

To be sure, China faces serious problems. These include the rising levels of protest that have accompanied the country's wrenching structural changes, intensifying corruption that some observers claim has turned the Chinese government into a "predatory state," the inability or unwillingness of co-opted private businessmen to push for democratic change, and the continuing lack of legal reform and abuse of individual rights. Collectively, such obstacles seem to present us with a China that is in a so-called trapped transition. Corruption and arbitrary rule, it is said, will come to threaten economic prosperity, while the impetus toward the democratic reforms essential for any lasting solution has been lost. Try as it might, China cannot escape the inherently logical contradiction of moving to a market economy within the framework of single-party rule. In the end, China's transition remains trapped by the fundamental contradictions between market liberalization and single-party dictatorship.[4]

There is nothing inherently wrong with having a broad conceptual framework within which to interpret China's path of reform. But there are problems with a perspective that, seemingly by default, interprets serious policy problems as irresolvable logical contradictions that threaten to derail or stall the entire reform process. Metaphysical assumptions have a consistently poor record of predicting either the policies pursued by China's leaders or their level of success or failure. Perhaps the logical contradictions that so many observers claim to see are between abstract concepts that exist primarily on paper and the more complex empirical reality of Chinese political and economic institutions. Serious policy dilemmas are not necessarily symptoms of irresolvable systemic contradictions. They may be nothing more than difficult policy problems for which solutions may or may not be found.

This volume seeks to push for a more analytic and empirical focus on the serious challenges facing China's reforms, and to develop a set of claims that are based less on metaphysics and more on sustained research and evidence. Some of the widely discussed problems that are thought to threaten China's reforms are in fact not as serious as many interpreters claim—and some have already been solved. Some widely noted problems truly are serious, and still others may loom on the horizon. The authors of this volume have all been asked to look at crucial problem areas in China's reforms, to examine the evidence of the problems' actual severity, and to assess the likelihood of near-term solutions. We seek to present a view that is not more or less optimistic than that commonly derived from metaphysical frameworks; we aim instead to develop a more *accurate* perspective. Which widely noted problems that plague China's reforms are in fact serious, or will become more serious with time? Which are less serious or will become less serious with time? And which are well on the way to being solved—or have already been solved—unbeknownst to many commentators?

Privatization and Marketization

The first section of this book contains four chapters on privatization and the creation of competitive markets. The first chapter, by Jean C. Oi, analyzes political constraints on the restructuring of state enterprises, and the methods by which these enterprises were steadily downsized and converted to other ownership forms between 1995 and 2005. Such downsizing and conversion were once viewed as the most irreconcilable contradiction in China's entire reform program. Chinese leaders, it was thought, could not possibly gather the political will to downsize the massive state sector. Even if they did so, it was a virtually impossible task, widely believed to be an intractable and insurmountable problem, both politically and economically. In 1998 the state sector was still bloated and inefficient, employing 122 million and losing money. But by 2006 the sector had been downsized to employ 76 million, and the number of firms still owned and controlled by the state had been reduced by two-thirds. Most notably, this reduced and reorganized sector was beginning to turn a profit.[5]

Oi begins by trying to reconcile two starkly different views about state enterprise reform. On the one hand, some observers have criticized reformers for being too slow and hesitant, avoiding the most difficult phases and delaying the inevitable, to the detriment of the program as a whole. On the other hand, many have argued that, once the reform process was underway, reformers moved too fast, laid off too many workers, and permitted managers to strip state assets. Oi shows how these conflicting views imposed political constraints—leaders felt impelled to push reforms through but simultaneously sought to avoid the political and social backlash that might imperil the entire process.

One particular kind of reform—corporate restructuring—was phased in gradually and deliberately, precisely to avoid these political problems. It took different forms, and the process was primarily pushed forward by the state itself. The least disruptive reforms were introduced first, and only later were the more challenging forms of privatization implemented. In the 1990s, privatization and bankruptcy were limited, while conversion to shareholding companies was relatively common. In the next decade, privatization and plant closures increased. The impact on workers was initially kept to a minimum. Before 2000 the majority of state-owned firms that restructured made every effort to keep all of their workers; those that did lay off workers had to pay sufficient compensation packages to resettle those who had lost their jobs. After 2000, however, firms were no longer required to keep all or even most of their employees and layoffs became much more common. Initially, and only rarely, managers obtained controlling shares of restructured firms, but this practice changed over time. A survey that Oi conducted in 2000 showed that slightly more that 4 percent of managers were the controlling shareholder, but by 2004 managers controlled more than half the restructured firms in her sample.

Overall, Oi describes a cautious process of restructuring and downsizing that was outwardly modest. Reformers eschewed the politically charged term *privatization* in favor of neutral terms, such as *shareholder cooperatives* and *joint stock companies*. But once these reforms were begun, they were carried out steadily. Thousands of China's state-owned enterprises (SOEs) have disappeared—some were closed down in bankruptcies, but the majority have been sold, converted to other ownership forms, or merged into larger new state-owned corporations, some of which are listed on stock markets. As of this writing, only 153 state-owned corporations are under the central government's control. Some of them have become very profitable in recent years and are even beginning to compete on world markets. The reform of the state-owned sector is by no means complete, but it is hard to avoid the conclusion that a problem that once seemed insurmountable has been reduced to manageable proportions.

The remaining three chapters in the first section describe how the state has withdrawn from an active role in allocating labor, food, and land. In chapter 2, Albert Park, Fang Cai, and Yang Du address three debates involving employment and labor markets. The first debate concerns the severity of the unemployment that the radical downsizing of the state industrial sector has created in Chinese cities. In recent years, they note, many have argued that unemployment has reached crisis levels, and that jobs are scarce for former state-sector workers, rural laborers from the interior, and even recent college graduates. Others, they note, have claimed that unemployment is actually relatively low and job creation robust. Marshaling an array of recent survey data, Park et al. show that while reemployment can be difficult for certain segments of the laid-off urban workforce, urban unemployment is modest by internationally accepted definitions, and has been falling in recent years. Job creation overall is healthy, and labor markets appear to be working. Future job creation will remain a challenge, and will depend on continued robust economic growth.

Park et al. also discuss a second debate: whether recently reported labor shortages and rising wages for unskilled workers in southern China and elsewhere are temporary phenomena that will subside when more workers arrive from the countryside, or whether China has reached a turning point where surplus labor is exhausted and real wages begin to rise. Park et al. find that rural wages are increasing and that many of the prime age cohorts (from 20 to 40) have high levels of off-farm employment, indicating that such employment is widely available, even for women. Some of the toughest remaining problems come from the demand rather than the supply side, and threaten industries that rely heavily on low-wage labor. However, Park et al. counter that labor productivity has so far risen even faster than wages, which means that off-farm industries have so far been able to compensate for rising labor costs. Somewhat ironically, the real challenge will come in future decades, when the size of age cohorts entering the labor force will drop dramatically and China will face a labor shortage.

Finally, Park et al. consider a third issue. Can China provide adequate social insurance for workers who are increasingly exposed to the risks and uncertainties of the market, as well as other unforeseen events such as illness? Here the authors find much less cause for optimism. The current social security system is broken, and currently proposed solutions are ambitious but suffer from obvious shortcomings. In sum, China is generating sufficient jobs to employ its workers, and is mobilizing enough labor-force entrants to remain internationally competitive. Even so, China has yet to establish the social insurance programs required to maintain a healthy, functioning labor market and to ensure adequate protections for its citizens' welfare. Increases in labor productivity and a shift toward production of higher-value-added items must continue, Park et al. find, if China is to enjoy improved living standards and remain globally competitive. Both are also necessary for China to be able to finance a well-functioning social insurance system in the future.

In chapter 3, Scott Rozelle and Jikun Huang look at efforts to create integrated, efficient, and competitive markets for agricultural commodities. They describe how reform policies have shifted between periods of liberalization and retrenchment over the past three decades, creating not only a great deal of confusion about the subject but also a widely held perception that China's agricultural policies remain highly restrictive. Rozelle and Huang argue that in fact there is now very little government interference in the operation of China's domestic or international markets, especially compared to the rest of the world. They point out, for example, that the state procurement system no longer exists, almost all output is procured and produced by private firms, almost all inputs are likewise marketed by private firms, there are millions of trading firms with few regulatory barriers, there are almost no cross-province barriers, and China's international tariff schedules are among the lowest in the world (less restrictive than Japan or Europe).

According to the authors, this surprising record of deregulation has created remarkably well-integrated, efficient, and competitive agricultural markets, which have demonstrably positive effects on the sector's general efficiency, productivity, and equity. As a result, in a country where there are ten million or more largely small traders buying from and selling to nearly two hundred million agricultural producers, competition drives traders to seek farmers who have the lowest production costs. This means that traders will go to remote and poor locations to procure crops and that poorer farmers are drawn into production for expanding and lucrative markets for agricultural products. Given this scenario, Rozelle and Huang assert that China's next challenge will be the likely temptation to return to greater regulation in the face of inflation or other policy imperatives. Moreover, the vast amalgam of small trading networks and informal marketing channels that produce current high levels of integration and efficiency also makes it more difficult to create institutions that can ensure food safety.

Another challenge that rural markets face is the issue of property rights over agricultural land. Linxiu Zhang, Songqing Jin, Scott Rozelle, Klaus Deininger, and Jikun Huang address this key issue in chapter 4. On the one hand, managing China's cultivated land has been a major success. With free labor and commodity markets, the key resource of farmland needs to be flexibly allocated to permit farmers to respond to new opportunities. Over the past three decades, the restrictions against land rentals have fallen sharply. In the 1980s, less than 2 percent of China's cultivated land was rented, but by the current decade the figure was above 10 percent. In Zhejiang Province, which enjoys the highest level of rural income, nearly 30 percent of cultivated land is now rented—a level comparable to market economies like the United States.

Zhang and her coauthors also assess the market traits, institutional features, and other entry barriers that either facilitate or prevent cultivated land markets from operating properly. They find that households with limited endowments of land and capital *can* gain access to land through rental markets, whereas those with higher levels of capital but lower ability and land endowment tend to establish nonfarm enterprises. Higher levels of out-migration also increase the number of land transactions, suggesting that rural farm and nonfarm development are linked by a positive feedback loop. In short, rental markets for cultivated land promote both efficiency and equity.

However, Zhang and her coauthors point out major remaining challenges in the security of land tenure. China has made little progress in shifting from a system based on collective ownership to one that provides enforceable rights. This lack of progress is not inadvertent: until very recently, it was not politically feasible to begin a debate about how to move to a system of private property rights over agricultural land. The authors do not believe that such a change will present a problem in the immediate future, and they admit that knowledge is meager about the costs of the current land-tenure system. Nevertheless, many believe that the move toward private property in land would be useful in the long run—both to help farmers finance their moves to the city as China urbanizes and to enable the country to insure itself against catastrophic illnesses and other large expenditures. Until recently this was not even open for discussion. The current policy keeps many rural families tied to the land, preventing them from moving to the cities, and it has associated costs that will rise as urbanization and industrialization proceed.

Overall, the chapters in this section outline changes that have been remarkably thorough and in many respects surprisingly successful. The downsizing and restructuring of the massive state sector—once dubbed a virtually impossible task—has been largely completed, in a cautious but steady manner. Moreover, restructuring has occurred without the catastrophic collapse of employment and welfare that most transitional economies in post-Communist regimes initially experienced. Relatively unregulated and robust markets for labor and agricultural commodities have finally emerged, and despite remaining restrictions on the privatization of land, land-rental markets that allow farmers a flexible response to market opportunities have emerged.

Major challenges still loom, of course, and many of them will require the state to play a heightened role: the creation of national welfare and national food safety systems, and the establishment of private property rights in land. There has been little progress in these areas, but none of these remaining problems expresses irreconcilable contradictions in China's chosen path of reform. These are challenges of economic development and institution building—growing pains that are by no means characteristic of only reforming socialist economies.

Governance

The second section of the book contains four chapters that address problems of governance. In chapter 5, Andrew Wedeman tackles the general issue of corruption, and in particular recent claims that corruption has intensified in China to the point that it threatens the integrity of the government and the future of the reform program. Wedeman emphasizes that while China suffers from widely recognized problems of official corruption, it does not rank as one of the most corrupt countries in the world. In 2006 it ranked near the middle of international indices of corruption, and the World Bank's governance index also places China near the middle of the pack. Wedeman argues that corruption clearly spread in the 1980s and intensified in the 1990s as market reforms proceeded, evidently a problem caused by reforming a socialist planned economy in a piecemeal fashion. He points out that many of the institutions for monitoring and dealing with corruption either had to be resurrected or constructed from scratch after the Cultural Revolution. However, the regime began rebuilding its monitoring capacity, launching several major anticorruption campaigns, and has poured resources into the effort almost continuously. Wedeman adds that it is hard to judge the overall effectiveness of these actions. The numbers that various authors cite as evidence of ineffective enforcement, he notes, are often incomplete and difficult to decipher. Despite the use of tactics and sentencing practices that are more draconian than in countries such as the United States, the most reasonable conclusion from available evidence is that China's anticorruption efforts have reached something of a stalemate. Corruption is a continuing challenge to the regime, but it is not an inherently irresolvable problem, nor are there grounds for concluding that it has intensified to crisis proportions. In short, the jury is still out.

In her chapter on village elections, Lily L. Tsai provides a national overview of the progress of implementing village elections—a phenomenon that has garnered considerable attention in recent years, though assessments have varied greatly. How common are these elections nationwide? Are they limited to a few model localities, or have they been deeply implemented? How effective have village elections been in ensuring regular turnover of officials in response to voter preferences? How competitive have these elections been, and have they been conducted fairly? How do rural residents view the elections?

In Tsai's view, her data justify "cautious optimism." Village elections have spread gradually over the fifteen years, but they are now widespread. The number of villages with elected rather than appointed leaders has increased considerably, and progressively larger percentages of villages have held elections with more than one candidate. The vast majority of villages have implemented the election procedures required by the revised Organic Law, and some villages have implemented additional election institutions such as fixed polling stations, which the law does not require. As a result, the turnover of village leaders has become more formalized and standardized. Instead of removing and installing village leaders at will, more and more township governments are constrained by the formal election process. Fewer village leaders are removed in the middle of an election term. Today, more village leaders leave office because they run for reelection and fail to get reelected, or because they finish their term and make a deliberate decision not to run again. Tsai sees this as a sign that village elections are becoming institutionalized. The period of the highest incidence of resignation or firing, which she interprets as an indication of higher-level intervention, was in the mid-1990s. Since then, better election implementation has apparently made citizens more interested and engaged in the election process. Villages in which election procedures are well run are more likely to have villagers who report that elections are "lively" and that people are excited about them.

At the same time, critical weak spots remain. Few villages have regulated proxy voting, which can easily be manipulated by individuals who vote on behalf of absent family members or pressure them to vote in certain ways. Even though most villages report that the upper levels do not interfere actively when villagers nominate candidates, most villages also report that the final slate of nominees is still subject to higher-level vetting. While corruption in the election process is a serious problem in some localities, it by no means represents a general pattern. Instead, these reports should be viewed as a way to pressure the state to continue grassroots political reforms. Elections are implemented most quickly and thoroughly when required by law, and especially when mandated by the central government. In areas where the central government has not explicitly specified what local governments are supposed to do, township officials often continue to intervene, particularly in the selection of candidates. One important example is the specified number of candidates. When there are specific central-level regulations requiring more candidates than seats, multicandidate elections are more frequent. However, when central regulations do not specify key details, there is more room for manipulation and corruption. This indicates that top-down enforcement is essential to grassroots democratization and that bottom-up initiative varies widely across localities. Perhaps the biggest barrier to grassroots democratization, Tsai concludes, is not central government capacity but the political will to implement procedural democracy more comprehensively at the grassroots level.

In chapter 7, Xueguang Zhou provides an ethnographic perspective on village elections that complements Tsai's survey-based analysis. Zhou describes a process in which the township government, increasingly stripped of its economic powers by recent economic reforms, gradually withdraws from active manipulation of leadership elections and increasingly relies on procedural fairness as a way to limit the conflict and instability that can appear during closely fought elections. Zhou also describes genuinely competitive contests in recent years—with high voter turnout and the serious concern of candidates over uncertain outcomes—that contrast sharply with earlier ritualistic elections.

Zhou argues that a quiet shift is taking place in the bases of local government legitimacy, creating for the first time a reservoir of legitimacy and power for village heads. Such legitimacy appears in sharp relief against the top-down authority of village party secretaries, who represent not the citizens but the higher levels of the party apparatus. Zhou suggests that this is a subtle breakthrough in rural governance that may have a more obvious and profound impact in future years—as he puts it, preparing "the battleground between the ruling party and the villagers, and between the township government and village leaders." In sum, he describes a shift in village governance that is not fully visible in Tsai's analysis, but is highly compatible with her overall conclusions. Again, we see that regulations and law are beginning to play a more important role. Townships have gone from manipulating the outcome of village elections to ensuring that the election process is fair. For Zhou, these profound changes will likely become "a major launching pad for China's political change" in future years. By this he means that unhinging village power structures from the state administration will not only reduce the potential for collective action in the villages and decentralize political pressures and risks, but also encourage future political reform in other arenas, especially in the urban areas.

In his chapter on the enforcement of rural fertility restrictions, Ethan Michelson describes a draconian program that affected vast proportions of China's rural population. It consumed enormous amounts of rural governments' time and resources, and for more than two decades, generated widespread disputes and considerable dissatisfaction with rural governments themselves. Michelson carefully examines evidence about the prevalence of disputes and their variation across regions and time periods, and concludes that the worst phase of conflict over these policies has now passed. He posits further that they will continue to diminish over time. He marshals impressive data to show that economic development, which reduces rural fertility, also diminishes the number of family planning disputes. This, he argues, will reduce overall levels of discontent with village government. He suggests that family planning conflict "will prove to be a growing pain," and may largely disappear with continued rural development and future policy changes. The more important general point is that the reduction of conflict over family planning will likely ease overall levels of dissatisfaction and political conflict in rural areas.

Public Goods Provision and Citizen Response

In the book's third and final section, three chapters address public goods provision and citizen response—with a focus on health care, environmental protection, and distributive justice, and the formidable challenges that China faces in these arenas. In chapter 9, Karen Eggleston focuses on health care and the provision of public health services. She argues that the reform of China's health-care system has lagged behind other areas of economic reform. The former system of public health has collapsed and the medical service infrastructure has deteriorated. Eggleston notes that effective reform will require that the distorted incentives embedded in the current system, which arose early in the reform era, be restructured. Following the success of dual-track reforms in other sectors, Chinese policymakers instituted policies intended to protect a "plan track" of access to basic health care for even the poorest patients, while allowing a "market track" of providers to allocate new, high-tech, discretionary services according to patient ability to pay and provider profit margins over regulated prices. The plan for basic access was neither defined nor protected in terms of risk pooling. When financing for health care largely collapsed—because it was linked to agricultural communes and soft budget constraints for SOEs—little was put in its place. Only in the early years of the current decade, thirty years into China's reforms, did the SARS crisis and other issues force policymakers to reassess the problems in China's health-care system as a whole. In Eggleston's view, these problems still beg solutions.

Leonard Ortolano describes challenges that are even more staggering in his chapter on environmental protection. Rapid economic growth and urbanization have generated an alarming trend of environment degradation. Ortolano demonstrates the extent of China's environmental degradation and discusses the bureaucratic response. He argues that the conflicting goals of economic growth and environmental protection, poor incentive design in the Chinese bureaucracy, and the environmental protection agencies' administrative dependence on local authorities all lead to ineffective regulation. As Ortolano looks to the future, he asserts that recent policies should improve the effectiveness of environmental protection, but the strong forces pushing for economic growth and expanding urbanization will more likely overwhelm these efforts for years to come. Both Eggleston and Ortolano describe a government bureaucracy ill-equipped to address serious problems effectively. Both fault the administrative capacity of the Chinese public sector, in which incentives are distorted, goals are in conflict, and policy implementation is ineffective. One concludes from their chapters that the process of building an effective administrative structure may be more challenging than creating markets that operate effectively.

Martin K. Whyte's chapter presents something of a contrast, and its conclusions are surprising in light of heightened attention to rising inequality and social tensions in China in recent years. In his national survey of public opinion on inequality and distributive justice, Whyte confirmed that although a majority of the Chinese population sees excessive overall income inequality, few observe excessive levels of inequality in their immediate work units or neighborhoods. Respondents clearly perceived increasing disparities in income and opportunity between rich and poor, as well as the lack of a social safety net for the most disadvantaged. They were remarkably tolerant, however, of market-based incentives and market-induced income differences. Whyte attributes this tolerance to rapid overall improvements in living standards that lend legitimacy to China's present course of market reform. He concludes, against the grain of much recent commentary on China's reforms, that rising inequality is offset by an open mobility structure that China's urban citizens still view as substantially fair. Ongoing debates, he says, "should be regarded as another manifestation of the 'growing pains' precipitated by market reforms, rather than harbingers of imminent political instability or social collapse."

Conclusion

It is hard to avoid the conclusion that many problems that were once viewed as inherently irreconcilable under continued CCP rule have already been basically solved. The state sector has been drastically downsized and reorganized, and the remaining firms have become more profitable. A massive wave of urban layoffs generated higher unemployment rates for several years, which have now largely passed with minimum political disruption. Robust rural markets for agricultural commodities, farm inputs, and labor have been created; they work well and are relatively unregulated by international standards. Corruption remains a serious concern but it is neither extreme by international standards nor is it clearly intensifying. Moreover, it appears not to have influenced public perceptions of the fairness of reform. Policies that once seemed unthinkable within the inherent limits of a ruling Leninist party, and problems that once seemed intractable without major political and social disruption have in fact proved amenable to steady piecemeal reform.

Ironically, many of the most serious remaining problems do not arise from the alleged conflict between a Leninist dictatorship and a liberal market economy. Instead, the biggest challenges result from unregulated market activities and institutions that are too weak to provide public goods and protect the rights of consumers and producers. The health-care system, environmental protection, and anticorruption efforts offer the most glaring examples. From a metaphysical perspective, this is something of a paradox: an insufficiently strong state administration is not part of the essential "logic" of a socialist regime. The biggest remaining challenges, in other words, are to bolster effective governmental mechanisms so they can effectively regulate the heavily market-oriented economy that has already grown up in the shadow of the abandoned state socialist model. Creating and funding a system of social security and health care, promoting environmental protection (and consumer safety), establishing a workable system of land tenure and dispute resolution, reining in official corruption—these issues do not exclusively characterize an economy that is making the transition away from state socialism. To a considerable extent, they are issues shared by a wide range of emerging market economies, from capitalist and (former) socialist regimes to dictatorships and democracies.

China's growing pains are problems of governance, but not necessarily problems of democratization. From a metaphysical perspective, China's transition is "trapped" because the democratization of national political institutions has been delayed and perhaps blocked indefinitely.[6] A democratic transition is surely appealing on normative grounds, but the implied assumption is that competitive elections will create a government that can effectively address the institution-building agenda identified in this book. It is not immediately clear whether a new multiparty electoral system would craft better health-care policy, environmental safeguards, and consumer protection laws, or could successfully gather the political will and consensus to implement bold new strategies. Multiparty electoral systems have proved highly compatible with incompetent national administration and all manner of corruption, both historically and today. Among the dozens of post-Communist states around the world, one of the least common paths for a post-Communist regime to follow is that of a well-functioning democracy. A small minority of these states are consolidated, effective democratic regimes—but most are corrupt dictatorships or unstable democracies. China's current state and future trajectory should not be defined by abstract conceptions of the alleged logic that underlies different political and economic systems. Rather, China must be assessed for what it is—a rapidly developing market economy with an authoritarian political system, which faces the same problems of institution building as every rising economic power in recent world history. The devil is in the details—not the metaphysics.

Notes

[1] See the arguments reviewed in Steven M. Goldstein, "China in Transition: The Political Foundations of Incremental Reform," *China Quarterly* 144 (December 1995): 1105–31.

[2] See the debates described in Andrew G. Walder, "China's Transitional Economy: Interpreting its Significance," *China Quarterly* 144 (December 1995): 963–79.

[3] See Barry Naughton, "SOE Policy: Profiting the SASAC Way," *China Economic Quarterly* 12 (June 2008): 19–26.

[4] For an energetic argument for this position, see Minxin Pei, *China's Trapped Transition: The Limits of Developmental Autocracy* (Cambridge, MA: Harvard Univ. Press, 2006).

[5] Naughton, "SOE Policy: Profiting the SASAC Way," and Gabriel Wildau, "Enterprise Reform: Albatross Turns Phoenix," *China Economic Quarterly* 12 (June 2008): 27.

[6] This is the central problem explored in a stimulating recent collection of essays on China's evolving political system. See Cheng Li, ed., *China's Changing Political Landscape: Prospects for Democracy* (Washington D.C.: Brookings Institution Press, 2008).

PRIVATIZATION AND MARKETS

POLITICAL CROSSCURRENTS IN CHINA'S CORPORATE RESTRUCTURING

Jean C. Oi

Many have lamented the incompleteness of China's efforts to break the so-called iron rice bowl, to free corporate firms from inefficient industrial practices, and to relieve those same firms of nonproduction expenses.[1] Mounting nonperforming loans (NPLs)—and the subsequent difficulties that asset management companies face in overcoming them—highlight the resilience of the old system.[2] Problems plaguing China's stock markets, which limit shares in circulation, also call into question how far China's industrial reforms have actually progressed, even after property rights reform made firms "private."[3] Is it hopeless to try to reform China's economy without far-reaching and rapid change, including the political reform that is needed to allow proper corporate governance to take hold?

Ironically, as incomplete and slow as the reforms seem to some, in recent years other critics have charged that China's reforms have been hasty and have gone too far. In 2004 Lang Xianping,[4] an economist in Hong Kong who also had a popular TV program in China, charged that, in the rush to restructure, state-owned enterprises (SOEs) have been subject to asset stripping, resulting in firms being "given away." He further asserted that a few—particularly factory managers—have become rich capitalists overnight through manager buyouts (MBOs), and by corruption and collusion with local officials. Instead of lamenting the state's resistance to step aside, Lang opposes privatization and argues for continued state ownership of China's assets.[5] Wang Hui, a professor at Tsinghua University and editor of *Dushu*, a monthly Chinese literary magazine, is another prominent critic, often associated with the New Left,[6] who argues that economic reforms and "market extremism" have propagated corruption, increased economic inequalities, weakened job security, and intensified social polarization.[7] Wang is quoted as saying that China is "caught between the two extremes of misguided socialism and crony capitalism, and suffering from the worst of both systems."[8] In summer 2007, ahead of the 17th Party Congress, seventeen retired senior cadres and old-school Marxist scholars published an open letter on the Web site *Mao Zedong's Flag* to President Hu Jintao and the party's Central Committee, charging the country's reforms have "gone badly offtrack." According to news reports, the letter warned that "Our socialist cause has been severely hindered and lost its direction. . . . Frankly speaking, the current reform model is trying to replace public ownership with private ownership and to transform China from a socialist country into a capitalist country. We're going down an evil road. The whole country is at a most precarious moment."[9] In the view of these critics, the workers—those who have been left unemployed and subject to layoffs, lack of health care, and even the loss of their promised pensions—are the real losers.

The divergent realities that the reforms have either been too slow and incomplete or too fast and too extreme reflect the political crosscurrents that have shaped China's corporate restructuring. Both views contain grains of truth but either taken alone is misleading. China's SOE reforms have been slow. Most restructuring only began in earnest in the mid to late 1990s, and some firms have yet to be restructured. Tremendous problems and inefficiencies are evident. At the same time, and in spite of the SOEs' many well-known problems, recent statistics indicate that returns are dramatically improving, including an increasing number of Chinese firms on the *Fortune* 500 list. Based on these developments, supporters of corporate reform and restructuring have reason to be optimistic.

Those with more socialist leanings, such as the New Left critics, have ample cause for concern about the fallout from recent restructuring. China's Gini coefficient, which is a measure of inequality, has risen to around 0.5. While this is not particularly high in global terms, it greatly exceeds that of the Mao period or the early reform period in the late 1970s. Some would argue that that even this fairly high Gini fails to reflect the true level of inequality that has emerged if one takes into account the gray economy.[10] Without question, layoffs and unemployment have grown. Worse, in stark contrast to the increasing inequality and poverty of some, cases of corruption by managers and officials are rampant.[11] Lang Xianping's high-profile accusations against Kelon Electrical Holdings Co., Ltd. board chairman Gu Chujun turned out to be accurate, and six executives of the firm, including Gu, were arrested.[12]

One can find plenty of anecdotal evidence to support both positions, however, both views taken to extremes are misleading and fail to grasp the complexity of China's corporate restructuring. The slow pace of this process has been due precisely to the leadership's unwillingness to lay off a large number of workers. Putting aside the issue of whether this reticence stems more from fear of social instability than concern for worker welfare, the fact remains that political restrictions—regardless of the desire for economic efficiency—have unavoidably tempered corporate reform. SOE reforms have necessarily been implemented in stages. China knows the most economically efficient strategies for cutting costs and the importance of autonomy and economic incentives for top management. However, those strategies are not always politically feasible.

More than any other country that has tried to change its centrally planned system, China is perhaps the most constrained because the ruling party still calls itself socialist. China's officials may be free of the pressures of electoral politics, but there are political repercussions from corporate restructuring. As China has tried to reform its debt-laden SOEs, pensioners who have been denied their due, along with an increasing numbers of laid-off workers, have engaged in various forms of protests and demonstrations. While not all laid-off workers participate in collective action, enough have done so to warrant officials receiving orders to safeguard stability (*wending*).[13] These disturbances highlight the underlying problem of how a still-Communist regime can change property rights—from public to private ownership—and yet maintain legitimacy. Considerable inefficiency remains in SOEs precisely because the state fears the social instability that would occur if all of the system's fat were trimmed away with one stroke of the knife.

Another difficulty in understanding China's corporate restructuring, as shown below, is that there is tremendous variation, not only over time, as different restructuring strategies have been implemented, but also in different regions and cities throughout the country. Moreover, there is variation in how different types of firms and their workers are treated.

This chapter draws on the findings from two surveys of China's industrial firms; one was conducted in 2000 and the other in 2005.[14] These two surveys were intended to provide an empirical assessment of China's corporate restructuring over time. The range of survey questions was broad, but to shed light on debates about the speed and depth of reform and the consequences for firms[15] and their workers and managers, I will limit my discussion to the responses to three questions:

- How has corporate restructuring proceeded in China?
- What happened to workers in the course of restructuring?
- How have shares been distributed between workers and managers?

How Has Corporate Restructuring Proceeded in China?

China's corporate restructuring has progressed through two distinct phases. For most of the 1990s, restructuring was slow because it had to include provisions for workers affected by the changes. Only over time, as necessary institutions and political contexts were put in place, has a shift occurred in the speed and content of restructuring.[16] This is shown in figure 1.1, which is based on the 2005 survey of five Chinese cities. There is a distinct upward trend in restructuring, starting in 1995 and reaching a high around 1997, when the 15th Party Congress gave private capital a greater social economic space, reaffirming and expanding the private sector's status in China's economy.

Patterns of Restructuring

In addition to its relatively slow acceleration, and in sharp contrast to Russia and parts of Eastern Europe, China's restructuring was gradual in terms of changes in forms of ownership. Instead of following a big-bang approach, selling off assets and creating immediate large stakeholders through insider privatization, for more than a decade China pursued more limited shareholding systems that were a long way from privatization. Up until the mid to late 1990s, only a small percentage of firms were transformed into fully private entities, and the state remained a major shareholder in the largest and most important ones. During these earlier phases there was significant restructuring but relatively little genuine privatization, two processes that were kept separate and distinct.

Figure 1.1 Most Important Firm Restructuring Since the 1990s

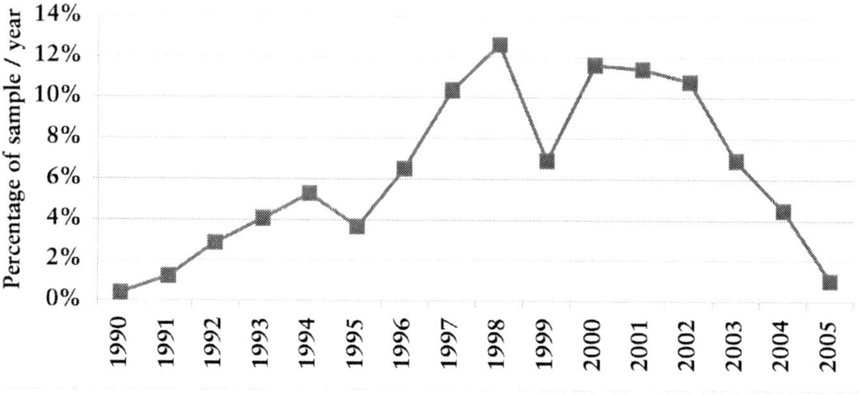

Source: Author surveys.

This gradual approach required the Chinese central state or its agents to control the reform process. Based on the 2000 and 2005 surveys, this is precisely what happened. Throughout the reform process, the state was able to remain the initiator of reform. Findings from the two surveys, conducted five years apart, show the stability of the government as the main initiator of firm restructuring. In both surveys, the government, including various state bureaucratic authorities, continued to initiate more than 60 percent of the restructurings.

Continued government control of restructurings had significant implications for China's ability to sequence when different types of restructuring would take place. As shown below, once local authorities resolved the political limitations to their pursuit of development and efficiency, it became possible to implement more radical reforms. By retaining control of the reform process, the Chinese state has been able to select appropriate forms of restructuring to achieve specific economic or political goals at different stages of the process. China thus carefully phased its restructuring, adopting the least disruptive forms first and privatizing later. The results of the 2000 survey show that in the 1990s, privatization and bankruptcy were limited, whereas shareholding was common.[17] In each of the five cities surveyed in 2000, privatization came last; however, over time, significant change did take place. The 2005 survey data show a substantial increase in privatization. Of the 521 firms that had been state or collectively owned in 1990, only 37 remained public by 2004.

It is also important to note that the rates of change in the number of firms in different ownership categories vary by city. The greatest change in public enterprises occurred in Wuxi, where the change was much larger than the sample as a whole. In contrast, the restructuring of public firms in Shenyang was less than the sample as a whole. This last finding is not surprising given that Shenyang is China's rust belt of old SOEs. There is significant variation in the rate of increase in private firms, with Wuxi in the lead, growing much faster than the sample as a whole. It remains for future research to explain why this city was able to successfully privatize its SOEs so rapidly and develop private enterprise.[18]

Institutional Obstacles to Corporate Restructuring

The slow pace of China's corporate restructuring seems all the more puzzling in light of some studies, which argue that, given the economic costs, local governments have incentives to privatize their SOEs.[19] Indeed, the incentives are real. Many officials would like to privatize their unprofitable enterprises, which are ongoing headaches that drive down their performance records. However, while local authorities have economic interests, they are still subject to political and economic constraints that limit their options. Local officials need to worry about disgruntled workers taking to the streets. A cadre's inability to maintain stability could negate other accomplishments (yipiao foujue) in the annual evaluations.[20] In China, economic expediency or efficiency cannot be the sole criterion for action. The sequencing and speed of China's corporate restructuring was tied to the political constraints that made certain aspects of the economic agenda impossible, at least at the start of reform.

The piecemeal nature of China's reforms has led to institutional disjunctures.[21] Only as new institutions were put in place to solve political problems could restructuring be accelerated. Unless local governments took over the provision of what in other systems are considered public goods, large SOEs had to continue to carry the burden of nonproductive expenditures, such as schools and hospitals, created under the work unit system (danwei). Problems arose when some local finance bureaus refused to pay.[22] Only recently, since state intervention allowed subsidized local governments to take over these public goods, have some firms finally shed such social costs.

Surprising as it may seem, China, long known for its iron rice bowl, lacked the social security and welfare institutions that are taken for granted in many developed economies.[23] This basic institutional gap shaped corporate restructuring, hindering deep and rapid corporate change, especially privatization. China's pre-reform socialist welfare was all-inclusive, but it was uniquely crafted for a system of central planning. The largest and best SOEs had prided themselves on providing workers and their families with jobs, housing, schools, canteens, and welfare benefits, including pensions and health care.[24] Benefits varied according to a worker's danwei. This firm-based welfare system worked well as long as firm sales were guaranteed under state plans. Production was planned, sales were automatic, and a stable stream of revenue flowed to the firm. All welfare entitlements in this system were accounted for annually as costs of production and were deducted from revenues before the calculation of the profits that were to be remitted to the state. In short, as long as central planning was in place, these extensive welfare guarantees were fully funded.

The reforms aimed to make enterprises economically self-sufficient but in the meantime they also left workers at the mercy of the firm-based welfare system. The state regulated the benefits pensioners should receive, stipulated the creation of worker retraining centers, and mandated subsidies for laid-off workers. In order to implement the payout policies, however, it was up to individual firms to fund these programs. The problem was that only the firms that were relatively robust economically had the resources to make the prescribed payments. Unless local governments could provide adequate support, firms that needed to lay off workers often were also those least likely to have the funds to pay the prescribed subsidies and benefits. Those enterprises that were on the brink of closure or that had stopped production were even less likely to be able to provide worker social security. Firms with many pensioners often found themselves in a vicious cycle, in which it was almost impossible to become profitable while also supporting many older, less-skilled workers and retirees. Our survey results from 2000 show that costs of pensions and salaries were increased in proportion to sales.

In the late 1990s the state began to create a unified welfare system, but even today it remains a work in progress.[25] The tremendous variation in wealth distribution across different localities has created impediments to an integrated national system of welfare. Like systems elsewhere, more affluent localities are unwilling to pay for the welfare of their poorer neighbors.[26]

It is not surprising, given the political and economic needs, especially during the early phases of reform, that shareholding emerged as one of the earliest and most widely used forms of restructuring. From an ideological perspective, it is most compatible with China's continued allegiance to socialism. Although there are different types of shareholding systems, employees—not outsiders—are the shareholders in most, if not all, of the systems. For instance, a shareholding cooperative sells shares in the firm only to its workers and managers.

What Happened to Workers in the Course of Restructuring?

Let us now consider the fate of workers. Concern about what has happened to workers is at the heart of the critiques that China's New Left have leveled at reform.

We know from various studies that workers have suffered. Work by Dorothy Solinger, C. K. Lee, Yongshun Cai, and others[27] clearly point to the difficulties that workers have had to endure as China attempts to reform its industrial structure. Some have been forced to leave their jobs before they reach the legal retirement age. This strategy, called internal retirement (*neitui*), has left those in their late forties—especially those with lower levels of education—particularly vulnerable, as they are considered too old to be retrained, and thus likely to remain jobless for the foreseeable future.[28] The stories are particularly heart-wrenching when both the father and the mother lose their jobs and are left with no means to support their family.

The severity of layoff and unemployment rates for the urban worker population as a whole has been somewhat difficult to ascertain. Unemployment figures show that the number of workers who have been permanently cut from their former units is on the rise, however, the exact percentage of the labor force that is unemployed has been subject to debate.[29] While we leave it to the economists to resolve these unemployment debates (see Park et al., chapter 2 in this volume), our surveys clearly show distinct phases and variation in how the state has tried to cope with worker layoffs and unemployment over time.

Phase I. Limited Worker Layoffs and Unemployment

During the early period of reform, great effort was made to minimize layoffs and unemployment, and to delink restructuring from layoffs. Although many might assume that layoffs automatically follow restructuring, analyses based on our 2000 survey show that that is not the case.

First, in the period before 2000, 75 percent of restructured firms in our sample kept all their workers and made no layoffs. More specifically, we found that:

(1) When firms were restructured to shareholding, were sold, or formed joint ventures with foreign firms, the firms themselves took on the majority of employees.[30]

(2) For leased firms, it was more likely that firms would retain only a portion of employees and leave it to the government to handle the rest. To a lesser extent, the same was true for joint ventures.

(3) The government was more likely to step in and take care of workers when a firm went bankrupt.[31]

These results are supported by the findings from a study by the International Finance Corporation (IFC), a member of the World Bank, which suggests that enterprise restructuring was in fact kept distinct from job loss, particularly during the 1990s.[32]

Second, multivariate analyses of our 2000 survey data indicate that restructuring and the laying off of workers each followed different logics and were affected by different factors. In the earlier years, economic factors like redundant employees and debt made firms more likely to undergo restructuring; however, as time went on, their predictive power faded. This implies that the forces behind restructuring have changed from economic factors to other causes. In contrast, the number of workers a firm lays off is, over time, more consistently

11

linked to economic factors, such as number of employees and profit level. When we tested the hypothesis of whether a firm's restructuring in previous years would affect the number of laid-off workers, we found that in only one out of five years was the effect statistically significant. A firm's decision to lay off workers depends more on its financial situation, regardless of whether it undergoes restructuring or not.[33] In short, given the internal turmoil or instability created in the society, a firm would not lay off workers unless it faced tremendous financial pressure and had no choice but to cut its redundant workforce.[34] The number of layoffs in each of the four cities that we surveyed in 2000 did vary, but in all cases it was below 1.5 percent of each city's population.

Just as our findings suggest some variation, earlier studies suggest that many laid-off workers were left to fend for themselves. What might explain the variation? As earlier studies have pointed out, programs meant to help laid-off workers were insufficiently funded. Many firms never had the funds to pay the required subsidies that the central authorities mandated to run the reemployment centers.[35] Giles, Park, and Cai found in their survey that many who were laid off never even registered and never got help. At the same time some who were still working did receive subsidies.[36] Thus, as with most other policies in China, problems arose with implementation. In addition to improper implementation of policies and unfunded mandates, we also now have evidence that there was a systematic bias that favored SOE workers.

As is true in Japan and South Korea, China employed different strategies for different types of firms. Cai conducted a study of the northeast, the rust belt, which shows the difference in the treatment of workers in state versus collective firms.[37] Workers in SOEs were much more likely to get assistance as the economy reformed, while those in collectively owned enterprises were essentially left to cope on their own, often receiving little or no help. This distinction is particularly relevant given the evidence from our 2000 survey. We found that there was a relationship between ownership and types of restructuring. First, collective firms were more likely to be restructured. In our 2000 survey sample, more than 80 percent of the collectively owned firms had been restructured. In contrast, more than 30 percent of the SOEs were not restructured in our 2000 survey sample. Second, shareholding was the most popular form of restructuring for both state-owned, urban collective firms and rural collective firms; joint ventures with foreign firms were more likely to be adopted by pooled firms. Finally, collective firms were more likely to be sold or leased than their state-owned counterparts.

Phase II. Increased Flexibility in Retaining Workers

Workers experienced a turn for the worse when privatization ramped up after the mid to late 1990s. Based on our 2005 survey results we know that new firm owners gained more flexibility with regard to retaining workers. Figure 1.2 shows the sharp change in commitment toward employees that took place during restructuring. In the 2000 survey, 95.7 percent of firms said they had to commit to keeping employees after restructuring. The 2005 survey, by contrast, reveals that only 11.28 percent of the firms made such a commitment.

Figure 1.2 Changing Commitment to Retain Workers, 2000 and 2005

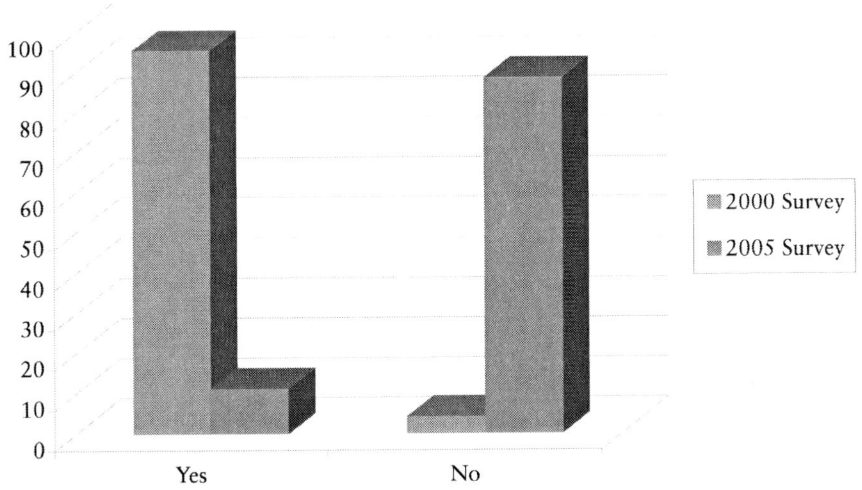

Source: Author surveys.

We should not conclude, however, that the political constraints so potent earlier were entirely gone. Even though a noticeable shift occurred in the commitment to keep workers, there is evidence that the issue was not moot. The identity of the new controlling shareholder seems to matter. Not surprisingly, if the firm was an employee shareholding company (represented by a shareholding board), then the likelihood that all employees would be kept was greater than our sample mean. The same holds true if the new controlling shareholder was the collective—meaning the township or the village. Perhaps most important, this was the case for external individuals who took over a firm. Our 2005 survey found that factory managers, as the new controlling shareholders, were less likely to be bound to hold on to workers. Even so, considerable variation persists across the sample.

How Have Shares Been Distributed between Workers and Managers?

Perhaps the greatest criticism that the New Left has leveled against corporate restructuring is undue benefit accrued by the factory managers. Given the large size of some of the firms that have come under the control of individuals, one can easily guess that preferential treatment for managers in attaining loans, at a minimum, would be a given. Interviews reveal that in some localities, loans

13

were arranged for managers to buy a controlling stake in restructured firms. The work of Ding Xueliang[38] or Minshin Pei[39] provides rich examples of corruption and the thief of enterprise assets. While we do not know how many corruption cases are related to corporate restructuring, the official tally involving party members is high.[40]

However, if one moves beyond individual cases to look at the overall trends, the story looks different (see also Andrew Wedeman, chapter 5 in this volume). Our data do not allow us to conclude anything about corruption or windfall profits for managers, yet we can shed light on the way shares were distributed during restructuring. Again, one finds that different patterns appear in the two distinct periods. Our surveys show that during the early period, the state was careful not to allow factory managers to own a disproportionate number of shares. There were, in fact, prohibitions that resulted in a relatively equal distribution of shares between factory managers and workers. Unlike in Russia or Poland, where managers gained large blocks of shares at the start of the process, China consciously adopted a more egalitarian policy, which prevented managers from immediately engaging in insider privatization at the outset of reform. Only in the later phases of restructuring has the trend emerged to promote the concentration of shares in the hands of management.

While most managers did not have a controlling share in the early phases of restructuring, there is evidence that the percentage of shares they controlled began to increase. The proportion of shares that top managers held in restructured firms increased from 21.5 percent upon completion of a firm's initial restructuring to 24.8 percent by 2000, the time of the first survey. The increase of top managers' share mainly happened in limited liability companies (3.45 percent increase on average), limited liability shareholding companies (4.71 percent increase on average), and in shareholding cooperative companies (4.88 percent increase on average). The shares held by ordinary workers, by contrast, decreased from 16.3 percent to 14.7 percent.

The state-imposed constraints on manager buyouts, at least initially, stemmed from a dual agenda. On the one hand, it allowed the regime to use shareholding as a means to minimize layoffs by offering workers the opportunity to help keep their firms afloat.[41] This served the political goal of keeping workers employed, but perhaps equally, if not more importantly during this period, it also provided an economic solution for firm finance. Shareholding served as a fund-raising scheme for firms to obtain extra capital.[42] The funds raised by the employee purchase of shares went directly to the enterprise. The sale of shares helped to fill the void left by decreasing the number of available bank loans. These had become more difficult to obtain, especially for ailing SOEs, as the state concurrently tried to solve the NPL problem by reforming the banks. On the one hand, for SOEs and the state, shareholding became a low-cost way to keep factories open and workers employed without relying exclusively on support from local governments. On the other hand, at least in theory, shareholding also held out the hope that if workers and managers became owners they would help turn around their factory, make it profitable, enable it to repay its debts, and forestall the need to lay off workers.

The change toward manager control became much more pronounced after 1997, when the speed of restructuring and privatization increased. As figure 1.3 shows, managers are now becoming the new controlling shareholders. According to the 2005 survey data, managers holding a controlling share, or even buying the entire enterprise was the most common type of restructuring (26.4 percent). Firms in which workers, including managers, take a controlling share or buy the enterprise ranked second (20.2 percent) in frequency. These findings point to a substantial loosening in the system of relatively equal share ownership practiced early in the restructuring process. Our 2000 survey showed that just over 4 percent of the managers were the controlling shareholder. After restructuring in these same factories, we found that by 2004 more than half of the managers had become the new controlling shareholder (see figure 1.3). Additional fieldwork conducted in 2005 suggests that in some parts of the country, manager buyouts are being instituted without first progressing through the earlier phase of equal shareholding. This change is explained as necessary, in part because effective corporate governance requires a major hands-on stakeholder.[43] An informed source indicated that in 2004 a central-level decision was made to stop allowing workers to own shares in their own enterprises. Ironically, this may also have been a reaction to criticism from the New Left, the logic being that these assets belonged to all the people and therefore should not be preferentially given to just these workers.[44] However, the managers—the target of New Left critiques—were not prevented from engaging in MBOs until the following year, 2005.

Aside from our data, which show an increase in MBOS, we also know from interviews that in some cases, local officials essentially "gave away" firms or sold them at a great discount. Are these clearly cases of asset stripping, as some would suggest? Obviously, letting a firm go for almost nothing raises suspicion. However, my research—in counties where officials openly told me about cases in which they sold or almost gave away factories—suggests that one needs to probe beyond the sale price to understand the full consequences of a restructuring deal. There is an alternative and quite plausible rationale to corruption for these quick sales, a practice often followed in market economies as well. There is no question that these sales netted the given localities very little in terms of direct compensation for the assets. However, the long-term benefits of these sales can arguably be seen as outweighing the short-term losses. For example, one county gave a factory/warehouse to an outside company, on the condition that the new owner agreed to revamp the building and turn it into a new feed-processing plant. This brought in new tax revenue for the locality. Without the giveaway, the plant would have continued to yield no taxes, as it had long stopped production. In addition, this scenario created new jobs and a market for locally grown corn.

Figure 1.3 Change in Controlling Shareholder, 2000 and 2005

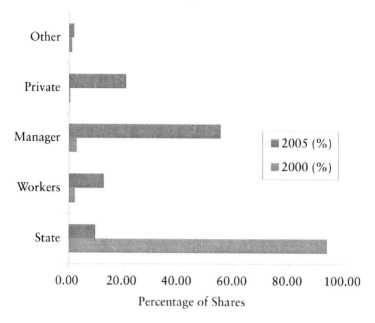

Percentage of Shares

Source: Author surveys.
Note: State includes state and public legal person shares. Workers includes all members of an enterprise, including managers and workers. Managers includes top manager or team of managers.

One can easily make the case for cheaply selling abandoned facilities or firms that had stopped operations, but what about seemingly healthy, still-functioning firms? For example, one county had a vehicle factory that was still doing quite well, employing workers and yielding tax revenues. Yet the county authorities decided to sell it to an outside company, in this case a much larger company from Beijing that produced similar types of vehicles. Local officials acknowledged that the selling price was relatively low. Was this a case of corruption or asset stripping? On the surface, by just looking at the selling price, one could believe the worst and reach a negative conclusion. Digging deeper, though, it becomes clear that the local company and officials knew the company would soon fail to compete effectively with the Beijing company, which had a much bigger market share and produced better vehicles. The county's strategy was to sell the firm sooner rather than later. The key caveat to the sale was that the Beijing buyer had to keep the factory in the locality and maintain all the workers. The locality thus faced a stark choice: no layoffs or a decrease in tax revenues. After the sale, it could look forward, instead, to increases in tax revenues, which did materialize after a few years. Such examples are telltale that the sale of firms may only be the beginning of a local development strategy, not the end.

In cases of restructuring where the outside firms are less willing to take all of a factory's workers, local officials take rather extraordinary measures to persuade workers to terminate their relations with a firm. This approach takes varied forms, and here, too, the shareholding system comes into play. Shareholding opened the door for the state to end its implicit social contract with state workers. Allowing workers to become investors demonstrated that the state was granting them the right to take ownership of the public firms to which they had devoted their working lives. To be sure, in some instances workers were coerced into buying shares, but overall, those who bought shares had the potential to earn significant revenues in the form of dividends and profits, provided the value of the shares increased. Regardless of the money that shares could potentially yield, this was an important political act. Workers became part owners of the public assets that they had worked hard to develop, and are now represented on both the boards of directors and the supervisory boards of many restructured enterprises.

In the past few years, as firms reach the second or third phase of restructuring, the political concerns that originally steered the state to favor relatively equal worker-manager shareholding systems are now sometimes seen as a problem that hinders further change. Interviews in 2004 and 2005 suggest that enterprise managers are increasingly frustrated by the power of employee shareholder associations, which block opportunities for sales or joint ventures.[45] What may have started primarily as schemes to raise money by selling shares to workers has, it seems, transformed over time into a means by which workers can block further restructuring.[46] The actually potency of such power remains to be investigated; it could also be why workers are no longer allowed to own shares in new restructurings.

Such strategic changes highlight the fact that local officials face political constraints during restructuring, but they also needed to heed counterpressures for economic development. After all, simply maintaining social stability does not guarantee an official's interests and ensure promotion. Increasingly, development is regarded as the first principle in assessment of cadre performance. Local officials thus had to strike a balance between the political consideration of keeping workers employed and the economic, efficiency considerations underlying the need to lay them off.

In cases where local authorities were extremely anxious to ensure that a firm could be sold, interviews reveal that they even gave workers extra money, based on years of service, to buy additional shares of the firm. However, the authorities then immediately offered to buy back all the worker shares, including those just purchased, in order to provide workers with a quick cash return if they wished. Why not just give workers the extra money? When asked why, the local authorities explained that allowing workers to have shares was a necessary step in the restructuring process. It marked an end to one stage in China's

17

history and the beginning of another—from a socialist planned economy to a capitalist market economy.

The preceding example suggests that creating and distributing shares to workers in China's SOEs became a symbolic fulfillment of the social contract between the state and its workers. One could argue that shares were distributed as a political payoff to state workers for their previous service to the firm and to the state. Such distribution might also help thwart charges of asset stripping, not to mention appease workers and maintain political stability. Making state workers shareholders changed their status (*shenfen*). The state could then affirm that workers had the right either to remain "owners" in the firm or to sell their shares for immediate cash and leave the firm. At that point their relationship with the firm (and the state) would be terminated. The decision rested with the workers. Obviously one can say that the entire procedure was nothing more than ritual. But such acts seem necessary in China in order to pave the way politically to transform formerly state-owned assets from public to private ownership.

On occasion, to placate workers and end the social contract, local authorities directly provide a severance package to workers who have to be laid off or fired. This buyout scheme—*maiduan gongling*—is based on the number of years of service that workers have given to the factory, and by extension to the public sector to which they would have belonged for the rest of their lives. Our 2005 survey in five cities found that this practice is still relatively rare, and the overwhelming majority of firms (86 percent) in our sample never engaged in it. Small- or medium-sized enterprises most often used this method to terminate employment for long-time workers. But, again, significant variation occurs. Of the five cities, Chengdu had the largest number of firms that used the *maiduan gongling*; Shenyang had the lowest incidence. We cannot yet explain the reasons for such differences, but possible relevant variables might be the number of SOEs, the number of workers who needed to be laid off, and the resources of local government. Shenyang, located in the heart of the rust belt region, has a large pool of surplus SOEs workers and only limited revenues, whereas in Chengdu the number of SOEs and their workers is much smaller. Interestingly, some officials complain that even after workers have been paid and agreed to a settlement, they sometimes still come back and ask for more.[47]

Growing Pains and Opportunities in Corporate Restructuring

Overall, the process of corporate restructuring in China has been relatively slow, not least because there were tremendous problems and obstacles to overcome. Gradually, however, and despite widespread fear that they would be insurmountable, many problems have been addressed and even solved in some cases. While the pace has been sequenced and the mechanisms ideologically more conservative than market advocates would like, dramatic changes in China's SOEs have taken place in the past decade. First, there has been a significant culling of the thousands of SOEs since 1979. Today, the State-owned Assets

Supervision and Administration Commission (SASAC) in Beijing controls fewer than 150 SOEs. Second, while problems remain, an increasing number of the remaining SOEs are not only becoming increasingly profitable but also able to compete internationally. In this sense, even as it experienced growing pains, China managed to turn this difficult period into an opportunity to restructure its key industrial sectors. Government statistics suggest that the various attempts at restructuring have had a positive impact, and that some of China's SOEs are doing very, very well. Indeed, according to the 2006 SASAC reports for 2004 to 2006, the biggest and most important enterprises—those under the central SASAC—have reported large increases in production, profits, and taxes paid to the state. A detailed breakdown shows just how successful the turnaround has been during those three years, 2004 to 2006.

The revenue from core businesses of the central SOEs increased 78.8 percent with an average annual growth rate of 21.4 percent; the total profits increased 140 percent with an average annual growth rate of 33.8 percent; the taxes-paid increased 96.5 percent with an average annual growth rate of 25.2 percent, the rate of preserving and increasing the value of state-owned assets reached 144.4 percent; and the returns on assets reached 10 percent, an increase of 5 percentage points. Over the past three years, the average annual increase of the total assets and sales revenue of the central SOEs registered 1.1 trillion RMB. The average annual increase of profits reached more than 100 billion RMB, and taxes-paid averaged an increase of 100 billion RMB annually. Thirteen central SOEs were ranked among the world's top 500 published by the American magazine, *Fortune*, in 2006. There were eight more than that in 2003.[48]

While China's SOEs have clearly turned a corner and survived their most difficult period,[49] the problems are far from being completely solved. Despite significant restructuring, significant fat remains in the industrial system. Political constraints continue to foster overemployment in some SOEs. While we do not have accurate figures on the number of surplus workers for all enterprises, one knowledgeable source who is closely involved with corporate restructuring at the central level noted that of the ten million workers in the state's centrally owned SOES, one-third are surplus. Our 2005 survey also concludes that firms still have surplus labor.[50] This hidden unemployment may be holding down wages. A number of central SOEs are still losing money.[51] Some have been allowed to declare bankruptcy, with the state taking care of the workers displaced. Others have been ordered to undergo further restructuring and to merge with profitable firms.

After culling a huge stock of SOEs and with the intentions to reduce the number under central control even further, the state wants to focus investments on making these key firms internationally competitive. Recentralization of control is evident here, as it has been in other sectors of the economy;[52] Li

Rongrong, head of SASAC, cites lax financial control among the reasons for the SOEs' continuing problems. Some firms reportedly had hundreds of bank accounts with little or no central oversight. In rooting out these problems, SASAC seems to be taking this opportunity to recentralize financial control in the big firms, much as the higher levels of the state banks have taken power away from lower-level branches. SASAC is also experimenting with having SOEs pay a percentage of their profits to the state, to create even stronger incentives for managers.[53]

These practices, of course, refer to China's national champions, those firms that are being primed to be internationally competitive. It is beyond the scope of this chapter to examine the impact of restructuring on individual firm performance—the profitability of firms is a complex issue best left to economists. This examination asks a broader question about the impact restructuring has had on China's firms as a whole. This study concurs with a 2006 World Bank study that finds that restructuring has had a positive impact, though that study questions whether the champion firms were stronger to begin with.[54] Restructured firms in our 2005 survey overwhelmingly confirmed that their performance improved, but those findings were based on self-reporting. Notably, the reason most often cited for firms' improved performance was restructuring. Particularly relevant for the questions addressed in this chapter is our finding that restructured firms paid more taxes.[55] In particular, these findings—along with the statistics given earlier on dramatically improved central SOE performance—suggest that China may have the resources to address the concerns of New Left critics. Indeed, it may be poised to move to the next stage of its institutional development. The question is how China will use these new revenues.

In sum, the growing pains are not entirely gone, and some have paid a heavy price during this transitional period. Moving forward, the question is not whether China should return to its old ways, but whether China can handle the much bigger challenge of remedying the problems and inequalities created by reforms. There are indications that at least some of the increased revenues generated by industry are being used to solve these problems. Expenditures on welfare and pensions have gone up significantly since 1998. A recent report by the Ministry of Finance provides some indication that the government is spending to free firms, once and for all, from the legacy of the *danwei* system.[56] Such state spending on social programs may allow China to calm the political crosscurrents that have hindered its corporate restructuring. Today's global economic crisis and the drop in exports questions how much revenue the state can mobilize and use to calm such currents.

Notes

[1] See, for example, Edward Steinfeld, *Forging Reform in China: The Fate of State-Owned Industry* (Cambridge Univ. Press, 1999); Nicholas R. Lardy, *China's Unfinished Economic Revolution* (Washington D.C.: Brookings Institution Press, 1998).

[2] Edward Steinfeld, "China's Program of Debt-Equity Swaps: Government Failure or Market Failure?" in Edward Steinfeld, Yasheng Huang, and Anthony Saich, eds., *Financial Sector Reform in China* (Harvard Univ. Press, 2005); Victor Shih, "Dealing with Non-Performing Loans: Political Constraints and Financial Policies in China," *China Quarterly*, no. 180 (2004): 922–44.

[3] See Carl Walter and Howie Fraser, *Privatizing China: Inside China's Stock Markets* (Singapore: Wiley, 2006), and Carl Walter, "Pandora's Box: Financial Reform and Corporate Restructuring in China," revised paper for conference volume, *System Restructuring in China* (ms.).

[4] He is sometimes known as the "Chinese Larry King," see Wieland Wagner, "Larry King's Chinese Twin: Challenging the Communists with 'Larry Lang Live'" *Der Speigel* (March 21, 2005) www.spiegel.de/international/spiegel/0,1518,347826,00.html.

[5] Chi Hung Kwan provides a useful summary, "The Huge Debate over Privatization and MBOs—Can the Drain on State-owned Assets Be Justified?" *China in Transition* (September 15, 2004), www.rieti.go.jp/en/china/04091501.html.

[6] Wang Hui himself denies such a categorization.

[7] See Wang Hui, *China's New Order: Society, Politics, and Economy in Transition*, translated by Theodore Huters and Rebecca E. Karl (Cambridge, MA: Harvard Univ. Press, 2003).

[8] Jehangir S. Pocha, "China New Left," *New Perspective Quarterly* 22, no. 2 (Spring 2005): 25–31.

[9] Ting Shi, "Old Guard Criticizes Beijing's Reforms," *South China Morning Post*, July 17, 2007: 6.

[10] Ma Guochuan, "Grey Income: A Report Causes an Uproar," *The Economic Observer Online*, October 6, 2007.

[11] In a special report from the 17th Party Congress, the Central Discipline Inspection Commission revealed that a total of 518,484 members of the Chinese Communist Party (CCP) were punished for corruption and other misconduct from December 2002 to June 2007. See "CPC [CCP] disciplines 510,000 Party members in 5 years," Xinhua News Agency (October 27, 2007), www.china.org.cn/english/government/229866.htm. For examples of corruption and asset stripping, see works by Melanie Manion, *Corruption by Design: Building Clean Government in Mainland China and Hong Kong* (Cambridge, MA: Harvard Univ. Press, 2004); Andrew Wedeman, "The Intensification of Corruption in China," *China Quarterly* no. 180 (December 2004): 895–921, Ding Xueliang, *"Illicit Asset Stripping of Chinese State Firms," China Journal* no. 43 (January 2000): 1–28; and Zheng Lu and Byung-Soo, "Spin-offs and Corporate Governance: Listed Firms in China's Stock Markets," revised paper originally presented at System Restructuring Conference in East Asia, Stanford University, Walter H. Shorenstein Asia-Pacific Research Center. June 2006.

[12] See Xinhua News Agency via Shenzhen Daily and China Daily (August 3, 2005). For an analysis and details, see "The Dramatic Collapse of Kelon Chairman Gu Chujun," *Caijing Magazine* 17, no. 16 (September 5, 2005); also see James V. Finerman, "New Hope for Corporate Governance in China?" *China Quarterly* no. 191 (September 2007): 590–612.

[13] See, for example, Yongshun Cai, *State and Laid-Off Workers in Reform China: The Silence and Collective Action of the Retrenched* (London: Routledge, 2006), as well as his article "The Resistance of Chinese Laid-off Workers in the Reform Period," *China Quarterly*, no. 170 (June 2002): 327–44. See also Ching Kwan Lee, "From the Specter of Mao to the Spirit of the Law: Labor Insurgency in China," *Theory and Society* 31

(2002): 189–228; Ching Kwan Lee, *Against the Law: Labor Protests in China's Rustbelt and Sunbelt* (Berkeley: Univ. of California Press), 2007; and Timothy Weston, "'Learn from Daqing': More Dark Clouds for Workers in State-Owned Enterprises," *Journal of Contemporary China* 11, no. 33 (2002): 721–34.

[14] The Institute of Finance and Trade Economics of the Chinese Academy of Social Sciences (CASS) conducted these two surveys. The 2000 survey was carried out in five cities (Wuxi, Zhengzhou, Jiangmen, Hangzhou, and Yancheng), five sectors (textiles, machinery, electronics, electrical equipment, and chemicals), and 451 firms with various forms of ownership. The research was generously supported by a grant from the Asian Development Bank Institute and a seed grant from the Stanford Institute of International Studies (now the Freeman Spogli Institute for International Studies), Stanford University. The second survey was done in 2005 in five cities (Wuxi, Zhengzhou, Jiangmen, Chengdu, and Shenyang), and five sectors (textiles, machinery, electronics, electrical equipment, and chemicals), with a total sample of 1,022 firms. This survey was generously supported by Stanford University and the Harvard Business School. I would like to thank Han Chaohua, with whom I have worked cooperatively on this project. Much of this chapter draws on our collaborative work.

[15] I leave the impact of restructuring on firm performance to another paper, for which see Han Chaohua and Jean C. Oi, "Zhongguo minyinghuade caizheng dongyin [Fiscal motivation for property rights restructuring of public enterprises in China]," *Jingji Yanjiu (Economic Research Journal)* no. 2 (February 2008): 56–68.

[16] Within the broad political constraints imposed by the absence of institutions such as social security, the state has maintained some flexibility and adopted a two-pronged strategy. It has allowed a few bold initiatives, including the creation of "private" firms to be spun off from its best SOEs. Some of these firms were listed on the stock exchange and have developed into national champions competing on the international market.

[17] The oft-quoted phrase, "grasp the large and let go of the small," suggests that the aggregate picture might mask a larger number of sales in smaller firms. However, even when the data are disaggregated, we find that, regardless of firm size, sale of firms totaled no more than 7 percent of total firms as of 2000. For more details on the 2000 findings, see Jean C. Oi, "Patterns of Corporate Restructuring in China: Political Constraints on Privatization," *China Journal* 53 (January 2005): 115–36.

[18] It is interesting to note that Wuxi, which was at the core of the collective model of development, privatized its township and village enterprises (TVEs) with similar speed.

[19] For example, see Yuanzheng Cao, Yingyi Qian, and Barry R. Weingast, "From Federalism, Chinese Style to Privatization, Chinese Style," *Economics of Transition* 7, no. 1 (1999): 103–31.

[20] Maria Edin, *Market Forces and Communist Power: Local Political Institutions and Economic Development in China* (Uppsala, Sweden: Uppsala University, 2000).

[21] This has also been a problem in China's rural reforms; see Jean C. Oi, "Old Problems for New Leaders: Institutional Disjunctures in Rural China," *The New Chinese Leadership: Challenges and Opportunities after the 16th Party Congress* (Cambridge: Cambridge Univ. Press, 2004), 141–55.

[22] The Ministry of Finance's new report on the budget alludes to this problem. See Ministry of Finance, "Report on the Implementation of the Central and Local Budgets for 2006 and on the Draft Central and Local Budgets for 2007," March 5, 2007, www.china.org.cn/english/government/203405.htm.

[23] China is not alone in this respect—most socialist states, as well as Asian economies such as Japan and Korea, lack many social welfare structures found in the United States and Europe.

[24] See Andrew Walder, *Communist Neo-Traditionalism: Work and Authority in Chinese Industry*, (Berkeley, CA: Univ. of California Press, 1986).

[25] Guidelines for the system's provisions can also be found in chapter 4 of Ross Garnaut, Ligang Song, Stoyan Tenev, and Yang Yao, *China's Ownership Transformation: Process, Outcomes, Prospects* (Washington D.C.: The International Finance Corporation, 2005).

[26] This problem is common in the process of welfare reform, and by no means unique to China. See Worawut Smuthkalin, "The Politics of State-Led Welfare Development: Health Insurance and Pension Institutional Reforms in Thailand, Taiwan, and China," unpublished manuscript, March 2005.

[27] See, for example, Dorothy Solinger, "Labor Market Reform and the Plight of Laid-off Proletariat," *China Quarterly* no. 170 (June 2002): 304–26; Ching Kwan Lee, "From Organized Dependence to Disorganized Despotism: Changing Labor Regimes in Chinese Factories," *China Quarterly* no. 157 (March 1999): 44–71; and Yongshun Cai, "The Resistance of Chinese Laid-Off Workers in the Reform Period," *China Quarterly* no. 170 (June 2002): 327–44.

[28] See John Giles, Albert Park, and Fang Cai, "How has Economic Restructuring Affected China's Urban Workers? *China Quarterly*, no. 185 (March 2006): 61–95.

[29] For the period 1995–2003, a World Bank study cites an increase of urban unemployment from 2.9 to 4.3 percent, which is in line with what official government sources list. See Ross Garnaut, Ligang Song, Stoyan Tenev, and Yang Yao, *China's Ownership Transformation: Process, Outcomes, Prospects* (Washington D.C.: The International Finance Corporation, 2005). However, John Giles, Albert Park, and Juwei Zhang ("What is China's True Unemployment Rate?" *China Economic Review* 16, issue 2 [2005]: 149–70) give the rate among urban permanent residents at the end of 2002 as 14 percent. In their *China Quarterly* article they note that "unemployment reached double figures in all sample cities and labor force participation declined by 8.9 percent" (p. 61). See Giles, Park, and Cai, "How has Economic Restructuring Affected China's Urban Workers?" One of the authors, Park, provides an update in this volume.

[30] Other empirical studies have also found that shareholding was less likely to result in unemployment and layoffs. See, for example, chapter 4 of Garnaut, Song, Tenev, and Yao, *China's Ownership Transformation*, especially pp. 98 and 101. These authors also found that employee shareholding reform resulted in significantly fewer layoffs than in firms that were sold.

[31] A more in depth discussion of the patterns of corporate restructuring can be found in my "Patterns of Corporate Restructuring: Political Constraints on Privatization," *China Journal*, January 2005, on which parts of this paper are based.

[32] See Ross Garnaut, Ligang Song, Stoyan Tenev, and Yang Yao, *China's Ownership Transformation: Process, Outcomes, Prospects* (Washington, D.C., The International Finance Corporation, 2005), chapter 4. One of their most important findings is that firms that restructure have fewer worker layoffs and unemployed than firms that do not. They also point out that it is incorrect to simply look at aggregate statistics on the changes in the number of workers in SOEs. Former state jobs may be reclassified as private-sector jobs.

[33] I would like to thank Zheng Lu for help with the statistical analysis.

[34] The most recent official government white paper reveals that "from 1998 to 2003, the accumulative total number of persons laid off from state-owned enterprises

was 28.18 million." See Information Office of the State Council of the People's Republic of China, *China's Employment Situation and Policies*, April 2004, www.china.org.cn/e-white/20040426/index.htm.

[35] See Cai, *State and Laid-Off Workers*.

[36] See Giles, Park, and Cai, "How has Economic Restructuring Affected China's Urban Workers?"

[37] See Yongshun Cai, "Distinguishing between the Losers: The Politics of Economic Restructuring in China," in Jean C. Oi, ed., *System Restructuring in China* (forthcoming).

[38] See, for example, Ding Xueliang, "Illicit Asset Stripping of Chinese State Firms," *The China Journal*, no. 43 (January 2000): 1–28.

[39] Minshin Pei, *China's Trapped Transition: The Limits of Developmental Autocracy* (Cambridge, MA: Harvard Univ. Press, 2006).

[40] The Central Discipline Inspection Commission reported that a total of 518,484 members of the CCP were punished according to Party discipline between December 2002 and June 2007. See "CPC [CCP] disciplines 510,000 Party members in 5 years," Xinhua News Agency, October 27, 2007. www.china.org.cn/english/government/229866.htm.

[41] Some enterprises—especially those that were ailing or loss-making—had difficulty persuading workers to buy shares. This is contrary to some earlier reports of how employee shareholders have benefited from shareholding arrangements. See Yingyi Qian, "Reforming Corporate Governance and Finance in China," in Masahiko Aoki and Hyung-Ki Kim, eds., *Corporate Governance in Transitional Economies: Insider Control and the Role of Banks* (Washington D.C.: The World Bank, 1995), 215–52. There is evidence to suggest that employees were required to purchase shares.

[42] In China, in contrast to a fully developed market system, this kind of fund-raising was done mostly within the factories; only a very few firms actually were listed.

[43] Jean C. Oi, personal interviews in Shandong, China (June–July 2005).

[44] Jean C. Oi, personal interviews in China (October 2007).

[45] For a different perspective on whether the employee shareholder associations have any influence at all, see Sally Sargeson and Jian Zhang, "Re-assessing the Role of the Local State: A Case Study of Local Government Interventions in Property Rights Reform in a Hangzhou District," *The China Journal*, no. 42 (July 1999): 77–99, especially 91–92.

[46] A small percentage of our respondents answered that worker shares should be abolished.

[47] At the central State-owned Assets Supervision and Administration Commission (SASAC) offices in Beijing, there is a special office devoted to receiving petitioners (*shangfang*).

[48] News release at the press conference held by the Information Office of the State Council General Information on Reform and Development of Central SOEs and Development of State-owned Assets Management System Reform, SASAC, December 19, 2006, www.sasac.gov.cn/eng/new/new_0143.htm.

[49] The year 2006 officially marked the completion of the corporate restructuring task.

[50] The estimated number of surplus workers in firms varies widely. Over 40 percent of firms said that their enterprise could cut up to 4 percent of their labor force without affecting performance.

[51] Speech given by Li Rongrong on January 5, 2007, and cited in "Central SOE Responsible Persons Meeting Convened in Beijing," www2.sasac.gov.cn/eng/new/new_0145.htm.

[52] Control over bank loans is one example.

[53] Firms that belong to a local SASAC pay those organizations; only the central-level SOEs pay the national SASAC.

[54] See Shahid Yusuf, Kaoru Nabeshima, and Dwight Perkins, *Under New Ownership: Privatizing China's State Owned Enterprises* (Stanford, CA, and Washington D.C.: Stanford Univ. Press and the World Bank, 2006).

[55] These findings are presented in Han Chaohua and Jean C. Oi, "Zhongguo minyinghuade caizheng dongyin" [Fiscal motivation for property restructurings of public enterprises in China], *Jingji Yanjiu* no. 2 (February 2008): 56–68.

[56] According to the Ministry of Finance, "[a] fund totaling 25 billion yuan was earmarked in the central budget for 2006 to support the policy-mandated bankruptcy of 93 SOEs and to make arrangements for the 410,000 laid-off employees. A base figure of 4.81 billion yuan was approved for subsidies for the work of relieving SOEs of the burden of operating social programs, and this work was basically completed in the second group of 74 central government enterprises." See Ministry of Finance, "Report on the Implementation of the Central and Local Budgets for 2006 and on the Draft Central and Local Budgets for 2007," www.china.org.cn/english/government/203405.htm.

CAN CHINA MEET ITS EMPLOYMENT CHALLENGES?

Albert Park, Fang Cai, and Yang Du

Concern is growing about employment, or the lack thereof, in China. Some suggest that unemployment in cities has reached crisis levels, citing the fact that workers from a range of backgrounds—former state-sector workers, rural laborers from China's vast interior regions, and even recent college graduates—are all having a hard time finding jobs. Others argue, pessimistically, that the economy cannot produce enough new jobs to employ the large numbers of new entrants to the labor market, let alone the newly unemployed. Still others point to large differences in income between urban/rural and coastal/interior regions, and to the persistence of China's residential permit (*hukou*) system, which links access to public services and benefits to where one is born, as evidence that those in the rural interior continue to be excluded from employment opportunities in China's booming cities and coastal areas. All of these observations indicate that a combination of failures, both market- and policy-related, may contribute to the system's inability to provide jobs equitably to all of China's able and willing laborers. China's success or failure in employing its workforce will have enormous impact on its future economic performance, social equity, and political stability, and can be considered the first of its major employment challenges.

Given the lively debate about rising unemployment, it is surprising that China also faces considerable controversy over labor shortages and rising wages for unskilled workers. Are these phenomena, reported in southern China and elsewhere, temporary? Will they subside as soon as more workers can be mobilized from the countryside? Or will they diminish once China reaches a Lewisian turning point, when surplus labor is exhausted and real wages begin to rise?[1] If the former is true, then temporary shortages provide additional evidence of labor-market immaturity. If the latter is true, it raises the question of whether China's low-cost advantage may disappear and threaten its export competitiveness. The continued mobilization of a cheap, educated, and disciplined labor force to support economic growth represents China's second key employment challenge.

A third major challenge is the provision of adequate social insurance for workers who are increasingly exposed, not only to market risks and uncertainties, but also to other unforeseen events such as illness. Social insurance—with its concomitant political implications[2]—is important for maintaining adequate security and well-being for all of China's citizens. An effective social insurance system can contribute directly to the productivity and flexibility of the workforce by ensuring the health and well-being of workers and by facilitating job transitions.[3] In China, employers or work unit systems (*danwei*) have traditionally provided great security to workers. Given the downsizing of the state sector, the rise of the private sector, and the high variability in the administrative and financial capacities of local governments, more and more Chinese lack access to unemployment insurance, health insurance, and social security in old age. Indeed, many dislocated workers and their families may be falling through the cracks.

These problems are much discussed, but often informed by anecdotal, outdated, or misleading evidence. By consulting the best available microdata and considering key measurement issues that affect how data from different sources are interpreted, this chapter seeks to shed empirical light on how China is meeting its three major employment challenges. In particular, the chapter analyzes an important new source of information—data from China's 2005 minicensus, which surveyed 1 percent of the Chinese population using a multistage sampling design. Like the 2000 census, the 2005 minicensus featured national coverage, but was unique in that it included information on wages. As in the 2000 census, the 2005 survey asked about persons living in the residence on October 31 of that year, and about work undertaken during the previous week. The newly available income data is particularly useful because it includes the incomes of migrants, who are severely undersampled in the annual urban household survey conducted by the National Bureau of Statistics (NBS), which is the source for official estimates of income and expenditure levels in China. The lack of previous census income data, however, makes it difficult to examine changes over time. For employment and migration outcomes, this chapter provides comparisons between 2005 and 2000, using the 2000 census data.

In addition to the 2005 minicensus and 2000 census data, the chapter also presents statistics and empirical analysis using NBS's annual labor-force surveys, NBS's urban and rural household survey data, and the Ministry of Agriculture's panel rural household survey data.[4] Because these are annual surveys, they are useful for tracking changes over time.

Can China Generate Enough Jobs?

In a neoclassical labor-market model with costless mobility, wages are set so that labor supply equals labor demand, and there is no involuntary unemployment. Explaining unemployment requires a theory of disequilibrium that considers the reality of labor adjustment costs, barriers to mobility, and/or wage rigidities. In such settings, shifts in labor demand or supply can influence not only the wage level but also the number of dislocated or unemployed workers. For example, it may be difficult for former state-sector workers to acquire the skills required in the new market economy and to find jobs at wages they find acceptable. If the government stipulates minimum levels of wages and benefits that are above market-clearing levels—as they have consistently done in the state sector—an excess supply of workers can result. This can be reduced in turn if labor demand is increased or labor supply decreased. Changes in labor supply are influenced by demographic shifts, and the supply of labor at different skill levels is determined in part by education: access to it, as well as its cost and quality. Labor demand is affected by changes in the quantity and types of goods and services produced in the economy, and the technologies used to produce them. Such changes can be significantly affected by economic growth and government policies that regulate factor prices (such as wages or interest rates), liberalize international trade and foreign direct investment (FDI), support the development of specific industries, or influence innovation and technology adoption. All of these factors have different impacts on different workers, depending on their distinct skill sets and education levels.

Unemployment and Labor-force Participation

The first way to investigate whether there is a shortage of jobs in China is to examine estimates of the unemployment rate. The lack of reliable and timely unemployment rate estimates consistent with internationally standard definitions presents a significant impediment to the design of appropriate macroeconomic and social insurance policies. Internationally, unemployed workers are typically defined as those who did not work in the past week; who were not temporarily on vacation, sick, or participating in training activities before going back to a job; and who actively looked for work in the past month. Both the 2000 census and 2005 minicensus asked about work in the past week and about the reason for not working if the respondent did not work. One possible response was that the respondent did not work but was looking for work. These questions can be used to construct unemployment rate estimates, even though the questions are not standard. Giles, Park, and Zhang estimate that, for five large cities surveyed using a specially designed instrument and based on an internationally standard definition, the census overestimated the unemployment rate by about 30 percent.[5]

Indeed, the evidence reveals that anectodal accounts of high unemployment in China's cities are alarmist. According to the 2005 minicensus data, China's urban unemployment rate on October 31, 2005, was 5.2 percent, down from 8.1 percent on October 31, 2000 (see table 2.1). If one adjusts for the upward bias in the census estimate relative to international norms, the unemployment rate was less than 4.0 percent. Using data from five large cities and extrapolating to all of China, following Giles, Park, and Zhang, we estimate the urban unemployment rate at 4.4 percent in 2005, compared to 7.3 percent in 2002. This finding independently verifies the downward trend in unemployment. However, as shown in table 2.1, estimates of the unemployment rate based on data from the NBS labor-force survey of the economically active and employed populations produces a somewhat different trend, with unemployment first

Table 2.1 Unemployment Rates and Labor-force Participation Rates in China, 1996–2005

	Unemployment rate, all (census)	Unemployment rate, all (AS)	Unemployment rate, all (GPZ)	Unemployment rate, urban residents (GPZ)	Labor-force participation rate (census)	Labor-force participation rate (AS)
1996	–	3.9	4.5	6.8	–	73.0
1997	–	4.3	5.0	7.7	–	72.0
1998	–	6.3	5.6	8.5	–	71.0
1999	–	5.9	5.9	9.0	–	73.0
2000	8.1	7.6	6.5	10.8	69.0	66.0
2001	–	5.6	7.0	10.8	–	67.0
2002	–	6.1	7.3	11.1	–	66.0
2003	–	6.0	–	–	–	63.0
2004	–	5.8	–	–	–	64.0
2005	5.2	7.0	4.4	6.7	65.0	63.0

Sources: Aggregate statistics are published in the *China Labor Statistical Yearbook* (Beijing, China Statistical Press, 2006). *Notes*: Census data calculations by the authors. AS = From aggregate statistics based on labor-force surveys. The unemployment rate is the difference between the economically active population and employed workers, divided by the economically active population. The labor-force participation rate is the economically active population divided by the working age population (above age 16). GPZ= Giles, Park, and Zhang (2005); figures for 2005 are the authors' calculations based on the second wave of the China Urban Labor Survey.

falling and then rising between 2000 and 2005, with a slight overall drop in unemployment from 7.6 percent in 2000 to 7.0 percent in 2005.[6] Still, the latter number is within shouting distance of the 5.2 percent minicensus estimate, though it remains unclear why there is a discrepancy at all, since both are presumably based on the same data.

According to the census data, the labor-force participation rate fell from 69 percent in 2000 to 65 percent in 2005, or by nearly a percentage point each year, as shown in the last column of table 2.1. Data from labor-force surveys show a similar decline, from 66 percent in 2000 to 63 percent in 2005. Over the past decade, the labor-force participation rate fell by 10 percent, a dramatic reduction. This decline might be cause for alarm if one believed that many of those leaving the labor force were doing so involuntarily and felt discouraged about finding a new job, and thus were similar to the unemployed. But another perspective is that adjustment was unavoidable, given a competitive market environment in which the government could no longer afford to subsidize nonproductive, or surplus, labor. As in other transitional economies, such an adjustment led naturally to a reduction in historically high labor-force participation rates. Neither perspective, of course, mitigates the pain experienced by older workers who developed their skills in an outdated system and held on to high expectations for their job security and other benefits. China's government has tried, with limited success, to cushion the shocks associated with such job loss.[7] Today, for better or worse, most workers dislocated by the major restructuring of the late 1990s have found new jobs, transitioned to retirement, or left the labor force. The most difficult part of the adjustment process appears to have passed.

Which groups of workers, then, currently have the hardest time finding work? Table 2.2 shows unemployment rates and labor-force participation rates in 2005 and 2000, respectively, broken down by gender, age, education, and region. In 2005 women had a higher unemployment rate than men, 6.1 percent compared to 4.4 percent, and a much lower labor-force participation rate, 57.1 percent versus 73.7 percent. These gender differences are similar to those in 2000. Unemployment rates tend to fall with age—they are highest for the youngest workers, aged 16 to 25 (9.1 percent). While this may reflect particular problems faced by new entrants to the labor force, unemployment rates for this group fell most sharply from the 2000 unemployment rate of over 15 percent. Also, younger workers in many countries tend to experience higher unemployment rates as they try to match their skills to employers and move more frequently from job to job.

Table 2.2 Urban Unemployment Rates and Labor-force Participation Rates, 2000 and 2005

	Unemployment rate (%)		Labor-force participation rate (%)	
	2000	2005	2000	2005
All	8.1	5.2	68.7	65.3
By gender				
Men	7.4	4.4	77.3	73.7
Women	9.1	6.1	60.0	57.1
By age				
16–24	15.8	9.5	91.9	85.1
25–34	7.1	5.3	88.7	86.3
35–44	7.5	4.6	88.1	85.9
45–54	5.1	3.8	71.0	69.3
55+	1.6	1.9	21.1	23.1
By education				
< Primary	2.1	1.4	26.8	29.7
Primary	4.0	2.6	60.4	58.1
Middle	9.6	5.7	78.9	74.3
High	10.9	7.6	83.4	74.8
Technical college	4.4	4.1	90.5	84.8
Regular college	2.0	2.5	84.9	85.3
Graduate	1.1	1.3	92.1	95.6
By region				
East	7.4	4.8	70.1	67.3
Central	9.8	5.9	66.3	62.0
West	7.7	5.1	68.4	65.0

Source: Authors' calculations using 2000 census and 2005 minicensus microdata.

Employment of College Graduates

Considerable media attention, both within and outside China, has focused on the difficulty that recent college graduates have encountered in finding desirable jobs. Many have attributed this to the surplus of graduates resulting from China's aggressive expansion of higher education in recent years. The number of graduates from regular institutions of higher education increased from 9.5 million in 2000 to a staggering 37.8 million in 2006.[8] Table 2.3 presents data on unemployment and labor-force participation rates for those aged 16 to 25, broken down by level of education. The data do show an increase in the unemployment rate and a decline in the labor-force participation rate for those graduating from regular college. The unemployment rate for this group increased from 6.3 percent in 2000 to 11.9 percent in 2005, while the labor-force participation rate fell from 96.3 to 90.1 percent over the same period. Interestingly, the increase in the unemployment rate contrasts sharply with declines in the unemployment rate for all other education levels over the same period. The decline in labor-force participation occurred for all education levels, perhaps reflecting the fact that people were pursuing higher levels of education or had a greater propensity to postpone or avoid employment.

Table 2.3 Labor-market Outcomes for Young Workers Aged 16–24, 2000 and 2005

	Unemployment rate (%)		Labor-force participation rate (%)	
	2000	2005	2000	2005
All	15.8	9.5	91.9	85.1
By education				
< Primary	7.7	3.3	52.5	41.1
Primary	10.4	5.9	87.4	80.0
Middle	14.6	7.7	91.7	85.3
High	20.4	13.0	92.8	84.5
Technical college	14.1	13.4	96.7	90.8
Regular college	6.3	11.9	96.3	90.1

Source: 2000 census and 2005 minicensus data.

On the one hand, the data support the argument that greater policy attention be directed toward facilitating the employment of recent college graduates. On the other hand, larger trends indicate that college graduates are being successfully absorbed into the workforce. The private return to college education compared to high school in urban areas has increased tremendously over time, from less than 12 percent in 1988 to 37 percent by 2001.[9] Younger cohorts enjoy even higher returns to schooling than older cohorts. This suggests that increases in demand for college-educated workers far outpace increases in supply. The national urban labor force that is college-educated remains less than 10 percent, even as global integration and rapid technological change increasingly place a premium on highly skilled workers. It is possible that college graduates need time to modify unrealistically high expectations about their first postcollege jobs, or that they are willing to wait for better matches because of the perceived importance of initial placements to future career development. Modest initial wages for college graduates are balanced by the fact that wages subsequently rise most steeply among younger members of the workforce.[10]

Industrial Policy, Financial Reform, and the Demand for Labor

As noted earlier, government policies can affect employment opportunities in the economy. During the period of economic restructuring, Chinese leaders sometimes felt frustrated that China's double-digit growth was not generating more new jobs. Relatively slow job creation can be partly linked to policies in other sectors that were formulated without consideration of their effects on aggregate labor demand. Industrial development strategy in particular has emphasized the development of heavy, capital-intensive industries (such as automobiles, machinery, and steel), which are viewed as keys to modernization, sustained GDP growth, and government revenue mobilization. In China, these sectors received preferential access to cheap credit, favorable tax treatment, and supportive public investments. Investments generally did not flow to light industries that had the capability to create more employment opportunities, especially for unskilled workers. Entry into nonindustrial, labor-intensive sectors, such as services, was often restricted, which in turn limited their development.[11] Especially after 1998—when the government initiated expansionary fiscal and monetary policies—the cost of investment funds for large enterprises was very low. For these reasons, industrial development has been very capital-intensive.[12]

Despite recent reforms in the banking system, large, capital-intensive firms have continued to receive favorable treatment from state-owned commercial banks. Banks had plenty of funds to lend, thanks to robust economic growth and large increases in personal savings. Under strong pressure to reduce nonperforming loans (NPLs), banks perversely had an incentive to steer funds to large, state-owned enterprises (SOEs) or to state-supported projects implicitly backed by the government. State-controlled interest rates were kept at below-market levels, creating incentives for firms to choose capital-intensive technologies. In addition to reducing overall labor demand, if capital is skill-biased, the demand for unskilled workers falls even more than that for skilled workers. Private enterprises, by contrast, many of which were small and medium sized, found it difficult to obtain loans from state commercial banks and instead turned to alternative financing channels, including FDI. Indeed, the private sector has accounted for the majority of new job creation since the mid-1990s, government restrictions notwithstanding.[13] Continued reform of the banking system through greater competition, including from foreign and private banks, could promote more lending to the private sector and increase labor demand.

Demography and Labor Supply

China has reaped a demographic dividend that has increased the size of the labor force each year. Because of the age structure of China's population, the labor force grew rapidly by 3 percent per year during the 1980s and early 1990s and at a slower rate of about 1.5 percent per year since then.[14] As the population pyramid for 2005 in figure 2.1 shows, China currently has more people entering their twenties (that is, joining the labor force) than entering their sixties (retiring). But after 2020 this will have reversed, so that the labor force will begin to decline in absolute numbers. As figure 2.2 illustrates, the dependency ratio, defined as the number of children and elderly relatives to the number of those of working age, will reach its low point sooner, in 2013, after which China will become a rapidly aging society. As that process occurs, the rising dependency ratio will slow per capita growth rates. However, China could reap a second demographic dividend as older citizens with greater savings enable the financing of investments that raise labor productivity, an important point to which we will return later in this chapter.[15] In summary, over the next fifteen years, labor force increases will be modest when compared to the speed of China's economic growth, but the labor force will subsequently shrink, leading to labor scarcity rather than surplus.

For urban labor markets, the large increase in rural migrant labor has been an even more important source of growing labor supply. This has been due in part to the relaxation of institutional restrictions on migration, yet it also reflects the biases of public investments, which have favored urban areas over rural areas. China's investment in agriculture is small compared with other countries at similar levels of development.[16] Through various channels—such as taxation, pricing policies, and credit allocation—significant resources have been extracted from the agricultural and rural sectors to support urban industrialization.[17] A key goal of the Hu Jintao government's new socialist countryside initiative, supported by increased public investments and social spending in rural areas, has been to reduce this urban bias, which could partly explain recent labor shortages in cities, as more rural laborers choose to remain in the countryside.

Has the Age of Surplus Labor Ended?

As noted earlier in the case of college graduates, the speed of real wage growth is another useful indicator of whether rising demand for labor is outpacing supply. Wage growth may also reflect increases in labor productivity or institutional changes that reverse practices that underrewarded workers relative to their productivity. Figure 2.3 plots mean real wages for China from 1978 to 2003 based on official data reported by work units. In contrast to most other transition economies, there are no large declines in mean real wages during the reform period. On the contrary, average real wages rose steadily in 1981, 1988, and 1989. Most remarkably, real wages increased at an accelerating rate (14 percent per year) after 1997, when state enterprise restructuring was at its high point.

Figure 2.1 China Population Pyramids, 2005 and 2020

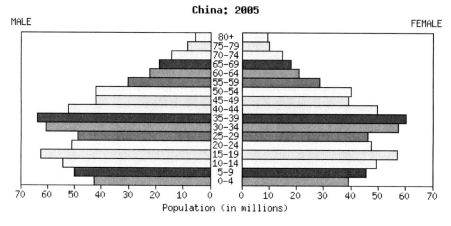

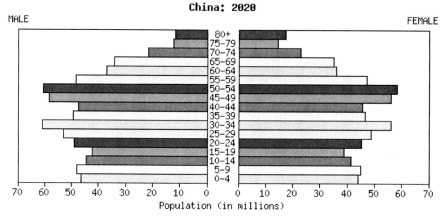

Source: Pyramids produced by U.S. Census Bureau, www.charlottediocese.org/customers/101092709242178/filemanager/docmgr/population_pyramids.pdf (downloaded August 20, 2009). Data underlying these pyramids available at www.census.gov/ipc/www/idb/.

These increases are probably overstated, because administrative reporting overlooks various types of informal employment that increased rapidly in the late 1990s. Nevertheless, figure 2.3 highlights the success of China's economic reforms in delivering amazing welfare gains for the average citizen. Focused government policies might well have been responsible for the continuously rising wages of government and SOE workers. Studies using urban household survey data also confirm the steady increase in real wages. According to NBS urban household surveys in six provinces from different regions, real wages climbed between 1988 and 2001, including increases of 9 percent on average between 1997 and 2001.[18] Studies describing trends in real urban income per capita support this finding.[19]

Figure 2.2 China's Demographic Dividend: Dependency Ratios, 1949–2049

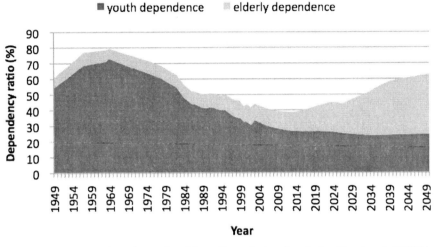

Sources: Pre-2003 data from the *China Population Statistics Yearbook* (2003); other years based on projections from the Institute of Population and Labor Economics, Chinese Academy of Social Sciences.

Figure 2.3 Real Wages, 1978–2003

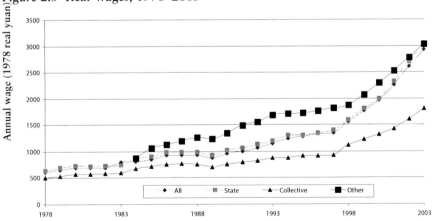

Source: NBS, China Statistical Yearbook, 2004. Wages deflated using the urban CPI (retail price index used prior to 1985).

What about increases in the wages of less-skilled workers, especially rural migrants? For many years, people doing business in China or visiting factories in the south reported that the wages for migrant factory workers remained stagnant and at a very low level (often between 300 and 600 yuan per month), thanks to the endless supply of cheap labor flowing in from the Chinese countryside. Despite numerous press accounts of labor shortage before the onset of the global economic crisis in 2007, many continue to argue that there remain hundreds of millions of underemployed (or surplus) laborers in rural areas.[20] It is true that coastal China historically tapped rural workers from nearby locations, beginning with local areas, and then progressing to neighboring provinces in central China. Only in the late 1990s did China witness significant increases in migration outflows from the western part of the country.[21] Does China still have the scope to mobilize more rural migrants from interior regions, or is the end of surplus labor with steady wage increases looming?

Let us consider the evidence. Table 2.4 shows that many of the sectors in which migrant workers are most prevalent have seen steady real wage increases over time, usually between 10 and 15 percent per year. However, these data are based on work unit reporting, which mixes skilled and unskilled workers and may underrepresent migrant laborers, who are often hired off the books. In the past several years, two national rural surveys—the Research Center for Rural Economy (RCRE, Ministry of Agriculture) Rural Panel Household Survey, and NBS's Rural Household Survey—began systematically collecting data on rural migrant wages. As detailed in table 2.5, the RCRE survey finds that mean real wages of migrant workers increased by -0.6 percent in 2004, 4.9 percent in 2005, and 9.8 percent in 2006. Wage increases accelerated particularly rapidly for middle and high school graduates in 2006—14.7 and 15.1 percent, respectively. The NBS survey finds that mean real (nominal) wages of rural migrants increased by 5.6 percent in 2003 and 7.6 percent in 2004.[22] The China Urban Labor Survey in five large cities in 2001 and 2005 underscored these statistics, indicating that the mean real hourly wages of migrants increased by 32 percent between 2001 and 2005 (an average of 8 percent per year), compared to an increase of 19 percent for local residents. For those with a middle school degree and below, the migrant hourly wage increases were somewhat slower, 22 percent—or 5.5 percent per year.[23]

Table 2.6 reports mean monthly and hourly wages for China according to the 2005 minicensus. For the entire country, the mean monthly wage was 1,021 yuan, and the mean hourly wage was 5.23 yuan. Men earned 23 percent more than women per month and 20 percent more per hour. There are similarly large differences in pay associated with disparities in education: college-educated workers earned twice as much as middle school graduates and 60 percent more than high school graduates. The age-earnings profile, however, is relatively flat, reflecting the higher mean education levels of younger workers.

Table 2.4 Annual Real Growth Rate of Average Wage in Select Sectors (%)

	Mining	Manu-facturing	Con-struction	Transport, storage, and post	Commercial and catering services	Comm-unity services
1995	5.34	3.33	1.20	4.54	2.82	1.90
1996	3.49	0.32	-0.72	4.11	0.85	4.14
1997	2.24	1.99	3.29	5.99	0.82	8.08
1998	6.63	19.78	12.71	14.74	21.79	10.99
1999	5.21	11.78	8.46	13.53	10.85	12.62
2000	10.01	11.37	8.56	11.19	11.15	10.73
2001	14.15	10.93	7.83	14.21	13.15	14.01
2002	16.09	13.69	9.48	14.39	15.88	14.88
2003	23.08	12.57	10.66	-1.34	n. a.	n. a.
2004	19.39	8.72	7.71	11.40	n. a.	n. a.
2005	20.32	10.52	10.52	14.34	n. a.	n. a.

Source: NBS, *China Labor Statistical Yearbook* (various years), and Ministry of Labor and Social Security (MOLSS), *China Labor Yearbook* (various years).

Table 2.5 Wages of Rural Migrants, by Education Level, 2003–2006

	Unit	2003	2004	2005	2006
Nominal monthly wage	yuan	781	802	855	953
	growth rate (%)	–	2.7	6.6	11.5
Real monthly wage	2003 yuan	781	776	815	895
	growth rate (%)	–	-0.6	4.9	9.8
By education level					
Primary and below	2003 yuan	687	705	750	801
	growth rate (%)	–	2.6	6.4	6.8
Junior high school	2003 yuan	728	732	757	867
	growth rate (%)	–	0.5	3.4	14.7
Senior high school	2003 yuan	878	849	846	973
	growth rate (%)	–	-3.3	-0.3	15.1
College and above	2003 yuan	1,098	1,080	967	1,027
	growth rate (%)	–	-1.6	-10.5	6.2

Source: RCRE panel household survey. Nominal prices deflated by the national urban CPI.

Table 2.6 Mean Monthly and Hourly Wages, 2005

	Monthly wage (yuan)	Hourly wage (yuan)
All	1,021	5.23
By gender		
Men	1,102	5.60
Women	899	4.68
By education		
Primary and below	734	3.51
Middle	867	4.15
High	1,062	5.51
College and above	1,603	9.10
By age		
< 30	960	4.80
30~39	1,061	5.40
40~49	1,049	5.48
> =50	1,005	5.42
By migrant status		
Migrant labor	1,125	5.52
Of which: rural-urban	952	4.30
Local labor	973	5.10

Source: Institute of Population and Labor Economics (CASS) Project Group, *Labor Market Supply and Demand Conditions and Social Insurance Problems: Analysis of the 2005 Mini-census Data*, unpublished report, 2007.

The advantage of the 2005 minicensus data is that it offers more comprehensive coverage for wage data than do other official sources. In particular, it has good coverage of migrants, who form an important part of the unskilled labor force in the manufacturing sector. Taking the mean manufacturing hourly wage for 2005 based on the minicensus data, adding a 27 percent premium for nonwage benefits in manufacturing as estimated by Banister for 2002,[24] and applying the official exchange rate in 2005 of 8.2 yuan, we calculate that China's mean hourly wage, as measured in U.S. dollars, was about 70 cents in 2005. To better illustrate the competitiveness of this wage level globally, figure 2.4 compares this wage with the hourly labor costs of workers in other countries, as reported by the U.S. Bureau of Labor Statistics. When stacked against countries such as Mexico, Chinese wages remain very low. Figure 2.4 makes clear that even with significant wage growth, China will remain competitive for some time to come.

Figure 2.4 Comparison of Manufacturing Unit Labor Costs Per Hour, 2005

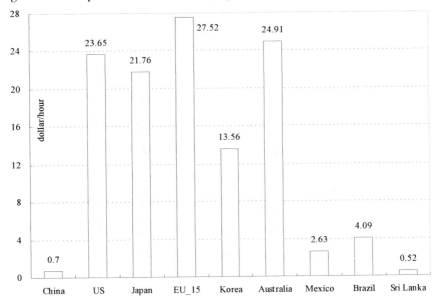

Sources: China manufacturing hourly wage calculated from 2005 1 percent minicensus data. Unit labor cost based on coefficient provided by Banister (2005)—1.27 times wage (for 2002). Yuan-dollar exchange rate for 2005 was 8.19 (*China Statistical Yearbook*). Cost for Sri Lanka is for the year 2004. Unit labor costs for other countries from U.S. Bureau of Labor Statistics, ftp://ftp.bls.gov/pub/special.requests/ForeignLabor/ichccsuppt02.txt.

Fretting over the effect of rising wages on China's competitiveness is unnecessary for several additional reasons. First, many foreign investors locate operations in China not only for low labor costs but also for proximity to the large China market, good infrastructure, and a stable, favorable policy environment. Second, even if one focuses on labor costs, it is important to remember that competitiveness depends not on the cost of labor per unit of time but on the cost of labor relative to labor's productivity. By maintaining higher labor productivity, China can preserve its competitive advantage over many countries in Africa and Asia, even though they have cheaper labor costs. Further, rising wages will not hurt competitiveness if they are matched by similar increases in productivity. One recent study that addresses data quality issues finds that labor productivity in Chinese manufacturing increased by over 20 percent per year between 1997 and 2003.[25]

Some have argued that despite the large number of migrants, there are still hundreds of millions of workers employed in agriculture who can be easily shifted to more profitable nonagricultural activities. According to official statistics, of the 485 million rural laborers, 297 million were not working in township and village enterprises (TVEs), private enterprises, or nonagricultural self-employment.[26] It is not clear how many of these individuals were actually working full-time in agriculture. Some may have migrated to urban areas, but were not categorized as such. The Ministry of Agriculture estimated the number of rural migrants (presumably mostly workers) to be 108 million in 2005. Others may have been engaged part-time in nonagricultural work. Rawski and Meade estimated that official numbers on agricultural labor overestimate actual labor time spent in agriculture by up to 25 percent.[27] Cai and Wang conduced similar exercises for the year 2005 and found that the number of full-time equivalent workers in farming and animal husbandry was about 190 million, assuming a 300-day work year.[28] This suggests that surplus labor time in 2005 could have ranged anywhere from 0 to 106 million workers, depending on how well official statistics captured migration.

And yet, these back-of-the-envelope calculations can be misleading. In China, young people are much more likely to migrate than older people, who often strongly prefer to live in their home villages. For their part, employers of migrants favor young workers. According to rural household surveys conducted in five provinces, by 2007 over 80 percent of those aged 16 to 30 were engaged in off-farm work, compared to about 70 percent for those aged 31 to 40 and 50 percent of those aged 41 to 50 (figure 2.5). Moreover, the number of young people who migrated increased significantly from 2000 to 2005, whereas less than 5 percent of people over the age of 45 elected to migrate. In other words, to the extent that surplus labor persists in China, workers are more likely to be older individuals who are both less willing to migrate and less desired by employers.

Figure 2.5 Share of Rural Labor Participating in Off-farm Work in 2007, by Age Group

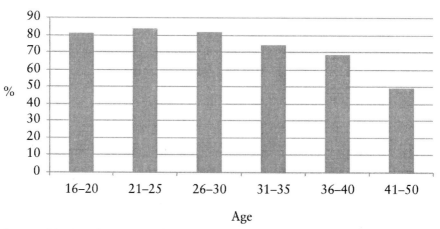

Source: Linxiu Zhang, Xiaofei Li, Scott Rozelle, and Jikun Huang, "China's Labor Transition and the Future of China's Rural Wages, Employment and Urbanization Shifts," unpublished manuscript, 2009.

Evidence on Labor-market Integration

To what extent has the Chinese labor market become integrated across regions? This key question helps us to evaluate whether observed labor shortages are temporary and region-specific or whether they reflect broad changes in the labor market as a whole. Greater integration would mean that rising wages are unlikely to reflect temporary shortages in a particular region. Integration also would promote more efficient labor allocation and create equal opportunities in the market for similarly qualified workers from different parts of the country. In this section, we review evidence from a number of different microdata sets, including the 2005 minicensus, all of which consistently show that labor markets have become highly integrated in recent years.

First, we consider evidence from the NBS's annual urban household survey. Analysis of a six-province subsample of the survey suggests that after the year 2000, interregional wage differences began to decrease. This can be seen in the narrowing dispersion over time of coefficients on provincial dummy variables included in Mincer-type wage regressions plotted in figure 2.6 (coefficients equal the percentage difference in earnings compared to the lowest wage province in the sample,

Figure 2.6 Provincial Urban Wage Differences, 1988–2003

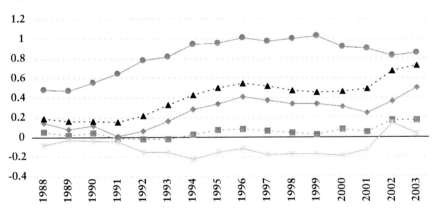

Source: Albert Park, Xiaoqing Song, Junsen Zhang, and Yaohui Zhao, "Rising Returns to Skill, Labor Market Development, and Rising Wage Inequality in China," unpublished manuscript, 2006.

Note: Differences relative to Sichuan as a percentage of annual wages of employed workers. Calculations based on Mincer regressions of annual earnings according to years of schooling, gender, potential experience, potential experience squared, and provincial dummy variables. Earnings are deflated by provincial CPIs to 1988 prices.

Sichuan). Conducting a similar analysis based on the full urban household sample in 2003, we find that coastal wages remained about 20 percent higher than elsewhere in real terms, although the differences among noncoastal regions were relatively small (figure 2.7).

Figure 2.7 Regional Urban Wage Differences, 2003

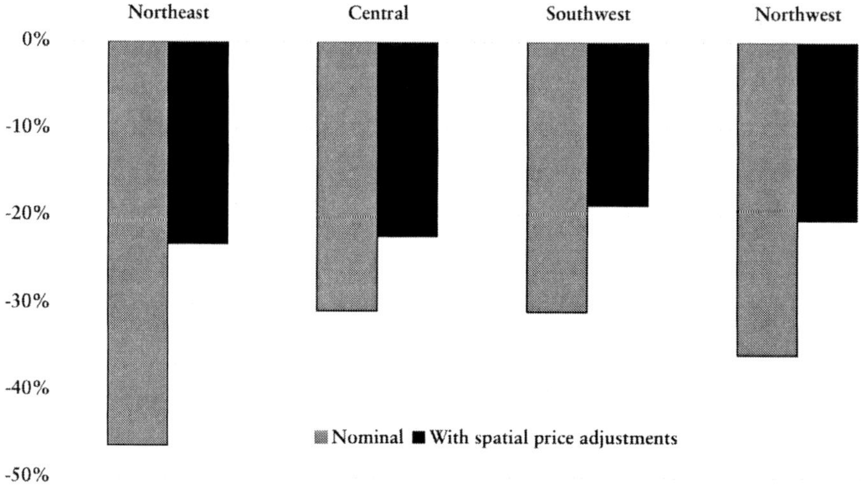

Source: Analysis of 2003 NBS urban household survey data.
Note: Percentage difference in wages relative to the coastal region. Calculations based on coefficients of regional dummy variables from Mincer regressions of annual earnings on years of schooling, gender, potential experience, and potential experience squared.

Next, we examine evidence from the Ministry of Agriculture's rural household surveys, with a particular focus on the earnings data for rural migrants, which were collected systematically beginning in 2003. As noted earlier, the NBS urban household survey significantly undersamples migrants. This gap in the evidence makes it difficult to study labor-market integration because migration is the mechanism that connects and integrates regional labor markets. As a first step, we decompose the inequality in wages into within-province and between-province components, using a set of general entropy measures that assign different weights to differing degrees of inequality. The best known of these measures, the Theil index, produces results similar to those using other measures. We control for differences in the cost of living across regions by using spatial price deflators for wages, as calculated by Brandt and Holz.[29] Throughout the period 2003 to 2006, interprovincial wage differences accounted for less than 10 percent of total inequality (table 2.7). This percentage was 7.2 percent in 2003, 9.3 percent in 2004, and 6.8 percent in 2005 and 2006. Thus, interregional market segmentation was relatively low and is declining over time. In table 2.8, we use a regression-based decomposition method to directly measure how specific factors contribute to inequality. Using this method, we find that the importance of regional differences increased from 14.4 percent in 2003 to 20.8 percent in 2004, and then declined to 19.0 percent in 2005 and 16.9 percent in 2006 (table 2.8).

Figure 2.8 The Rise of Informal Employment in Urban China (% of urban employment by employer type)

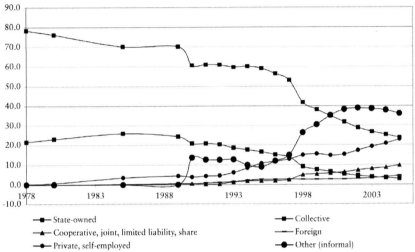

Sources: NBS 2006 and *China Statistical Yearbook*, 2006.
Note: The "other" category is obtained residually as the difference between total urban employment (as estimated from labor-force surveys and that reported by state and collective units), and registered private businesses and self-employed individuals. This category primarily relates to those in some kind of informal employment in urban areas.

Table 2.7 Decomposition of Rural Labor Wage Inequality between and within Provinces (Theil index)

	2003	2004	2005	2006
Total inequality	0.263	0.237	0.204	0.205
Within provinces	0.244	0.215	0.189	0.190
Between provinces	0.019	0.022	0.014	0.014

Source: Calculations using Research Center for Rural Economy panel household survey data and Brandt and Holz (2006) provincial spatial price deflators. For results without spatial price deflation, see Fang Cai, Yang Du, and Changbao Zhao, "Regional Labor Market Integration since China's World Trade Organization Entry: Evidence from Household-level Data," unpublished manuscript, 2007.

Table 2.8 Theil Regression-based Decomposition of Rural Labor Wage Inequality

Components of inequality	2003	2004	2005	2006
Theil entropy	0.263	0.237	0.204	0.205
Regional factors (%)	14.4	20.8	19.0	16.9
Individual factors (%)	-63.7	-54.3	-36.4	-29.4
Constant (%)	-11.4	-27.5	-64.4	-43.6
Residual (%)	160.7	161.1	181.7	156.1
Total (%)	100.0	100.0	100.0	100.0

Sources: Calculations using Research Center for Rural Economy panel household survey data and Brandt and Holz (2005) provincial spatial price deflators. For results without spatial price deflation, see Cai, Du, and Zhao, "Regional Labor Market Integration since China's World Trade Organization Entry."

As a final exercise to study wage patterns across regions, we turn to the 2005 minicensus data, which includes wage data for both local residents and migrants. We present separate results for workers with different education levels. Again, spatial price differences have been controlled for using Brandt and Holz's indices.[30] Classifying the decomposition of wage variation into between- and within-province components, we find that interprovincial wage differences accounted for between 8 and 13 percent of total wage differences for primary, middle, and high school graduates, depending on the education level and entropy measure (table 2.9). Interprovincial differences were least important for middle school graduates—by far the largest category of migrants. In contrast, they accounted for 22 and 26 percent of wage inequality for college graduates.

Is this pattern of wage convergence across regions consistent with other indicators of the magnitude and nature of migration? Table 2.10 presents estimates of the scale of migration in 2000 and 2005 using the census and minicensus data. Total migration increased from 73 million in 2000 to 97 million in 2005, a growth of 32 percent. Interestingly, migration by urban dwellers increased three times faster than the rural population, by 65 percent compared with 22 percent. Nonetheless, in 2005 rural migration still accounted for 70 percent of all migration. While migration increased rapidly over this period, it was still the case that migrants remained a relatively small portion of the total population (7.5 percent). Compared with other measurements of the number of migrants, these are on the low side, perhaps because they are based on migration in the past five years.[31] Table 2.11 also breaks down the types of labor flows that characterized migration in 2000 and 2005. In both years, the majority of migrants moved to another province, with this share increasing slightly from

2000 to 2005. Overall, the data support the story of increased migration and greater labor-market integration in the 2000s. Other research has found similar evidence of convergence in the rates of return to education across regions and ownership sectors,[32] as well as wage convergence across industrial sectors.[33]

Table 2.9 Male Manufacturing Wage Inequality Decomposition by Education Level, 2005

	Within province (%)	Between province (%)	General entropy index of inequality
Primary and below			
GE(-1)	89.43	10.57	0.16
GE(0)	88.34	11.66	0.14
GE(1)	89.31	10.69	0.15
GE(2)	92.03	7.97	0.20
Middle school			
GE(-1)	90.67	9.33	0.13
GE(0)	89.96	10.04	0.12
GE(1)	90.78	9.22	0.13
GE(2)	92.88	7.12	0.16
High school			
GE(-1)	87.72	12.28	0.16
GE(0)	86.80	13.20	0.14
GE(1)	87.84	12.16	0.15
GE(2)	90.43	9.57	0.19
College and above			
GE(-1)	77.55	22.45	0.24
GE(0)	74.02	25.98	0.20
GE(1)	74.16	25.84	0.20
GE(2)	77.36	22.64	0.22

Source: Institute of Population and Labor Economics (CASS) Project Group (2007), analyzing the 2005 minicensus data.

Table 2.10 The Scale of Migration, 2000 and 2005

	Total population	Rural population	Urban population
Million persons			
2005	97.28	68.60	28.68
2000	73.38	56.00	17.38
Increase (%)	32.6	22.5	65.02
Migration rate (%)			
2005	7.44	7.06	8.54
2000	5.79	5.88	5.5
Composition (%)			
2005	100	70.52	29.48
2000	100	76.32	23.68

Source: Peking University CCER Project Group (2007), analysis of 2005 1 percent minicensus data. Population estimates based on ratios calculated from survey data and base figures from the *China Statistical Yearbook*. Rural and urban defined by *hukou* (residential permit) status.

Table 2.11 Migration by Origin and Destination Type and by Migration Distance, 2000 and 2005

		Origin and Destination Type				Migration distance	
	Total	Rural to urban	Rural to rural	Urban to urban	Urban to rural	Within province	Between province
Million persons							
2005	97.28	55.26	13.34	26.30	2.38	45.37	51.91
2000	73.38	42.18	13.93	14.34	2.93	34.75	38.62
Increase (%)	32.57	31.01	-0.04	83.4	-18.8	30.6	34.4
Composition (%)							
2005	100	56.81	13.71	27.04	2.45	46.64	53.36
2000	100	57.48	18.98	19.54	3.99	47.35	52.63

Source: Peking University CCER Project Group (2007), analysis of 2005 1 percent minicensus data. Population estimates based on ratios calculated from survey data and base figures from the *China Statistical Yearbook*. Rural and urban defined by *hukou* status.

Are Rising Wages a Good Thing?

From a broader development perspective, rising wages should not be viewed negatively, even if labor productivity growth does not fully match the increases. After all, rising real wages are the key to increasing living standards for China's rural citizens. Rising wages for unskilled workers in China also reduces inequality between the educated and the uneducated, and between those who live in urban and rural areas. Rising wages do not mean that competitiveness will be lost. Rather, they indicate that China is ready to move up the product chain and produce higher-value-added goods—a natural and desirable progression of development. Viewed in this light, the end of surplus labor in China can be viewed as a tremendous economic achievement.

Social Insurance for All of China's Workers?

Urban workers today lack employment security, and urban families now find themselves vulnerable to market forces out of their control. In contemporary urban China, having an unemployed worker in your family is a strong predictor of being poor (table 2.12). Even though only 15 percent of all urban people live in a household with a unemployed worker, those 15 percent account for the majority of the urban poor (using a $2 per day poverty line benchmark).

In the past, employment guaranteed pensions, health care, and housing benefits. But reforms have dismantled that system, and it is now critical to establish effective social insurance and social assistance programs that will protect citizens from hardship in the face of volatile market forces or other unforeseen events such as illness. The Hu government has introduced a number of new programs intended to enhance the coverage and level of support for unemployed citizens. In particular, reforms have attempted to shift the management of social insurance programs from work units to local governments, and to scale up social assistance programs targeted at the poor. Concern persists, however, that coverage rates remain low and access to benefits varies tremendously across regions.

To date little systematic evidence exists on the extent of social insurance program coverage. Fortunately, the 2005 minicensus asked several direct questions about whether each member of interviewed households participated in pension, health insurance, and unemployment insurance schemes. As table 2.13 shows, the national coverage rates for these three programs were 18 percent, 33 percent, and 14 percent, respectively, which means that the vast majority of Chinese citizens have no access to basic social insurance programs. Coverage is highest in cities, lower in towns, and negligible in rural villages. But even in cities, coverage extends to less than 50 percent for each of the three programs: 42 percent for pensions, 47 percent for health insurance, and 23 percent for unemployment insurance. Table 2.13 also indicates that social insurance coverage is highly regressive, with the poorest individuals having virtually no coverage while most of the very rich enjoy all three types of social insurance.

Table 2.12 Employment Status and Relative Poverty in Urban Areas, 2003

Those living in households with/without	% with per capita income below			
	$2 per day		$3 per day	
	With	Without	With	Without
An adult not working	4.3	1.0	13.8	5.5
Who is out of the labor force	3.3	2.3	11.2	8.6
And who is unable to work	11.9	2.6	28.1	9.6
Who is unemployed	9.5	1.5	26.8	6.6
			Share (%) of those with per capita incomes below	
Those living in households with	Share in urban population (%)		$2 per day	$3 per day
An adult not working	50.6		81.3	72.0
Who is out of the labor force	42.3		51.3	49.0
And who is unable to work	0.5		2.4	1.6
Who is unemployed	15.3		53.8	42.1

Source: World Bank, *From Poor Areas to Poor People: China's Evolving Poverty Reduction Agenda* (2009); based on estimates from the national sample of NBS's 2003 Urban Household Survey. See http://web.worldbank.org/WBSITE/EXTERNAL/COUNTRIES/EASTASIAPACIFICEXT/CHINAEXTN/0,,content MDK:22131856~pagePK:141137~piPK:141127~theSitePK:318950,00.html.
Note: The poverty lines in yuan per person per year are at 2003 all-China urban prices, and poverty is in terms of per capita income.

Why are coverage rates so low and so regressive? First, social program coverage remains closely linked to employment status, which is in turn highly correlated with poverty status. To rectify this problem, China began an experimental program in 2007 to expand health insurance coverage to dependents for the first time. A second challenge is that employment has become increasingly informal in nature. According to the 2005 minicensus, 53 percent of urban workers were employed without a formal labor contract, with the percentage being higher in townships than in cities and also higher among migrants (table 2.14). Employers can avoid payroll charges for social insurance programs by hiring workers informally, off the books, and young workers may prefer cash wages to benefits that they may never use—young workers, for example, tend to be relatively healthy and therefore may not demand health insurance. Rural migrants traditionally never received extended access to urban social insurance or social protection programs. Today, even though China's 1994 Labor Law allows for all city workers to join social insurance schemes, most local governments assign low priority to meeting the needs of migrants, who are considered outsiders. Workers in the rapidly growing private sector, including the self-employed (many of whom are migrants), usually lack access to the three basic programs. The bottom of table 2.13 shows, using the 2005 minicensus data, that coverage rates of informal sector workers are dramatically lower. For hired workers, the informal worker coverage rate was 20 percent for pensions, 27 percent for health insurance, and 8 percent for unemployment insurance, compared to 74 percent, 78 percent, and 55 percent for formal employees. The China Urban Labor Survey, conducted in twelve cities in 2005, found similar results: migrant workers, the poor, and those employed informally had extremely low rates of coverage.[34]

The low level of pooling and the lack of enforcement represent a third set of difficulties. Contributions into social insurance funds are typically pooled only at the local government (municipality or city) level, which creates incentives for local governments to not enforce regulations in order to attract enterprises and leads to sizable disparities in benefit levels across cities. Local governments may fear that high contribution rates and strict enforcement will drive away businesses to other jurisdictions. Low-level pooling has the effect of tying local social insurance expenditures to local revenues. Analysis of provincial-level data finds that provincial per capita expenditures on pensions and medical care appear to be largely limited by per capita contributions within the province, so that richer (or poorer) areas are able to raise larger (or smaller) revenues to sustain their social insurance expenditures. Per capita spending at the top end (Shanghai Province) is 6.4 times higher than at the bottom end (Jiangxi Province).[35]

A final challenge for China's evolving social insurance schemes is portability. The current system does not allow workers to take their benefit entitlements with them if they decide to take a job in another city. Making benefits portable requires national-level coordination of programs, which up to now have been highly decentralized. A new system to make migrant workers' benefits portable nationally was initiated in 2007 but has yet to be implemented widely.

The Chinese government recognizes the importance of meeting these challenges and has aggressively increased the national funding and scope of social assistance programs for both urban and rural areas.[36] Even so, China is still a long way from establishing a truly effective set of social insurance and social protection programs. The programs are still plagued by inequity, difficulties in enforcement, and incomplete coverage; and solving these problems will require strong central leadership, the mobilization of enormous resources, and repairing fundamental fissures in the public finance system. The longstanding division of populations and programs between urban and rural has made it difficult to design an effective method for covering migrant workers in the cities. Likewise, little headway appears to have been made in designing a plan that will eventually harmonize the rural and urban programs. Likely elements should include gradually extending benefits to long-term migrants in urban areas, and gradually reducing the gap between benefit levels of rural and urban citizens.

Table 2.13 Urban Social Insurance Coverage, 2005 (%)

	Pensions	Health Insurance	Unemployment
All	17.9	32.9	13.6
By location type			
• Cities	42.4	47.1	23.1
• Towns	19.7	32.8	10.2
• Rural	3.9	25.3	2.7
By income group			
• Poorest decile	1.5	19.8	2.6
• Second decile	1.8	20.8	3.6
• Third decile	1.6	21.7	7.2
• Fourth decile	3.8	23.1	5.6
• Fifth decile	6.6	25.6	8.5
• Sixth decile	12.0	28.1	9.6
• Seventh decile	20.9	35.5	15.2
• Eighth decile	32.6	46.0	21.7
• Ninth decile	45.8	62.2	32.4
• Richest decile	54.5	65.7	41.6
By employment formality (urban)			
Formal employment			
• Hired	73.8	78.0	54.7
• Employer	26.6	30.5	10.2
Informal employment			
• Hired	19.5	26.6	7.9
• Self-employed	11.8	21.2	2.6
• Household labor	11.5	19.9	2.4

Source: Institute of Population and Labor Economics (CASS) Project Group, *Labor Market Supply and Demand Conditions and Social Insurance Problems: Analysis of the 2005 Mini-census Data*, unpublished report, 2007.

Table 2.14 Situation of Urban Informal Employment (%)

	Local residents	Rural migrants	Urban migrants	All
Cities	43.7	68.1	35.8	48.2
Townships	60.4	70.8	50.1	61.6
All urban	50.1	68.8	38.1	52.6

Source: IPLE Project Group (2007), analyzing 2005 1 percent minicensus data. Informal employment includes self-employed.

Conclusion

In this chapter, I have sought to assess key challenges that China faces with respect to employment and unemployment. Based on the evidence available, I conclude that China is well positioned to meet its first two employment challenges—generating sufficient jobs to employ its workers, and mobilizing workers to remain internationally competitive. However, China is currently in a weak position to tackle its third challenge—establishing strong social insurance programs for a healthy, functioning labor market and ensuring adequate protections for citizen welfare. The evidence from the 2005 1 percent sample minicensus and other microdata sources tells a compelling story of rapid labor-market development, increasing labor-market integration, and increasing labor scarcity in China. In the future, increases in labor productivity and in the production of higher-value-added items will support continued improvements in living standards. Building a well-functioning social insurance system is a difficult challenge, complicated by a host of institutional and historical factors, but it will be critical if China is to remain globally competitive over the long term.

Notes

[1] See Arthur Lewis, "Economic Development with Unlimited Supplies of Labour," *The Manchester School* 22, no. 2 (1954): 139–91.

[2] One could add here the importance of guaranteeing the rights of labor to bargain collectively; redress grievances fairly; work in safe, clean environments; and achieve other minimum labor standards. These issues are outside the scope of this chapter.

[3] Social insurance can also create disincentives to work. See John Giles, Albert Park, and Zhang Juwei, "What Is China's True Unemployment Rate?" *China Economic Review* 16, no. 2 (2005): 149–70.

[4] Collected by the Research Center for Rural Economy (RCRE) under China's Ministry of Agriculture.

[5] See Giles, Park, and Zhang, *What Is China's True Unemployment Rate?*

[6] Tabulations from the NBS labor-force surveys can be found in the *China Labor Statistical Yearbook* (Beijing: China Statistical Press, various years).

[7] See John Giles, Albert Park, and Cai Fang, "How Has Economic Restructuring Affected China's Urban Workers?" *The China Quarterly* 0, no. 177 (2006): 61–95.

[8] National Bureau of Statistics (NBS), *China Statistical Yearbook* (Beijing: China Statistical Press, 2006).

[9] See Junsen Zhang, Yaohui Zhao, Albert Park, and Xiaoqing Song, "Economic Returns to Schooling in Urban China, 1988 to 2001," *Journal of Comparative Economics* 33, 4 (2005): 730–52; John Giles, Albert Park, Wang Meiyan, and Zhang Juwei, *The Great Proletarian Cultural Revolution, Disruptions to Schooling, and the Returns to Schooling in Urban China*, unpublished manuscript, 2007; and Li Hongbin and Zhang Junsen, *Why Doesn't Education Pay in Urban China?*, unpublished manuscript, 2007.

[10] See Fang Cai, Albert Park, and Yaohui Zhao, "The Chinese Labor Market in the Reform Era," in Loren Brandt and Thomas G. Rawski, eds., *China's Economic Transition: Origins, Mechanisms, and Consequences* (Cambridge: Cambridge Univ. Press, 2008).

[11] Kesha Guo, "Aggregate Demand or Structural Problems? How Distorted Economic Structure Constrains China's Economic Growth," *Jingji yanjiu* [Economic research] 9 (1999): 15–21.

[12] See Xuejun Liu and Fang Cai, "Institutional Transition, Technology Choice, and Employment," *Zhongguo laodong jingjixue* [China labor economics] 2 (2004): 1–24.

[13] See Thomas G. Rawski, *Recent Developments in China's Labor Economy*, report prepared for International Policy Group, International Labor Office, Geneva, 2002.

[14] Feng Wang and Andrew Mason, "The Demographic Factor in China's Transition," in *China's Economic Transition: Origins, Mechanisms, and Consequences.*

[15] Wang and Mason, "The Demographic Factor in China's Transition."

[16] Jikun Huang, Keijiro Otsuka, and Scott Rozelle, "The Role of Agriculture in China's Development: Past Failures, Present Successes, and Future Challenges," in *China's Economic Transition: Origins, Mechanisms, and Consequences.*

[17] Fang Cai and Justin Yifu Lin, *Zhongguo jingji: Gaige yu fazhan* [The Chinese economy: reform and revelopment] (Beijing: Zhongguo caizheng jingji chubanshe, 2003).

[18] See table 2 of Zhang, Zhao, Park, and Song, "Economic Returns to Schooling in Urban China, 1988 to 2001."

[19] Meng Xin, Robert Gregory, and Wang Youjuan, "Poverty, Inequality, and Growth in Urban China, 1986–2000," *Journal of Comparative Economics* 33, no. 4 (2005): 710–29.

[20] This argument is summarized in "Reserve Army of Underemployed" *The Economist*, September 4, 2008. Earlier reports of labor shortages include Thomas Fuller, "China Feels a Labor Pinch," *New York Times*, April 20, 2005; David Barboza, "Labor Shortage in China May Lead to Trade Shift" *New York Times*, April 3, 2006; and Simon Montlake, China's Factories Hit an Unlikely Shortage: Labor" *Christian Science Monitor*, May 1, 2006.

[21] Yang Du, Albert Park, and Sangui Wang, "Migration and Rural Poverty in China," *Journal of Comparative Economics* 33, no. 4 (2005): 688–709.

[22] Calculated from mean nominal wages reported in Laiyun Sheng, and Liqun Peng, Liqun, "The Population, Structure, and Characteristics of Rural Migrant Workers," *Rural Migrant Labor Research on Rural Labor of China* (Beijing: National Bureau of Statistics, 2005), deflating by urban CPI (retail price index used prior to 1985). See NBS, *China Statistical Yearbook.*

[23] Fang Cai and Meiyan Wang, "Growth and Structural Changes in Employment in Transitional China," unpublished manuscript, 2007.

[24] Judith Banister, "Manufacturing Earnings and Compensation in China," *Monthly Labor Review* 128, no. 8 (August 2005): 22–40.

[25] Adam Szirmai, and Ren Ruoen, "Measuring Labour Productivity in Chinese Manufacturing: Statistical Problems and Solutions," unpublished manuscript, 2007.

[26] This is somewhat less than the 341 million workers reported to be primarily engaged in the primary sector, a number that could include farmers living in urban areas.

[27] Thomas G. Rawski and Robert W. Mead, "In Search of China's Phantom Farmers," *World Development* 26, no. 5 (1998): 767–81.

[28] Fang Cai and Wang Meiyan, "Growth and Structural Changes in Employment."

[29] Loren Brandt and Carsten Holz, "Spatial Price Differences in China: Estimates and Implications" *Economic Development and Cultural Change* 55, no. 1 (2006): 43–86.

[30] Brandt and Holz, "Spatial Price Differences in China."

[31] See Cai, Park, and Zhao, "The Chinese Labor Market in the Reform Era."

[32] See Zhang, Zhao, Park, and Song, "Economic Returns to Schooling."

[33] See Fang Cai and Yang Du, "Labor Market Integration: Evidence from Wage Convergence in Manufacturing," in Ross Garnaut and Ligang Song, eds., *China: Is Rapid Growth Sustainable?* (Canberra, Australia: Asia Pacific Press, 2004).

[34] World Bank, *From Poor Areas to Poor People: China's Evolving Poverty Reduction Agenda* (2009). The report is available online; see http://web.worldbank.org/WBSITE/ EXTERNAL/COUNTRIES/EASTASIAPACIFICEXT/CHINAEXTN/0,,contentMDK:22 131856~pagePK:141137~piPK:141127~theSitePK:318950,00.html.

[35] World Bank, *From Poor Areas to Poor People.*

[36] Though beyond the scope of this chapter, similar issues arise with respect to China's urban minimum living standards subsidy (*dibao*) program. In addition to the urban *dibao* program and expansion of urban health insurance to dependents, in rural areas the Hu government enlarged several programs to national levels, such as the rural *dibao* program, scaled up a new rural cooperative medical insurance program, and introduced new assistance programs for the poor to subsidize compulsory education costs and pay medical bills. See Shaohua Chen, Martin Ravallion, and Youjuan Wang, "*Di Bao*: A Guaranteed Minimum Income in China's Cities," World Bank Policy Research Working Paper 3805 (Washington D.C.: World Bank, 2006); and World Bank, *From Poor Areas to Poor People.*

THE MARKETIZATION OF RURAL CHINA: GAIN OR PAIN FOR CHINA'S TWO HUNDRED MILLION FARM FAMILIES?

Scott Rozelle and Jikun Huang

The initial reforms in China and other successful transition nations centered on improvements to property rights and transforming incentives, but the other, equally important task of reformers was to create more efficient institutions of exchange.[1] Markets—whether classic competitive ones or their workable substitutes—increase efficiency both by facilitating transactions among agents to allow specialization and trade and by providing information through a pricing mechanism to producers and consumers about the relative scarcity of resources. But to function efficiently, markets require supporting institutions that ensure competition, define and enforce contracts, ensure access to credit and finance, and provide information.[2] These institutions either were absent in the Communist countries or, if they existed, were inappropriate for a market system. In assessing the successes and failures of twenty-four transition nations during their first decade of reform (measured from the first year of reform in different countries), Swinnen and Rozelle demonstrate that improved institutions of exchange were absolutely essential for nations to make progress.[3] The continued success of all transition nations, including China, during the second decade of reform and beyond will almost certainly depend on continued market development.

Somewhat surprisingly, despite the importance of market performance in the reform process, relatively little empirical work has been done on the success that China (or any other transition nation, for that matter) has had in building markets. Instead, studies of market performance have largely relied on anecdotal accounts, with mixed results. On the one hand, China has frequently been praised for promoting market competition among the state-owned, collective, and private sectors.[4] Authors have also described an explosion in exchange activity in China's rural sector.[5] DeBrauw et al. have shown the positive effect that market development has had on the efficiency of China's agricultural producers and their welfare during the 1980s and early 1990s.[6]

On the other hand, Young argues that changing patterns of the provincial economic structure suggest that China's markets became less, rather than more, integrated during much of the reform period due to internal trade barriers.[7] Poncet suggests that this is also true in agriculture—though it should be noted that Young and these other researchers were working with data from before the mid-1990s.[8] Others studying trade in agricultural commodities using traditional measures of price comovement have raised different concerns. In their view markets have developed, but China's institutional structures have benefited the rich and left out the poor. In particular, many Chinese researchers fault marketization for subjecting farmers' fortunes to the forces of supply and demand.

In this chapter we attempt to make sense of these contradictory views. In doing so, we have two broad objectives. First, drawing on a large number of our own studies of different commodities—including research efforts on grain, oilseeds, fruits, vegetables, and fertilizers—we seek to understand how agricultural markets have developed in terms of integration, efficiency, and competition. Second, we assess how the expansion of markets has helped or hurt the rural economy, looking at a wide spectrum of indicators, including the efficiency of the sector and the incomes of farmers. We also consider a number of the distributive consequences of China's marketization and seek to discover if markets have benefited the poor or not. The overall goal is to understand if the emergence of markets is a positive force that will reinforce China's drive for development or a floundering institutional form that could be a source of tension in the coming years.

In brief, we find that China's agricultural markets have begun to get integrated, efficient, and competitive. Whether out of benign neglect or on the basis of a promarket economic strategy, few regulations exist in today's rural China, and buyers and sellers can enter every segment of the marketing chain with relative ease. If our findings are correct, it means that China has almost made the complete transition—at least in agriculture—from a socialist economy with no markets to an economy whose markets are among the most unfettered in the world. And while markets do expose farmers to price variability, in this chapter we document that their emergence has had positive effects as well, leading to increases in productivity, specialization, and income.

Before we begin, several caveats are in order. Given its relatively straightforward nature and the homogeneity of major crops such as maize and soybeans, agriculture lends itself well to any study of integration and market efficiency. Still, it represents only a small part of China's economy. In 2005 the agricultural sector accounted for less than 15 percent of China's gross domestic product (GDP) and less than 50 percent of employment.[9] In addition, although we were able to examine agricultural markets for some commodities at the national level, for other commodities we were able to look at only regional markets because we had to use our own survey data. What is true in these regions may not be true for all of China. Finally, we do not look at international markets—though, in fact, many of the conclusions for domestic markets in this chapter apply to international markets as well.

Liberalization and Retrenchment: Twenty-five Years of Stop-and-go Marketing Policies

In addition to reforming property rights and transforming incentives, policymakers must create more efficient institutions of exchange. These institutions were either absent in almost all Communist countries or, if they existed, were inappropriate for a market system. In China, as in most countries with central planning agencies directing production and other economic transactions, planners enforced contracts involving exchanges among agents in the chain. Market liberalization requires the elimination of central planning, but to be successful, the process should allow producers continued access to inputs and marketing channels while the necessary market-supporting institutions emerge.

In this section we examine the policy path that China has taken in its effort to liberalize markets. The most prominent characteristic of China's market-liberalization policies is the gradual way in which they have unfolded. Because these policies have been documented elsewhere in detail, we touch on some of the most important policy shifts here only briefly.[10] Later in the chapter, we seek to determine whether China has been successful in creating markets that are competitive, efficient, and equitable.

In contrast to transitioning countries in Central and Eastern Europe, leaders in China did not dismantle the planned economy in favor of liberalized markets in the initial stages of reform.[11] In fact, the major changes to agricultural commerce in the early 1980s almost exclusively centered on increasing the purchase prices of crops.[12] The decision to raise prices, however, cannot be considered a move to liberalize markets, since planners in the Ministry of Commerce made the changes administratively and the price changes were mostly executed by the national network of grain procurement stations acting under the direction of the State Grain Bureau.

An examination of the policies and the extent of marketing activity in the early 1980s illustrates the limited extent of changes in the marketing environment of China's food economy before 1985. It is true that reformers did allow farmers increased discretion to produce and market crops in ten planning categories, such as vegetables, fruits, and coarse grains. Moreover, by 1984 the state asserted control over only twelve commodities, including rice, wheat, maize, soybeans, peanuts, rapeseed, and several other cash crops.[13] However, while this may seem to represent a significant move toward liberalization, the crops that remained almost entirely under the planning authority of the government still accounted for more than 90 percent of the sown area in 1984. Hence, by state policy and practice, agricultural output and marketing was still, for the most part, directly influenced by China's planners.

Reformers proceeded cautiously when they began loosening restrictions on free trade. The decision to permit the reestablishment of free markets came in

1979 but initially allowed farmers to trade only vegetables and a limited number of other crops and livestock products within the boundaries of their own county. Reformers did gradually reduce restrictions, however. Skinner writes that the local rural periodic markets were the predominant marketing venue during the early 1980s.[14] Farmers also began to sell their produce in urban settings, but free markets in the cities did not appear until 1982 and 1983. and even then traders could not market any of the commodities that were still under the control of the state procurement stations.

The record of the expansion of rural and urban markets confirms the hypothesis that market liberalization had yet to begin in the mid-1980s. Although agricultural commodity markets were allowed to emerge during the early years of reform, their number and size made them small players in China's food economy. In 1984 the state procurement network still purchased more than 95 percent of the marketed grain and more than 99 percent of the marketed cotton.[15] In all of China's urban areas, there were only two thousand markets in 1980 and only six thousand in 1984.[16] In Beijing in the early 1980s, there were only about fifty markets transacting around 1 million yuan of commerce per market per year. Each market site would have had to serve, on average, about two hundred thousand Beijing residents, each transacting only 5 yuan of business for the entire year. In other words, it would have been impossible for such a weak marketing infrastructure to even come close to meeting the food needs of urban consumers.

After 1985, however, market liberalization began in earnest. Changes to the procurement system, further reductions in commodities-trading restrictions, moves to commercialize the state grain-trading system, and calls for the expansion of market construction in rural and urban areas led to a surge in market-oriented activity.[17] For example, in 1980 only 241,000 private and semiprivate trading enterprises were registered with the State Markets Bureau; by 1990 more than 5.2 million were registered.[18] Between 1980 and 1990, the per capita volume of commercial transactions in Beijing's urban food markets rose almost two-hundred-fold. Private traders handled more than 30 percent of China's grain by 1990, and more than half of the rest was bought and sold by commercialized state grain-trading companies, many of which had begun to behave as private traders.[19] China moved equally slowly in its liberalization of input markets.[20]

Even after the start of liberalization in both output and input markets in the mid to late 1980s, the process was still partial and executed in a stop-and-go manner.[21] For example, in the case of fertilizers, Ye and Rozelle show that after an early attempt at market liberalization in 1986 and 1987, perceived instability in the rural economy in 1988 led to sharp retrenchments.[22] Agricultural officials did not take controls off fertilizer marketing and encourage private trade until the early 1990s. Lin et al. argue that leaders were mainly afraid of the disruption that would occur if the institutions through which leaders controlled the main goods in the food economy (such as fodder, grain, and fertilizers) were eliminated without the institutions in place to support more efficient market exchange.[23]

The foundations of the state marketing system began to be undermined when the right to private trading was extended to include the surplus output of all categories of agricultural products after contractual obligations to the state were fulfilled.[24] During the late 1980s, the second stage of price and market reforms gradually began to limit the scope of government price and market interventions and enlarge the role of market allocation. By the early 1990s, reformers had begun to eliminate planned procurement for crops other than rice, wheat, maize, soybeans, oilseeds, and cotton; government commercial departments still existed, but they could continue to buy and sell only in the market. For grain, incentives were introduced through reducing the quota volume and increasing procurement prices. In subsequent years, although mandatory procurement of rice, wheat, maize, soybeans, oilseeds, and cotton continued to provide greater incentives for farmers to raise productivity and to encourage sales to the government, quota procurement prices were raised over time.[25]

True to the spirit of gradualism, as grain production and prices stabilized in the early 1990s, plans to abolish the grain ration system led to a new round of reforms.[26] Urban officials discontinued sales at ration prices to consumers in early 1993. Although the state compulsory quota system was not eliminated, in most parts of China in the mid-1990s, leaders once again lowered the procurement level. The share of compulsory grain quota procurement in total production was kept at only 11 percent in the mid-1990s. Local government grain bureaus and stations were encouraged to trade on their own accounts as a way to increase not only the marketing of agricultural commodities but the incomes of grain bureau officials.[27]

The start-and-stop process was still not over. As food prices rose in the mid-1990s, another round of retrenchment-oriented polices was announced. For example, the "Rice Bag" responsibility system replicated the policies of the late 1980s and early 1990s, once again restricting grain flows among provinces and attenuating market activity to force local officials to make their districts more self-sufficient in the area of food production.[28] Zhu Rongji pushed the policies further in the late 1990s when he issued an edict strictly limiting the free trade of agricultural products. Grain bureaus were directed to remonopolize grain trade and collect and store vast amounts of grain to ensure the nation's supply of food, as the rest of the economy was growing by an astounding 10 percent per year.

The policies in the late 1990s, however, worked in the same way as they had in the 1980s.[29] At the local level, private traders emerged as an economic force that was difficult to suppress, despite considerable policing. In fact, many of the efforts to restrict the flow of grain were not successful. Market flows continued as the share of the total government procurement in domestic production fell; trade was driven by the profits that traders could earn by shipping grain from low- to high-priced areas.[30] Personnel in the grain bureaus that had been partially privatized in the early period were among the most avid traders. The grain bureaus that did follow government edicts amassed enormous stocks of grain, and the debt of these bureaus and their local government counterparts rose to astronomical levels.

In the early 2000s, marketing reforms were once more allowed to proceed, although initially with little public encouragement.[31] Restrictions on marketing were removed, and efforts to commercialize the grain bureaus resumed. Government intervention in grain prices was eliminated in those regions where it had been present. In short, a new attempt was made to push the policy environment to be even more market oriented and to encourage farmers to begin a period of structural adjustment (*jiegou tiaozheng*).

It was not until the new government of Hu Jintao and Wen Jiabao came to power in 2002, however, that Zhu's policies were officially reversed and another round of market-liberalization policies was sanctioned.[32] During this period, officials exhorted producers to shift their output to crops in which they had a comparative advantage. Private trade was legalized. Grain bureau reforms were implemented with unprecedented aggressiveness, and finally, between 2003 and 2004, the grain bureaus were shut down completely. The size of the grain storage system was reduced dramatically. The explicit goal of the government was to make the agricultural economy fully market driven.

In summary, China's agricultural marketing policy has been on a roller-coaster path. Since the early 1980s, leaders have liberalized markets and retrenched, reliberalized, and re-retrenched—there have been at least three cycles. China's policymakers have gradually, over the course of more than twenty years, condoned the market and market prices as the main determinants of production.[33] But it is unclear how effective the policies have been in creating a functional market system—one that is relatively integrated, efficient, and competitive. Unsurprisingly, during this time there has been a debate about whether or not markets have in fact emerged. It is to this question that we now turn.

Data

In assessing China's markets over the past ten years, we use data from a number of different sources. First, we use a set of price data (data set 1) collected by China's State Market Administration Bureau (SMAB). Nearly fifty sample sites from fifteen of China's provinces report prices of agricultural commodities every ten days. This means there are thirty-six price observations available for each market site for each commodity each year. The prices are the average price of transactions that day in the local rural periodic markets. The Ministry of Agriculture assembles the data in Beijing and makes them available to researchers and policymakers. Unfortunately, after 2000, the quality of the data has deteriorated.

Using the SMAB data, we can examine rice and soybean prices from the early 1990s to 2000 and maize prices from the early 1990s to 2000. The three crops are produced and consumed in nearly every province in China. Rice price data are available for thirty-one markets. Because of quality differences among rice varieties in different regions of China, we look at price integration among markets within four regions: South China (South), the Yangtze Valley (YV), the North China Plain (and Northwest China, NCP), and Northeast China (NE). For the provinces included in the sample, rice prices are available for more than 90 percent of the time periods. Prices for maize and soybean data are available for thirteen and twenty markets, respectively.[34] Product homogeneity in the case of maize and soybeans makes it possible to examine price integration among markets across a broader geographic range. We compare our results for the late 1990s (1996 to 2000) to results from 1988 to 1995 that were produced with the same data and published in Park et al. (2002).[35]

The second source of data on China's domestic market (data set 2) comes from price data collected by the Jilin Province Grain and Oil Information Center (GOIC). For maize, we use data on prices that were reported on a weekly basis between August 10, 1998, and February 24, 2003, for fifteen of China's main maize production and consumption provinces, including Heilongjiang, Jilin, Liaoning, Hebei, Shandong, Jiangsu, Zhejiang, Shanghai, Hubei, Sichuan, Hunan, Fujian, Guangdong, and Guangxi.

To examine maize markets in the northeast regions of China and between major producing and consuming regions of the country after its ascension to the World Trade Organization (WTO) we use another set of data collected by the Jilin Province GOIC (data set 3). This data set is from October 26, 2001, through February 25, 2003. It is more detailed than data set 2 for two reasons. First, it is more spatially disaggregate. Data set 3 includes prices from three markets in Heilongjiang, three from Jilin, three from Liaoning (including two in production regions and Dalian), as well as market sites in Guangdong, Fujian, Jiangsu, and Hubei. In addition, data set 3 includes data reported more frequently, typically twice a week.

The soybean data come from the same source, the Jilin Provincial GOIC, but are collected a bit differently (data set 4). Soybean data are only available on a monthly basis, from twenty markets. Similar to the maize data in data sets 2 and 3, the soybean data are complete and, overall, their quality appears to be high.

Although we do not have consistent price data over time for fruit and vegetable production, we have collected two data sets on horticultural production in the Greater Beijing Area and in Shandong Province. The data sets were both collected using a stratified randomized approach used to provide a representative regional picture of horticultural production and marketing in two of northern China's most important producing areas.[36] During the same survey efforts, data were collected on horticultural traders and wholesalers.

Price Trends and Spatial Patterns of Market Emergence

In this section, we use our price data to sketch a picture of China's agricultural markets. We divide our analysis into two parts. The first looks at the rise in the integration and efficiency of markets. The second examines the competitiveness

63

of markets in the late 1990s and 2000s. We will then, in the following section, examine whether or not the rise of these markets has benefited producers, especially those in poor households.

To look at whether markets are becoming integrated and efficient, we first plot the data over time and examine how prices move together in markets in the same geographic region and in markets separated by long distances. Next, we examine how price data points from different markets across space (during the same time period) relate to one another graphically (which is done by tracing out transportation gradients in China's rice, maize, and soybean markets). To put the results in perspective, we examine them over time and compare transportation gradients in China's markets with those in U.S. markets. Our assumption is that if prices in different regional markets across China move together and if they create spatial patterns similar to those found in more market-oriented economies (such as the United States), this implies that China's markets are becoming increasingly integrated and efficient.

Examining Integration: Price Trends

Maize

Using data set 3, it can be shown that prices in different markets closely track one another in Northeast China. In figure 3.1 we plot the Dalian domestic price versus the prices in the two Heilongjiang market sites (chosen because they are the farthest northeast from Dalian). While varying over time, the Dalian domestic price remains between $120/metric ton (mt) and $130/mt in December 2001–February 2003. During the same period, the prices in both the Heilongjiang markets move in almost perfect concert with each other; maize prices in Heilongjiang stay between $110/mt and $115/mt. Most importantly, visual inspection shows that although the markets in Dalian and Heilongjiang are more than a thousand kilometers apart and prices vary by $12/mt to $17/mt, the prices in many periods are moving together. That is, when the prices in Dalian move up (down), the prices in Heilongjiang tend to move up (down).

Similar patterns of price movements are found between the two markets in western and central Liaoning and Dalian (not shown in figure 3.1). In fact, the prices in the two Liaoning producing areas track each other even more closely than the markets in Heilongjiang, a finding that is perhaps not surprising given that Liaoning is a smaller province with better transportation and communication infrastructure. The comovements of prices among the producing areas in Liaoning and the consumption center of the province, Dalian, are also clear. Narrower price gaps among producer (lower trend lines) and consumer areas (higher trend lines) reflect smaller distances (see, for example, the narrower gaps in figure 3.1, panel B, versus panel A).

Figure 3.1 Maize Prices in Heilongjiang and Dalian (yuan/mt), October 2001–February 2003

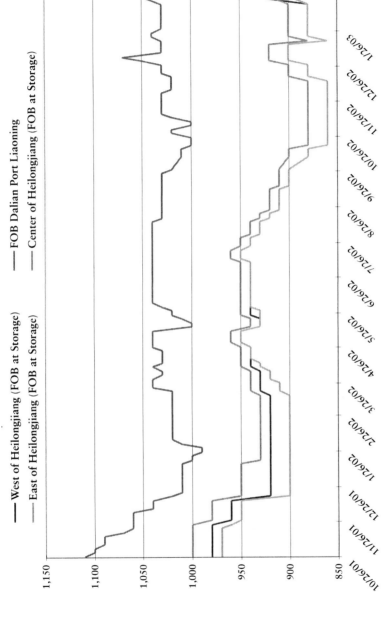

Source: Data set 3.

65

Figure 3.2 Maize Prices in Guangdong, Fujian, and Dalian, January 1996–
February 2003

Panel A. Maize Prices in Dalian and Guangdong

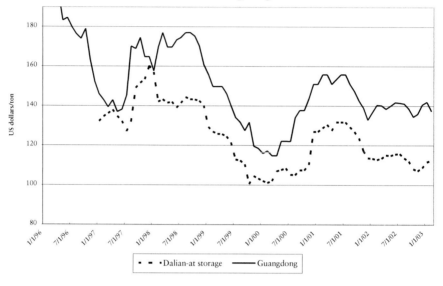

Panel B. Maize Prices in Dalian and Fujian

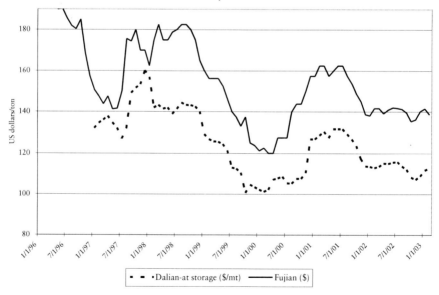

Source: Data set 2.

Using data set 1, we see that the patterns of price movements across other areas of China are similarly close (figure 3.2, panels A and B). While prices have moved together since the mid-1990s between Dalian and Guangdong and between Dalian and Fujian, the tracking among markets appears to be even closer in recent years. Almost every turning point in pricing in Guangdong and Fujian can be found in the Dalian market. With the advent of private shipping and commercial trading, there are now many shipping lines and trading companies that move grain between northeast (Dalian) and south China's main consumption areas (Guangdong/Fujian). Comparing figure 3.2, panels A and B, with figure 3.1 shows that prices in Heilongjiang appear to depend on shifts in feed demand and corn availability in Guangzhou and Fujian.

Soybeans

Using data set 4, we find that soybean prices also move together across markets both in the same region and across space. The bottom two price series in figure 3.3 trace the price trends for soybeans in Heilongjiang and Jilin. The two series are almost indistinguishable from one another, though Heilongjiang prices are slightly lower for almost the entire period. The Shanghai price series, the top line in the figure, also shows that Chinese prices move in concert with one another even when the markets are thousands of kilometers apart. In only two short periods—early 2000 and late 2002—does the gap between the two markets deviate from a fixed margin that is almost equal to the transport price between the northeast and the south.

In a more rigorous cointegration analysis, the results of the descriptive statistics are confirmed. It can also be seen that China's markets have integrated over the 1990s into the early 2000s. In this analysis we examine the degree of integration across all pairs of markets in our rice, maize, and soybean samples.[37] In the case of rice there are more than three hundred pairs of markets; in the case of maize and soybeans there are more than five hundred pairs.

According to our data, only around 25 percent of maize, soybean, and rice markets were integrated before 1995 (table 3.1, column 1). By 2000 the degree of integration had risen to above 50 percent for rice and around 70 to 90 percent for maize and soybeans (column 2). Interestingly, our results are consistent with those of Park et al. (2002), who find that markets were becoming more integrated even in the late 1990s when the retrenchment policies of Zhu Rongji were being implemented. These results suggest that once the genie was let out of the bottle (once private traders began to trade), there was no turning back.

Figure 3.3 Soybean Prices in Heilongjiang, Jilin and Shanghai (yuan/mt), January 1999–September 2003

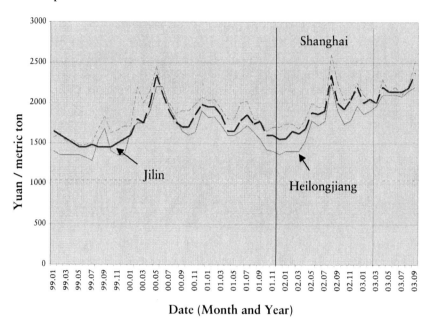

Date (Month and Year)

Source: Data set 4.

Table 3.1 Percentage of Market Pairs in Rural China that Test Positive for Integration (Based on the Dickey-Fuller test), 1989–2003

Commodity	1989–1995	1996–2000	2002–2003
Maize	28	89	98
Soybeans	28	68	99
Japonica rice (Yellow River Valley)	25	60	–
Indica rice (Yangtze Valley and South China)	25	47	–

Source: Data sets 1, 3, and 4.
Note: Results in columns 1 and 2 are from the same data set. For 1989–1995 results for maize and rice, see Park et al. 2002. Rice results are for the whole country in 1989–1995. Results for soybeans for 1989–1995 and all results for 1996–2000 are from the authors. Results for column 3 are from Rozelle and Huang 2004 for maize and Rozelle and Huang 2005 for soybeans.

By 2003 the impact of the market-liberalization policies of the Hu and Wen regime were even clearer (table 3.1, column 3). In the case of the maize and soybean markets, nearly all pairs of markets had become cointegrated. This meant that during any one-week period (or so), if the price in one market moved, those in another would do likewise.

Importantly, the results in this chapter are also found to hold for villages in China's poorest areas.[38] In other words, prices are not only integrated across provinces and between traders in major marketing towns but also in China's poor villages. When poor areas suffer production shocks (for example, a sharp fall in their output due to some natural disaster) it is found that there is no change in the price that is not associated with shifts in outside prices. This is in stark contrast to Mexico, where most of the nation's poorest villages exist in their own subsistence economies.

Examining Integration: Price Patterns across Space

We can also use our data descriptively and in conjunction with relatively simple multivariate analysis to examine price behavior across space, holding time constant. If China's markets function well, then there should be well-defined relationships across space. At any given point of time, the price in the consumption center should be the highest, while the price in the most remote production location the lowest. If all prices are plotted as a function of their distance from the consumption center, the plot of these points traces out a "transportation gradient," so called because in the absence of other distortions, the fall of the line reflects rising transportation costs. Higher per-kilometer transport costs and distance-varying distortions and other costs will also increase the steepness of the line. Thus, the transportation gradient can be used to gauge the efficiency of China's markets (and its transportation systems).

A simple plotting of the relationship between the prices of maize in Dalian and those in Liaoning, Jilin, and Heilongjiang during the postaccession period (after December 2001) illustrates a price contour that indicates well-functioning markets (figure 3.4). Since Dalian is the main demand center in the northeast, the point of export for maize to foreign markets, and the point of transshipment to south China, one would expect that in an integrated marketing system, as a market becomes more remote, the price should fall according to a well-defined transportation gradient.[39] Indeed, the price in a market a thousand kilometers away from Dalian (for example, the Jilin market) is, on average, about 70 yuan/mt less, or 6 percent lower, than the price in Dalian.

Figure 3.4. Changes in Maize Prices across Northeast China as Markets Increase Distances from the Port of Dalian, 2000–2003

Panel A. Transportation Gradient, Maize in Northeast China, 2002

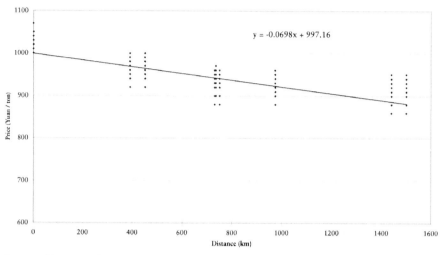

$y = -0.0698x + 997.16$

Source: Data set 3.

Like maize, a simple plotting of the relationship between the price of soybeans in China's ports (Beijing/Tianjin/Hebei, Shanghai, or Guangdong) and those in the inland producing and consuming areas (for example, Heilongjiang, Jilin, Henan, Shandong, or Jiangxi) during the study period, 1999–2003, illustrates a price contour of well-functioning markets (figure 3.5). Since the main demand centers are in the vicinities of the ports, one would expect that in an integrated marketing system, as a market became more remote from the ports, the price should fall. Indeed, the average price in a market in the port (2,250 yuan/mt—say, Hebei/Beijing/Tianjin) and one that is a thousand kilometers away from port (2,100 yuan/mt—say, Jilin) is, on average, about 150 yuan/mt different. In percentage terms, this means the price of Jilin soybeans is about 6 to 7 percent less than the price of soybean in the Beijing area.

When looking at *average transportation gradients* from 1998 to 2000 for maize, soybeans, and rice in China and the United States, table 3.1 suggests that China's markets are indeed performing relatively efficiently.[40] First, the transportation gradients for all crops are falling over time. Although we cannot pinpoint the exact source of the fall in the transportation gradient, according to Park et al. the patterns indicate improving infrastructure and more competitive markets.[41] Second, the results show that the transportation gradients in China are similar to those found in the United States. When plotting similar data and running similar regressions on corn in the Mississippi River Valley, we find price patterns similar to those in China—especially in the case of maize. According to our analysis, then, China's maize, soybean, and rice markets after 2000 are as efficient as (or nearly efficient as) those in the United States. It appears that the marketing reforms during the 1980s and 1990s (as well as aggressive investment in roads and other infrastructure) have dramatically improved the ability of traders to move agricultural commodities (maize in particular) around China at costs that rival those of the United States.[42]

Figure 3.5 Price of Soybeans (yuan/mt) Measured by Distance from the Ports of Tianjin, Shanghai, and Guangdong, 1999–2003

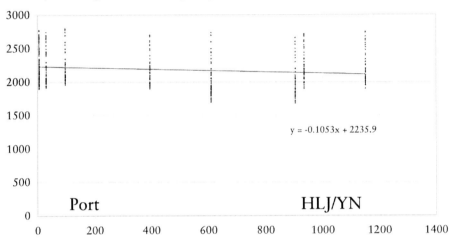

y = -0.1053x + 2235.9

Source: Data set 1.

Competitiveness

In addition to better infrastructure, the increasing integration that is observed throughout the 1990s and early 2000s could also be a function of increasing competitiveness. In this section, we look at competitiveness by examining the number and nature of traders, as well as their pricing behavior.

Perhaps the most convincing metric of the rising competitiveness of China's markets is the increasing number of traders. According to our interviews in the markets from which data sets 2 to 4 derive, tens of thousands of private traders were dominating grain trade by 2001 and 2002 (despite government attempts to remonopolize grain trade in the mid-1990s). According to a survey by Xie, in 2001 there were more than two thousand private rice wholesaler traders in Beijing, more than three thousand in Shanghai, and more than five thousand in Guangzhou.[43] Nearly all rice, maize, and soybean moved through their hands, completely bypassing the state. During our interviews in wholesale markets in 2005 and 2006, most guessed that the number of grain traders had doubled since 2000.

Table 3.2 Supply and Marketing Channels of Horticultural Markets in Greater Beijing Area, 2004

Panel A: First-time buyers (percent)

	Modern supply chains			Traditional supply chains		Other supply chains		
	Super-markets	Specialized suppliers	Processing firms	Small traders	Farmers selling in local periodic markets	Cooperatives	Consumers purchasing direct from farmers	Others[1]
Horticultural crops	0	2	2	79	8	0	7	2
Vegetables	0	3	5	82	5	0	1	3
Fruit	0	1	1	75	11	0	9	3
Nuts	0	6	0	88	3	0	3	0

Panel B: Location of first transaction (percent)

	Farmers' fields	Village center	Roadside	Periodic markets	Wholesale markets	Urban wetmarkets	Others[2]
Horticultural crops	65	9	3	6	11	4	2
Vegetables	64	0	3	6	18	9	0
Fruit	60	12	3	9	12	3	2
Nuts	86	11	0	0	0	0	4

(Table 3.2 continued)

	Modern supply chains			Traditional supply chains		Other supply chains	
Panel C: Second-time buyers (percent)	Super-markets	Specialized suppliers	Processing firms	Small traders	Traders selling to consumers in periodic markets	Cooperatives	Others
Horticultural crops	3	3	10	49	13	0	22
Vegetables	6	0	6	57	11	0	20
Fruit	1	2	9	46	16	0	26
Nuts	3	10	19	50	6	0	12

Source: Honglin Wang, Xiaoxia Dong, Jikun Huang, Scott Rozelle, and Thomas Reardon, "Producing and Procuring Horticultural Crops with Chinese Characteristics: A Case Study in the Greater Beijing Area," World Development (forthcoming).

Note: [1] "Others" (first-time buyers) includes purchases by agents of hotels or restaurants, gifts to other farmers, or procurement by organized groups (such as enterprises for distribution to their workers).

[2] "Others" (second-time buyers) includes sales to other villages, to market sites that supply processing, and to other food firms.

Inputs—fertilizer in particular—are increasingly dominated by the private sector, and the number of traders has grown over time. By the mid-1990s, about 50 percent of fertilizer was sold by private traders. In 2000, according to a national representative survey of twelve hundred households in six provinces, fertilizer sales at the farmgate level were almost exclusively handled by the private sector. In a 2004 survey of fertilizer use and procurement by households in eight provinces, the Center for Chinese Agricultural Policy found that all fertilizer was purchased from private individuals and that the number of traders was rising dramatically.[44] During the preplanting season, in almost any village in China scores of fertilizer traders can be found in permanent shops, periodic markets, on roadsides, and acting as itinerant traders moving from village to village selling door to door.

Perhaps the most competitive markets are those for horticultural products. According to our data, despite the rise of supermarkets, restaurants, and processors—that is, the dominant actors in the downstream segments of horticultural marketing chains—in China's villages during the harvest season nearly all fruits and vegetables are sold by small producers and bought by small traders. Although there is much discussion about the potential effect of the rise of modern supply chains on rural areas, according to our data, supermarkets are completely absent in these areas (table 3.2). Indeed, none of the 201 village leaders that we interviewed reported the use of supermarkets for the procurement of any horticultural goods (panel A, column 1). Likewise, village leaders reported that of total procurement from farmers, only 2 percent was by specialized suppliers and 2 percent by processing firms (columns 2 and 3). Hence, in the Greater Beijing Area, in 2004 only 4 percent of all horticultural goods were procured by firms that could be described as part of the modern supply chain. Although not shown, the data from households that took part in a survey of 50 villages in Greater Beijing show the exact same patterns: households sold almost all of their output to small traders—either villages or in local wholesale markets. No household reported that it sold to a supermarket or a specialized supplier.

A similar picture emerges from the focus groups of farmers in the seventy-two Shandong tomato- and cucumber-producing villages (table 3.3). Ninety-nine percent of farmers in the Shandong tomato-producing village in both 2000 (22—row 1+77—row 2) and 2004 (15—row 1+84—row 2) stated that they sold their tomatoes to small traders that either visited their village or traded in local wholesale markets (columns 1 and 2). While the percentage that was sold to small traders in the wholesale market rose (from 77 to 84 percent, shifting from direct sales to small traders in the village), less than 1 percent of sales remained in all other channels. Meanwhile, more than 90 percent of cucumbers were to small traders in the village or wholesale market (columns 3 and 4). Interviews with trading firms (which, on average, consisted of four employees, almost always family members or close friends) in the wholesale markets in both Beijing and Shandong confirm that the procurement channels between the farmer and the wholesale market have changed very little and that the supply of horticultural products in China flow largely through traditional, small, trader-dominated supply chains.[45]

Table 3.3 Procurement Channels at the Farmgate: Buyers of Tomatoes and Cucumbers Produced in Sample Shandong Village, 2000 and 2005

	Tomato villages		Cucumber villages	
	2000	2005	2000	2005
	(%)	(%)	(%)	(%)
Small traders	22	15	14	14
Wholesalers	77	84	77	78
Special suppliers	0	0.004	0.4	0.3
Processing firms	0	0.2	1	3
Supermarkets	0.1	0.3	0	0.1
Associations	0	0	0	2
Exporters	0	0	2	1
Consumers	1	0.4	5	1

Source: Authors' survey.
Note: Data are from a question posed to farmers in the focus group: "To whom did you sell your tomatoes/cucumbers?"

Not only was there little evidence of procurement from farmers by the newly emerging players in the retail segment of the supply chain, there was almost no change in the contractual terms under which most transactions took place. In the Greater Beijing sample there was nearly no contracting over either price or quantity, and no provision of input or credit by the buyer. All transactions took place on a cash, spot-market basis in both 2000 and 2004. In the Shandong tomato- and cucumber-producing villages, the exact same pattern held for both 2000 and 2005. In sum, our study sites, which cover some of the most productive and commercialized horticultural areas in China, show little penetration by actors in modern supply chains.

In fact, judging by the number of traders to whom farmers can sell without even leaving their village, it seems that horticultural markets are extremely competitive. For example, producers in a hundred and twenty randomly selected villages in Shandong estimated that, on average, farmers in each village had a choice of selling their crop to more than a hundred different traders. Interviewed independently, village leaders gave similar estimates.

The profit margins of traders between the village and markets and between rural and urban wholesale markets confirm the competitiveness of China's horticultural markets. Profit margins are razor thin; traders often make one or two fen (1/100th of a yuan) per kilogram. The income of the typical small trader of horticultural commodities in China is only somewhat higher than the average producer. When we interviewed traders in Beijing who were handling commodities from Shandong we found that the wholesale prices in Beijing and wholesale prices in Shanghai differed only by the transportation cost plus 3 percent. There was almost no difference among traders inside the market on any given day for a commodity of the same quality.

A quantitative study by Park et al., supplemented by qualitative interviews, confirms that the transaction costs of moving commodities across space have fallen over time.[46] While increasing competitiveness is only one possible reason for this, it is consistent with this observation. Both empirical work (and qualitative interviews) suggest that the sales of grain between production/surplus and consumption/deficit areas are only made after many phone calls and that the price gap between the two is close to the transportation cost.

When one observes how the selling price in a village is struck between a buyer and seller, it is clear that most sellers are aware of the going market rate in the locality and that buyers are constantly calling their home offices to check on the highest bid price allowable (always denominated in fen). In a recent survey in one hundred and forty villages in Shandong, although farmers wished they had better price information, they mainly wanted to know what the price would be in the future. Almost no one mentioned selling without good knowledge of the current market. Against other production and marketing constraints, Shandong farmers ranked "price discovery at the time of crop sale" far down the list in terms of importance of problems that they faced. Discussions with more than thirty focus groups of grape, apple, tomato, and cucumber producers across Shandong found that most farmers had a very good idea of what the price was at the time that they sold it. There are many sources of price discovery in a market that is made up of thousands of traders and many market sites.

In sum, it is little wonder that China's markets are so efficient. The competitiveness of grain, input, and horticultural markets are clearly very high. All markets are dominated by private individuals. Most traders work for themselves (in groups of two to six) or as incentivized agents for a downstream buyer. Wholesale markets are also dominated by hundreds if not thousands of traders.[47] With so many traders moving around the country, the integration analysis suggests that when small gaps in prices between two regions appear, the margins are quickly arbitraged away. With the increasing concentration in the food markets in the United States, European Union (EU), and Japan, China's markets may be more efficient, competitive, and integrated than those of most developed countries.

Performance

It is often said that the market is a two-edged sword.[48] Since the job of a well-functioning market is to transmit information about shifts in supply and demand ("price signals") quickly throughout the region or nation, the net impact that a rise in markets will have on producers will depend on the nature of the supply and/or demand shocks in the economy as a whole. Therefore, in the case of positive supply shocks (oversupply) or negative demand shocks (reduced demand), aside from helping farmers (when price rises are transmitted to farmers and farmgate prices rise), markets are responsible for reducing the farmgate price of agricultural commodities.

It could be argued that the emergence of markets has not, in fact, been good for farmers and that farmers in a very real sense have been a victim of their own success in raising productivity. Between 1980 and 2005—with the exception of price spikes in 1988 and 1995—the real price of rice, wheat, and maize fell as supply outpaced demand.[49] As shown by a regression approach to measure trends, grain prices fell in real terms by 33 percent (maize) to 45 percent (wheat) between the late 1970s and early 2000s. The falling prices of agricultural products have been tied to the flagging performance of agriculture during the 1980s and 1990s.[50]

In horticultural markets, too, emerging markets may be tied to adverse welfare consequences. Nationally, the real prices of fruits and vegetables have fallen over time.[51] There are endless stories of farming communities that have spent enormous time and effort on expanding orchards or greenhouses only to find that the prices on which they based their initial investments had collapsed and that they were earning much lower profits than originally anticipated (or even incurring losses). Intraseason price variability—a natural phenomenon in almost all fruit and vegetable economies due to the perishable nature of crops—was noted in focus groups as the major price concern of producers.

In a broad sense, then, markets will not necessarily raise incomes. If markets are emerging and transmitting information in the form of lower prices (due to underlying supply and demand), everything else held equal, poverty could be exacerbated rather than alleviated. In fact, well-functioning markets should be expected to be neutral in terms of their effects on farmers. Markets merely transmit prices. It should be noted that whether those prices are higher or lower is a function of other factors—outside of markets—and so should not be blamed on the functioning of the markets themselves.

The Positive Effects of Improved Markets

Although few authors have attempted to quantify the gains of market liberalization, the few studies that do exist on this subject show that farmers have gained from increased allocative efficiency. For example, both Lin and Huang and Rozelle argue that marketization has a positive effect on productivity.[52] Both sets of authors conjecture that the gains are in part due to market specialization and increased efficiency. Unfortunately, these conjectures are not made on an empirical basis. In this section, we seek to provide an empirical analysis of how the emergence of markets has affected farmers' specialization, efficiency, and productivity.

Markets and Specialization

In order to try to understand whether or not specialization has occurred since the mid-1990s (when markets began to emerge and integrate), in 2004 we conducted a randomized, nationally representative survey of four hundred communities.[53] In the survey of community leaders we asked the question Are farmers in your village specializing in any particular crop or livestock commodity? The question was asked for the years 1995 and 2004. If the respondents answered affirmatively, we asked about the commodity in which they were specializing. If the farmers in the community were specializing in a cropping activity, we asked for the area sown with the specialty commodity.

The results of our survey show that China's agricultural sector has indeed become specialized. Between 1995 and 2004, the percentage of villages specializing in an agricultural commodity increased sharply in every province we studied (table 3.4, columns 1 and 2). On average, throughout our sample from across China, 30 percent of China's villages were specializing, up from 21 percent in 1995. When examining the output of the villages that are specializing, it is clear that the rise in the demand for horticultural and other specialty products is what is driving the specialization. In our sample, 60 percent of specializing villages were producing either fruits (28 percent), vegetables (13 percent), or other cash crops (28 percent—for example, sugarcane, tobacco, and cotton). Other villages were specializing in livestock commodities, oilseeds, forest products, and other commodities. Our 2006 Shandong community survey found that more than 60 percent of villages were specializing in a crop or other agricultural commodity.

Table 3.4 Percentage of Villages and Sown Area Specialized, by Region

	Percentage of villages		Percentage of sown area	
	1995	2004	1995	2004
Average	21	30	14	24
• Hebei	18	19	20	24
• Henan	22	23	4	9
• Shanxi	51	74	11	22
• Shaanxi	4	5	23	32
• Inner Mongolia	9	17	38	40
• Liaojing	15	32	13	29

Source: Jikun Huang and Scott Rozelle, "Market Development, Commercialization and Small Farmers in China," Working Paper, Center for Chinese Agricultural Policy, Institute of Geographical Sciences and Natural Resource Research (Chinese Academy of Sciences, Beijing, China, 2005).

Markets, Efficiency, and Improved Welfare

The only truly systematic attempt to measure how efficiency improves markets and the overall performance of the economy was made by deBrauw et al. (2004).[54] The authors develop measures of increased responsiveness and flexibility within a dynamic adjustment cost framework to estimate the returns to market liberalization reforms, holding incentive reforms and other factors constant. They find that the behavior of producers in China has been affected by market liberalization. Gains in responsiveness (measured by price elasticities of factor demand for variable inputs—in this case, fertilizer) between the early and late reform periods are attributed to the gradual market-liberalizing changes of the late 1980s. Farmers also have increased their speed of adjustment of quasifixed factors (which in the case of China's agriculture include labor and sown area) to price changes between the early and late reform period.

DeBrauw et al. also measure how increased flexibility and responsiveness affect overall welfare. Although by 1995 the direct gains were relatively small (as might be expected given the gradual nature of market changes), it is found that the magnitude of gains in efficiency due to increased responsiveness and flexibility in the late reform period (between 1985 and 1995) is positive and statistically significant.

Structural Adjustment and Improved Incomes

If the increased flexibility of markets and the reduced restrictions on farmers' choice of crop or activity are allowing more and more farmers to shift into the production of new commodities (such as fruits, vegetables, livestock, and dairy), an emerging empirical literature shows that the farmers producing these nontraditional crops are increasing their incomes. For example, in Greater Beijing it has been shown that both producers and traders of fruits and vegetables have higher incomes, *ceteris paribus*.[55] The same results are found for grape, apple, tomato, and cucumber producers in Shandong Province.[56]

Producers that shift into livestock commodities are also shown to increase their earnings. Bi et al. demonstrate that hog and poultry producers have higher incomes, ceteris paribus, than their counterparts who are mainly producing grain.[57] Huang et al. show that dairy production enhances income—even among farmers with five and fewer dairy animals.[58] To the extent that structural adjustment policies have allowed specialization, especially in the production of crops and animal activities, the rise of markets is surely associated with a significant improvement in rural welfare.

Perhaps most important, Wang et al. show that—contrary to the fears of policymakers who worried that only the rich benefit from the new opportunities in the production of higher-valued commodities—at least in some areas of China, it is the poor who have benefited. According to our data, farmers in poor villages and independently poor farmers are actually increasing their share of the production of horticultural crops.[59] To show this, we divide the villages in our Greater Beijing sample into quartiles, divided by reported income per capita. Between 2000 and 2004 we find that farmers in the very poor and poor village categories (that is, those farmers living in villages with incomes below the median income level) have increased their share of total sown area. In fact, by 2004, farmers in very poor and poor villages produced more than half of horticultural crops in Greater Beijing. Even more significant, farmers in the very poor villages increased their share of vegetables, fruits, and nuts between 2000 and 2004 from 15 percent to 22 percent

A similar picture emerges when examining different categories of horticultural crops. For example, in the case of fruit, production is dominated by farmers in very poor and poor villages. In contrast, farmers in average-income villages produce most of the vegetables. Of course, one of the most interesting findings of table 3.2 is that farmers in the richest villages are not the largest producers (or beneficiaries) of vegetables, fruits, or nuts.

Work in other parts of China and in other sectors produces similar findings. Our results from Shandong show that farmers were equally able to enter the horticultural market in rich and poor villages in the 2000s. In our Beijing sample, we find that it is the poor who are increasing production of hogs.[60] In fact, in a much broader sample, Chen et al. show this trend throughout China's hog-producing regions.[61]

Conclusion

Disproving the past findings of some researchers, China's domestic markets—at least in agriculture—have become increasingly integrated, efficient, and competitive. Regulations are few and entry is easy. In fact, compared with the often highly regulated agricultural markets in many other countries, China (somewhat surprisingly) can now be considered part of a group of nations that includes Australia, New Zealand, and Brazil—some of the most competitive, free agricultural markets in the world. This is remarkable, given that thirty years ago there were almost no free markets in China where agriculture was part of the planned economy. Equally remarkable is that, except for the emergence of a grain-subsidy program since 2004 (which in many parts of the country is being run as a decoupled income-transfer scheme), the state has almost completely disappeared from agricultural markets.

So, what has been the impact of these liberalized, flourishing markets? As do markets anywhere, good markets merely transmit signals about supply, demand, and uncertainty that are inherent in the fabric of the economy. On the downside, markets have exposed farmers to fluctuation—both good and bad—that in the past may have gone unnoticed by those living in isolated localities. Farmers, exposed to the larger forces of markets, now have less control of their lives. But, as we have seen, there have been many positive effects: rising productivity, rising specialization, and rising incomes as farmers move into new specialty crops. Above all, one of the most surprising findings is that these new, competitive markets, far from excluding poor farmers, have sought them out and given them new opportunities to become a part of China's thriving economy.

Marketization in Rural China: Source of Crisis or Opportunity?

So what is the final word? At least in the agricultural sector, farmers appear to be gaining a lot of information from the emergence of markets. Not all of the information that they receive, of course, is positive. At the very least, because China is changing so fast, this information will challenge farmers to adapt.

Is there more gain or more pain? To the extent that change is difficult, there will be pain. And, of course, some households and communities will be better able and willing to adjust than others. But we have also shown that there is a lot of gain. There is increased specialization, improved efficiency—and income gains, linked to new activities that markets have allowed farmers to move into.

Fast-growing economies striving for modernization are defined by change. Urbanization, industrialization, and globalization imply growth. And with growth come changes in preferences and in the demand put on China's agricultural producers. Most likely, farmers will have to undergo more changes, many of them difficult. However, if the rural population wants to be part of China's modernizing surge, markets are an integral part of the process.

In short, there will be pain. But, we believe that our findings are consistent with the view that most of the unavoidable changes will, ultimately, be good ones. They might best be tagged as "growing pains."

Notes

[1] See John McMillan, John Walley, and Lijing Zhu, "The Impact of China's Economic Reforms on Agricultural Productivity Growth," *Journal of Political Economy* 97 (1989): 781–807; Shenggen Fan, "Effects of Technological Change and Institutional Reform on Production Growth in Chinese Agriculture," *American Journal of Agricultural Economics* 73 (1991): 266–75; Justin Yifu Lin, "Rural Reforms and Agricultural Growth in China," *American Economic Review* 82 (1992): 34–51; John McMillan, "Markets in Transition," in David Kreps and Kenneth F. Wallis, *eds.*, *Advances in Economics and Econometrics: Theory and Applications*, vol. 2 (Cambridge: Cambridge Univ. Press, 1997: 210–39).

[2] See McMillan, "Markets in Transition."

[3] See Johan Swinnen and Scott Rozelle, *From Marx and Mao to the Market: The Economics and Politics of Agrarian Transition* (Oxford: Oxford Univ. Press, 2006).

[4] Yingyi Qian and Chenggen Xu, "Innovation and Bureaucracy under Soft and Hard Budget Constraints," *Review of Economic Studies* 65, no. 1 (1998): 151–64.

[5] See Terry Sicular, "Redefining State, Plan, and Market: China's Reforms in Agricultural Commerce," *China Quarterly* 144 (1995): 1020–46.

[6] See Alan deBrauw, Jikun Huang, and Scott Rozelle, "The Sequencing of Reforms in China's Agricultural Transition," *Economics of Transition* 12, no. 3 (2004): 427–66.

[7] Alwyn Young, "The Razor's Edge: Distortions and Incremental Reform in the People's Republic of China," *Quarterly Journal of Economics* 115 (November 2000): 1091–135.

⁸ Sandra Poncet, "Measuring Chinese Domestic and International Integration?" *China Economic Review* 14, no. 1 (2003): 1–22, www1.elsevier.com/homepage/sae/econworld/econbase/chieco/frame.htm.

⁹ *Zhongguo Tongji Nianjian* 2006 [China Statistical Yearbook 2006] (Beijing: Zhongguo Tongji Nianjian Chubanshe, 2006).

¹⁰ For example, Terry Sicular, "Agricultural Planning and Pricing in the Post-Mao Period," *China Quarterly* 116 (1988): 671–703; Sicular, "Redefining State, Plan, and Market," 1020–46; deBrauw, Huang, and Rozelle, "The Sequencing of Reforms."

¹¹ Swinnen and Rozelle, *From Marx and Mao to the Market.*

¹² See Sicular, "Agricultural Planning and Pricing in the Post-Mao Period"; Sicular, "Redefining State, Plan, and Market"; Dwight Perkins, "Completing China's Move to the Market," *Journal of Economic Perspectives* 8.2 (Spring 1994): 23–46; and Lin, "Rural Reforms and Agricultural Growth in China."

¹³ See Sicular, "Agricultural Planning and Pricing in the Post-Mao Period."

¹⁴ See W. Skinner, "Rural Marketing in China: Repression and Revival," *China Quarterly* 103 (1985): 393–413.

¹⁵ See Sicular, "Redefining State, Plan, and Market," 1020–46.

¹⁶ See deBrauw, Huang, and Rozelle, "The Sequencing of Reforms," 427–66.

¹⁷ Sicular, "Redefining State, Plan, and Market," 1020–46.

¹⁸ See deBrauw, Huang, and Rozelle, "The Sequencing of Reforms," 427–66.

¹⁹ See Scott Rozelle, Albert Park, Jikun Huang, and Hehui Jin, "Bureaucrat to Entrepreneur: The Changing Role of the State in China's Transitional Commodity Economy," *Economic Development and Cultural Change* 48, no. 2 (2000): 227–52.

²⁰ Bruce Stone, "Developments in Agricultural Technology," *China Quarterly* 116 (December 1988): 767–822; Qiaolun Ye and Scott Rozelle, "Fertilizer Demand in China's Reforming Economy," *Canadian Journal of Agricultural Economics* 42, no. 2 (May 1994): 191–208.

²¹ Sicular, "Redefining State, Plan, and Market," 1020–46.

²² Ye and Rozelle, "Fertilizer Demand in China's Reforming Economy," 191–208.

²³ Justin Yifu Lin, Fang Cai, and Zhou Li, *The China Miracle: Development Strategy and Economic Reform* (Hong Kong: Chinese Univ. Press, 1996).

²⁴ Sicular, "Redefining State, Plan, and Market," 1020–46.

²⁵ See Jikun Huang, Scott Rozelle, and Min Chang, "The Nature of Distortions to Agricultural Incentives in China and Implications of WTO Accession," *World Bank Economic Review* 18, no. 1 (2004): 59–84.

²⁶ Rozelle et al., "Bureaucrat to Entrepreneur," 227–52.

²⁷ See Albert Park and Scott Rozelle, "Reforming State-Market Relations in Rural China," *Economics of Transition* 6, no. 2 (1998): 461–80.

²⁸ See A. Nyberg and S. Rozelle, *Accelerating China's Rural Transformation* (Washington, DC: World Bank, 1999)

²⁹ Albert Park, Hehui Jin, Scott Rozelle, and Jikun Huang, "Market Emergence and Transition: Arbitrage, Transition Costs, and Autarky in China's Grain Market," *American Journal of Agricultural Economics* 84, no. 1 (February 2002): 67–82

³⁰ Huang, Rozelle, and Chang, "The Nature of Distortions to Agricultural Incentives in China," 59–84.

³¹ Huang, Rozelle, and Chang, "The Nature of Distortions to Agricultural Incentives in China," 59–84.

[32] Scott Rozelle, Jikun Huang, and Keijiro Otsuka, "The Role of Agriculture in China's Development: Past Failures; Present Successes and Future Challenges," in Tom Rawski and Loren Brandt, eds., *China's Great Economic Transformation*, (London: Oxford Univ. Press, forthcoming).

[33] In fact, the reader should be aware of an alternative interpretation. Although we attribute many of the observed changes in China's marketing policy to the effectiveness of state policies, others say that the government simply "abandoned" the countryside. In this interpretation, the expansion of produce markets we observe today is less a conscious policy choice than the result of state neglect, and whatever benefits farmers may be experiencing now may evaporate in the future. But the huge effort that has been put into rural development since the Hu Jintao and Wen Jiabao government took power in 2003 suggests that the government is actively interested in the future of the rural economy.

[34] Since we use data over time, we need to convert prices to a real basis. Nominal prices from our data set are deflated using the monthly consumer price indices calculated and reported by the China National Bureau of Statistics. Deflation facilitates transaction cost comparisons across time and allows us to disregard transaction cost increases within periods associated with inflation.

[35] To produce the results, we run cointegration tests on each pair of markets using the data for each year. So, in other words, we use 36 observations (since the price data are available every 10 days) and count the number of pairs of markets that are cointegrated in a statistically significant way (see next endnote and text for explanation of testing). For example, this means in the case of soybeans, for the late 1990s (1996 to 2000), we are examining the extent of integration between 190 (20*19/2) pairs of markets in each of the 5 years, which equals a total of 950 pairs of markets. Hence, since we found that prices in 646 markets were integrated (according to the testing procedure), we report that 68 percent of markets are integrated in the late 1990s. Since we use only 36 observations per test, and since cointegration tests typically perform better with longer time series, by splitting our data into annual increments, we are biasing the results against accepting integration. We do this in order to make our analysis comparable to Park et al., "Market Emergence and Transition," which follows a similar procedure.

[36] For detailed descriptions of the data, see Honglin Wang, Xiaoxia Dong, Jikun Huang, Scott Rozelle, and Thomas Reardon, "Producing and Procuring Horticultural Crops with Chinese Characteristics: A Case Study in the Greater Beijing Area," *World Development* (forthcoming); and Jikun Huang, Xiaoxia Dong, Yuhua Wu, Huayong Zhi, Xianfang Nui, Zhurong Huang, and Scott Rozelle, "Regoverning Markets: The China Meso-level Study," Working Paper, Center for Chinese Agricultural Policy (Chinese Academy of Sciences, Beijing, China, 2007).

[37] For a complete set of results, see Huang, Rozelle, and Chang, "The Nature of Distortions to Agricultural Incentives in China," 59–84.

[38] Huang, Rozelle, and Chang, "The Nature of Distortions to Agricultural Incentives in China," 59–84.

[39] China's custom data demonstrate overwhelmingly that most of China's maize is exported from Dalian (more than 90 percent over the past 5 years). By far most of the maize from the northern part of the nation that moves to the southern part of the nation also flows through Dalian.

[40] An average transportation gradient (reported in table 3.1 for maize, soybeans, and rice for China from 1998 to 2000, and for maize and soybeans for the United States for 1998) is the coefficient on the "distance variable" (a variable that is measuring the distance in 1,000 kilometers from the port to the location of the market) from regressions that explain commodity-specific prices for each year (in logs) as a function of the distance variable and a series of period dummies (one for each week of the year). In other words, the coefficient is the average percent change in price for each 1000 kilometers that a marketing site is removed from the port, holding constant the average price change for all sites during each week of the year. Regression results available from authors upon request.

[41] Park et al., "Market Emergence and Transition."

[42] Renfu Luo, Linxiu Zhang, Chengfang Liu, and Scott Rozelle, "The Emergence of Agricultural Commodity Markets in China," *Chinese Economy* 39, no. 4 (July–August 2006): 57–84.

[43] Yuping Xie, "An Analysis of China's Grain Markets," Masters Thesis, Chinese Academy of Sciences (Center for Chinese Agricultural Policy, Beijing, China, 2002).

[44] Linxiu Zhang, Jikun Huang, Fangbin Qiao, and Scott Rozelle, "Do China's Farmers Overuse Fertilizer?" Working Paper, Chinese Academy of Sciences (Center for Chinese Agricultural Policy, Beijing, China, 2005).

[45] Tables not shown, but available in Wang et al., "Producing and Procuring Horticultural Crops."

[46] Park et al., "Market Emergence and Transition."

[47] Wang et al., "Producing and Procuring Horticultural Crops."

[48] Huang, Rozelle, and Chang, "The Nature of Distortions to Agricultural Incentives in China," 59–84.

[49] Rozelle, Huang, and Otsuka, "The Role of Agriculture in China's Development."

[50] Scott Rozelle, "Stagnation without Equity: Changing Patterns of Income and Inequality in China's Post-Reform Rural Economy," *The China Journal* 35 (January 1996): 63–96.

[51] Huang, Rozelle, and Chang, "The Nature of Distortions to Agricultural Incentives in China," 59–84.

[52] Lin, "Rural Reforms and Agricultural Growth in China"; Jikun Huang and Scott Rozelle, "Technological Change: Rediscovering the Engine of Productivity Growth in China's Rural Economy," *Journal of Development Economics* 49 (1996): 337–69.

[53] For a complete description of this survey, see Jikun Huang and Scott Rozelle, "Market Development, Commercialization and Small Farmers in China," Working Paper, Center for Chinese Agricultural Policy, Institute of Geographical Sciences and Natural Resource Research (Chinese Academy of Sciences, Beijing, China, 2005).

[54] See deBrauw, Huang, and Rozelle, "The Sequencing of Reforms," 427–66.

[55] Wang et al., "Producing and Procuring Horticultural Crops."

[56] Huang et al., "Regoverning Markets."

[57] X. Bi, Jikun Huang, and Scott Rozelle, "Producing China's Hogs and Poultry in China's Rural Economy," Working Paper, Center for Chinese Agricultural Policy (Chinese Academy of Sciences, Beijing, China, 2007).

[58] Huang et al., "Regoverning Markets."

[59] Wang et al., "Producing and Procuring Horticultural Crops"; Elizabeth M. M. Q. Farina and Eduardo Luiz Machado, "Government Regulation and Business Strategies in the Brazilian Fresh Fruit and Vegetable Market," Paper Presented to the International

Food and Agribusiness Management Association (IFAMA) Congress, Florence, Italy, June 1999.

[60] Bi, Huang, and Rozelle, "Producing China's Hogs and Poultry in China's Rural Economy."

[61] Jing Chen, Scott Rozelle, and Colin Carter, "Market Emergence and the Rise and Fall of Backyard Hog Production in China," Working Paper, Freeman Spogli Institute of International Studies (Stanford University, Stanford, 2005).

Rights and Rental: Are Rural Cultivated Land Policy and Management Constraining or Facilitating China's Modernization?

Linxiu Zhang, Songqing Jin, Scott Rozelle, Klaus Deininger, and Jikun Huang[1]

China's rural economic reform, widely regarded as one of the most successful transitions of the past two decades, radically altered land tenure in rural China.[2] The initial reforms (initiated in the late 1970s and early 1980s) triggered an unprecedented acceleration of agricultural growth in China. Empirical studies[3] attribute a significant part of this increase to the incentives associated with better residual income rights. Growth slackened after 1984, however, especially for grain production.[4]

The deceleration in the late 1980s and early 1990s prompted considerable debate. Some observers blamed China's land-management system—the one dimension of the farm economy that had been altered relatively little since the initial reforms. Insecure tenure, for example, reportedly discouraged investment in agriculture and lowered growth.[5] Such perceived problems sparked calls for either land privatization or for the extension of land contracts to thirty years or more (this last option was institutionalized in the early 2000s).[6]

While growth rebounded in the mid to late 1990s, the nature of China's land rights still require consideration. As China goes industrial, urban, and global, it will need to find a way to increase farm incomes even as hundreds of millions of households move to the cities. Without being able to increase protection against imports from other countries at the border, due to its World Trade Organization (WTO) commitments,[7] the only feasible way to increase the incomes of those left in farming is to increase farm sizes. Since land cannot be bought or sold (due to policy constraints implemented by national leaders), this means that China's cultivated rental markets need to be improved. In the 1980s and even the 1990s, restrictions on renting kept the number of rental contracts extremely small.[8] In recent years, however, rental markets seeM to have emerged in a vibrant way. Unfortunately, China's national statistic surveys offer almost no systematic information on the scope of current rental markets or on the ways that local governments and village leaders discourage or encourage them.

The overall goal of this chapter is to describe the organization and utilization of China's cultivated land resources in order to better weigh China's policy options. In particular, we will look at cultivated land rights and cultivated land rentals. From a policy perspective, the critical question is how effective both have been in providing households the necessary incentives and flexibility to ensure rational land use and investment, while simultaneously helping local communities meet distributive objectives. We will try to assess what the literature says about the effects of China's land rights and rentals on the efficiency, equity, and overall development of the rural sector. Ultimately, we want to know if rural land-management practices must be transformed to avoid chronic unrest or if only gradual adjustments are required to promote economic growth and societal well being.

Data

Of the four data sets used in this chapter, the first three deal with land rights in general, and the fourth focuses on land rentals in particular.

First and foremost, in 1996, we collected a community-level data set that, because of its widespread coverage, provided a rough estimate of nationwide trends and heterogeneity. We also based some of our insights and findings on a household data set that we collected from the Liaoning and Hebei provinces in 1995.

This community-level data set (data set 1) covers two hundred and fifteen villages in eight representative provinces across China. On the coast—the most developed area in China—the sample includes the Liaoning, Shandong, and Zhejiang provinces. Inland, the agricultural heartland of the upper and middle Yangtze River Valley, the sample includes the Hebei, Hubei, and Sichuan provinces. In the northwest and southwest, China's poorest regions, the sample includes the Shaanxi and Yunnan provinces. In all of these provinces, counties were stratified on the basis of per capita industrial output. Eight counties per province were randomly selected—two from each of the quartiles of the ranked list of counties. A similar sampling procedure was used in each county to select two sample townships and in each township to select two sample villages.

In each village, the enumerators elicited a broad array of detailed data from three village leaders: the party secretary, the chairman of the village committee or the village leader, and the village accountant. These three leaders were chosen because they were usually able to answer most questions about current and past village institutions. The ten-section survey instrument included questions on off-farm labor, land management, local industrial management, local credit markets, periodic markets, agricultural input and output markets, and the local political environment. We collected data on two years—1988 and 1995—and looked for changes since household farming was reintroduced in the late 1970s and early 1980s. We collected detailed information on the frequency, average size, and timing of each village's land readjustments, and about its rental activities and related institutions, including local rules concerning renting, how many households participated in the rental process, and how much land was engaged in rental transactions.

To study the impact of tenure types and land rights on production behavior, a survey of seven hundred and eighty households from thirty-one villages in six counties in the Hebei and Liaoning provinces was also conducted in the summer of 1995 (data set 2). The Hebei and Liaoning provinces, located in north and northeast China, are two of China's major agricultural provinces, and the six sample counties are located in the major agricultural areas of the two provinces. Most agricultural producers in the sample counties depend on grain or cash-crop production. Farmers primarily grow maize—which accounts for about 70 percent of the total sown area—and also cultivate soybeans, rice, and cotton.

For each of the surveyed households, enumerators recorded detailed information about household characteristics and agricultural production activities. The total land holdings of each household were enumerated on a plot-by-plot basis. After obtaining basic information about each plot, the supervisor of the enumeration team selected two plots from each household for more detailed investigation. An effort was made to ensure that the two plots were being farmed under different tenure forms (e.g., one plot was a private plot, and the other plot was contracted to the household from the collective). The enumerators systematically surveyed the two selected plots from each household, eliciting information about the plots' tenure status, specific land rights, all inputs and outputs, and land quality. After data cleaning, the sample consisted of 1,073 plots from 612 households.

These data on land rights were updated in data set 3, collected by the authors in 2000. This data set covers sixty villages across six nationally representative provinces—Hebei, Liaoning, Shanxi, Zhejiang, Hubei, and Sichuan. There are twenty sample households from each village, for a total of one thousand two hundred households. Since the survey is designed to analyze land tenancy issues in China, this data set provides rich information on land rights, land-rental transactions, and family labor endowments. The data set includes the results of several recall questionnaires on particular issues, such as allocated land holdings in earlier years. This information indicates tenure insecurity. The data are available by plot, for all holdings of cultivated land and orchards in the sample households.

The data on cultivated land rentals (data set 4) come from China's Rural Household Income and Expenditure Survey (HIES), a nationwide survey of rural households carried out annually by China's National Bureau of Statistics (NBS). Like most household surveys, the sample (prepared by NBS) uses a two-stage sampling procedure. In the first stage, sampling villages are drawn randomly from the survey. Sample villages in 2001 came from twenty-six provinces. In the second stage, ten households were drawn from each administrative village in the sample, using an equal-distance sampling methodology.

While the main aim of the HIES is to provide a detailed record of household consumption and production activities, each year the survey team undertakes a series of special interviews that provide information on other household variables. In 2001 the NBS added one-time questions related to household land-rental activities. In particular, enumerators asked households whether they rented land in or out and, if they did, the size of the rental transaction. In addition, there is a block of the survey (added in the 1990s) that records information on labor allocation, including whether a member of the household worked off the farm and, if so, where he or she lived. If a household member earned a wage while living outside of the home, we counted him or her as part of the migrant labor force.

We use both panel data and cross-sectional data for our analysis in this chapter. The descriptive statistics that we present are derived from a 2001 data set that includes the *entire sample* for nineteen of the NBS's twenty-six sample provinces. As part of our agreement with the NBS, we used only a *subsample* from the same nineteen provinces (28 percent of the entire sample of the nineteen provinces) for our econometric analysis of the determinants of land rental and migration. Since the households in our subsample were chosen from those interviewed in both 2000 and 2001, the NBS allowed us to create a panel that included variables that could be used to estimate a production function. With these data, we were able to derive a measure of the household's productive efficiency in farming, as done by Deininger and Jin (2002).[9] The land-rental and migration activities analyses use only the subsample of data for 2001.

Tenure, Rentals, and Other Land Rights

In this section, we focus our attention on three rights: security of tenure, transfer or rental rights, and crop selection and land conversion. The rights (all of them) most likely affect both short- and long-run productivity. Our description of security and crop selection relies mainly on data set 1 and is updated by references to data set 3. While rental rights between 1988 and 1995 are looked at in data set 1, a fuller description of land rentals in 2001 relies on data set 4.

Security of Tenure

Tenure security is typically associated with long-term rights to land and protection from the arbitrary loss of these rights without compensation. In most villages, rights to land are lost (or gained) in the process of villagewide reallocations. Land is taken back from some households and redistributed to others. For example, leaders shift land from a household whose newly married daughter has just departed to her in-laws to one welcoming the birth of a new child. In this process households are typically not compensated for the investments they may have made in the land. Tenure security is therefore inversely related to the frequency of these reallocations. The effect of insecurity, however, may be attenuated if the timing and the scope of the reallocations are established in advance.

Our data confirm that the right to reallocate land is typically vested in the village. Considerable differences existed in the 1990s among provinces in the average number of reallocations per village since the household responsibility system (HRS)—a reform that decollectivized farming, making the household responsible for cultivating the land—was introduced in the late 1970s and early 1980s. During the time between the implementation of the HRS and the 1995 survey, the national average for land reallocations was 1.7 times. Local leaders in the Liaoning, Shaanxi, and Hubei provinces made adjustments at a higher-than-average rate, while those in the Yunnan and Sichuan provinces intervened relatively infrequently. Examining a histogram for the number of reallocations per village, in sixty of the two hundred and fifteen villages in our survey, the land had *not* been readjusted between the start of the HRS and the mid-1990s; in a small number of villages, reallocation occurred almost annually (figure 4.1). In a quarter of all the villages, land was reallocated once during the 1980s and early 1990s, and in a fifth of the villages, reallocation was conducted two times.

Figure 4.1 Percentage of Villages Undertaking Land Reallocations Since Reform Began in 1983

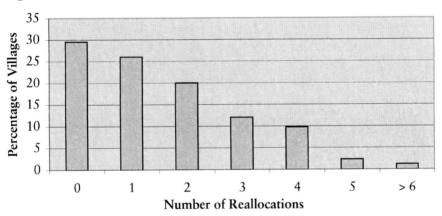

Source: Authors' data.

In some parts of China, the decision to reallocate is made at the township level. In Yunnan, two-thirds of the villages reported that reallocation decisions were made by higher administrative levels, while in Hebei and Liaoning a third and a quarter of surveyed villages, respectively, reported that township leaders made these decisions. Overall, however, 85 percent reported that these decisions were village-based. This number did not change much between 1995 and 2004 (according to data sets 3 and 4).

The pattern of reallocations over time indicates that villages and townships were making the decisions to reallocate in a decentralized way, without much regard for national policies mandating that land allocations be maintained for fifteen-year periods. Figure 4.2 shows the percentage of villages in our sample that reallocated land for each year between 1983 and 1995. In any year between 1980 and 1995, slightly less than 10 percent of all villages, on average, reallocated land. While there is no definitive long-term trend, reallocation behavior appears to be slightly cyclical. Leaders make land adjustments more commonly in years associated with major macroeconomic retrenchment policies, as in 1989–1990 and 1994–1995.[10] Data reported in Deininger and Jin (2007) suggests that between 1995 and 2002, the pace of reallocation did not change.[11] There may have been a downward shift, however, after the passage and implementation of the 2003 Rural Land Contracting Law (which unfortunately cannot be verified given the absence of data since 2003).

Figure 4.2 Villages Carrying Out Major Land Reallocations in China, by Year

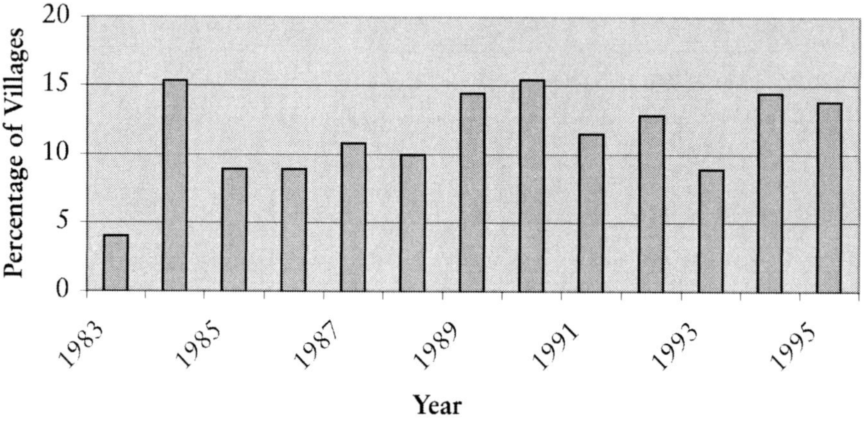

Source: Authors' data.

Reallocations differ in size and scope across China's rural communities. On average, a reallocation was found to involve slightly more than half the village's land and to extend to two-thirds of its households. In villages experiencing more than one reallocation between 1980 and 1995, the sizes of the reallocations were highly correlated with each other (for example, the amount of land reallocated each time was fairly similar). On average, slightly more than half of all cultivated land in our sample of villages (53.4 percent) had been reallocated at least once (figure 4.3). The distribution was also bimodal; about 40 percent of village leaders reported that nearly all or none of the land had been reallocated since the HRS. Interestingly, according to data set 3, between 1995 and 2000, the nature of reallocations continued along this same pattern and at the same level of intensity. While not as detailed, data from a Center for Chinese Agricultural Policy (CCAP) study appear to be consistent with these patterns, too. Similarities in reallocation patterns can be best observed over time (in other words, if a locality reallocated land in a particular way in the early 1990s, it is likely that it reallocated land in the same way in the early 2000s, despite the national policy and legal efforts to establish a uniform national rural cultivated land system).

Figure 4.3 Percentage of Cultivated Land Reallocated Since 1983 Reform

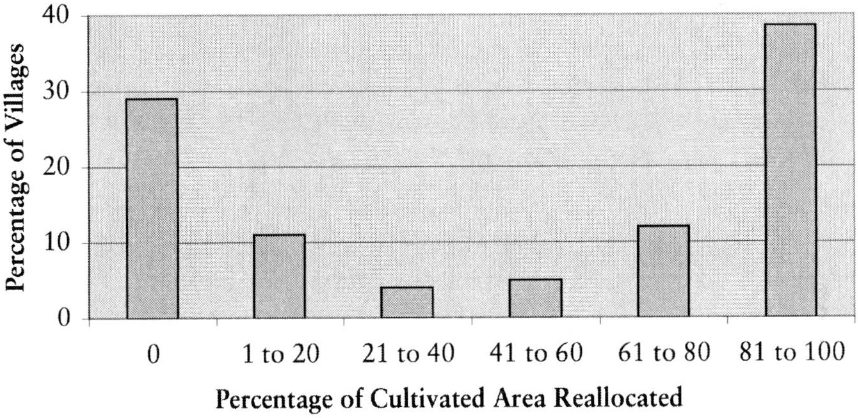

Percentage of Cultivated Area Reallocated

Source: Authors' data.

Insecure tenure is associated with a higher frequency of cultivated land reallocation; the more that land has been reallocated in a village, the more likely that a farmer will have lost a particular plot of land. Tenure insecurity is also exacerbated if the dates of villagewide adjustment are not known, since this increases farmers' uncertainty. From the survey, we know that leaders should have announced the date of the first adjustment at the time that they implemented the HRS. In nearly half of all villages, however, a date was not announced. A similar percentage of villages also reported that households did not know the date of the next adjustment during the survey period. All three factors—the frequency, size, and uncertainty of the next reallocation—potentially contribute to a farmer's concerns regarding his rights to the land.

While tenure security changed little from the early 1980s through the mid-1990s, farmers' security in their land-use rights began to increase after 1998 and was strengthened by the passing of the Rural Land Contracting Law (RLCL) in 2002.[12] By 2000 the percentage of farmers that claimed to believe that they would be able to keep their land for the full thirty years of their contract rose in all provinces. But it is important to point out that there is still much reallocation going on in most areas of China. So, while the passing of the RLCL strengthened property rights, it has not made tenure perfectly secure.

Crop Selection and Land Conversion

During the 1980s, many leaders were involved in making decisions on planting and land use.[13] Even into the 1990s, leaders imposed restrictions on how farmers used the land, including on crop alternations (table 4.1, column 4). Although in nearly 75 percent of villages, households claimed they could freely decide on crop mix in 1995, there were many that had to follow the decisions of local leaders. In several sample provinces—and in Hubei, Shandong, and Yunnan provinces in particular—leaders intervened in crop decisions. Even as late as the late 1990s in Zhejiang, farmers showed us a directive from township leaders requiring all farmers in the village to plant a two-season (summer and fall) variety of rice under threat of a fine, even when the trend in the area was to use one-season varieties or move into horticultural production.

During the mid-1990s, obligations such as mandatory grain or cotton delivery quotas also affected crop choice. In surveyed villages in Liaoning Province, for example, grain quotas in 1995 averaged nearly 25 percent of gross output, and officials typically did not allow farmers to satisfy their obligations with a cash payment, but instead insisted on delivery. Cotton quotas in parts of Hebei, Hubei, and Shandong provinces may also have had a similar effect on land use. Some of the farmers in the surveyed areas complained that they would rather plant cash crops than grain or cotton, as they were required to do.

Local leaders placed even more severe constraints on converting land to alternative uses (table 4.1, column 5). For example, during the 1990s, rules often prohibited farmers from converting cultivated land to orchards, fish ponds, greenhouses, or brick kilns. Officials in Liaoning Province were especially strict, and throughout China only about half of the farming population was to make significant permanent changes to its land use without the authorization of local leaders.

After 2000, however, these rules changed dramatically. According to data set 3, by 2000, village leaders were intervening in crop-choice decisions in only about 10 to 15 percent of villages (down from 25 percent in 1995). Reductions in procurement quotas made village leaders much less interested in telling farmers what to do. By 2000 the average procurement quota affected only 9 percent of gross output. Rules were also beginning to be relaxed on conversion of land to orchards and other uses.

In 2005 and 2006, two surveys by the authors in the Greater Beijing Area and Shandong Province found almost no leader intervention in the decision-making process.[14] Ninety-seven percent of farmers in Greater Beijing and 96 percent in Shandong said that crop choice and land conversion were up to them. The only farmers that said they did not have a choice were those that were renting orchards that belonged to a collective. In other words, by 2006, the right to choose a crop or convert land had devolved to the household.

Table 4.1 Nonresidual Property Rights in China's Villages, 1988 and 1995

Province	Unencumbered right to rent (% of villages)	Percentage of land rented in 1988	Percentage of land rented in 1995	Right to decide crop mix (% of villages)	Right to convert land to alternative uses (% of villages)
Zhejiang	93.8	1.6 (3.3)	6.9 (10.3)	74.1	40.7
Sichuan	93.8	0.2 (0.5)	2.1 (2.6)	93.1	68.9
Hubei	59.4	0.3 (1.1)	3.6 (8.3)	66.7	41.4
Shaanxi	65.6	0.8 (2.1)	2.2 (2.9)	93.3	84.4
Shandong	46.5	N/A	1.1 (1.8)	60.0	60.7
Yunnan	66.7	1.3 (0.5)	0.9 (2.2)	66.7	45.8
Hebei	80.0	0.3 (0.6)	2.1 (2.2)	84.6	53.8
Liaoning	62.3	0.1 (0.3)	3.6 (5.0)	93.8	6.3
Total	71.6	0.6 (1.8)	2.9 (5.8)	73.4	53.6

Source: Authors' field survey.
Note: Standard errors are reported in parentheses.

Transfer or Rental Rights

Zhuanbao, literally "passing on a contract," refers to the transfer of land-use rights between two households and is comparable to the notion of a land rental. Since the 1980s this transfer has been typically short term and usually entails the payment of a fee and the assumption of tax and quota liabilities (when present) by another household, in return for use of the land. In 1995, 71.6 percent of villages reported that households had complete freedom to transfer land-use rights, about the same as in 1988 (table 4.1, column 1). In the remaining 28.4 percent of villages, households faced some sort of constraint, most often in the form of restrictions on renting to nonvillagers or the need for households to obtain prior authorization from village leaders. Leaders only rarely imposed a complete moratorium on rental transactions.

Despite the high percentage of villages reporting that households had unconstrained rights to rent their land, before 2000 a remarkably low percentage of land was rented in and out by farmers (table 4.1, columns 2 and 3). In 1988 only 0.5 percent of cultivated land was rented in rural China; nearly three-quarters of villages reported no land rental. By 1995, although more than 75 percent of local leaders reported rental activities in their villages, farmers still rented less than 3 percent of their land, most often to relatives.

China's emerging markets for cultivated land in 2001

The descriptive statistics produced from our new national-level data for 2000 and 2001 (data sets 3 and 4) are close to the overall figures generated by the NBS and are broadly supportive of our hypotheses on the productivity and equity effects of the emergence of land and labor markets in China. For example, table 4.2 provides information on household income composition, the participation of household members in different types of economic activities and land endowments, and rental market participation. The average rural income per capita is almost the same as in the 2001 statistical yearbook. The national shares of income from agricultural production (37 percent) and land holdings per capita (1.62 mu—where 1 mu is 1/15th of a hectare)—two variables also reported regularly in published statistical sources—are nearly the same as the published figures.[15] Our data also show how diversified China's rural income sources are in 2001. Agriculture, still the largest contributor to overall rural household income (37 percent), is followed by income from local wage employment and migration (25 percent and 9 percent, respectively) and local nonfarm self-employment (29 percent).

96

Table 4.2 Key Indicators of Labor and Land Market Activity in China's Main Regions, 2001

	All China	North and Northwest	Coast	Central	Southwest
Income level and composition					
Mean per capita income (yuan)	2,681	2,646	3,894	2,392	1,794
Agricultural production (%)	37	38	28	41	41
Wage employment (%)	25	28	31	21	19
Remittance (%)	9	6	10	13	8
Nonfarm self-employment (%)	29	28	31	25	32
Participation in activities (%)					
Households with nonfarm enterprise	10.7	7.3	14.4	11.1	9.2
Households who migrate	37.0	25.0	35.0	47.0	37.0
Months in nonfarm activity	10.0	8.3	13.7	9.2	7.6
Months spent in migration	4.1	2.3	4.5	5.4	3.6
Agricultural endowments	32	32	53	59	46
Land endowment (mu/capita)[2]	1.62	2.14	1.00	1.31	1.37
Share of households renting in	9.50	7.10	9.40	10.40	7.50
Share of households renting out	6.20	4.90	8.80	5.10	5.70
Rented-to-own land ratio[1]	0.51	0.48	0.59	0.50	0.44
Number of households in sample	54,590	12,390	14,680	14,860	12,660

Sources: Authors' computation from the NBS national 2001 household survey.
The *North and Northwest* region includes the provinces of Hebei, Shanxi, Liaoning, and Henan; the *coastal region* includes Jiangsu, Zhejiang, Fujian, Shandong, and Guangdong; the *central region* includes Anhui, Jiangxi, Hubei, Hunan, and Guangxi; and the *southwest* includes Sichuan, Guizhou, Yunnan, Shaanxi, and Gansu.
Note: [1] Only for households that are renting in. [2] 1 hectare equals 15 mu.

With information from the survey data, the emergence of land markets is confirmed. The 2001 NSB survey shows that 9.5 percent of households nationwide rented land in, while 6.2 percent rented land out. Although there are considerable regional differences, there are nontrivial amounts of rentals across all regions. Around 10 percent of households rented land in China's central and coastal regions, versus about 7 percent of households in other parts of China.[16] Land-rental activities are becoming increasingly common in China, approaching levels in more market-oriented economies.

At a number of different levels of disaggregation, our data not only show rising levels of land rentals but also a positive correlation between activities in the land and labor markets. Across China's major regions, those with the highest levels of migration (the central and coastal regions) also have the highest rental levels (table 4.2, row 8 versus row 10). The correlation between the share of labor that is in the migrant labor force and the share of cultivated land that is rented is more than 0.80. This becomes more than 0.90 when migration and other types of off-farm activities are included. Moreover, trends at the regional level are supported by province-level data. For example, rental markets tend to be more active in the provinces in which emigration is most common (for example, Jiangxi, Henan, Hubei, Hunan, and Anhui). The relationship is also evident in the coastal region if the definition of off-farm employment is expanded to include both migration and local wage earnings. The correlation coefficient between migration and land rental at the province level is 0.54. Examining the differences among households supports our findings on the relationship between migration and land rental (see table 4.2), as well as showing that the emergence of land markets has helped those with less land endowment. T-test results show that households who rent land out spend significantly more time in migration and have significantly fewer land holdings than those who rent land in. Both tests are at a 1 percent significance level.

Our data also indicate that land markets are pro-poor. Households renting out, when compared with those renting in, have the highest level of nonfarm assets (557 versus 237). Even more notable, the per capita income of those renting out (3,024) is higher than of those renting in (2,636).

The empirical evidence also suggests a link between nonagricultural activity and land-rental market participation. It can be seen that once households allocate more of their available labor time to work off the farm, the propensity to rent out land increases. To see this, we note that households who rent out spend, on average, 4.7 and 12.2 months in migration and nonagricultural self-employment as compared to 3.7 and 9.9 months for autarkic households (or households that do not have members working outside of agriculture). This illustrates the importance of potential linkages between land and labor markets.

Land Rights Formation: Identifying the Determinants

A popular view expressed in some of the earlier work on land is that rights and land policies are uniformly determined by the central government. Policy pronouncements by the state council on issues such as tenure security convey this impression. The observed heterogeneity in property rights, discussed in the previous subsection, essentially undermines this view. Land security and transfer rights not only differ among provinces, but also from township to township within a county and among villages within a township. In terms of land reallocations, in thirty-nine out of the forty-four sample counties (87 percent), townships within a county reported different frequencies of land readjustment at the village level. In fifty-two out of ninety-two townships (57 percent), villages within a township reported different frequencies in readjustment. Similar patterns appear with respect to land-rental rights. In thirty out of forty-four counties (68 percent), townships within a single county reported different land-rental rights at the village level. In thirty-three out of ninety-two townships (36 percent), villages within a township reported different rental rights. In our sample of thirty-one villages drawn from six counties in Northeast China, land resources were organized in almost twenty different ways. Qiao (1997) discovered that leaders in forty Yunnan and Fujian villages managed their forest land in nearly thirty different ways. Throughout China, heterogeneity is observed at every administrative level, suggesting that central or regional policymakers are not the final arbiters in land-management issues.

Instead, the pattern of land rights suggests that the real source of this widely observed heterogeneity is differences at the village level. This interpretation is consistent with several recent studies that find central policymakers to be less effective in implementing local development programs due to the increased independence of village leaders.[17] Some argue that decision-making powers have already shifted from central to local and village authority to such a degree that China is now one of Asia's most decentralized countries.[18]

Empirical Work on Rights Impacts and the Determinants of Rental

Our empirical work, along with that of others, helps illuminate a number of the issues raised. This work has focused on several key areas and can be divided into three empirical exercises: (A) measuring the extent of inefficiency resulting from the current land-allocation system; (B) identifying the effects of the current property-rights regime on dynamic incentives; and (C) explaining the determinants of land rental. We will now examine the impact of land security on efficiency and output (empirical exercises A and B). The final section empirically examines the determinants of market-rental transactions (empirical exercise C).

Land Rights and Inefficiency (Empirical Exercise A)

Inefficiency arises because of the misallocation of resources across households; in the case of China, the reasons for such misallocation are relatively straightforward. At the outset of decollectivization, the land was allocated in a fairly egalitarian way to reflect household size and composition and, in some cases, off-farm labor supply. Over time, however, changes such as births, deaths, marriages, family divisions, and labor-supply shifts affected households' demographic structure.[19] Demographic changes and differential access to off-farm opportunities led to growing inefficiencies and a less-than-perfect fit between households' land holdings and endowment of labor.

The key questions are: do these inefficiencies exist and, if so, what mitigates or exacerbates them? It is possible that households rent land out or in (or hire farm labor out or in) to offset these differences, but recall that cultivated land-rental markets are thin in most of our survey areas. Village reallocations could accomplish the same thing. If land is *not* allocated so that all households have the same land-labor ratio, land-scarce households might be induced to supply more labor per unit of land—a symptom of static inefficiency. In principle, this can give rise to an inverse relationship between farm size and land productivity, with output per unit of land higher on smaller farms. In fact, the presence of the inverse relationship is evidence of static inefficiency.

Using our data, we examined this inverse relationship as an indicator of inefficiency.[20] And, in fact, we do find that as farm size increases, labor use per unit of land falls and output per unit of labor rises. These findings can only be reconciled by a view that there is inefficiency in the use of labor. Constrained farmers apply more labor per unit of land and earn relatively little in return for their extra time. Inefficiencies indeed exist. We also examined whether the severity of the relationship is correlated with key institutional factors, such as the nature of village land reallocation. We find that villages that undertook larger and more comprehensive village land reallocations mitigated labor inefficiency. One interpretation of this result is that reallocations are partially mimicking the outcome of a functioning land-rental market. Even after the reallocations, however, we find that some inefficiency remains.

Importantly, we also find that well-functioning local labor markets and other sources of off-farm employment significantly help to reduce the inefficiency in farm labor use. Since low productivity is essentially a product of underutilized labor, it appears that less labor is wasted where its opportunity cost is greatest. Together, our findings suggest that there are some efficiency gains to be realized from reallocating land from land-rich households to land-poor ones—a move that equalizes the marginal product of labor across households and enables the same level of output to be produced with less labor.

Are these inefficiencies serious? While the findings also suggest that there is a cost associated with the current property rights regime, Carter and Yao, drawing on data for two hundred rice-farming households in Zhejiang, suggest that the cost of allocative inefficiency arising from restrictions on transfer rights is around 2 percent of output.[21] Because of the relatively well-developed off-farm opportunities in these areas, the costs are probably lower than they are in other areas where income from farming is much more important.

Perhaps the most information to be gleaned from measuring the impact of reallocation on household welfare is that inefficiency does not have to come at the cost of rising inequality. On the basis of our work, and that of Carter and Yao, it is fair to say that there is room for reallocations that improve both efficiency *and* equity. This conclusion and any policy implications that might follow, however, are based on the assumption that land-rental markets do not operate well. The presumption here is that better-defined rights to rent might alleviate the problem. As noted earlier, it might be that high transaction costs cause the problem, not village-level policy. Why such limited amount of land is transacted through the rental markets will be more carefully examined in the next subsection.

Investment Incentives and the Costs of China's Rights Regime (Empirical Exercise B)

The major rationale for calls to extend land-rights tenure to thirty years during the early 2000s was the anticipated effect of enhanced tenure security on household investment decisions. In addition to our own work, several studies have examined the effects of tenure security and related rights on household investment behavior.[22] While the results of our studies are useful, we should point out that they are done with imperfect data, address only some issues, and are based on a small sample in only one region of China.

There are several kinds of investments in which we are interested, all of which can affect land productivity and output growth. On the one hand, there are investments that augment land quality. These include expenditures on irrigation, drainage, wells, and on organic fertilizers and manure to enhance long-term soil fertility. Empirically, the key is to link levels of investment to the land rights that households enjoy, notably security of tenure and freedom of rental, while simultaneously controlling for household characteristics and inherent differences in land types and quality that may influence household investment decisions. We used plot-by-plot data collected in Hebei and Liaoning provinces to analyze the incentive effects of long-term property rights on household input use and investment. Because of the nature of our data, we could analyze only one household investment decision—the use of organic fertilizer. Other kinds of land-quality-improving investments were excluded from the analysis. In fact, with the exception of our (unpublished) analysis using data set 3, there is no empirical study of the effect of land tenure on any type of land-specific investment except organic manure.

In a subsample of our data drawn from one county in Hebei Province, we found that farmers had significantly higher yields from their private maize plots (plots that are given to farm households to use without being subject to reallocations) than their responsibility maize fields (plots that are given to farm households to use, which are subject to reallocations in some villages). On average, private plots yielded 25 percent more than responsibility plots. Also, the difference in output appears linked to differences in input use. When cultivating their private plots, farmers applied more labor (11 percent), draft animal input (3 percent), nitrogen fertilizer (5 percent), organic fertilizer (35 percent), and phosphates (22 percent). Note that the greatest differences are observed in organic fertilizer and phosphate use, the two inputs with the greatest long-term impact on the land.

To what degree can these differences in inputs be attributed to property rights? A key difference between private plots and responsibility plots in the sample (both planted with maize) is the length of tenure. For private plots, the average length of tenure was over twice that for responsibility land (21 years versus 9 years). Also, for nearly 40 percent of the responsibility plots, the household's contract was expected to expire the following year. Security of tenure, as captured by these two variables, appears to be much better on private plots. However, several other factors, such as the size of the plot, the quality of the land, and the distance of the plot from the homestead, may also be important. In fact, differences in yield and input intensity may be a product of differences in inherent plot characteristics and unrelated to property rights.

Interplot comparisons are made using regression analysis. Controlling for differences in land quality and other key variables, we find that weaker property rights, either in the form of poorer tenure security or constraints on rental rights, adversely affect farmers' incentives to invest in medium-term inputs, such as soil-building organic manure. In fact, these two variables explain much of the difference in organic manure use between the two kinds of plots. The effect of these same variables on other current inputs was insignificant, as might be expected. The relatively low effect of organic fertilizers on output suggests that only a relatively small percentage of the differences in output between the two kinds of plots is related to property rights per se.

One problem with the above results is that the length of time that a household has held a plot may not be a perfect measure of tenure; it could be that the longer one has held a plot, the more likely the land will be taken away. To overcome some of the simplifying assumptions, we used the same data and undertook a new empirical exercise.[23] More specifically, we performed a hazard analysis of individual plot tenures that relates the predicted probability of having a plot expropriated to land-specific investment, specifically organic fertilizer use. We can do this analysis since our plot-by-plot tenure data collected in Hebei and Liaoning reflect the recent history of land expropriation. Using our analytical framework, we can create an objective measure of tenure insecurity and assess the social benefits of policies designed to reduce tenure insecurity.

Our empirical results support the view that heightened expropriation risk dampens investment in rural China, although the impacts may not be large. Farmers living in villages with more frequent land reallocations—or those who are at higher risk of losing a plot, for example, because they have greater land holdings than the average farm household in the village—use organic fertilizer less intensively. The opposite is true of chemical fertilizers, which are known to have no long-lasting effects on soil quality. Despite having a negative impact on investment in soil quality, periodic land reallocations do not appear to entail a substantial cost—only about 5 percent of production, a figure that is above that of Carter and Yao, but still relatively low.

Determinants of Land-market-rental Transactions (Empirical Exercise C)

In this last subsection, we study another crucial dimension of land rights—the right to rent. In particular, we look at whether the improvement in transfer rights (which were improved by policy edicts that acknowledged the farmer's right to rent their cultivated out) has increased land rental. We also seek to identify who benefits from new opportunities for rental—the poor or the well-off. In a country like China, land rental is essential for the long-term health of agriculture, since trade policy restrictions do not allow China's leaders to raise domestic prices through border protections.

Econometric evidence

The econometric results reported in tables 4.3 and 4.4 perform fairly well. The results are robust regardless of which dependent variable is used. The results are also consistent when using different estimation techniques. Many of the estimated parameters are consistent with our prior expectations, as well as with other analyses of households in rural China and elsewhere in the world. For example, the coefficient on the education variable is positive and significant in the equation explaining the participation in migration of both the household head (table 4.3, row 5) and children of the household heads, suggesting that education has a strong and significant effect on the ability of household members to access a job in the migrant labor force. Similar results are found in other studies of migration in China[24] and for Mexico.[25]

Table 4.3 Determinants of Household Head's Participation in Migration/Local Nonfarm Employment

	Probit models		Tobit models	
	Participation in migration	Participation in local nonfarm employment	Months of migration	Months of local nonfarm employment
Agricultural ability	-0.057*** (7.70)	-0.205*** (12.30)	-3.668*** (7.73)	-2.883*** (18.22)
Owned land per capita	-0.001 (1.46)	-0.005** (2.11)	-0.098*** (3.05)	-0.099*** (9.47)
Value of agricultural assets (log)	-0.003** (2.36)	-0.013*** (7.21)	-0.198*** (3.25)	-0.160*** (7.71)
Value of nonagricultural assets (log)	-0.004*** (3.94)	0.018*** (4.75)	-0.242*** (4.93)	0.230*** (14.77)
Years of education obtained by head	0.007** (2.48)	-0.006 (0.91)	0.394** (1.98)	-0.123** (2.01)
Head's education squared	-0.001*** (2.96)	0.001*** (3.16)	-0.027** (2.26)	0.021*** (5.66)
Head's age	0.009*** (3.89)	0.019*** (5.27)	0.530*** (4.44)	0.193*** (5.51)
Head's age squared	-0.000*** (6.75)	-0.000*** (8.48)	-0.010*** (7.36)	-0.003*** (9.19)
Household expenditure at village mean	-0.001 (1.24)	0.001 (0.59)	-0.031 (.14)	0.038*** (4.58)
Number of children at working age	-0.010** (2.20)	-0.010 (1.52)	-0.499*** (3.13)	-0.030 (0.60)
Constant			-15.477*** (5.59)	0.282 (0.33)
Observations	13,598	13,598	13,598	13,598
Pseudo R-squared	0.12	0.09	0.07	0.04
Log likelihood	-4,296.65	-8,538.31	-8,494.70	-26,805.94

Source: Authors' survey data.

Note: Robust z statistics in parentheses. * significant at 10 percent; ** significant at 5 percent; *** significant at 1 percent.

Table 4.4 Determinants of Household Participation as Renter (that is, of cultivated land) and Area Rented by Renter

	Probit (participation)		Tobit (area rented in)	
	Base model	Expanded model	Base model	Extended model
Agricultural ability	0.160*** (11.41)	0.157*** (9.55)	3.294*** (13.73)	3.225*** (13.43)
Owned land per capita	-0.011*** (9.28)	-0.011*** (5.10)	-0.085*** (5.38)	-0.085*** (5.41)
Own draft animal	0.057*** (6.41)	0.058*** (3.77)	1.028*** (6.41)	1.048*** (6.54)
Value of agricultural assets (log)	0.007*** (3.54)	0.006 (1.62)	0.098*** (2.92)	0.095*** (2.83)
Value of nonagricultural assets (log)	0.000 (0.27)	0.001 (0.32)	0.012 (0.51)	0.018 (0.75)
Education attained by head	-0.000 (0.05)	-0.000 (0.04)	-0.005 (0.06)	-0.005 (0.05)
Education attained by head squared	-0.000 (0.39)	-0.000 (0.34)	-0.001 (0.10)	-0.001 (0.12)
Head's age	0.012*** (4.12)	0.013*** (4.50)	0.141*** (2.88)	0.167*** (3.37)
Head's age squared	-0.000*** (4.83)	-0.000*** (5.07)	-0.002*** (3.74)	-0.002*** (4.11)
Share of households migrating in the village, except the current village	0.039*** (2.66)	0.060*** (3.04)	0.389 (1.40)	0.823*** (2.78)
Share of households working off-farm in the village, except the current village	-0.003 (0.26)	0.006 (0.23)	-0.259 (1.23)	-0.089 (0.39)
Household expenditure at village mean	-0.001** (2.04)	-0.001 (1.31)	-0.021* (1.67)	-0.018 (1.43)
Months migrating out in the previous year		-0.003*** (3.67)		-0.056*** (4.65)
Months working nonfarm in the previous year (separate from above)		-0.001 (1.22)		-0.027** (2.35)
Constant			-4.965*** (4.07)	-5.655*** (4.58)
Observations	13,598	13,598	13,598	13,598
Pseudo R-squared	0.05	0.05	0.02	0.02
Log likelihood	-7,211.71	-7,201.00	-14,558.61	-14,545.85

Source: Authors' survey data.

Participation in off-farm migration

The regressions—both probits and tobits for the household head—confirm that labor markets enhance both efficiency and equity (table 4.3, columns 1 and 3). On the one hand, migrant labor markets are providing a way for farm households that have invested more in education to access the off-farm labor market (table 4.3, row 5). On the other hand, emerging migrant labor markets are also places for households less able to engage in agriculture. In all of the labor-market regressions, the sign on the agricultural ability variable is negative and highly significant (row 1). In fact, the least able households in the sample are 5 percent more likely to migrate than the most able ones. These two findings are consistent with efficiency improvements at both the macro- and microlevels. From society's point of view, when labor markets are able to shift those with higher human capital and less efficient farming abilities into the more productive industrial and service sectors, welfare will improve. From the household's point of view, when the household can send its members into the off-farm labor market, its investment in education will generally earn a higher return.

Migration labor markets, however, also provide opportunities for the poor. In our results, we show in all our equations that those households with less land and lower levels of wealth (as measured by the value of their nonagricultural assets) are more likely to migrate (table 4.3, rows 2 and 4). Our results also show that villages that are poorer (as measured by the average level of expenditures) have more migrants (row 9). Although such findings are not new, they have important policy implications and should help resolve the debate on reforms that seek to facilitate greater migration.[26]

Participation in nonfarm employment

The regression examining the determinants of nonfarm employment generally supports the findings of the migration equations for both household heads and their children, especially in the ways that nonfarm labor markets are enhancing efficiency (table 4.3, columns 2 and 4). Specifically, the nonfarm employment markets appear to enhance efficiency by attracting those with relatively poor ability—but with relatively large families—to engage in agriculture (rows 1 and 10). Moreover, those with moderate levels of education have a tendency to move away from nonfarm employment. This may be because, for these intermediate levels of education, the best opportunities are in the migrant market. However, when levels of education reach relatively high levels (for example, above three years for the household head and nine years for children), there is a tendency for households to begin their own businesses.

The local nonfarm employment markets, however, do not enhance equity to the same degree. Those with less land are more likely to become self-employed, perhaps due to poorly functioning capital markets (see row 2); unlike migration markets, it appears that those with greater levels of nonagricultural assets (or wealth) are able to finance the start-up of their own businesses (row 4). Whether because of poor liquidity or the demand pull of local wealth, wealthier villages are likely to have a larger self-employed sector (row 9). Hence, while the nonfarm employment market enhances efficiency, employment opportunities in the sector more often go to those with higher levels of wealth, living in wealthier areas.

Land-market participation

Perhaps more than any other single result, our analysis shows the effectiveness of cultivated-land-rental markets in increasing the efficiency of production in China's rural economies. Although the information problems that affect land rental are well known, our results show how land-rental markets allow those with higher agricultural abilities to systematically rent in more land (table 4.4, row 1). In contrast, those households with inferior abilities in agricultural systematically rent out their land (table 4.4, row 1). The results are robust regardless of whether we examine the probit (columns 1 and 2) or tobit regressions (columns 3 and 4) and no matter the composition of the explanatory variables (the partial model—columns 1 and 3—versus the full model—column 2 and 4). Such findings are consistent with other findings inside China[27] and elsewhere in the world.[28] In Deininger and Jin, the effectiveness of rental markets in raising efficiency (as we have defined it) is shown to be far greater than administrative moves by village leaders to reallocate land among households.

Our results also show that rental markets shift land toward those with the means to improve the productivity of farming. Farm households with draft animals and other assets that can be used in agricultural production are more likely to rent land in. In contrast, households with fewer draft animals (with coefficients significantly different from zero) and those with fewer other agricultural assets (nonsignificant) are more likely to rent out.

While it is possible that the emergence of efficiency-enhancing markets could hurt the poorer households in our sample, we instead find evidence that land-rental markets are doing little to limit the access of land by the poor and even improving equity. According to our findings, the wealth of a household does not play a significant role in gaining access to land (table 4.4, row 4). Essentially, there is no detectable relationship between the value of the nonagricultural assets of the households and their propensity to rent in land. In other words, the poor and the rich appear to have equal levels of participation. Moreover, the findings in both the rent-in and rent-out equations support the hypothesis that rental markets in China farm households with less cultivated land to expand their holdings. *Ceteris paribus*, families that have less land given to them by the village are more likely to rent land in (table 4.4, row 5). In short, the findings of our study show that, in fact, households with small holdings are at least beginning to increase their access to cultivated land.

Conclusions and Policy Implications

The allocation of property rights is widely recognized to have important implications for resource use and the distribution of household welfare. The introduction of the HRS in the early 1980s extended rights of use to cultivated land on a fairly egalitarian basis. In the two decades that followed, control over the land allocation to households remained in the hands of local leaders. To evaluate China's land-tenure system from a policy perspective, we must first ask how effective the system has been in providing households with the necessary incentives to ensure rational land use and investment, while simultaneously helping local communities meet distribution objectives. Moreover, how well has the system fit the needs of China's rapidly evolving economy?

Our surveys suggest enormous heterogeneity in household land rights at the village level. In some villages, farmers seem to hold relatively long term tenure, and most of the rights—for example, right to crop selection, right to convert to alternative agricultural uses, right to rent—are typically associated with a private property regime, short of being able to buy or sell the land. In other villages, tenure is more short term, and farmers' use of the land appears to be constrained in a variety of ways.

We have examined a number of alternative explanations for this heterogeneity. Underlying the reallocation behavior are a number of factors, including quota fulfillment, the desire to maintain equal access to land among villagers, poorly functioning rental markets, and rent-seeking behavior on the part of local leaders. The role of reallocations in assuring equal access can explain only a small portion of the reallocation behavior; other factors, all linked to the incentives of local leaders, appear to be far more important in explaining decisions on the timing and size of reallocations. These incentives, in turn, are directly tied to state policy, as well as officials' rent-seeking behavior.

So, has China's land-management system succeeded in increasing efficiency and equity? Our work (and that of others) on the impact of the land-tenure system on growth, efficiency, and distribution is limited, but a number of observations can be made. First, the impact on growth of tenure security's effect on investment appears relatively modest. One possibility is that leaders are "internalizing" these costs in making decisions; in other words, in areas in which the potential costs of tenure insecurity are high, reallocation is less likely. Some villages have also invested heavily in agriculture. Since we do not have the basis for estimating investment, crop choice, and output under a counterfactual in which households enjoy all of the rights associated with private property, we hesitate to push this conclusion too far.

The system may have a much greater effect on efficiency, however. Although villagewide reallocations help move land to households that have a higher marginal product of land, and are thus efficiency enhancing, the allocation of land across households remains inefficient. This can be linked to the thinness (or absence of a lot of activity) of rental markets, and more generally, to the difficulty of administrative methods to efficiently allocate resources. The latter difficulty is almost certainly tied to informational problems and the transaction costs of carrying out the reallocations.

Land allocation also has important distributive implications. In the 1980s, equal access to land played an important role in enabling households to meet basic nutritional needs at minimum cost in an environment in which food markets were highly imperfect and off-farm opportunities were limited. This feature of the system, however, has probably become less important as grain markets have developed, off-farm opportunities expanded, and rural incomes increased. All of these developments, in some sense, have taken pressure off the land. Ironically, in the changing economic environment in China, the current land-tenure system may actually be adversely affecting income distribution. Households differ considerably in their ability to access rapidly emerging off-farm opportunities. This ability is linked to the age of individuals and human capital. Hence, it is likely that poorly developed rental markets have prevented households that are limited in their ability to access off-farm opportunity from more fully utilizing their labor and income potential by expanding the size of their farming operations. More generally, the land system may have discouraged households from specializing in agriculture. This issue will become more important during the first and second decades of the twenty-first century as the farm labor force continues to shrink both in absolute and percentage terms, as reorganization in farm structure is required, and as food markets grow more competitive both domestically and on a global scale.

In the long run, most economists believe that China needs a land-tenure system that provides long-term security and promotes the efficient use of land. The move to provide households with security for thirty years (which was granted in the mid-2000s) and allow only small adjustments to accommodate population changes is a step in that direction. In the meantime, keeping the door open for small adjustments (whether sanctioned by the new contracting law or not) may be enough to meet distributional concerns. As noted above, only a small percentage of land is reallocated with the goal of equal access, and so small adjustments can likely meet this need. Secure use rights and the expansion of rental markets can help facilitate the reorganization that is required in the farm sector.

If the past is any clue, however, this policy will be effective only if the incentives of local leaders are aligned in this direction (for example, if there are fewer incentives for leaders to undertake major reallocations). Interestingly, the decline in farm prices over the late 1990s and early 2000s—and the conversion of the quota tax into a subsidy—has worked in that direction by reducing the "rents" and other benefits that local leaders originally had from maintaining control over land. Rental activity appears to have increased as a consequence, with potentially important benefits for both efficiency and distribution. Without secure land rights, however, leaders' waning interest in land reallocation could be short-lived. A rise in farm prices and a reintroduction of the quotas would

109

once again put a premium on control over land, and likely reverse the trend when there are lower prices. As long as land is not privatized—and that raises a separate set of issues—additional reforms (including an elimination of the quota) and additional checks on leader behavior (such as that provided through genuinely contested elections) are likely needed to sustain current trends. This highlights, once again, how embedded the property rights that households enjoy are in the local political economy, and how reform of the local political economy is required to provide farmers the kind of property rights that a rapidly growing economy requires.

Land Rentals

We have explored the question of whether increasing reliance on market forces, in the context of rapid globalization, provides an avenue for China to increase rural productivity—as well as to improve the welfare of the poorest households. Our findings suggest that markets do, in fact, move things in the right direction. At a more fundamental level, we have shown that the emergence of land rights and the appearance of labor and land markets have enhanced both efficiency and equity. Efficiency is enhanced since market forces tend to allow households with limited farming skills and poor capital endowments to migrate. In the meantime, those with great agricultural abilities are able to rent land from those with poorer agricultural abilities. In all of our regressions, we see those households and individuals with higher levels of education able to break more easily into the migrant and self-employed labor markets. In this way we see a movement of resources—both land and labor—toward those with the ability to best use them.

There are also a number of equity-enhancing elements in China's labor and land markets. Those with little land are getting access to land. Those with little wealth are going into the migrant labor force. But while the poor tend to benefit, the efficiency side of the market essentially means that we might be able to conclude that it is actually the *productive poor* that are benefiting. Those with education in poor areas are finding migrant jobs. Those with high levels of agricultural skills and high levels of agricultural capital are the ones that are able to rent land. From a policy point of view, this means that markets can help alleviate poverty, but only if policymakers can provide access to the human and physical capital that are needed to take advantage of the opportunities provided by China's growth.

Finally, we see the connection of labor and land markets. Higher levels of nonfarm activity, whether migration or self-employment, appear to play a direct role in activating land-rental markets. This implies that land and labor markets in rural areas interact to improve overall economic health. And, it gives hope, as China begins to fulfill its promises for entering the WTO, that China will not only enjoy the rising efficiency that comes from such agreements but that it might be able to avoid some of the negative consequences of closed trade policies by giving some of those who are not able to take advantage of the greater levels of employment a chance to access land through land-rental markets.

Notes

[1] The authors would like to thank Loren Brandt, Alan deBrauw, Carl Gotsch, Hongbin Li, Fangbin Qiao, Jean Oi, Guo Li, Albert Nyberg, Matt Turner, Dwayne Benjamin, Albert Park, Minggao Shen, Jeffrey Williams, Changbao Zhao, and Fred Zimmerman for help in collecting the data, discussing and providing input on the issues, and reviewing earlier versions of this work. Rozelle is a member of the Gianinni Foundation, University of California.

[2] Gale D. Johnson, "China's Rural and Agricultural Reforms in Perspective," Working Paper No. 01-01, Department of Economics (University of Chicago, Chicago, 1996); Justin Yifu Lin, "Rural Reforms and Agricultural Growth in China," *American Economic Review* 82, no. 1 (1992): 34–51.

[3] John McMillan, John Whalley, and Lijing Zhu, "The Impact of China's Economic Reforms on Agricultural Productivity Growth," *Journal of Political Economy* 97 (1989): 781–807; Lin, "Rural Reforms and Agricultural Growth in China," 34–51; and Jinkun Huang and Scott Rozelle, "Technological Change: Rediscovering the Engine of Productivity Growth in China's Rural Economy," *Journal of Development Economics* 49, no. 2 (1996): 337–67.

[4] *Zhongguo Nongye Nianjian* 1996 [China Agricultural Yearbook 1996] (Beijing: Zhongguo Tongji Chubanshe, 1996).

[5] Roy Prosterman, Tim Hanstad, and Li Ping, "Can China Feed Itself?" *Scientific American* (November 1996): 90–96.

[6] X. Chen, "Issues in Land and Management of Land Rights in China," Paper presented in the 1999 Conference on Land Rights, China Institute of Reform, Haikou, China, January 15–16.

[7] Jinkun Huang, Scott Rozelle, and Min Chang, "The Nature of Distortions to Agricultural Incentives in China and Implications of WTO Accession," *World Bank Economic Review* 18, no. 1 (2004): 59–84.

[8] Loren Brandt, Jinkun Huang, Guo Li, and Scott Rozelle, "Land Rights in China: Facts, Fictions, and Issues," *The China Journal* 40 (January 2002): 67–97.

[9] Klaus Deininger and Songqing Jin, "Securing Property Rights in Transition: Lessons from Implementation of China's Rural Contracting Law," Working Paper No. 1447 (World Bank, Washington, DC, 2007).

[10] As discussed below, quota fulfillment is a major motivation for land reallocation. During boom periods, grain prices have typically increased, as has the implicit tax associated with the quota. This makes quota fulfillment more difficult, and effectively reduces the demand for land on the part of farmers. The slight increase in the incidence of reallocations may be related to both of these factors.

[11] Deininger and Jin, *Securing Property Rights in Transition.*

[12] Deininger and Jin, *Securing Property Rights in Transition.*

[13] Terry Sicular, "Redefining State, Plan and Market: China's Reforms in Agricultural Commerce," *China Quarterly* 144 (1995): 1020–46; Scott Rozelle, "Decision-making in China's Rural Economy: The Linkage between Village Leaders and Farm Households," *China Quarterly* 137 (1994): 99–124.

[14] Honglin Wang, Xiaoxia Dong, Jikun Huang, Thomas Reardon, and Scott Rozelle, "Producing and Procuring Horticultural Crops with Chinese Characteristics: A Case Study in the Greater Beijing Area," *World Development* (forthcoming); and Jikun Huang, Xiaoxia Dong, Yuhua Wu, Huayong Zhi, Xianfang Nui, Zhurong Huang, and Scott Rozelle "Regoverning Markets: The China Meso-level Study," Working Paper No. WP004, Center for Chinese Agricultural Policy (Chinese Academy of Sciences, Beijing, China, 2007).

[15] *Zhongguo Tongji Nianjian* 2002 [China Statistical Yearbook 2002] (Beijing: Zhongguo Tongji Nianjian Chubanshe, 2002).

[16] Not surprisingly, the spatial variations widen when we disaggregate regions. For example, 20 percent of households in Zhejiang rented in land. During the same year, only 2.9 percent of households in Gansu did so.

[17] Daniel Kelliher, "The Chinese Debate over Village Self-Government," *The China Journal* 37 (January 1997): 63–86.

[18] Michael Carter, Shouying Liu, and Yang Yao, "Dimensions and Diversity of Property Rights in Rural China," Working Paper No. 359, Department of Agricultural and Applied Economics (Univ. of Wisconsin-Madison, Madison, 1995).

[19] Deaths of the elderly and births do not affect the number of individuals of working age in the household, but can affect how much other members of the family decide to work through a variety of channels, for example, the number of individuals that need to be fed.

[20] Dwayne Benjamin and Loren Brandt, "Property Rights, Labor Markets and Efficiency in a Transition Economy: The Case of Rural China," *Canadian Journal of Economics* 35, no. 4 (2002): 689–716. In a related paper they also utilize the inverse relationship, but only look at output and not labor input and labor productivity because of data limitations. See Robert Burgess, "Land, Welfare, and Efficiency in Rural China," Working Paper No. 9 (London School of Economics, London, 1997). He finds support for a fairly severe inverse relationship in Sichuan but only a small one in Zhejiang, which he attributes to differences in off-farm opportunities in the two provinces. Failure to control for land-quality differences, as well as missing information on labor input, leave these results open to several interpretations.

[21] Michael Carter and Yang Yao, "Property Rights, Rental Markets, and Land in China," Working Paper, Department of Agricultural and Applied Economics (Univ. of Wisconsin-Madison, Madison, 1998).

[22] See R. Burgess, "Land, Welfare, and Efficiency in Rural China;" Michael Carter and Yang Yao, "Property Rights, Rental Markets, and Land in China;" and Prosterman, Hanstad, and Li, "Can China Feed Itself?" .

[23] Hanan G. Jacoby, Guo Li, and Scott Rozelle, "Hazards of Expropriation: Tenure Insecurity and Investment in Rural China," *American Economic Review* 92, no. 5 (December 2002): 1420–47.

[24] Alan deBrauw, Jikun Huang, Scott Rozelle, Linxiu Zhang, and Yigang Zhang. "The Evolution of China's Rural Labor Markets during the Reforms," *Journal of Comparative Economics* 30, no. 2 (June 2002): 329–53.

[25] Edward J. Taylor and Antonio Yunez-Naude, "Selectivity and the Returns to Schooling in a Diversified Rural Economy," *American Journal of Agricultural Economics* 82, no. 2 (May 2000): 287–97.

[26] William L. Parish, Xiaoye Zhe, and Fang Li, "Nonfarm Work and Marketization of the Chinese Countryside," *China Quarterly* 143 (1995): 697–730; Scott Rozelle, Guo Li, Minggao Shen, Amelia Hughart, and John Giles, "Leaving China's Farms: Survey Results of New Paths and Remaining Hurdles to Rural Migration," *China Quarterly* 158 (June

1999): 367–93; Alan de Brauw and Scott Rozelle, "Reconciling the Returns to Education in Off-farm Wage Employment in Rural China," *Review of Development Economics* 12, no. 1 (2008): 329–53.

[27] Klaus Deininger and Songqing Jin, "The Potential of Land Rental Market in the Process of Economic Development: Evidence from China," World Bank Policy Research Paper 2930 (World Bank, Washington, DC, 2002); Benjamin and Brandt, *Property Rights, Labor Markets and Efficiency*, 689–716.

[28] See, for example, Klaus Deininger and Songqing Jin, "Land Sales and Rental Markets in Transition: Evidence from Rural Vietnam," World Bank Policy Research Paper 3013 (World Bank, Washington, DC, 2003); and Klaus Deininger, Songqing Jin, Berhanu Adenew, Samuel Gebre-Selassie, and Mulat Demeke, "Market and Nonmarket Transfers of Land in Ethiopia: Implications for Efficiency, Equity, and Nonfarm Development," World Bank Policy Research Paper 2992 (World Bank, Washington, DC, 2003).

GOVERNANCE

GUILT AND PUNISHMENT
IN CHINA'S WAR ON CORRUPTION

Andrew Wedeman

In the three decades since Deng Xiaoping and his confederates wrested control of the Chinese Communist Party (CCP) from Hua Guofeng and pushed through a round of economic reforms, the Chinese economy has grown tremendously. According to the International Monetary Fund (IMF), the gross domestic product (GDP) per capita has increased at an average annual rate of 8.77 percent—more than four times the global average of 1.82 percent. As a result, between 1980 and 2007, per capita GDP in China increased a total of 854 percent, more than twelve times the 68 percent gain that the American economy enjoyed.[1] In this same period, according to the conventional wisdom, corruption has become endemic. Even a superficial reading of the media seems to confirm this view. Over the past few years, for example, the party secretary of Shanghai and concurrent member of the CCP's Politburo, Chen Liangyu, was convicted of allowing the diversion of 4 billion yuan from the municipal pension fund into risky loans for his cronies and sentenced to eighteen years in prison; the head of the State Food and Drug Administration (SFDA), Zheng Xiaoyu, was executed for taking bribes from pharmaceutical companies; Jia Renqing, the finance minister, was sacked for sexual misconduct; Tian Fengshan, the minister for land resources, was sentenced to life in prison for accepting bribes while serving as the governor of Heilongjiang; and Admiral Wang Shouye of the Chinese Navy was also convicted on bribery charges and sentenced to life in prison. Moreover, senior government officials and party cadres in Beijing, Tianjin, Anhui, Heilongjiang, Sichuan, Guangdong, Hebei, Hunan, and Guizhou have faced a variety of criminal charges for misconduct in office.

Despite this rash of high-level, high-profile cases, the total number of officials and cadres charged with corruption each year, which I term the "revealed rate of corruption" (RRC), actually leveled off about a decade ago, and indices of corruption compiled in recent years by Transparency International (TI), the Political and Economic Risk Consultancy (PERC), and the World Bank suggest that the "perceived level of corruption" (PLC) in China has actually remained stable for much of the past decade (see figure 5.1).[2] Such a leveling off would suggest that although the initial stages of economic transition from a planned economy to a semimarketized economy fueled rising corruption, the deepening of reform and intensified enforcement have prevented corruption from spiraling out of control. Mounting corruption, in other words, appears to be a growing pain associated with the immature stages of economic reform, not a crippling disease that threatens the survival of economic reform or the power of the CCP.

Figure 5.1 Trends in Corruption, 1980–2006

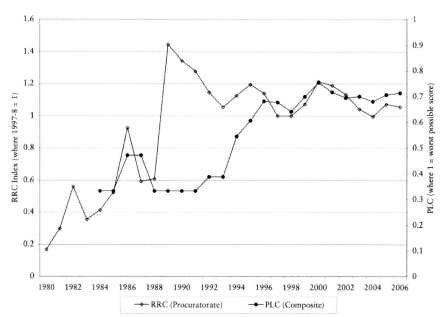

Sources: Composite PLC Index based on data from Transparency International (TI), "Corruption Perceptions Index," www.transparency.org/; Political and Economic Risk Consultancy, "Corruption in Asia," www.asiarisk.com; and World Bank, "Governance Index," www.worldbank.org/wbi/governance. Normalized RRC based on data in Zhongguo Jiancha Nianjian, [China Procuratorial Yearbook] (Beijing: Zhongguo Jiancha Chubanshe, various years).

Notes: RRC=revealed rate of corruption; PLC=perceived level of corruption. Composite PLC represents the average of individual indices, with the original scores normalized as a percentage of the maximum possible score. TI and World Bank indices are inverted so that the "worst" score (most corrupt) is the maximum score. The RRC has been normalized to control for changes in the legal definition of corruption resulting from the 1997 revision of the PRC Criminal Code. Scores for years prior to 1997 were thus normalized as a percentage of the number of cases filed in 1997, and scores for years after 1998 were normalized as a percentage of the number of cases filed in 1998. The author's assumption here is that, adjusting for the change in definitions, the revealed rate of corruption was roughly the same in 1997 and 1998.

Such a benign assessment is contrary to most thinking. To begin with, the spikes in the RRC evident in 1982, 1986, and 1989 result from the launching of anticorruption campaigns. The government has mounted only one major campaign since. That campaign, launched in 1993, resulted in a significant increase in the number of senior officials prosecuted but not the aggregate number of cases filed.[3] The leveling off of the RRC and PLC in the mid-1990s is thus possibly due to the ceasing of the campaigns. It should not be assumed, however, that anticorruption efforts slackened after 1993. The number of senior officials indicted for economic crimes, in fact, increased thirteenfold, rising from 186 in 1988 to 2,528 in 2006.[4] The number of senior officials tried for economic crimes rose twelvefold, from 76 in 1993 to 926 in 2006.[5] The number of senior cadres punished by the party's Discipline Inspection Commission (DIC) almost quadrupled from 1,530 in 1991 to 5,916 in 2004.[6]

Pei's recent work presents a radically different picture of China's handling of corruption. He maintains that the aggregate "leveling off" of the number of officials charged with corruption masks a failing anticorruption effort. Investigation rates, he argues, are extremely low; only one in four tips from the public about corruption are ever investigated. Those that are investigated result in formal charges less than 40 percent of the time, and punishment rates are lower still. As a result, according to Pei, only 5 to 7 percent of CCP members accused of corruption are actually convicted.[7] Officials, he concludes, face a "negligible probability" of punishment. Moreover, according to Pei, the probability of punishment has decreased significantly since the mid-1990s. He argues that even though the number of officials assigned to the procuratorate increased significantly in the decade preceding the mid-1990s, the number of cases it accepted for investigation declined 50 percent between 1990 and 2003.[8] China's "lagging enforcement efforts" are so ineffectual, he concludes, that the Chinese state has degenerated into a decentralized collection of "predatory . . . local mafia states" and is in danger of becoming "incapacitated."[9]

Although Pei's statistics are certainly evocative, they are not conclusive evidence that corruption continues to surge out of control or that China's anticorruption effort is a paper tiger. Even if, as Pei argues, the party's DIC only referred a mere 6 percent of its cases to the Supreme People's rocuratorate for criminal investigation between 1998 and 2005, more than 140,000 individuals stood trial on charges of graft, bribery, or misappropriation. Based on the more complete sentencing data we have for economic crime—of which these 3 corruption-related offenses constitute an important subset—it is likely that nearly 30,000 of these went to prison for 5 or more years; 50,000 received prison sentences of less than 5 years; and 48,000 received a variety of "noncriminal" sanctions including detention, probation, and supervision.[10] Of the remaining, some 7,000 were likely found guilty but exempted from criminal punishment, receiving administrative punishments instead.[11] Presumably, only some 1,500 were found innocent.

From Pei's perspective, we might dismiss the 80,000 individuals who went to prison as a mere drop in the bucket—the unlucky small fry who were dumb enough to get caught but had no powerful friends to protect them. This seems unwarranted. To begin with, not all those tried for corruption were low-ranking officials. Between 1994 and 2003, 4,354 senior officials stood trial for economic crimes, including 32 who held senior provincial or ministerial posts (省部) and 634 who held positions at the prefectural or bureau levels (地厅).[12] Moreover, over the years, the Chinese government has executed hundreds of officials convicted on corruption charges, including a number of very senior officials.[13] It is also important to recognize that when economic reforms were initiated, China had, at best, a rudimentary set of anticorruption agencies and had only just drafted a formal criminal code that defined corruption. Since then the regime has progressively tightened and refined the laws governing official conduct and greatly increased the number of investigators and prosecutors tasked with rooting out corruption. China's anticorruption efforts cannot be dismissed as mere theatrics.

My purpose here is to try to assess whether the apparent leveling off of the RRC and the PLC over the past decade represents an end to the rapid growth in corruption observed in the 1980s or the effects of slackened enforcement and the ceasing of major anticorruption campaigns in 1993.

Specifically, I examine data drawn from the three major institutions responsible for implementing China's war on corruption.[14] First, I track the investigation rate, which I define as the caseload of the DIC and its state counterpart, the Ministry of Supervision.[15] Second, I track the prosecution-indictment rate, which I define as the caseload of the procuratorate, China's prosecutorial institution. Third, I track the punishment rate, which I define as the caseload of the people's court system. In theory, by examining the relationship between these three sets of data, it should be possible to evaluate the relationship between accusations of guilt and actual punishment—and from that to make certain inferences about the efficacy of China's anticorruption efforts. In simple terms, the closer the punishment rate is to the investigation rate, the more rigorous the effort.

Multiple Jurisdictions, Institutional Processes, and Slippage

Attempting to measure the correlation between investigation and punishment is formidable. As a corruption case goes from accusation to criminal conviction, it must make its way through three institutional layers: the disciplinary-supervisory system, the procuratorate, and the court. Understanding the intricacies of the process at each stage is crucial to analyzing the data from these institutions and—ultimately—to judging their effectiveness against corruption.

In theory, when a party member or state employee is accused of corruption, the DIC or Ministry of Supervision is responsible for conducting an investigation and determining whether the accusations had merit and, if so, whether the offense warrants disciplinary action. If the offense constitutes a violation of party or state regulations but not the law, then the investigating body may impose sanctions, such as a reprimand, a demotion or expulsion from the party, or a dismissal from office. If the offense is more serious, the case will be remanded to the procuratorate for a preliminary investigation to determine if criminal charges are warranted. If they are, the procuratorate "files the case" (立案) and issues an indictment. Then the procuratorate must decide whether the case meets the threshold for criminal prosecution. If not, the procuratorate is authorized to impose administrative sanctions or may return the case to the disciplinary-supervisory system. If so, it is referred to the court, where court officials conduct a review to determine if the accused should be bound over for trial. If they find problems, the case may be dismissed or returned to the procuratorate for further investigation or administrative adjudication.

Not all cases end up in court. Some may be terminated because the allegations prove false or for lack of evidence. Others may end with administrative punishments or may be "continued" due to inconclusive evidence. As a result, we must expect some degree of "slippage" between accusation and conviction.

Moreover, the jurisdictions of the three major anticorruption systems do not line up. In particular, the disciplinary-supervisory organs have a much broader mandate than the judicial organs. They are charged with enforcing a wide range of party and state regulations that include not only corruption but also, in the case of the DIC, political offenses (for example, failing to support the party line), and, in the case of the Ministry of Supervision, administrative infractions (for example, insubordination), neither of which necessarily constitute criminal offenses and thus may not require the involvement of the procuratorate or the court.

Gaps in the data present another difficulty. In general, the most complete data come from the procuratorate. Data from the courts are reasonably good, at least at the aggregate national level, but data from the DIC are less complete. Nevertheless, the data are sufficient to allow us to assess the ratio—or what we might call the "gearing"—among investigation, prosecution, and conviction, and hence the efficacy of China's anticorruption campaign.

Going Beyond Fuzzy Math

The various jurisdictions and processes involved in corruption cases make it especially difficult to relate data from the disciplinary-supervisory system to data from the prosecutorial system (for example, the procuratorate) and the judicial system (the people's court). Unless one carefully follows the different paths that cases take, it's easy to slip into a bit of "fuzzy math" to conclude that the odds of punishment are low. This is not to say that observers such as Pei have misrepresented the data or that his figures are wrong. Other studies have also found that only a small percentage of Party members investigated by the DIC are remanded to the procuratorate for criminal investigation and that the procuratorate files criminal charges in only half the cases it accepts for investigation.[16]

121

It is hard, though, to track cases from accusation to conviction, as a preliminary examination of the data reveals. In 2003, for example, the DIC disciplined 174,507 Party members, of whom it remanded 8,691 to the judicial system (移送司法机关) for criminal investigation. The following year it disciplined 164,831 party members,[17] handing 4,775 individuals over to the prosecutor.[18] As is evident, the percentage of party members found guilty of infractions who ended up facing criminal investigation was quite small, ranging from 4.9 percent in 2003 to 2.9 percent in 2004.[19]

These low figures are potentially misleading. To begin with, not all party members disciplined by the DIC were charged with corruption. Studies have suggested that "economic offenses" constituted about a third of party disciplinary cases during the 1990s.[20]

Taking all the minor disciplinary cases out of the equation, the real referral rate for economic crimes becomes higher but not dramatically so—13.5 percent in 2003 and 7.89 percent in 2004 (assuming that the ratio was similar in 2003 and 2004 and that all those handed over to the procuratorate were charged with economic crimes.)

Data from the procuratorate and the courts, however, imply that more party members were charged and tried for corruption than just those referred by the DIC. In 2003 the procuratorate "accepted" 54,024 graft (贪污), bribery (贿赂), or misappropriation of public funds (挪用公款) cases for preliminary investigation. The following year, it accepted 52,123 corruption cases.[21] Even assuming all DIC referrals were investigated, they constitute only a small fraction of the total investigations (15.9 percent in 2003 and 9.2 percent in 2004). We can assume though that a great deal of the other investigations involve party members as well, since a majority of public officials presumably belong to the party.

Corruption is not, moreover, the only type of crime the procuratorate and courts deal with. They also have jurisdiction over a class of offenses known as "disciplinary crimes" (法纪罪) or "malfeasance" (渎职罪) that includes abuse of power (滥用职权), official negligence (玩忽职守), and nepotism (徇私舞弊). Most forms of official malfeasance correspond to offenses covered by the disciplinary-supervisory system. In 2003 the procuratorate accepted 15,699 cases of alleged official malfeasance for investigation and indicted 8,568 individuals. The following year, it accepted 15,395 cases for investigation and indicted 8,726 individuals. Assuming that some significant percent of the officials accused of malfeasance were concurrently party members, the gap between the number of party members the disciplinary-supervisory system remanded to the judicial system and the number investigated and indicted by the procuratorate was even wider. Court reports show that the number of state officials tried on all charges (for example, not only for corruption and abuse of power but also for ordinary crimes) has risen steadily since the mid-1990s (see figure 5.2).[22]

Figure 5.2 State Employees Tried by Court (all charges)

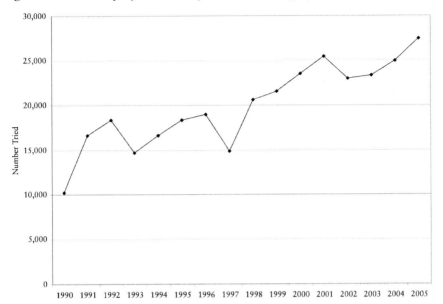

Source: *Zhongguo Falu Nianjian*, various years.

Further complicating the picture, the procuratorate also refers cases back to the disciplinary-supervisory system, either for independent administrative action or for concurrent disciplinary action.[23] The extent of overlap is not, however, clear. The disciplinary-supervisory system, finally, has the power to investigate the procuratorate and the courts.[24]

It seems clear that considerably more party members are prosecuted for corruption and official malfeasance than the number the DIC handed over for criminal investigation. If so, the odds of prosecution must be higher than the 6 percent argued by Pei.

The link between investigation and indictment is also unclear. Of the 54,024 corruption cases initiated by the procuratorate in 2003, it filed formal charges in 31,468 of them (58.2 percent). In 2004 it filed charges in 30,042 of 52,123 cases (57.7 percent). Roughly two in five investigations ended without criminal indictments. Of those, in 2003, the procuratorate decided not to seek indictments in 1,379 cases and closed 1,576 others.[25] The following year it decided not to seek indictments in 1,106 cases and closed 1,168 others.[26] The fate of some 19,500 investigations in 2003 and 19,800 in 2004 is unspecified. Interviews suggest that in the bulk of these cases, the accused were found guilty of misconduct, but their offenses did not meet the standard for criminal prosecution. These individuals were given "administrative punishments" (行政处罚) ranging from

123

a warning to dismissal from office.[27] In the absence of hard data, the severity of such sanctions cannot be evaluated. Even so, it suffices to recognize that these individuals did not escape penalty.

The math linking indictments to convictions is slightly clearer. In 2004 the procuratorate investigated 30,042 cases involving 34,308 individuals. Of these, the procuratorate prosecuted 26,131 (76 percent), and of the 22,178 cases it prosecuted, it took 16,710 (75 percent) to court for trial, which suggests a fairly high prosecution rate. Nevertheless, about a quarter of those indicted were not tried. Once again, it is not entirely clear how we should account for this gap. It is likely, of course, that some not insignificant number of cases were held over to the next calendar year.[28] Others were returned to the procuratorate for further investigation. And in others, the accused may have agreed to cooperate with authorities, delaying prosecution.

Once cases reached the courts, most resulted in some form of formal punishment. In 2004, for example, the courts tried 18,894 individuals on charges of graft and bribery (贪污贿赂罪). (The discrepancy between the number of corruption cases taken to court by the procuratorate and the number of economic crimes cases tried by the courts is also due to differences in how the two systems report data.) Of these, a mere 187 (1 percent) were found innocent. Of those convicted, 4,044 (21 percent) were sentenced to five or more years in prison and 2,818 (15 percent) to fewer than five years.[29] Just over half of those convicted (10,024) received "noncriminal" punishments, including short-term detention (up to six months), probation, and supervision. An additional 1,821 (9.6 percent) were "exempted from criminal punishment" (免予刑事处罚). Presumably, most of those "exempted" received alternative administration penalties. According to Chinese sentencing guidelines, individuals convicted of offenses involving less than 5,000 yuan may be exempted from criminal punishment or sentenced to a period of supervision by their unit. Such cases may also be referred to the supervisory authority, which can use its discretion in determining punishment. However, if such an offense is deemed serious (for example, because the accused has repeatedly engaged in acts of petty corruption; has been involved in the theft of certain types of property, including safety equipment and military equipment; refuses to admit to his guilt; attempts to shift the blame onto others, or destroys evidence), the individual may be sentenced to up to two years in prison.[30]

Also, in 35 to 40 percent of the cases tried, those convicted were subject to fines and/or the confiscation of illicitly obtained funds and property (附加判处罚金和没收财产).[31] There seems to be evidence of some amount of potential slippage during the investigation and prosecution stages, but much less during the punishment stage.

Let us now see how this analysis compares with earlier findings. True, there is a considerable gap between the number of individuals investigated by the DIC and the procuratorate and the number convicted. In 2004 the ratio of individuals investigated by the procuratorate to the number eventually sent to prison was

7.6 to 1, or about 13 percent. We may recall Pei's claim that the authorities only investigate one in four allegations of corruption. If so, that would put the odds of getting punished at considerably less that one in thirty. However, we ought not assume that all the tips prove to be reliable. Nor should we assume that each tip fingers a different official. Moreover, not all tips necessarily relate to corruption.[32] The number of tips authorities receive from the public is thus not necessarily a solid indicator of the extent of corruption and hence we should not read too much into the gap between the tips and the investigations.

Similarly, it may not be justified to assume that enforcement is slack because the procuratorate filed charges in only 60 percent of the cases it investigated. Although cross-national comparisons are fraught with problems, data from the U.S. Federal Bureau of Investigation (FBI) shows similar slippage rates. Between 1989 and 2000, 36 percent of the corruption cases referred to the FBI for investigation were eventually prosecuted, of which 72 percent resulted in convictions.[33] Of those convicted, 45 percent were sent to prison. Overall, 13 percent of referrals ended up with prison sentences handed down.

In China, on the other hand, the procuratorate filed criminal charges in 47 percent of the cases it accepted for investigation during 2003–2005.[34] Eighty-three percent of the indictments resulted in conviction, and of those, 56 percent received prison sentences. In all, roughly 20 percent of the investigation resulted in prison sentences, a higher ratio than in the United States.

It is worth noting that between 1986 and 2000, the average prison sentence for public corruption in the United States was about sixteen months. In China, 37.5 percent of those given prison sentences received a minimum of five years (or sixty months); the remaining 62.5 percent received terms of less than five years. Without more detailed data we cannot accurately estimate the average sentence in China. Nevertheless, even a crude "guesstimate" suggests that the average sentence in China was considerably more than sixteen months.[35] Chinese law also allows for the death penalty in corruption cases, while American law does not.

Also, recall that of the 87 percent who were suspected of corruption but did not go to prison, the majority did not simply walk away scot-free. Most were sentenced to various forms of detention, supervision, and probation—punishments similar to those imposed by American courts for corruption cases that do not warrant prison. Others received administrative sanctions such as dismissal from office or disciplinary supervision by their units. All those accused were presumably disgraced. Even those who were ultimately exonerated, at a minimum faced a grueling and harrowing investigation that might well have included periods of indefinite detention at the hands of the DIC.[36] People accused of corruption had more to fear than a sly wink and a nod or perhaps a friendly slap on the wrist, as studies like Pei's imply. Simply to be accused of corruption carries negative consequences.

It is important to recognize that many of the cases that did not result in prison sentences may have involved bad behavior rather than criminal activity. Petty corruption is common and might be called, for lack of a better term, "bad conduct in office." Chinese officials and cadres are notorious for taking advantage of their authority to create "perks." Excessive banqueting at the expense of either the public or private citizens is one such example; accepting gifts is another. In many such instances, officials do not accept cash; nor do they provide a quid-pro-quo favor. Banqueting and gifts are used instead to "build relationships" (关系). They are repaid through a process of "diffuse reciprocity," most often in the form of help at some point in the future. Relationships may also be built indirectly, with a private citizen lending a hand to an official's relatives, friends, or spouse. In other cases, assistance may be rendered to an official organization rather than to a specific individual. In fact, savvy officials are apt to be very careful not to engage in quid-pro-quo exchanges, which both reduces the possibility of prosecution and allows them to avoid becoming "trapped" in relationships with specific individuals. Other types of bad behavior, such as drunkenness, womanizing, and frequenting prostitutes may be disgraceful but do not necessarily constitute an abuse of power or even (with the exception of visiting prostitutes) criminal activity. They may be construed, however, as violating the rules governing proper conduct. In the past, in fact, the supervisory system listed "degeneracy" (腐化堕落道德败坏) as a punishable offense.

Of course, accusations are sometimes ignored, cases dropped for lack of evidence, misdeeds covered up, the guilty protected, slap-on-the-wrist punishments handed down. Obstruction of justice is clearly a major problem. In recent years, in fact, the regime has launched repeated attacks on the "protective umbrellas" (保护伞) that shield corrupt officials, suggesting that even Beijing recognizes that enforcement can be arbitrary and that the scales of justice in China are frequently balanced with a heavy thumb. Rather, it serves to remind us that some degree of slippage is unavoidable. What we cannot be sure of, however, is how much the degree of slippage in contemporary China deviates from the ideal. We also cannot, it must be recalled, determine how much the rates of investigation, indictment, and imprisonment deviate from the actual rate of corruption (ARC). The ARC, though, is essentially unknowable since corruption, by its nature, strives to remain hidden.

In sum, the relationship between accusations of corruption and prison sentences is complex. We can only relate these two points through some admittedly imprecise math. To a considerable degree, my calculations are "fuzzy," but whereas Pei bases his claim of chronic low rates of punishment on a questionable link between macrolevel "inputs" (accusations of official malfeasance and misconduct) and specific "outputs" (party members remanded to the judiciary for possible criminal prosecution), my analysis works through the various intermediate "inputs" and outputs in order to more accurately interpret the relationship between macro-inputs and specific outputs. This approach provides for better tracing and hence reduces the level of fuzziness that relates inputs to outputs. In the end, however, the result is a general statement about the efficacy of enforcement, which indicates that the degree of slippage is far less than suggested by Pei and others. Moreover, we still lack a metric that would allow us to determine whether the investigation-indictment-punishment ratios are "reasonable" or whether they suggest a slack and potentially failing anticorruption effort (that is, unless we are willing to assume that the overwhelming majority of those initially accused are in fact guilty). Such an assumption might not seem overly bold in the contemporary environment, where many people (such as taxi drivers and other common sources of street knowledge) are inclined to believe that most, if not all, officials are corrupt. This widely held view is, however, ultimately an assumption that rests on an impressionistic "sense" of the ARC.

Changing Gear?

Although it might be difficult to assess the efficacy of China's anticorruption campaign from the investigation-indictment-punishment ratios alone, evidence of significant changes in the ratio over time might provide a telling indicator. *Ceteris paribus*, if the ratio of accusations to convictions increases, we may assume that enforcement is becoming more lax. If it decreases, on the other hand, we might assume that investigators and prosecutors are more vigorously pursuing corruption.

Using aggregate trend data is fraught with a variety of difficulties. As mentioned previously, the data on the activities of the combined party disciplinary and state supervisory systems are at best limited and incomplete. Aggregated data are reported annually in the *Yearbook of the People's Republic of China* (中华人民共和国年鉴). *Xinhua* generally reports on the DIC's annual national conference and publishes a summary of the DIC's report to the Central Committee's yearly plenum. However, the DIC does not provide a breakdown of its caseload. Nor does it report the number of corruption-related cases it investigates each year.

Similar problems arise with the procuratorate and the court. Although both publish yearbooks containing data on the number of cases accepted, indictments, trials, and convictions, definitional variations make it difficult to compare data. The procuratorate, for example, reports data on the number of economic crime (经济犯罪) cases it handles each year, which, according to its definition, include graft, bribery, misappropriation public funds, tax evasion, and copyright violations. The first three categories account for more than 95 percent of the cases accepted since 1989 and 98 to 99 percent of cases accepted since 1997. In an analysis of procuratorate activities, the category of economic crime provides a near-perfect proxy for corruption.

The court, on the other hand, defines economic crime more broadly, including offenses that do not necessarily constitute corruption, such as fraud, smuggling, certain forms of theft, and other offenses. The *Law Yearbook* provides data on graft and bribery cases but aggregates misappropriation of public funds, which account for approximately a quarter of the procuratorate's corruption caseload, with other forms of white-collar crime. Even though we can break down the data in ways that help us piece together the relationship between the procuratorate's caseload and the court's, we cannot rigorously match inputs (investigations and indictments by the procuratorate) to outputs (convictions and sentences handed down by the courts). Ultimately, we are forced to continue to rely on some amount of fuzzy math to assess the efficacy of China's anticorruption efforts.

As Pei notes, the number of economic crime cases accepted by the procuratorate has declined since the early 1990s (see figure 5.3). In part, the decrease can be attributed to the 1997 revision of the criminal code, which decriminalized a variety of less serious offenses.[37] Such cases are now handled by the disciplinary-supervisory system. Shifting cases out of the judicial system and into the displinary-supervisory system caused the DIC caseload to increase, and thus decreased that of the procuratorate, with the secondary result that the gap between their caseloads widened. Since 2003 a drop in the DIC caseload has caused the gap to narrow. At the same time, the number of cases the procuratorate accepts for investigation has decreased while the number of indictments has remained relatively constant; as a result, its investigation-indictment ratio has decreased. Finally, the ratio of indictments to trials has not changed significantly.[38] In combination, these changes suggest that while the initial investigation rate has fallen, the odds of indictment and conviction have increased. There has, finally, been a marked decrease in the ratio of tips from the public to cases accepted by the procuratorate in recent years.[39] The significance of the drop is unclear.

The drop in the number of corruption cases investigated by the procuratorate is troubling. It mirrors a drop in the number of civil lawsuits that began in the late 1990s,[40] but it's unclear what linkage—if any—exists between the two. It should be noted that the caseload from 1989 to 1990 was "inflated" by a burst of greatly intensified enforcement during 1989 and 1990. The regime had launched a major anticorruption campaign in the summer of 1989 in the immediate aftermath of widespread antigovernment demonstrations—fueled in part by anger over perceived increases in official corruption. The leveling off of caseloads in recent years might, therefore, be interpreted as the result of a shift from a reactive "firefighting" approach to anticorruption work to a more standardized, routine "police-patrolling" approach.[41] Yet, the decrease came at a time when the overall number of criminal prosecutions and the overall crime rate continued to rise at fairly substantial rates (see figure 5.5).

Figure 5.3 Procuratorial Economic Crime Caseload

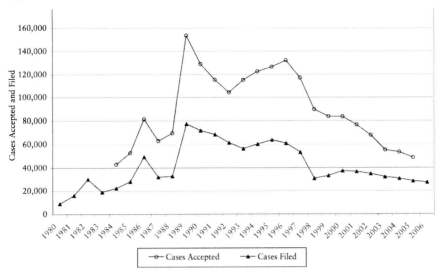

Source: *Zhongguo Falu Nianjian*, various years.

Figure 5.4 Procuratorial Caseload: Tips versus Indictments

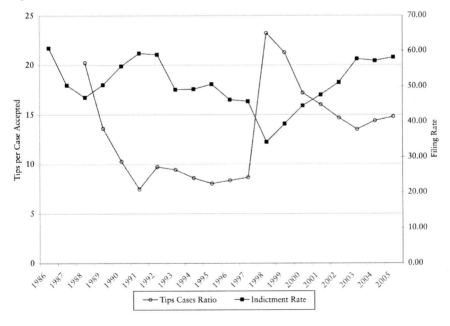

Source: *Zhongguo Jiancha Nianjian*, various years.

Figure 5.5 Ordinary Crime: Cases Tried versus Convicted

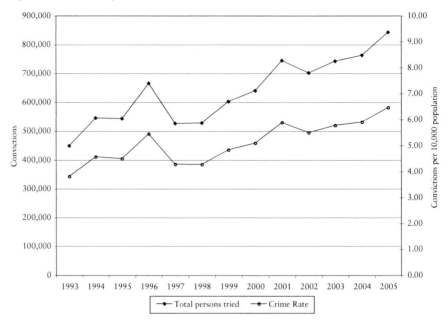

Source: *Zhongguo Jiancha Nianjian*, various years.

There has been a fairly significant drop over time in the severity of sentences handed down for economic crimes. Of those convicted of economic crimes in the mid-1990s, 29 percent received prison sentences of five or more years; from 2002 to 2003 only 20 percent received such heavy sentences (see figure 5.6). In the mid-1990s, roughly a third of those convicted received prison sentences of less than five years; that figure increased to 37 percent from 1999 to 2000, and returned to about a third from 2002 to 2003. The share of nonprison sentences increased from 38 percent in 1995 to 48 percent in 2005, while the number of persons who were exempted from criminal punishment rose from 3.5 percent in the mid-1990s to almost 6 percent in 2005. (One percent or less of those tried for economic crimes were found innocent.)

Compared to those convicted of ordinary criminal offenses, between 1988 and 2005 those convicted of economic crimes were less likely than people convicted of ordinary criminal charges (25 percent versus 30 percent) to receive prison sentences of five or more years (see table 5.1). They were considerably less likely (32 percent versus 46 percent) to receive lesser prison sentences.[42] They were more than twice as likely to be exempted from punishment (4 percent versus 1.5 percent) and almost twice as likely to receive nonprison sentences (21 percent versus 39 percent). They were also twice as likely to be declared innocent (1 percent versus 0.5 percent).

Figure 5.6 Sentencing for Economic Crime, 1988–2005: Five or More Years

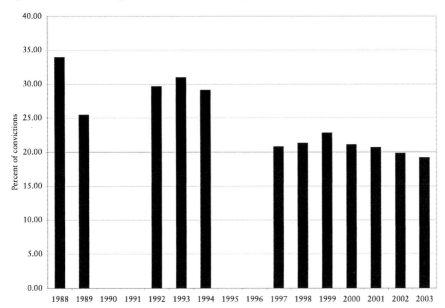

Source: *Zhongguo Falu Nianjian*, various years.
Note: Data on shorter prison sentences prior to 1991 may not be comparable with later years as they may contain sentences subsequently classified as not requiring prison time.

Over time, the imbalance in sentencing has decreased. In 1995, 38 percent of those convicted of ordinary crimes received sentences of five or more years while 30 percent of those convicted of economic crimes received sentences of five or more years. Ten years later, this 10 percent gap had disappeared and 19 percent of those convicted of either ordinary or economic crimes were sentenced to five or more years. Similarly, whereas in 1995, 16 percent of those convicted of economic crimes received nonprison sentences—while 38 percent of those convicted of economic crimes received nonprison sentences in 2005—32 percent of those convicted of ordinary crimes received nonprison sentences while 47 percent of those convicted of economic crimes received nonprison time. The share of those convicted of ordinary crimes who received sentences of less than five years, however, rose from 45 percent in 1995 to 48 percent in 2005 while the share of those convicted of economic crimes who received sentences of less than five years dropped from 32 in 1995 to 28 percent in 2005.

Table 5.1 Comparison of Sentencing

	Five years or more		Less than five years		Nonprison sentence		Exempted		Innocent	
	All crime	Economic crime	All crime	Economic crime	All crime	Economic crime	All crime	Economic crime	All crime	Economic crime
1988	30.79	26.67		55.15				1.40	0.55	0.58
1989		30.51		50.08				1.61		0.27
1990	36.99	33.91		45.22			1.25	1.55	0.33	0.31
1991	36.20	25.43		30.08			1.49	3.72	0.39	1.02
1992	34.61	24.09		28.46			1.62	3.97	0.51	1.53
1993										
1994	38.04	29.65	44.60	32.18	15.65		1.40	3.21	0.39	
1995	40.14	30.94	42.41	26.83		37.71	1.45	3.53	0.35	0.99
1996	43.05	29.09	40.56	30.52	14.66	35.88	1.38	3.39	0.34	1.12
1997	39.51									
1998	27.94									
1999	25.89	20.77	48.03	37.18	23.63	36.75	1.49	4.06	0.97	1.24
2000	25.28	21.28	47.62	37.16			1.51		1.02	1.14
2001	25.11	22.77	49.15	35.56			1.41		0.88	1.23
2002	22.69	21.08	48.87	34.20			1.59		0.70	1.14
2003	21.22	20.66	47.92	30.24			1.59		0.65	
2004	19.04	19.80	47.27	28.01	32.46	46.74	1.61		0.64	0.73
2005	18.93	19.16	46.78	27.65	21.28	38.51	1.58	5.89	0.26	0.57
Average	30.34	24.55	46.32	31.95			1.49	3.97	0.57	1.02
<1997	37.42	29.80	42.52	29.84	18.22	35.85	1.43	3.46	0.41	1.04
1997 >	22.59	20.79	47.95	32.86	27.19	40.37	1.54	4.98	0.73	1.01
Change	-14.82	-9.02	5.42	3.02	8.97	4.52	0.11	1.51	0.32	-0.04

Source: Zhongguo Falu Nianjian, various years.

132

Table 5.2 Changes in Sentencing

	All crime	Economic crime	Gap (All vs. economic)
Five or more years			
< 1997	37.42	29.80	7.62
1997 >	22.59	20.79	1.80
Fewer than five years			
< 1997	42.52	29.84	12.68
1997 >	47.95	32.86	15.09
Nonprison sentence			
< 1997	18.22	35.85	-17.63
1997 >	27.19	40.37	-13.18
Exempted			
< 1997	1.43	3.46	-2.03
1997 >	1.54	4.98	-3.44
Innocent			
< 1997	0.41	1.04	-0.63
1997 >	0.73	1.01	-0.28

Source: Zhongguo Falu Nianjian, various years.

Nevertheless, sentences for economic crimes have generally been somewhat lighter than those for other offenses, which might suggest that corrupt officials are getting off easy. It should be borne in mind, though, that it may be legitimate for corrupt officials who commit white-collar crimes, as they are called in the United States, to be punished less harshly than violent criminals, murderers, rapists, and armed robbers.

To sum up, there has been a significant change in the gearing of China's anticorruption efforts since the mid-1990s. Investigation rates by the disciplinary-supervisory bureaus and by the procuratorate have fallen significantly. A wide gap still exists between the caseload of the disciplinary-supervisory system and that of the procuratorate. Yet the number of indictments filed by the procuratorate and the number of cases brought to trial have not changed dramatically. As a result, the percentage of procuratorial investigations leading to indictments and convictions has gone up. Of those convicted of corruption, the percentage sentenced to prison has decreased and the percentage receiving nonprison sentences or exemptions from penal sanction has increased. There have been changes in the overall pattern of criminal sentencing as well. Sentences handed down for corruption are now more in line with those handed down for other crimes. Finally, the number of government officials convicted of criminal offenses, including noncorruption offenses, has increased significantly since the mid-1990s.

Conclusion

Assessing the success or failure of China's war on corruption—and whether China has perhaps weathered the worst of its postreform corruption problems—is difficult. The fundamental problem is that we cannot determine the ARC, the actual rate of corruption. Because of that we cannot be sure of how to interpret changes in the RRC (for example, the number of officials caught and punished). If the number of corruption arrests rises, does it mean that the government has become more corrupt or that the authorities are pursuing corruption more vigorously? Conversely, if the number goes down, does it mean that fewer officials are corrupt or that more of them are getting away with their crimes? Asking experts to provide their best guess of the severity of corruption provides an alternative measure, but ultimately such polls derive from their subjective beliefs and assumptions about both the ARC and the RRC. A significant jump in the RRC, after all, is likely to cause observers to assume that corruption has worsened or that their previous estimates of the PLC were too low. However, they might dismiss a decrease in indictments as either insignificant or as evidence of slackening enforcement and be hesitant to revise their estimates of the PLC downward, even in the face of a real decrease to the ARC. Certainty is difficult even under the best of circumstances.

Globally, China is not an outlier when it comes to corruption. Although TI ranked China as the fifth-most corrupt country in the world in 1995 and the sixth-most corrupt in 1996, throughout most of the reform period China has not been in the upper quartile of any of the various corruption indices. Its high rankings in 1995 and 1996 were largely the result of samples that omitted many more corrupt countries. When countries of the former Soviet bloc states were added to the sample in 1997, China fell to twelfth; in 1999 it had dropped to thirty-ninth.[43] As of 2006, it was ranked 88th out of 163 countries. The World Bank's Governance Index also places China in the middle of the pack. And yet these two rankings differ on the direction corruption has taken in China in recent years. TI's index shows China moving from the upper-quartile boundary down toward the mean, while the World Bank's has it moving from the mean toward the upper quartile.[44]

That China is not—by international standards—extremely corrupt is another factor that makes it hard to assess the progress of China's war on corruption. Discussions about corruption in China often fail to make cross-country comparisons, including with developed countries such as the United States. Corruption in China clearly spread in the 1980s and intensified in the 1990s. After initially ignoring the growing threat of corruption, the government launched two limited attacks on corruption in 1982 and 1986 and then a major anticorruption effort in 1989. It has almost continuously poured resources into the fight and implemented a variety of new rules and regulations designed to reduce the opportunities for corruption and facilitate the detection and punishment of those caught engaging in illegal or improper activities. In theory, as the regime's anticorruption assets increase and the legal system plugs loopholes, the need for short bursts of intensified enforcement should decrease as routine policing more effectively serves to deter and detect corruption. The absence of campaigns after 1993 might thus be interpreted as evidence of a more mature anticorruption system, but only if the government is making headway in its efforts to reduce corruption. If, instead, its anticorruption efforts are failing to keep pace with corruption, then the leveling off of the RRC over the past decade simply masks an increase in corruption. This is, in fact, the critical question: have the regime's anticorruption efforts failed to keep pace with rising corruption or are they successfully mitigating it?

This question is not easy to answer, absent the ability to measure the ARC. And yet, focusing on whether the regime is winning or losing its fight against corruption makes it possible to reformulate the question into classic hypothesis testing terms. We can thus divide the question of whether China is winning or losing the war on corruption into two rival hypotheses:

H1: The regime is winning its war on corruption.
H2: The regime is losing its war on corruption.

The key is given by the null hypotheses, which are defined as:

$H1_0$: The regime is not winning its war on corruption.
$H2_0$: The regime is not losing its war on corruption.

"Not winning" is defined as the absence of clear evidence of winning. Conversely, "not losing" is defined as the absence of clear evidence of losing. We thus draw a middle ground between winning and losing that we can think of as a "zone of ambiguity" in which the struggle against corruption continues but in which the outcome remains unclear.

The importance of recognizing the existence of this zone of ambiguity is critical because the data on changing rates of investigation, indictment, and conviction do not yield a clear picture. As such, they do not provide convincing evidence that China's quarter-century-long war on corruption is failing, as Pei argues. Nor do they provide solid evidence that the government is making headway. Frankly, the data are inconclusive. Their contradictory mix of positive and negative indicators allows us to reject both H1 (the regime is winning) and H2 (the regime is losing) and accept the twin null hypotheses of not winning and not losing.[45] The data are, therefore, actually consistent with a period of ambiguous "protracted warfare" in which the balance of power has not yet tipped either for or against the government. Manion's work suggests that such a balance indicates success, in the sense that the government has managed to prevent corruption from "spiraling out of control."[46] But, as Manion further implies, the balance shows a lack of significant progress in reducing corruption or significantly reducing the institutional weaknesses that create both opportunities and incentives for officials to misuse the power vested in their offices for personal advantage.[47]

We can only conclude that China's war on corruption has reached a stalemate. This forces us, in turn, to consider what a stalemate means in the context of an economic and systemic transition, such as that ongoing in China. It is important to recall that when the party initiated economic reforms in the late 1970s and early 1980s, the government lacked the institutional capacity to control corruption. At the time economic reforms were first initiated, China lacked a functioning legal system. The criminal law drafted during the early 1950s had effectively lapsed in the wake of the 1957 Anti-Rightist Campaign. A new code was enacted in 1979, but did not come into effect until the following year. The procuratorate had all but ceased to function even prior to the Cultural Revolution, and in 1975 prosecutorial authority was assigned to the public security organs. It was not until 1978 that it was formally reestablished. The courts had been transformed into revolutionary tribunals during the Cultural Revolution and were staffed largely by untrained judges. The DIC, which had been established in 1949, had lost most of its independent authority in 1955 and was not made an independent party organ until the 11th Party Congress in 1977.[48] At that time, however, the disciplinary committees were placed under the direct supervision of the local party committee, thus making them subordinate to the institution they were charged with investigating. It was not until 1982 that a new party constitution placed the DICs under the dual supervision of the Central Discipline Inspection Commission in Beijing, giving them some degree of independence from the party committees.[49] The Ministry of Supervision, finally, was not established until 1987, almost a decade after the advent of economic reform and thus well after the surge in corruption. In sum, China had to construct an entirely new legal system at the same time that economic reform and the rise of corruption were placing new and more daunting demands on anticorruption work. Given the underdeveloped nature of China's legal and anticorruption institutions in the early 1980s, what is perhaps most surprising is not that corruption increased, but rather that it did not overwhelm the system,

Thus, finding that the war on corruption is stalemated actually suggests that the authorities have succeeded at the toughest job of all: they have managed to implement a functioning anticorruption regime even in the face of mounting corruption. At the same time, a twenty-five-year lack of substantial headway in reducing corruption cannot be viewed as evidence of deep institutional strength. While we might conclude that the apparent leveling off of corruption reflects an emerging balance, we must also recognize that the outcome of the war remains in doubt.

Cast in terms of the broader question asked by this volume, the leveling off of corruption in the past decade suggests that the surge in the first decades of reform was in fact a transitory growing pain caused by the sudden and radical restructuring of the Chinese economy. Concluding that the surge in corruption has ended does not, however, tell us whether its current level poses a threat to the vitality of the Chinese economy or the political stability of the CCP. Even if we conclude that corruption is not worsening, it is clear from recent cases that high-level corruption remains a serious problem. In theory, extensive high-level corruption might be tolerable, particularly if the economy continues to grow rapidly. If, however, the economy slows down, corruption could prove a more serious and perhaps even a debilitating drag. Even in the absence of a slowing economy, over a prolonged period of time the current level of corruption could slowly sap the economy of its vitality and undermine the legitimacy of the CCP. The political consequences of corruption are, however, difficult to assess. Corruption does not appear to have a continuous and linear political effect. Discontent over corruption might reach critical levels and produce nothing more than grumbling and griping because ordinary citizens are afraid to speak out publicly or take to the streets in protest. At present, the Chinese public appears to see extensive corruption as normal, with the result that corruption remains a latent political threat. Changing circumstances (for example, a significant economic downturn) could, however, trigger shifts in perception that would render this same level of corruption politically unacceptable and thus trigger greater unrest.

Notes

[1] International Monetary Fund, *World Economic Outlook Database*, October 2007, www.imf.org/external/pubs/ft/weo/2007/02/weodata/index.aspx.

[2] Caution must be exercised in evaluating changes in the perceived level of corruption (PLC) because evaluators' estimates are apt to be based in part on previous scores. As a result, year-to-year changes in estimates may understate the magnitude of real change. Moreover, it is likely that changes in the PLC lag behind changes in both the actual rate of corruption (ARC) and the revealed rate of corruption (RRC). It seems most prudent, therefore, to assess trends over a number of years rather than focusing on short-term fluctuations. See Transparency International (TI), "The Methodology of the Corruption Perceptions Index 2007," www.transparency.org/policy_research/surveys_indices/cpi.

[3] In Chinese legal usage, "senior" officials are those holding leadership positions at the county level and above.

[4] *Zhongguo Jiancha Nianjian* [Prosecutorial Yearbook of China] (Beijing: Zhongguo Jiancha Chubanshe, various years).

[5] *Zhongguo Falu Nianjian* [Law Yearbook of China] (Beijing: Zhongguo Falu Chubanshe, various years).

[6] "Congress Work Reports Show China has 'Intensified Efforts' Against Corruption," *Xinhua*, March 9, 2005.

[7] Minxin Pei, *China's Trapped Transition: The Limits of Developmental Autocracy* (Cambridge, MA: Harvard Univ. Press, 2006), 150–3; and Minxin Pei, "Corruption Threatens China's Future," Carnegie Endowment Policy Brief No. 44 (October 2007).

[8] Pei, *China's Trapped Transition*, 151. Between 1986 and 2000, the total number of procuratorial personnel increased from 140,000 to 228,000. After 2000 the number fell and as of 2005, procuratorial personnel totaled 214,000 (*Zhongguo Jiancha Nianjian*, various years).

[9] Pei, *China's Trapped Transition*, 150, 159–66.

[10] See *Youqi tuxing, juyi huanxing de zhixing* [Implementation of suspended sentences], http://china.findlaw.cn/info/xingxi/xsss/39674.html. Chinese criminal law does not differentiate between felonies and misdemeanors, but instead designates less serious offenses as "noncriminal." Conviction for such offenses does not mandate prison time but can result in a variety of other punishments. Many ordinary petty crimes are adjudicated by the public security system and never enter the judicial system. For economic crimes, however, even noncriminal cases are generally referred to the procuratorate. See Ian Dobinson, "Criminal Law," in Wang Chenguang and Zhang Xianchu, eds., *Introduction to Chinese Law* (Hong Kong: Sweet and Maxwell, 1997), 147–8.

[11] In the case of an exemption from punishment, after being found guilty the accused is released without further punishment. Fu Hualing, "Criminal Procedure Law," in Wang and Zhang, *Introduction to Chinese Law*, 1009–10.

[12] *Zhongguo Falu Nianjian*, various years.

[13] Between 1980 and 2007, at least 1,000 individuals were sentenced to death or have received suspended death sentences for corruption-related offenses (estimates based on the author's database). For the years 1997–2000 data came from Amnesty International's "Death Log China" and for other years were derived primarily from Lexis-Nexis searches. As the data on the number of death sentences is incomplete and imperfect, the author's figure of 1,000 likely represents a minimal estimate.

[14] In recent years, the State Audit Administration (国家审计署) has begun to play an important role in detecting financial irregularities and providing referrals to both the disciplinary/supervisory and judicial systems. The number of referrals appears to be small and the relationship between the audit system and the other anticorruption systems requires additional study before the audit system can be brought into the analysis of the overall war on corruption.

[15] The state Ministry of Supervision (监查部) (established in 1987) is tasked with investigating wrongdoing by state officials. Because most state officials are also party members, the jurisdictions of the supervisory and disciplinary organs overlap. After operating in parallel for several years, the two institutions were functionally merged in 1993, with the Discipline Inspection Commission (DIC) taking primary responsibility for investigating individuals suspected of corruption. As a matter of convenience, I sometimes refer to it as the DIC even though more properly speaking, it should be called the "disciplinary-supervisory system." See *Zhonggong Zhongyang Jilu Jiancha Weiyuanhui, Jiancha Bu guanyu Zhongyang Zhishu Jiguan he Zhongyang Guojia Jiguan Jijian, Jiancha Jiguo Shezhi de Yijian* (Opinion of the DIC and Ministry of Supervision Regarding the Organization of the Disciplinary and Supervisory Systems), May 18, 1993, www.kxdj.com/16d/1021-19.htm.

[16] Andrew Wedeman, "The Intensification of Corruption in China," *China Quarterly* 180 (December 2004): 895–921. Three recent studies found that the time between an official's first involvement in a corrupt activity and his arrest has increased significantly since the mid-1990s, which would indicate that corrupt officials face a decreased risk of detection. See Guo Yang, "Corruption in Transitional China: An Empirical Analysis," Paper presented at the Workshop on Building Clean Government at the City University of Hong Kong, May 17–18, 2007, Hong Kong; Yan Sun, "Cadre Recruitment and Corruption: What Goes Wrong?" *Crime, Law and Social Change* 49, no. 1 (February 2008): 61–79; and Andrew Wedeman, "Win, Lose, or Draw? China's War on Corruption," *Crime, Law and Social Change* 49, no. 1 (February 2008): 7–26.

[17] *Zhongguo Renmin Gongheguo Nianjiani* [Yearbook of the People's Republic of China] (Beijing: Zhongguo Renmin Gongheguo Nianjian She, 2005), 290.

[18] In 2005 the number of party members disciplined by the DIC fell to 147,539, a decrease of 10 percent. The number of individuals remanded to the judicial system, however, was 15,177, a more than threefold increase. There is some question, however, if these data are comparable with those of previous years.

[19] Aggregate data for the periods 1992–96 and 1997–2002 show remand rates of 5.6 percent and 4.5 percent respectively. See "Work Report of CPC Central Committee Discipline Inspection Commission Presented at the 16th Party National Congress (adopted by the 16th CPC National Congress on November 14, 2002)," *Xinhua*, November 19, 2002; and "Circular on Stepping Up Anticorruption Drive: 120,000 Expelled from Party," *Xinhua*, September 27, 1997.

[20] Wedeman, "The Intensification of Corruption in China."

[21] *Zhongguo Jiancha Nianjian* 2005: 512–3.

[22] The number of government officials tried in 2005 was, in fact, 87 percent higher than the number tried in 1993.

[23] *Zhonggong Zhongyang Jiwei. Zuigao Renmin Jiancha Yuan, Jiancha Bu, "Guanyu jiwei jiancha jiquan he jiancha jiguan zai fanfubai douzheng zhong jiaqiangxiezuo de tongzhi"* [Notice regarding the strengthening of cooperation between the disciplinary, supervisory, and procuratorial systems], November 5, 1993, www.law-lib.com/law/law_view1.asp?id=9930.

[24] In 2003, for instance, the disciplinary-supervisory system investigated 449 members of the procuratorate for violations of party or administrative regulations, subjecting 169 to party disciplinary action and 338 to administrative action. The following year, the DIC took disciplinary action against 345 members of the procuratorate; in 2005 it disciplined 292 (*Zhongguo Jiancha Nianjian* 2005: 295 and *Zhongguo Jiancha Nianjian* 2006: 320–21).

[25] *Zhongguo Jiancha Nianjian* 2004: 247.

[26] *Zhongguo Jiancha Nianjian* 2005: 240.

[27] According to the Criminal Procedure Law, if the procuratorate decides that a punishable offense has occurred but that criminal prosecution is not warranted, it may refer the case back to other state organs with a recommendation for sanctions. Fu, "Criminal Procedure Law," 148. In a sense, the procuratorate has powers analogous to those of the magistrate courts in the British legal system or district courts in the American system, in that it can make summary judgments and impose penalties without taking a case to trial.

[28] Over the past 15 years, on average about 30 percent of those indicted in the United States on charges of public corruption were listed as "awaiting trial" at the end of each reporting year. United States Justice Department, Public Integrity Section, Criminal Division, "Report to Congress on the Activities and Operations of the Public Integrity Section for 2005," www.usdoj.gov/pin.

[29] *Zhongguo Falu Nianjian* 2005.

[30] Gao Gezhu, *Ding zui yu liangxing* [Conviction and penalty measuring] (Beijing: Zhongguo Fangzheng Chubanshe, 2001), 984–95. Prior to 1997, bribery cases involving sums of less than 2,000 yuan were considered to fall below the level of criminality and were normally dealt with administratively. In 1997 the revised criminal code raised the threshold to 5,000 yuan. Meng Qinghua, *Shou Hui Zui Yanjiu Xin Dongxiang* [New trends in research on the crime of accepting bribes] (Beijing: Zhongguo Fangzheng Chubanshe, 2005), 4–5. The regulations governing the misappropriation of public funds

are more complicated. Such offenses involve the "misuse" or diversion of public resources, rather than the embezzlement (outright theft) of public funds. State agencies, state-owned companies, and social organizations routinely put "idle" funds into a variety of short-term interest accounts, usually, but not always, in state-owned banks. Funds may be lent to other state units, placed on account with investment brokerages, or even lent to individuals. Officials and financial managers can take advantage of this practice to earn illicit profits by either pocketing interest earned from legitimate loans and investments, or making unauthorized risky, high-interest loans and then skimming off the inflated returns. So long as the funds can be recovered, the offenders are charged with misappropriating the interest or other income they illegally obtained. Sentencing, however, is based on the amount of money they diverted. As a result, there appears to be a wild disparity between the monetary thresholds for sentencing in bribery and embezzlement cases and those for misappropriation. Although further analysis is needed, much of the disparity vanishes if one compares the amount of illegal income from the illicit loans with the amounts gained through bribery or embezzlement. Misappropriation is also complicated by the fact that many public organizations maintain substantial off-the-books slush funds (known in Chinese as "small treasuries," 小金库), from which they make a variety of loans and investments. The shady and slippery nature of short-term institutional investing frequently creates situations in which it is hard to tell if officials and managers are engaged in legitimate financial management or illegal activity. Meng Qinghua, *Nongyong Gongkuan Zui Xin Dongxiang* [New tendencies in the study of the crime of misappropriating public funds] (Beijing: Beijing Daxue Chubanshe, 2006), 74–115.

[31] Data on confiscations for 2004 are not available. In 2002, 41 percent of those convicted on corruption charges were subject to confiscation and 36 percent the following year.

[32] According to data provided by the Liaoning DIC, between 1994 and 2000, 17 percent of the tips it received were redundant (重复), and 32 percent related specifically to graft, bribery, and embezzlement. An additional 10 percent related to violations of financial regulations (违反财经纪律) and 15 percent to other economic offenses. Of the remaining 43 percent, nearly half were for unspecified problems. *Liaoning Jijian Jiancha Zhi (1949–2000)* [Liaoning provincial almanac of disciplinary inspection and supervision] (Shenyang: Liaoning Renmin Chubanshe, 2005), 302.

[33] FBI data from the Transactional Records Clearing House (TRAC) database, http://trac.syr.edu/tracfbi/index.html.

[34] Data from *Zhongguo Jiancha Nianjian* (various years) and *Zhongguo Falu Nianjian* (various years). The lack of easily comparable data makes estimating the input-output (referral-prison) ratio difficult in the Chinese case. Estimates are based on comparisons of the number of economic crime cases accepted by the procuratorate and the number of cases in which it filed criminal charges. Estimates of the ratio of convictions-to-indictments are based on the number of graft and bribery cases filed by the procuratorate and the number of such cases concluded by the court, with an adjustment for the small number of cases in which the accused were found innocent (which occurred in about 1 percent of the cases). The prison-to-conviction ratio estimate was based on the percent of persons convicted for economic crimes who received prison sentences.

[35] For instance, if we assume for analytical purposes an average sentence of 7.5 years (90 months) for those given 5 or more years and 2.5 years (30) months for those given less than 5 years, then the average sentence would work out to approximately 50 months or about 4.25 years.

140

[36] In recent years, a provision known as *shuanggui* (双规), "dual regulations," gives the DIC (and the Ministry of Supervision, because it operates in concert with the DIC) the authority to summon individuals suspected of infractions for questioning. Because the summons does not involve criminal charges, suspects are not protected by the criminal procedure law, which limits the length of time that a suspect can be held without being formally arrested and charged. As a result, the disciplinary and supervisory organs have the ability to detain individuals virtually indefinitely. More critically, *shuanggui* places the accused in the position of having to convince investigators of their innocence.

[37] In 1996 new regulations also placed new restrictions on the range of offenses that the procuratorate could investigate.

[38] Because almost all trials result in convictions, I have omitted data on court cases concluded.

[39] The percentage of party members disciplined by the DIC by expulsion from the party rose significantly during 2004 and 2005. Between 1992 and 1996, 18.2 percent of those disciplined were expelled from the party; 16.3 percent were expelled between 1997 and 2002. The percentage rose to 29.7 in 2004 and 30.3 in 2005. In 2006, however, there was a marked decrease in the expulsion rate, with just 21,000 expelled out of the 123,489 party members disciplined (17.0 percent). See *Zhongguo Renmin Gongheguo Nianjian*, 2004 and 2005; "China's Anti-Corruption Campaign Drive Successful, Says Report," *Xinhua*, September 23, 1997; "Work Report of CPC Central Committee," *Xinhua*, November 14, 2002; and "Circular on Stepping Up Anticorruption Drive," *Xinhua*, March 9, 2005.

[40] See Xin He, "The Recent Decline in Economic Caseloads in Chinese Courts: Explorations of a Surprising Puzzle," *China Quarterly* 190 (June 2007): 352–74.

[41] See Mathew D. McCubbins and Thomas Schwartz, "Congressional Oversight Overlooked: Police Patrols versus Fire Alarms," *American Political Science Review* 28, no. 1 (February 1984): 165–79.

[42] In the United States, 40 percent of those convicted in the state court on felony charges received prison sentences. An additional 30 percent received short-term jail sentences and 28 percent were released on probation. Among those prosecuted on public corruption charges, 18 percent were not convicted, 48 percent were sentenced to prison, and 36 percent received probation. Based on data from the "U.S. Department of Justice, Office of Justice Statistics," www.ojp.gov/bjs/pub/html/scscf04/tables/scs04102tab.htm.

[43] See TI, "Corruption Perceptions Index," www.transparency.org.

[44] The authors of the World Bank's Governance Index (www.worldbank.org/wbi/governance) argue that because of the inherent imprecision in estimating the level of corruption, it is only possible to differentiate scores that are far apart. Scores with overlapping standard errors, they assert, cannot be assumed to be statistically significant independently. This suggests to me that while we can easily distinguish the upper quartile of the distribution from the bottom quartile, it is much more difficult to distinguish scores within the middle two quartiles. See Daniel Kaufmann, Aart Kraay, and Pablo Zoido-Lobaton, "Governance Matters," World Bank Working Paper 2196 (October 1999): 11.

[45] Although my analysis suggests rejection of both positive hypotheses, it should be noted that there is a possibility of a type II error (that is, rejection of the positive hypotheses when they are true). In this case, because both positive hypotheses cannot be simultaneously true, this means accepting the null hypothesis that the regime in not winning when in fact it may be (1) winning or (2) losing.

[46] Melanie Manion, "Issues in Corruption Control in Post-Mao China," *Issues and Studies* 34, no. 9 (September 1998): 1–21; and Melanie Manion, "Corruption by Design:

Corruption Control through Enforcement Swamping," Paper presented at the American Political Science Association Annual Meeting, September 2–5, 1999, Atlanta. Also see Mark R. Kleiman, "Enforcement Swamping: A Positive Feedback Mechanism in Rates of Illicit Activity," *Mathematical Computer Modeling* 17, no. 2 (1993): 65–75; and Francis T. Lui, "A Dynamic Model of Corruption Deterrence," *Journal of Public Economics* 31, no. 2 (November 1986): 215–26.

[47] Melanie Manion, *Corruption By Design: Building Clean Government in Mainland China and Hong Kong* (Cambridge, MA: Harvard Univ. Press, 2004).

[48] Ting Gong, "The CCP's Discipline Inspection: Evolving Trajectory and Embedded Dilemmas," *Crime, Law and Social Change* 49, no. 2 (March 2008): 139–52.

[49] Manion, *Corruption by Design*, 122–3.

GOVERNING ONE MILLION RURAL COMMUNITIES AFTER TWO DECADES: ARE CHINA'S VILLAGE ELECTIONS IMPROVING?

Lily L. Tsai

Theories of democracy tell us that government officials should be more responsive to the interests of citizens when citizens can vote those they want into office and those they do not want out of office. Well-implemented election procedures help ensure that voters can actually elect the candidates they want. Institutions such as public vote counts, tamper-resistant ballot boxes, and the regulation of proxy voting help make sure that voters will not be forced into voting for people they do not support and that their choices will be accurately represented and reported.

Since 1988, when the Chinese government first implemented direct elections for village leaders, social scientists, policymakers, and international organizations have been enamored with them and their potential for fostering grassroots democratization in rural China. Numerous studies have examined why the central government implemented these local political reforms,[1] where they have been implemented most effectively,[2] and the extent to which they are, as Kelliher puts it, "the real thing."[3]

The literature is rich in empirical fieldwork and anecdotal case studies but lacks systematic, nationally representative data on the actual implementation of village elections nationwide, collected independent of the Chinese government. As Pastor and Tan have noted, "What is missing is a national picture." Without that, it is impossible to evaluate the progress of grassroots democratization and local political reform (or lack thereof), or to determine if they are in fact going through "growing pains," and if so, what kind.[4] An accurate national picture is also needed to assess the capacity and will of the central government to implement election laws and regulations, and the extent to which the implementation of village elections has been a bottom-up or top-down process. Local studies are well suited for looking at political processes in detail and examining specific cases of political and electoral change over time. However, they cannot address questions about the central government's ability to elicit compliance from local governments, central-local power dynamics in general, or regional variation in local democratic initiatives.

In the absence of reliable information on the state of village elections nationwide, we remain vulnerable to the impressions given by the most recent case studies and popular media reports. The official Chinese media, for example, has, in recent years, promoted an increasingly pessimistic picture of village elections. In 2006 and 2007, a rash of articles highlighted cases of corruption, vote rigging, and bribery in election administration.[5] But are these isolated incidents or representative of a nationwide phenomenon?

Objectives

So what is the actual state of village elections in China? Drawing on data from a unique, nationally representative survey conducted in 2005, this chapter seeks to provide a definitive assessment. Furthermore, it compares the results of the 2005 survey with previous estimates on election implementation published in top English and Chinese academic journals. The survey data help us put these previous estimates in perspective and establish a benchmark for evaluating future changes in implementation.

The chapter also uses the 2005 survey data to assess what citizens themselves think about the quality of village elections. Are citizens more interested and excited by elections with well-implemented procedures, and do they participate actively in such elections? In other words, are such elections more meaningful and substantively important to citizens themselves?

Data

The data from the 2005 China Rural Governance Survey, administered by the Center for Chinese Agricultural Policy (CCAP) at the Chinese Academy of Sciences (CAS) under the direction of Linxiu Zhang and Scott Rozelle, come from a nationally representative sample of 101 villages in 5 provinces. One province was randomly selected from each of China's major agro-ecological zones: Jiangsu from the eastern coastal region, Sichuan from the southwest, Shaanxi from the northwest, Hebei from the central region, and Jilin from the northeast. Each province's counties were stratified by per capita gross value of industrial output (GVIO); then a stratified random sample of five counties was selected from each province.[6] The same procedure was used to select two townships from each county and two villages from each township. In sum, through a stratified clustering strategy, one hundred villages were randomly selected from fifty townships in twenty-five counties in five provinces. Interviews with village officials and focus-group discussions with villagers constitute the key sources of data. Within each village, survey enumerators interviewed village officials about the implementation of specific election procedures, and two enumerators held a focus group with twelve villagers, asking them to evaluate the competitiveness and fairness of the most recent election in their village.

The Current State of Village Election Implementation

To start with a basic question, just how common are village elections in China? Has implementation reached the point where most villages in rural China attempt to hold some form of election? Estimates, even from the same time period, have varied widely. O'Brien and Li cite an estimate by the editor of the magazine *Xiangzhen Luntan* that in 1997 "no more than 10 percent" of villages have held democratic elections.[7] Their own opportunistic survey of people from 478 villages in 7 provinces, conducted in late 1997, suggested that leaders were elected in 45 percent of the villages.[8] Pastor and Tan report that when the minister of civil affairs was asked informally how many village elections are conducted according to the election laws, he replied, "Perhaps, 50 percent of all the village elections, but frankly, we do not know."[9] Of eighty-seven villages opportunistically sampled from twenty-five provinces in a 1999 survey, Li estimated that 68 percent of the villages had held elections.[10] In 2000 Wang Zhenyao, the former director of the Department of Basic-level Governance within the Ministry of Civil Affairs (MCA) and the official who was responsible for the initial implementation of direct village elections, estimated that 30 to 60 percent of all villages had started to implement democratic reforms—and he acknowledged that this estimate was an optimistic one.[11]

Given that these estimates are based on personal experience or opportunistic samples, it's not surprising that they vary widely. Data from the 2005 survey give us a reliable, recent estimate of the percentage of villages that currently hold direct elections for village leaders. In each village, the survey asked respondents how their village leaders since 1991 had come to office—whether by direct election by all villagers, election by village representatives, election by village committee cadres, election by party branch cadres, or appointment by higher levels of government. Figure 6.1 shows the percentage of villages that directly elected their leaders each three-year election cycle since 1991.[12] As we can see, the percentage has been increasing since that time. The spread of direct elections was slower during the 1990s but has been more rapid since 2000.

The marked increase since 2000 can be attributed at least in part to the November 1998 revision of the Village Organization Law by the National People's Congress. The original version, passed in 1988, permitted but did not require direct election of village officials. The revised version required that all villages hold direct elections. In the late 1990s, only 17 percent of village leaders came to office through direct election in the sampled villages. By the early 2000s, the number had increased to 42 percent, and in 2004 it stood at around 75 percent.

The rapidly changing conditions in the late 1990s and early 2000s help account for the widely varying estimates of village election implementation. Figure 6.1 graphs the data by three-year election cycles (provinces hold village elections once every three years), giving a clearer representation of the overall trend nationwide over time. In contrast, figure 6.2 graphs the data year by year,

145

highlighting the variation in election implementation across provinces. We can see from figure 6.2 that the time period with the most variability was 1999–2001. In 1999, among the surveyed villages, 31 percent of the leaders who took office were directly elected. In 2000, when a different set of provinces held village elections, only 15 percent were directly elected. In 2001, 54 percent were directly elected. It is not surprising that researchers focusing on different provinces during that period gave wildly varying estimates of election implementation. Such dramatic variation underlines the dangers of drawing broad conclusions based on data from one or two provinces.

Figure 6.1 Percentage of Village Leaders Who Were Directly Elected During this Election Cycle

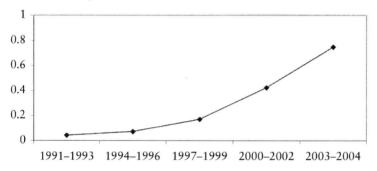

Source: 2005 China Rural Governance Survey, Center for Chinese Agricultural Policy, Chinese Academy of Sciences.

Figure 6.2 Percentage of Village Leaders Who Were Directly Elected

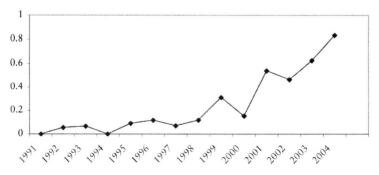

Source: 2005 China Rural Governance Survey, Center for Chinese Agricultural Policy, Chinese Academy of Sciences.

Implementation of Specific Village Election Institutions

From 1991 to 2004, more and more village leaders took office through direct elections by all villagers, but how "good" or "real" are these elections? Are elections contested by multiple candidates? To what extent are people free to choose whom they elect? And do all of the candidates have a fair chance of winning? [13] One way to evaluate the quality of an election is to examine whether it incorporates the specific components of a "free and fair" election, such as having multiple candidates for each position, using secret ballots, counting votes publicly, regulating proxy voting, and using fixed polling stations (rather than mobile ballot boxes brought to individual homes). These institutions prevent voters from being coerced into voting for a candidate they do not want and ensure that their votes are accurately tallied and reported. It is also necessary to look at the institutions governing the election process. Is the election administered impartially, or is there interference from higher levels? Do governing institutions make sure that incumbents allow their opponents to run for office? Are candidates popularly nominated by the electorate, or are nominations dictated by higher levels? Do higher levels respect the electorate's choice of nominees, or is higher-level approval required for the final slate of candidates?

Table 6.1 presents descriptive figures on the implementation of specific election procedures in 2005 in the 101 villages surveyed. These particular procedures are commonly identified by social scientists as critical to ensuring free and fair elections. [14] By 2005 some key procedures had become almost universal. In their most recent elections, 95 percent or more of the villages in the survey had multiple candidates for village leader, used a secret ballot, and held public vote counts. Other voting procedures were far less commonplace. Candidates gave campaign speeches in less than half of the villages. Sixty-three percent of the villages reported that they used fixed polling stations exclusively, but a significant minority still used less-secure mobile ballot boxes, which are more susceptible to voter coercion and election fraud.

Even more problematic was the regulation of proxy voting. Only one-third of the villages required written documentation from a voter for a proxy to vote on his or her behalf. Elsewhere, oral permission, given in person or over the phone, sufficed. As a result, men often submitted ballots for their wives and adult children as well as for themselves. Often, villagers also submitted multiple ballots on behalf of migrant family members working outside the village and unable to return for the election.

Institutions ensuring that candidates are nominated freely and elections are administered impartially were also less commonplace. In most villages, higher levels did not intervene in the nomination process, but approval of the final slate of candidates *was* required. Moreover, only 9 percent of the villages reported that their election-administration committee was composed entirely of noncadres.

Table 6.1 Descriptive Statistics on the Implementation of Specific Election Institutions

	Percentage of villages in 2005 (standard deviation)	Standard deviation	Number of villages
Voting institutions			
* Multiple candidates for village leader	99%	10%	99
* Anonymous ballots	96%	20%	101
* Public vote count	95%	24%	101
Regulated proxy voting	33%	47%	86
Use of fixed polling stations only	63%	49%	99
Campaign speeches	44%	50%	99
Preelection institutions			
Lack of cadre participation in village election administration committee	9%	29%	101
Lack of higher-level intervention in the nomination of candidates	69%	46%	101
Higher-level approval of final slate of candidates *not* required	34%	48%	99

Source: 2005 China Rural Governance Survey, Center for Chinese Agricultural Policy, Chinese Academy of Sciences.
Note: When the number of villages equals less than 101 for a particular indicator, 1 or more villages were missing data for that indicator.

Such variation is not surprising, considering that the revised Village Organization Law of 1998 requires only some of these institutions. It mandates that the number of candidates exceed the number of positions, that voting must be by secret ballot, and that winning candidates have to obtain an absolute majority of the votes cast. Subsequent government directives mandated a public vote count, the immediate announcement of election results, publication of a voter-registration list twenty days before the election, that the final slate of candidates be determined by some form of primary election, and that an election administration committee be elected by the villagers or their representatives (General Office of the CCP [Chinese Communist Party] Central Committee and General Office of the State Council 2002).[15] Outside of these requirements, provincial governments implemented other election institutions, such as campaign speeches, fixed polling stations, and proxy voting, as they saw fit.[16] As is usually the case, regulations vary widely from province to province.

Not surprisingly, localities are more likely to implement those election institutions mandated by the central government. (Centrally mandated election institutions are marked with an asterisk in table 6.1.) Institutions explicitly mandated by the revised law of 1998 have been implemented by 95 percent or more of the villages in the sample; others have been implemented in anywhere from 9 to 69 percent of the villages. Moreover, intervention in the village election process by higher-level and incumbent village officials tends to come in forms that are not explicitly prohibited by the central government. For example, though central government directives hold that the final slate of candidates be determined by primary elections, they do not forbid higher levels of government from requiring that they approve the final slate before election day. As a result, most of the villages surveyed—66 percent—report that they must seek such approval from the township. Similarly, though the election committee must be popularly elected, central government regulations do not forbid cadres from becoming committee members. Not surprisingly, in only 9 percent of villages were the election committees free of cadres.

This cross-sectional snapshot suggests that village elections have become commonplace in rural China. At a minimum, in most villages, voters have some choice of candidates, can generally vote without fear of intimidation or reprisal from another faction, and can be relatively confident that the declared winner actually received the most votes. However, regulation of proxy voting remains a weak point (as mentioned, only one-third of the villages required written permission). As a result, the preferences of many villagers are not necessarily being taken into account.

These numbers suggest that central government regulations have a substantial impact on election institutions. When the central government requires a particular procedure, local governments are very likely to implement it. When the central government gives localities discretion over implementation, however, township officials are able to exert a significant degree of control over the village election process.

Previous Estimates of the Implementation of Specific Election Institutions

Using the nationwide 2005 survey as a benchmark, we can look at estimates for previous years, allowing us to take an educated guess at whether implementation of various election institutions have gotten better or worse over time.[17] A review of the relevant literature yielded nineteen English articles and twenty-four Chinese articles with at least one descriptive statistic or estimate based on anecdotal evidence on the implementation of village elections. Only ten of these dealt with the core election institutions discussed in this chapter.

The most commonly reported statistic in previous studies was the percentage of villages with multiple candidates running for the office of village leader. Figure 6.3 charts the estimate from the nationally representative 2005 survey of one hundred villages along with those from previous studies. Previous estimates vary widely, which is again not surprising given that some are based on very small samples from within a single province. Overall, the numbers suggest that village leader elections with multiple candidates gradually became more commonplace between 1990 and 2005. The 2005 estimate lies directly on the trend line, suggesting that when taken together, the figures do form a coherent picture of change over time.

Figure 6.3 Percentage of Villages with Competitive Village Leader Elections in 2005 Compared to Previous Estimates

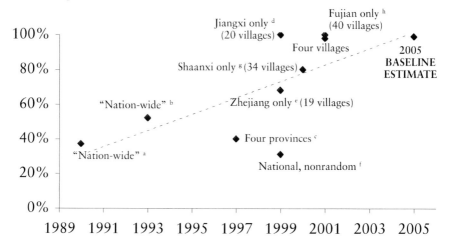

Sources: [a] Shi, "Village Committee Elections in China," 386. Survey respondents were villagers. Sampling unknown.

[b] Shi, "Village Committee Elections in China," 386. Survey respondents were villagers. Sampling unknown.

[c] Melanie Manion, "Democracy, Community, Trust: The Impact of Elections in Rural China," *Comparative Political Studies* 39, no. 3 (2006): 310. Electoral data obtained from village officials and available village records in 1997 about the most recent three village elections. Fifty-seven villages randomly sampled from twenty counties in Hebei, Hunan, Anhui, and Tianjin. The statistic used is the percentage of villages in the sample that "consistently feature elections with choice."

[d] Lianjiang Li, "The Empowering Effect of Village Elections in China," *Asian Survey* 43, no. 4 (July/August 2003): 653. Data collected by election observers in twenty villages selected from one county in Jiangxi.

[e] Baogang He and Youxing Lang. 2005. "Competition in Villager Elections: An Analysis of Case Studies from Zhejiang," *Huazhong Normal University Journal* 39 (2005): 23. Survey of 111 village leaders selected in Zhejiang.

[f] Li, "Elections and Popular Resistance in Rural China," 96. Survey conducted by university students returning to a nonrandom sample of eighty-seven home villages for school holiday.

[g] Kennedy, "The Face of 'Grassroots Democracy' in Rural China," 463. Survey of thirty-four villages randomly sampled from six counties in Shaanxi with both villager and village official respondents.

[h] Hu, "Economic Development and the Implementation of Village Elections in Rural China," 432. Survey of 913 villagers in 40 villages randomly sampled from 2 counties in Fujian.

[i] Tsai, *Accountability without Democracy*, 206. Survey of village officials in 316 villages randomly sampled from 8 counties in Shanxi, Hebei, Jiangxi, and Fujian.

Figure 6.4 Percentage of Villages with Anonymous Ballots in 2005 Compared to Previous Estimates

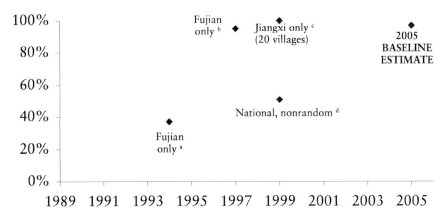

Sources: [a] Pastor and Tan, "The Meaning of China's Village Elections," 500. Data from interviews with the director of the Division of Basic-level Government in the Fujian Department of Civil Affairs.

[b] Pastor and Tan, "The Meaning of China's Village Elections," 500. Data from interviews with the director of the Division of Basic-level Government in the Fujian Department of Civil Affairs.

[c] Li, "The Empowering Effect of Village Elections in China," 653. Data collected by election observers in twenty villages selected from one county in Jiangxi.

[d] Li, "Elections and Popular Resistance in Rural China," 96. Survey conducted by university students returning to a nonrandom sample of eighty-seven home villages for school holiday.

Figure 6.5 Percentage of Villages with Public Vote Counts in 2005 Compared to Previous Estimates

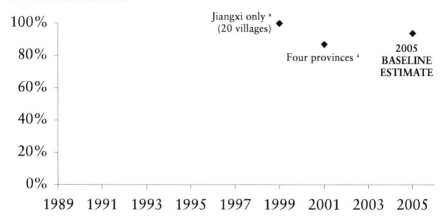

Sources: [a] Li, "The Empowering Effect of Village Elections in China," 653. Data collected by election observers in twenty villages selected from one county in Jiangxi.
[b] Tsai, *Accountability without Democracy*, 207. Survey of village officials in 316 villages randomly sampled from 8 counties in Shanxi, Hebei, Jiangxi, and Fujian.

Figure 6.6 Percentage of Villages with Regulated Proxy Voting in 2005 Compared to Previous Estimates

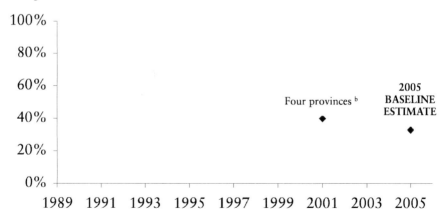

Source: [a] Tsai, *Accountability without Democracy*, 207. Survey of village officials in 316 villages randomly sampled from 8 counties in Shanxi, Hebei, Jiangxi, and Fujian.

Figure 6.7 Percentage of Villages Using Only Fixed Polling Stations in 2005 Compared to Previous Estimates

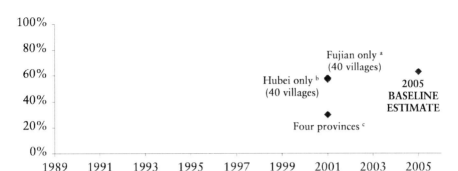

Sources: [a] Hu, "Economic Development and the Implementation of Village Elections in Rural China," 435. Survey of 913 villagers in 40 villages randomly sampled from 2 counties in Fujian. Seventeen villages missing data.
[b] Xuefeng He, "An Investigation and Analysis on the Procedures of Village Committee Elections: A Report on the Data Verification of the Village Committee Election in 40 counties in Hunan Province," *Rural China Villager Self-Government Information, Statistical Analysis*, June 28. As cited by Kennedy, "The Face of 'Grassroots Democracy' in Rural China," 464. Survey of 40 counties in Hubei.
[c] Tsai, *Accountability without Democracy*, 207. Survey of village officials in 316 villages randomly sampled from 8 counties in Shanxi, Hebei, Jiangxi, and Fujian. Two villages missing data.

Existing data on the implementation of preelection institutions such as impartial election administration committees and free and fair candidate nomination processes are also scarce, but they do suggest some improvement over time. As we can see in figure 6.9, the estimated percentage of villages with no cadre participation in the election committee increased from 1 percent in 2001 to 9 percent in 2005. More data are available on the implementation of candidate nomination processes. Figure 6.10 indicates that the nomination of candidates without cadre intervention has become substantially more common since 1999, and the majority of the villages in the 2005 survey reported no cadre participation. Even when cadres refrain from nominating candidates directly, they may still subject the final slate of candidates to their approval before allowing the election to proceed. Figure 6.11 shows that the estimated percentage of villages whose final slate did not require cadre approval seems to have increased somewhat since 1999, but perhaps not as much as there was in the area of nomination without cadre intervention.

Figure 6.8 Percentage of Villages with Campaign Speeches in 2005 Compared to Previous Estimates

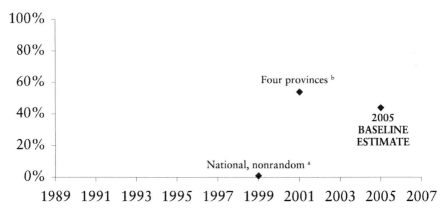

Sources: [a] Li, "Elections and Popular Resistance in Rural China," 97. Survey conducted by university students returning to a nonrandom sample of 87 home villages for school holiday.
[b] Tsai, *Accountability without Democracy*, 207. Survey of village officials in 316 villages randomly sampled from 8 counties in Shanxi, Hebei, Jiangxi, and Fujian.

Figure 6.9 Percentage of Villages with No Cadre Participation in Election Administration Committee in 2005 Compared to Previous Estimates

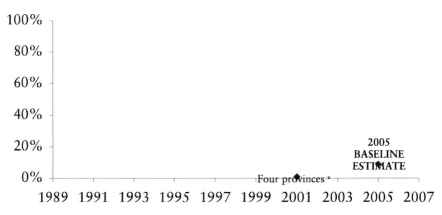

Source: [a] Tsai, *Accountability without Democracy*. Survey of village officials in 316 villages randomly sampled from 8 counties in Shanxi, Hebei, Jiangxi, and Fujian.

Figure 6.10 Percentage of Villages with No Cadre Intervention in Nomination of Election Candidates in 2005 Compared to Previous Estimates

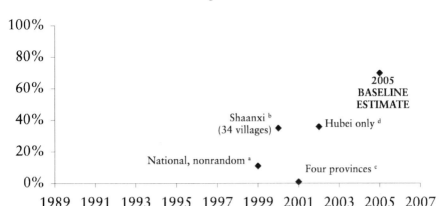

Sources: [a] Li, "Elections and Popular Resistance in Rural China," 97. Survey conducted by university students returning to a nonrandom sample of 87 home villages for school holiday.

[b] Kennedy, "The Face of 'Grassroots Democracy' in Rural China," 463. Survey of 34 villages randomly sampled from 6 counties in Shaanxi with both villager and village official respondents.

[c] Tsai, *Accountability without Democracy*. Survey of village officials in 316 villages randomly sampled from 8 counties in Shanxi, Hebei, Jiangxi, and Fujian.

[d] Lei Hong and Shuzhi Hu, "Research on Villagers' Evaluations of Village Committee Elections: A Survey of 1,281 Rural Residents in Hubei's Yangxian County," *Zhongnan Minzu University Journal* (June 2004): 102–05. Survey of villagers in seven villages selected from Changyang County in Hubei.

Overall, the data suggest that implementation of most village election institutions has improved at least slightly since 1990. Although estimates from previous studies are often based on information collected from a single province, taken together, they can suggest minimum and maximum thresholds for the actual level of nationwide implementation prior to 2005. (Comparing previous estimates taken together to the baseline descriptive statistics of implementation provided by the 2005 survey thus allows us to take an educated guess at trends in implementation over time.) As the graphs above show, the baseline point estimate provided by the 2005 survey data is generally similar to or higher than previous estimates taken together. Graphing the 2005 data with previous estimates also enables to see which of the previous estimates seem to be relatively low or high compared to the 2005 and surrounding estimates.

Figure 6.11 Percentage of Villages with No Cadre Approval of Final Election Candidates in 2005 Compared to Previous Estimates

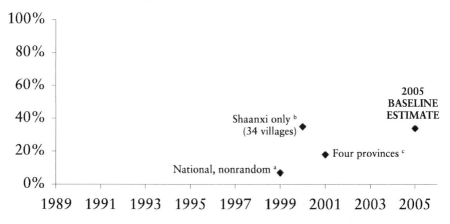

Sources: [a] Li, "Elections and Popular Resistance in Rural China," 97. Survey conducted by university students returning to a nonrandom sample of 87 home villages for school holiday.
[b] Kennedy, "The Face of 'Grassroots Democracy' in Rural China," 463. Survey of 34 villages randomly sampled from 6 counties in Shaanxi with both villager and village official respondents.
[c] Tsai, *Accountability without Democracy.* Survey of village officials in 316 villages randomly sampled from 8 counties in Shanxi, Hebei, Jiangxi, and Fujian.

Do Village Elections Determine Village Leader Succession?

So, more villages have been holding elections, and more of these elections feature multiple candidates. Nomination and voting procedures ensuring that villagers can elect the leaders they want are perhaps slowly becoming more commonplace.

But what happens after the election? Do township officials and higher levels of government respect the outcome of the election even if the winner proves a problem to them? Are elections the primary institutional mechanism by which village leaders gain and hold office? Or are they appointed and removed by higher levels at will?

The 2005 survey provides data on the ways in which village leaders leave office. Specifically, the survey asked the following question: For all the village leaders since 1991, why did each step down?

- He was fired.
- He resigned during the term.
- He was appointed party secretary.
- He did not run again at the end of this term.
- He did run for another term at the end of this term but lost the election.

The percentage of village leaders leaving office because they were fired increased in the early years of village election implementation, peaking at 22 percent between 1994 and 1996 (see figure 6.12). That figure, however, has steadily decreased since the mid-1990s. This decrease coincides with the spread of village elections and progress in the implementation of election institutions, suggesting a correlation between their growth and an increasingly institutionalized and formal process of village leader succession.

Figure 6.12 Percentage of Village Leaders Fired, by Election Cycle

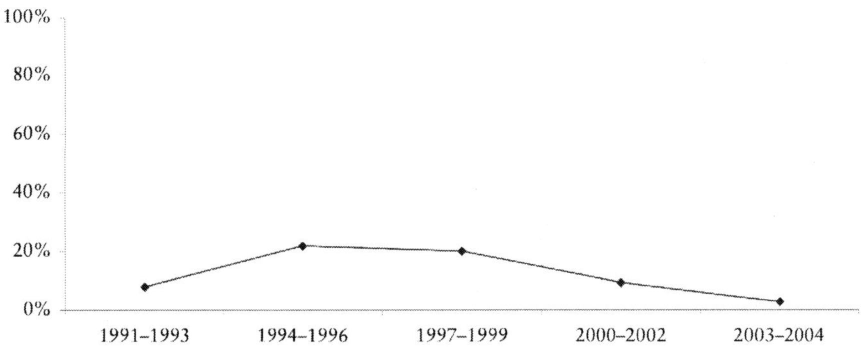

Source: 2005 China Rural Governance Survey, Center for Chinese Agricultural Policy, Chinese Academy of Sciences.

When a village leader is fired in the middle of his term, it is obvious that higher levels have directly intervened. The situation is not as clear when a village leader resigns—the leader may have done so for his own reasons. Interviews with both cadres and villagers, however, suggest that most resignations are prompted by a request, or an order, from higher levels. Having accepted the position, the village leader is under considerable pressure from the community and from higher levels to fulfill his public responsibilities and serve to the end of his term. Upon occasion, village leaders are impeached by villager representatives, but these cases seem to be quite rare. In a survey of 316 villages in 4 provinces that I conducted in 2001, only 45 percent of the villages allowed impeachment, and the vast majority had never taken advantage of the institution.[18]

Not surprisingly, the figures for midterm resignation follow a pattern similar to those for firings. As figure 6.13 shows, the percentage of village leaders leaving office by resigning rose in the early years of village election implementation, peaking at 24 percent during the 1994–1996 cycle, and then declined steadily. Together, the percentage of village leaders who leave office because they are fired or resign peaks at 46 percent in 1994–1996 and declines to only 14 percent during the 2003–2004 period. The decline indicates that both higher-level and village officials consider village elections as the appropriate vehicle for choosing a new leader, suggesting that elections are becoming more institutionalized.

Another way higher-level officials intervene in succession is by offering the village leader an appointment as village party secretary in exchange for relinquishing his or her current position. As shown in figure 6.14, the percentage of village leaders who left their position to be appointed party secretary has also decreased over time, from 26 percent of all village leaders leaving office in 1991–1993 to 14 percent in 2003–2004.[19]

Figure 6.13 Percentage of Village Leaders Resigning in Middle of Term, by Election Cycle

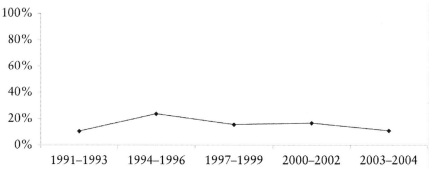

Source: 2005 China Rural Governance Survey, Center for Chinese Agricultural Policy, Chinese Academy of Sciences.

Interpreting this trend, however, is complicated. On the one hand, some higher-level officials see village elections as a convenient way of identifying individuals with leadership potential and popular support for integration (and co-optation) into the formal party-state apparatus. Throughout the 1990s, the norm of separating the party and government dictated that the village leader could not also serve as party secretary.[20] Townships that wished to appoint a village leader as party secretary had to ask him or her to step down from that position. A significant proportion of village leaders left office through this route, but again this proportion declined over time. Starting in around 2000, however, it became more common for one person to hold the positions of both village leader and party secretary concurrently. Forces at work behind the change included pressure to reduce the villagers' tax burden by cutting the number of cadres on the village payroll and the increasingly common belief that concurrent office-holding or *yijiantiao* (literally, "two posts on one shoulder") reduced conflict between the village party branch and village committee.[21] This new official practice explains some of the decline since 2000 in the proportion of village leaders leaving to take the party position. Since the decline began in 1991, though, we can also interpret some of the recent decline as a sign that higher levels may be less likely to summarily switch out village leaders.

Figure 6.14 Percentage of Village Leaders Who Left to Become Party Secretary, by Election Cycle

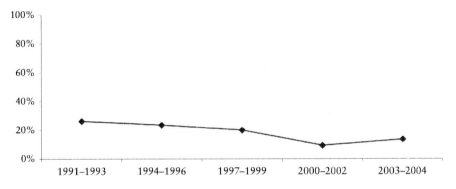

Source: 2005 China Rural Governance Survey, Center for Chinese Agricultural Policy, Chinese Academy of Sciences.

In contrast, the percentage of village leaders who leave at the end of their term of office has increased as the number whose removal was due to ad hoc actions by higher levels has decreased. As figure 6.15 shows, the percentage of village leaders leaving because they ran for reelection but lost increased from 13 percent in 1991–1993 to 35 percent in 2003–2004. Likewise, the percentage who finished their term but decided not to run again increased from 7 percent in 1997–1999 to 22 percent in 2003–2004 (see figure 6.16). Taken together, the majority of all village leaders—57 percent—leave office because their term has ended.

To summarize, more and more villages are now using elections to choose their leaders. From 1990 to 2005, village leaders have become more likely to finish out their full election terms and less likely to leave their positions because of actions taken at higher levels. These trends, too, suggest that choosing village leaders through village elections has become increasingly institutionalized and formalized.

Figure 6.15 Percentage of Village Leaders Who Left Because They Were Not Reelected, by Election Cycle

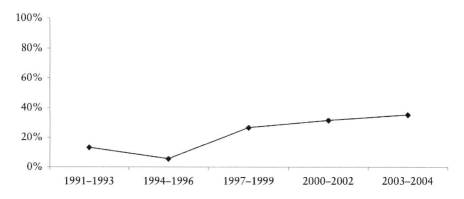

Source: 2005 China Rural Governance Survey, Center for Chinese Agricultural Policy, Chinese Academy of Sciences.

What Do Citizens Think of Election Implementation?

Village election implementation is gradually improving and village leaders are increasingly determined through the formal institutional process of village elections. But what do citizens think of election implementation? Even when the formal institutions have been implemented rigorously and thoroughly, higher levels may manipulate the process behind the scenes. It may be obvious to everyone that the eventual winners have been determined informally far in advance of the actual vote. Citizens enthusiasm and interest in the elections is an important criterion for evaluating their quality, but, as Pastor and Tan note, there has been a dearth of appropriate and reliable data.[22]

The 2005 survey asked citizens to evaluate the "liveliness," or *renao*, of the most recent election in their village. Future surveys will continue to gauge this factor as election procedures and institutions are implemented more completely.

Figure 6.16 Percentage of Village Leaders Who Declined to Run for Reelection, by Election Cycle

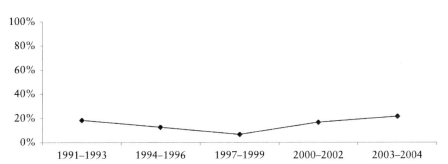

Source: 2005 China Rural Governance Survey, Center for Chinese Agricultural Policy, Chinese Academy of Sciences.

Data and Measurement

Citizen Evaluations of Village Elections

In each village, two survey enumerators held focus groups with twelve randomly sampled villagers to discuss a variety of issues relating to village governance. Enumerators asked villagers to discuss the level of *renao* of the most recent election until all of them came to an agreement on a score. Stated criteria for liveliness included active participation by villagers in the election process, the villagers' interest in the election, and intense competition among the election candidates. (As the rewards of holding village office have declined in many places, it has become common for only one candidate to be truly interested in the position; the others are nominal candidates who have been asked by the local government to stand for election to comply with the letter of the law.)

Table 6.2 shows the results of these discussions. A score of 1 indicates that the election was not lively at all, while a score of 5 indicates that the election was very lively. We can see that there is significant variation across the villages in their perception of election liveliness, and that the distribution leans toward the lively end of the range.

Summary Indices for Village Election Implementation

To measure village election implementation, I used principal component analysis (PCA) to construct an index summarizing the implementation of the voting and preelection institutions described above. PCA standardizes each of the variables on a single scale and calculates how each variable should be weighted so that, together, they account for the greatest possible amount of variance or information in the original variables.

Table 6.2 Distribution of Villages by Citizen Evaluation of Election Liveliness

	Number of villages	Percentage of villages (%)	Cumulative percentage of villages (%)
1 Not lively at all	4	4	4
2	10	10	14
3	13	13	27
4	42	43	70
5 Very lively	29	30	100
Total	98	100	100

Source: 2005 China Rural Governance Survey, Center for Chinese Agricultural Policy, Chinese Academy of Sciences.

Analysis

In this section, I examine whether objective measures of village election implementation correlate with subjective evaluations of their quality by the citizens who participated. Because the measure of citizen evaluations is in ordinal categories rather than true continuous variables, I used ordinal probit regression to examine this relationship. When citizen evaluations of election liveliness are regressed on the index of village election implementation in a simple bivariate regression, they correlate positively and significantly (p-value = 0.001).

To give us a sense of the magnitude of this positive relationship, table 6.3 shows that citizens are much more likely to give their village elections a much lower liveliness score when election implementation is relatively poor (one standard deviation below the mean) and a much higher score of 5 when it is relatively good (one standard deviation above the mean). For example, when the implementation of village election procedures is relatively poor, a village election has only a 13 percent probability of receiving a liveliness score of 5. In contrast, when implementation procedures are relatively good, the probability of the election receiving a 5 increases to 41 percent.

In sum, better-implemented election institutions are associated with an increase in citizen perception of election liveliness. We should keep in mind, however, that these are simple correlations without controls. There may be other omitted variables that correlate with election implementation and its evaluation. There may also be differences in villagers' expectations and standards of election liveliness. Without further research into such factors, we can only make tentative conclusions about the possible relationships between the implementation and evaluation of elections. These results, however, do give us more confidence that tracking the progress of the implementation of election institutions is in fact meaningful.

Table 6.3 Predicted Probabilities of Election Liveliness at Low and High Levels of Election Implementation

	Low level of election implementation	High level of election implementation
1 Not lively at all	.015 (.048)	.015 (.011)
2	.195 (.059)	.060 (.026)
3	.161 (.048)	.081 (.030)
4	.415 (.061)	.438 (.058)
5 Very lively	.129 (.050)	.406 (.070)

Source: 2005 China Rural Governance Survey, Center for Chinese Agricultural Policy, Chinese Academy of Sciences.

Note: Predicted probabilities based on ordinal probit estimates when election liveliness is regressed on an index for election implementation with robust standard errors. Low and high values of election implementation are defined as one standard deviation below and above the mean. The values in parentheses are standard errors for the predicted probabilities.

Conclusion

Overall, what do these data tell us about the state of village election implementation in rural China? Is grassroots political reform suffering from growing pains, and if so, what kind? Has election implementation been improving, or should we read recent media reports of election fraud and bribing of election administration officials as representative of a national trend?

The data presented here give us reason for cautious optimism. Improvement in village election implementation has been slow but definite. Between 1990 and 2005, the number of villages with elected rather than appointed village leaders gradually increased. More and more village elections have more than one candidate on the ballot. The vast majority of villages have implemented the election procedures required by the revised Village Organization Law of 1998, and some have implemented additional institutions, such as fixed polling stations, which are not mandatory by law.

As election implementation has improved, the succession of village leaders has become more formalized and standardized. More and more township governments are constrained by the formal election process—they are removing fewer and fewer village leaders at will in the middle of their elected terms. And more and more village leaders are completing their elected terms, leaving office because they decide not to run again or they do run but fail to get reelected.

In villages with well-implemented procedures, villagers are more likely to be report that elections are lively and to be excited about them.

At the same time, critical weak spots in village election implementation still remain. Only a minority of the villages surveyed have regulated proxy voting, without which the process of representation can easily be distorted. Even though higher-level officials do not actively interfere in the nominating process in most villages, the majority report that the final slate of nominated candidates is still subject to higher-level approval.

Though reports of corruption represent serious problems in particular places, they should not be interpreted as illustrations of a general pattern. They are perhaps better seen as pressure on the state to continue grassroots political reforms and progress in election implementation. This pressure may be well timed and useful. The national picture of village election implementation presented here suggests that the growing pains are perhaps best addressed by central state leaders. Localities implement election institutions most thoroughly and most quickly when they are required by state law. Where the central government has not been explicit, township officials often continue to intervene, particularly in the areas of candidate and the election-committee selection. These findings indicate both that top-down enforcement of local political reforms is essential to grassroots democratization and that bottom-up initiative varies widely across localities, which suggests that perhaps the biggest growing pain in the process of grassroots democratization is not the capacity but the willingness of the central government to institute the next round of reforms needed to bring more complete procedural democracy to China's million villages.

Notes

[1] Tianjian Shi, "Village Committee Elections in China: Institutionalist Tactics for Democracy," *World Politics* 51, no. 3 (1999): 385–412; Kevin J. O'Brien and Lianjian Li, "The Struggle Over Village Elections," in Merle Goldman and Roderick MacFarquhar, eds., *The Paradox of China's Post-Mao Reforms*, (Cambridge, MA: Harvard Univ. Press, 1999: 129–44); X. Drew Liu, "A Harbinger of Democracy: Grassroots Elections in Rural China," *The China Strategic Review* 2, no. 3 (1997): 50–75; and Jean C. Oi, "Economic Development, Stability, and Democratic Village Self-Governance," in Maurice Brosseau, Suzanne Pepper, and Tsang Shu-ki, eds., *China Review 1996* (Hong Kong: Chinese Univ. Press, 1996), 125–44.

[2] Kevin O'Brien, "Implementing Political Reform in China's Villages," *The Australian Journal of Chinese Affairs* 32 (July 1994): 33–59; Daniel Kelliher, "The Chinese Debate over Village Self-Government," *The China Journal* 37 (January 1997): 63; Amy B. Epstein, "Village Elections in China: Experimenting with Democracy" in E. Bliney, ed. *Crisis and Reform in China* (New York: Nova Science Publishers, 1997), 135–50; Shi, "Village Committee Elections in China"; Rong Hu, "Economic Development and the Implementation of Village Elections in Rural China," *Journal of Contemporary China* 14, no. 44 (2005): 427–44.

[3] Kelliher, "The Chinese Debate over Village Self-Government"; Liu, "A Harbinger of Democracy"; Jude Howell, "Prospects for Village Self-Government in China," *Journal of Peasant Studies* 25, no. 3 (April 1998): 86–111; Kevin J. O'Brien and Lianjiang Li, "Accommodating 'Democracy' in a One-Party State: Introducing Village Elections in China," *The China Quarterly* 162 (June 2000): 465–89; Jean C. Oi and Scott Rozelle, "Elections and Power: The Locus of Decision-Making in Chinese Villages," *The China*

Quarterly 162 (June 2000): 513–39; Robert A. Pastor and Qingshan Tan, "The Meaning of China's Village Elections," *The China Quarterly* 162 (June 2000): 490–512; John James Kennedy, "The Face of 'Grassroots Democracy' in Rural China," *Asian Survey* 42, no. 3 (2002): 456–82; Richard Levy, "The Village Self-Government Movement: Elections, Democracy, the Party, and Anticorruption—Developments in Guangdong," *China Information* 17, no. 1 (2003): 28–65; Qingshan Tan, "Building Institutional Rules and Procedures: Village Election in China," *Policy Sciences* 37, no. 1 (March 2004): 1–22.

[4] Pastor and Tan, "The Meaning of China's Village Elections."

[5] "Progress and Problems Mark Village Elections," *China Daily*, July 10, 2007; "Rural Elections Undermined by Bribery, Official Manipulation: Lawmakers," Xinhua News Agency, March 13, 2006; "Inner Mongolia Village Elections See Rampant Bribery," Xinhua News Agency, October 10, 2006.

[6] Per capita gross value of industrial output is often more reliable than official statistics on rural net per capita income and one of the best predictors of standard of living. See Scott Rozelle, "Stagnation without Equity: Patterns of Growth and Inequality in China's Rural Economy," *The China Journal* 35 (January 1996): 63–92.

[7] O'Brien and Li, "Accommodating Democracy," 465–89.

[8] O'Brien and Li, "Accommodating Democracy," 486.

[9] Pastor and Tan, "The Meaning of China's Village Elections."

[10] Lianjiang Li, "Elections and Popular Resistance in Rural China (Revised Version)," *China Information* 16 (2002): 89.

[11] Lily L. Tsai, *Accountability without Democracy: Solidarity Groups and Public Goods Provision in Rural China* (Cambridge: Cambridge Univ. Press, 2007).

[12] Village elections are conducted every three years. Each year a different set of provinces holds its village elections, creating a three-year cycle. Graphing by the three-year cycle gives a more accurate representation of the overall trend. Because the survey asked for data over 14 years, the last election cycle consists of only 2 years of data.

[13] For a definitive examination of what constitutes free and fair elections, see Robert A. Dahl, *Polyarchy: Participation and Opposition* (New Haven: Yale Univ. Press, 1971).

[14] Pastor and Tan, "The Meaning of China's Village Elections," 493–99

[15] "Circular Concerning Improving Villager Committee Election," Reference No.14, General Office of the CPC Central Committee and General Office of the State Council, 2002. See www.chinaelections.org/Eng/readnews.asp?newsid={A8769297-13E5-45EB-96EA-FB3E7671B6D5.

[16] See Article 13, the Organization Law of Villagers' Committees, the Fifth Meeting of the Standing Committee of the Ninth NPC, November 4, 1998.

[17] For English-language academic journals, a literature search for articles since 1990 containing the key terms "village election" and "China" was conducted in the JSTOR and Proquest academic journal databases. For Chinese-language academic journals, a literature search for articles since 1990 containing the key words "election" and "democracy" was conducted in the Weipu (维普) and Zhongguo Qikan Wang (中国期刊网) databases. Articles focusing on a single village were eliminated, and articles in the following journals were prioritized: *Zhongguo Nongcun Guancha* (中国农村观察), *Zhongguo Nongcun Jingji* (中国农村经济), *Jingji Yanjiu* (经济研究), *Guanli Shijie* (管理世界), *Zhongguo Nongye Jingji Pinglun* (中国农业经济评论), *Diaoyan Shijie* (调研世界), and *Shehuixue Yanjiu* (社会学研究).

[18] Tsai, *Accountability without Democracy.*

[19] Pastor and Tan, "The Meaning of China's Village Elections."

[20] Zhenglin Guo and Thomas P. Bernstein, "The Impact of Elections on the Village Structure of Power: The Relations between the Village Committees and the Party Branches," *Journal of Contemporary China* 13, no. 39 (May 2004): 257–75.

[21] In the villages surveyed, 14 percent of all village leaders since 1991 were also party secretary during some part of their term; 25 percent of all village leaders were also party secretary during some part of their term.

[22] "The Normalization of China's Village Elections," *People's Daily*, January 9, 2008.

[23] Pastor and Tan, "The Meaning of China's Village Elections," 507.

CAN A FALLING LEAF TELL THE COMING OF AUTUMN? MAKING SENSE OF VILLAGE ELECTIONS IN A TOWNSHIP . . . AND IN CHINA

Xueguang Zhou[1]

一叶知秋 (A falling leaf tells the coming of autumn).

—Chinese proverb

One chilly morning in the early spring of 2006, I arrived in FS Township with great excitement and anticipation. It was the beginning of elections for the twenty-seven villages in this agricultural township in northern China. I had visited this township many times in the past two years to conduct participatory observations of the daily lives of villagers and local cadres, and of the societal changes affecting them. Over time, I had learned a great deal about the experiences, problems, and grievances of the inhabitants of some of these villages. However, these grievances and tensions were frequently suppressed, diverted, or ignored, either by means of subtle social pressures or deliberate government maneuvers.

During my visits, I stayed in a room in the township government and interacted extensively with local cadres in the township government and nearby villages. As a result, I learned a good deal about the problems and issues from the views of these cadres. But I knew far less about the views of the villagers. Although I had contact with ordinary villagers on different occasions, such exchanges were casual and less systematic. The hidden side of the villagers, the "silent majority," had been just that—hidden and silent—until the occasion of this village election. Established by the Organic Law of Village Committees in 1987 and revised in 1998, the institution of local elections provides opportunities for open, legitimate political mobilization and leadership change in China's villages.[2] Elections offer villagers the chance to bring multiple and latent forces to the surface—to speak out or stay silent—in time with an election cycle every three years. I felt as if I was watching a poker game between the cadres and peasants. I had a clear view of one hand of cards—that of the township cadres—but knew little about the villagers' hand. On the occasion of this village election, it was time to learn the outcome of the game.

167

The courtyard of the FS Township government vibrated with anxiety and anticipation. The corridors where the office staff usually gathered to chat were empty, and only occasionally did a few staff members hurry through, speaking in lowered voices. Township party secretary Jin's spacious office now served as a war room—staff members rushed in and out to update him on elections taking place throughout the villages in his township. At the same time, Mr. Jin could be heard yelling at a village head who faced defeat in the current election. As soon as I put down my luggage, I was swept onto the back of a motorcycle to several villages where elections were being held that day. Wherever we went, we saw crowds, slogan posters, ballot boxes wrapped in red paper, the familiar faces of the township officials I had met before, and, of course, the village cadres whose facial expressions reflected their decided fate. The curtain had finally lifted to reveal the stage of the village election, and the drama was on full display. Everyone was excited about how these elections would play out and what they would mean for village governance in the future.

Election events have implications that reach far beyond the village boundaries. Rural China has been rich soil for social-science research on China's transitional economy, and important theoretical and empirical research has been developed in this context.[3] Among various institutional changes in China, village elections have attracted enormous and sustained attention from social-science researchers, especially among political scientists, notably in the special issue of the *China Quarterly* on "Elections and Democracy in Greater China."[4] In theory and in practice, village elections—the open, direct, "one person, one vote" election of leaders—come close to the democratic, electoral process that Western societies practice. What implications, then, do these elections have for China's future? Does the institution of village election indicate a move forward? Is it an indicator of a democratic political system, or merely a symbolic, but ultimately empty act? Scholars diverge in their research of this institutional practice now emerging in China, using in-depth interviews, large-scale social surveys, or participatory observations.[5] They also differ in their focus on the various stages and aspects of this phenomenon, from the sources of variations in election implementation to the consequences of the elections.[6]

This study is based on my ethnographic research in FS Township, and provides a close assessment of the events, processes, and implications of village elections. Both the location—an agricultural town in northern China—and the time—2006—are worth emphasizing here. The former cautions us that this is but a small corner of rural China; the latter reminds us of the temporal nature of my analytical focus, which presents a glimpse into the ongoing changes in rural China. These axes of time and place help us situate this study in the larger context of institutional changes in China. Although the research site is local, the research issues are far broader: What processes and mechanisms are at work in these village elections? In what ways do these episodes inform us of the large processes of institutional change in China?

This study is an effort to address these issues. Viewing the selected episodes of village elections through a microscopic lens, my goal is to understand the specific processes through which institutions are being transformed and the implications for understanding societal transformation in China. I organize my discussions around the evolving role of the township government in village elections. I use the lens of organizational analysis to examine how the role of the township government has evolved in response to changing relationships with its environment and changing incentives within the Chinese bureaucracy. I argue and demonstrate that such changes have been the consequences of larger processes taking place in other, often not directly related, areas.

As I argue and illustrate below, the episodes of village elections highlight several important lessons for understanding institutional changes in China. First, institutional changes take time, may not be continuous, and seldom follow a linear or monotonic trend. This observation implies that, if we probe different points of time over these long processes, we will draw different lessons and arrive at different conclusions. Second, institutional changes involve multiple, often disparate processes, which are often distinct and separate and evolve in their own realms with no direct link to village elections. However, their interactions at specific axes of time and place can generate the kinds of conditions that facilitate (or disrupt) the institutionalization of village elections. Without careful attention to these diverse streams of events and processes over time and in different areas, the outcomes may be seen as surprising, incoherent, and at odds with an imagined order imposed by our intellectual exercise. In order to better explain for the ongoing changes in China, we must adopt those conceptual and analytical tools of social-science research that can better capture the dynamics of multiple, interactive processes.

This chapter is organized as follows: First, I describe select episodes to introduce the issues and complexities involved in village elections. Second, I draw upon research on organization-environment relationships to make sense of the processes and mechanisms that generated the observed patterns of change. Finally, I discuss the implications of village elections in order to assess larger processes of institutional change in Chinese villages, and in China.

Inside the Dynamics of Village Elections

To interpret village elections in a meaningful way, it is important to locate them in a specific institutional context. In this section, I describe select episodes of village elections in FS Township in order to familiarize readers with the background, processes and emerging issues in this setting. These episodes serve as the empirical basis for analyses later in the chapter. To provide some context, I first introduce the village government structure and official election procedures.

Village elections emerged in the context of a long-standing rural governance structure that was set up under state socialist rule. Since the People's Republic of China (PRC) was established in 1949, the extent of political control gradually increased in rural China, and culminated in the institution of the People's Commune.[7] The villagers' daily lives and work were organized by production teams within the village (production brigades), under the leadership of the village party committee (村支部) and headed by the party secretary. Since the decollectivization era began in the late 1970s, the land-tenure reform has made households the primary decision-making agents in farming activities. The introduction of village elections in 1987 gave rise to an emergent institution, the village committee (村委会), which became a potentially competing authority. The distinction between these two lines of authority is key to understanding the significance of village elections. In this chapter, I use the terms "party secretary" (村支书) and "village head" (村主任) to refer to the respective heads of these two village-level offices (village party committee and village committee). In the Chinese government structure, villages are not a formal level of government, but rather a self-governance entity under township leadership, the lowest level of government.

When village elections were first introduced in the late 1980s, they were intended as a countervailing force that would check the behavior of village cadres from the bottom. The timing seemed perfect. In rural areas, land reform in the late 1970s had returned the authority to make major decisions to the households, and as a result the role of village government drastically diminished. Moreover, in areas where village government still mattered, it was usually the case that local governments (at the township or county level) were also highly effective. This means that village elections could be firmly controlled—procedures tailored, candidates handpicked, and votes orchestrated—to yield the desired results. For many years, this is exactly what happened in this region; until recently, the government of FS Township effectively dictated village elections.

The dynamics have changed significantly since the late 1990s. Elections have grown more and more competitive and moved beyond the control of the local government. On the one hand, in the areas of taxation, land seizure, and abuse of power, grievances and tensions have accumulated among the state, local governments, and peasants. On the other hand, few effective institutional channels exist for peasants to voice their complaints and seek solutions. The village election cycle gives villagers, every three years, the opportunity to engage in legitimate, open contests to settle scores, to voice their dissatisfaction, and to challenge the existing authority order. It is not surprising that the township government views village elections as a ticking time bomb.

Village elections, true to their name, are village-bound, and consist of two formal stages. At the first, preliminary election (预选) stage, villagers nominate and vote for candidates who will be put on the ballot for the formal vote during the second stage, the formal election (正式选举). At that point, villagers cast their votes to select three of the candidates on the ballot to be members of the village committee (村民委员会). In practice, the first stage is the more critical; hence, it is more competitive and often becomes contentious. The processes vary hugely across villages—even in the same town—and this is also true of

FS Township. For example, some elections ran smoothly and reelected the current cadres with little fanfare; others went through intensive mobilization and confrontation, which led to the toppling of the entire village committee. In other cases, the villagers stubbornly refused to participate and defied the township government's efforts to carry out the election process. I turn now to select episodes of village elections in FS Township.

The Willow Village

Tucked away in the corner of a mountainous area, more than 15 kilometers away from the town center, Willow Village appears remote and marginal to those in the township government, where its name and affairs seldom surfaces in casual conversations or serious discussions. All of this suddenly changed in the early days of the election season when, in the preliminary election, the then village committee—the party secretary, the village head, and the accountant—all faced serious challenges. Mr. Wang, the party secretary, who also stood for village committee election, narrowly made it to the second round; his partner, the village head, failed to win enough votes to advance. This shocked the township government for several reasons. First, the collective authority in this village had been in relatively good standing in recent years. A few years prior, an outside investment project infused the village with significant financial resources in exchange for land use. The exchange enabled the village to pay off a collective debt of 120,000 yuan (about $17,500) and even to maintain a surplus of 40,000 yuan (about $5,850) in the collective account—an enviable financial situation for most village governments in this region. Second, since there had been no signs of trouble before, such unexpected results suggested considerable, behind-the-scenes organizing efforts beyond the village government's control. The township government panicked. The election of unexpected new faces into the village committee meant that township officials would have to deal with strangers. Indeed, if elected in the second round, the young challenger might cause problems for the township government officials for years afterward.

The dreaded second round—the formal election—finally came. During our long ride to the village, Mr. Chen, the head of the government work team, was worried and dispirited. He informed his team members that Mr. Wang had called him the night before and told him that the young challenger in his village had been working hard in recent days, mobilizing his kinship network and handing out promises. To make things worse, Mr. Wang had few kinship ties to rely on; his was an outside family that had moved into the village, albeit many years ago. Almost resigned to the certain defeat of Mr. Wang and the other incumbents, Mr. Chen bitterly complained of the villagers: "They don't care about the cadres' performance. In the end, they only vote along kinship lines."[8]

When we arrived in the courtyard of the village government, the election committee, comprised mostly of the current village committee members, was already busy working—hanging up banners, posting prescribed election slogans, and setting up the voting booth. In his late fifties, Mr. Wang was quiet, soft-spoken, and unpresumptuous, unlike some of his peers whom I had previously met. I had learned much about him on our ride to the village. Mr. Wang was a veteran village cadre, and had worked as one since the collective era. Because of his good performance, he was later appointed to head a township-government-owned enterprise. The township government then asked him to return to his village to take charge of village affairs as the party secretary. According to Mr. Chen, Mr. Wang had done an excellent job in his position and significantly improved the living conditions of his villagers.

When the voting started, the air in the crowded village courtyard turned tense. I overheard a bystander remark, half-jokingly, that whoever would be willing to pay him 100 yuan would get his vote. Others laughed in agreement. In a corner away from the crowd, Mr. Wang stood alone, awkward and resigned. I walked over to him and he eagerly struck up a conversation, complaining in a low voice that he expected to fail in the election and that the villagers did not appreciate what he had done for the village because they were loyal only to their own kin. His bitter remarks echoed what Mr. Chen had said earlier, or was it the other way around?

The voting lasted several hours. Slowly the villagers dispersed, voices quieted, and the courtyard emptied. At around two o'clock in the afternoon, the number of ballots cast well exceeded the legal requirement of at least 50 percent of the eligible voters, so the voting booths were closed and ballot counting began.[9] Members of the election committee, the township government work team, and several "concerned villagers" from the challenger's side were present to count the ballots or to inspect the process. The names on each ballot were simultaneously broadcast through the loudspeakers to the entire village. I was told that, in the past, many in the village had carefully followed these counting announcements and kept track of the count on their own. At times, some would reportedly rush to the village office to correct errors in the official counting process.

The final result: Mr. Wang got the most votes, 150 out of the total 251 valid ballots. His partner, the village accountant, received 149, the second-largest number of votes, and the challenger received 133 votes. The three candidates who won the most votes—two incumbents and one contender—were elected into the next village committee. As the outright winner of the election, Mr. Wang was selected to head the village committee—a pleasant surprise to him, to those on the township government work team, and especially to Mr. Chen, the head of the work team. "After all, the eyes of the masses are discerning," noted Mr. Chen, quoting a well-known expression in Chinese politics, with a relieved smile.

The Boulevard Village

Boulevard Village is one of four adjacent villages that make up the center of the township. For many years, Boulevard Village was a headache for the township government. In 2003 the township government dismissed the former village party secretary from his position for abuse of power. However, with the backing of a strong kinship base, he refused to hand over the seal that signified the party secretary's authority. Worried about his influence, the township government dared not hold a meeting of village party members to elect a new party secretary. As a result, the party branch was paralyzed and the township government had to rely on Mr. Liu, the elected head of the village committee, for cooperation. Tensions between those who supported the former party secretary and those who backed the village head persisted for many years and from time to time erupted into open confrontation.

Village elections offered the chance of an open, legitimate contest, and both sides ferociously mobilized their votes. On the eve of the election, Mr. Liu appeared to be the front-runner. Resentful of this expected outcome, the other side—the supporters of the old party secretary—made a desperate effort to disrupt the preliminary election: several villagers stormed into the voting site, tore apart the ballot boxes, and threw away the ballots already collected in these boxes—all of which temporarily halted the voting process. But the election committee, backed by the township government, quickly printed new ballots and restarted the voting process. The first round of election concluded with no further incidents, and all members of the incumbent village committee were voted in to stand for the second, final election.

The morning of the formal election came and went uneventfully. Perhaps in response to the disruptions in the first-round election, a larger-than-usual crowd came to the voting site. As more and more villagers entered the village courtyard, the single-file line of those waiting in front of the voting booth became longer and longer, twisting and wrapping around the courtyard, as villagers chatted and laughed. It was difficult to imagine that just a few days before, serious confrontation and the destruction of ballots and ballot boxes had occurred in this same location. By the end of the election process, Mr. Liu received 91 percent of the votes, a number he often proudly cited on subsequent occasions.

The high turnout and overwhelming outcome solidified Mr. Liu's position and forced his opponents to retreat. A few weeks after the village election, the party branch election was formally held, and a new party secretary was elected. Everything soon calmed down and there were no more confrontations. In Boulevard Village, it appears that the village election has finally brought closure to a contentious past, ending a chapter—indeed an era—of open conflicts.

The Bao Village

To the township government, Bao Village has been a long-running nightmare. Mr. Ren, the current village head, was elected to office three years ago, after he mobilized his fellow villagers to overthrow the previous party secretary and his team. Incessant, intensive fighting engulfed kinship groups within the village and strained the village's relationship with the township government. Mr. Ren was especially despised because, as some government officials alleged, he repeatedly bypassed the township government and petitioned the higher authorities (上访) directly. In a much-talked-about episode, a county government bureau promised to provide 40,000 yuan (about $5,850) to develop a project in the village, but never followed through. When Mr. Ren found out that the bureau had falsely reported this promise as an accomplishment to the media, he immediately filed complaints with the county government and insisted that the bureau fulfill its promise. Later, the bureau grudgingly complied under pressure. Mr. Ren was noncooperative in other ways as well. Three years prior, in the previous election, he announced over loudspeakers that if elected, he would lead Bao Village in resisting the collection of government taxes and fees. Many township government officials saw him as a thug.

Meanwhile, the township government was tactfully building its case to discredit him. Government aid to the village was withheld, funds from government programs were not allocated, and outside investment opportunities were diverted to other villages. For example, funds from the Sloping Land Conversion Program—an important source of government funding to peasant households in this area—were not awarded to Bao Village at all, whereas most villages received funds sufficient to cover a large proportion of their land. Even when government funds that were specifically designated for the Bao Village arrived, the township government was reluctant to make them available to Mr. Ren's village committee. All of this was done under the pretense that, as one official put it, village governance was so erratic that no one could be sure that the funds would be distributed appropriately. But the real motive behind these efforts was to cultivate grievances against the current village committee so that Mr. Ren and his team would be voted out of office in the election.

Election time finally came. When I asked Mr. Jin, the township party secretary, if he anticipated that the village head in Bao Village would be voted out, he confidently said, "Of course," and added, "The villagers should know what is in their best interests. With this kind of village head, no outside opportunities will land in this village." To facilitate the desired election outcome, the township government hastily appointed a new party secretary in the village and nominated him as a candidate to challenge Mr. Ren. Anticipating potential confrontations and disruptions, the township government cautiously postponed the Bao Village election until after other villages had completed their elections.

The Bao Village preliminary election was held on a cold morning, just before the last snowfall of the season. The village courtyard was crowded with villagers wrapped up in bulky winter clothes. The atmosphere was tense: an unusually large number of the government work-team members were deployed, clearly marked police cars were parked in the village courtyard, uniformed local police were present to deter altercations, as was a videotaping crew that had been hired to record the whole process. As the election proceedings commenced, the confrontations began. First came loud, bitter voices from the crowd; then two or three men emerged at the front, where Mr. Ren was presiding over the meeting. They pointed fingers at him and demanded that he explain to the whole village why he had not secured the kind of government aid that other villages had received. The shouts and gestures were so fierce—and very nearly physical in nature—that the township government officials had to step in from time to time to calm both sides. As the shouting came in waves, one voice after another, Mr. Ren quietly advised his supporters: "Don't pay attention to what is going on here, go and cast your vote." An interesting scene ensued. At the center of the courtyard the shouting continued, but on the other side, the voting line snaked around the noisy crowd. In a few hours, the township government received an unequivocal message: Mr. Ren gained the most votes (189 out of 341) in the preliminary election. His successful reelection in the formal election followed a few weeks later. Soon afterwards, his challenger—the township-appointed village party secretary—resigned from his position, packed his belongings, and left the village.

*   *   *

After the village elections concluded, Mr. Jin, the party secretary of the township government, declared the election season a great success. There were good reasons for self-congratulation—all villages except one had carried out elections and new village governments were up and running. A tough job had been completed. With only a few exceptions, most elected village cadres were the same familiar faces that the township government had either worked with before or was willing to work with. Moreover, through the election process, several difficult cases—such as the governance crisis in Boulevard Village—were resolved to the satisfaction of the township government. Finally and most importantly, there were no major incidents in the election processes that threatened social stability or led to petitions outside of the township boundaries.

As an outside observer, I too see the elections as a surprising success story, but for different reasons. First, in most cases, the election procedures were meticulously implemented. On many occasions, official instructions were followed to the letter—beginning with the formation of the village election committee and moving through voter certification, two rounds of voting, and the process of counting, registering, and sealing ballots. One particular scene stuck in my memory. Election time was approaching on a chilly morning in a village courtyard, but villagers were still in their houses or scattered in small gatherings far away. Facing an almost empty courtyard, the current village head—who had failed in the preliminary election a few days before—bravely began to read the script that the government had prepared for this special occasion:

Dear voter comrades:
    On behalf of the village election committee, I now preside over today's election meeting. Starting on [insert date/month], our village has engaged in the event of village committee election. Through broad communication

175

and mobilization, and the full participation of the voters, we elected the formal candidates for the village committee on [insert date/month]. Today, we hold our election meeting, and elect a new village committee.

To ensure the smooth election progress, I now announce the basic procedures for today's election meeting.

The announcement was broadcast over loudspeakers and lingered in the cold sky. Drawn by these pleading calls, villagers gradually appeared and converged on the village center, filling the courtyard with greetings, chatting, and laughter. As I listened and watched, I felt strongly the solemn power of the formal procedures that sustain the institution of Chinese village elections.

Although these formal procedures were often ceremonial, the progress made over time was real and substantive. At the voting site in one village, a township official pointed to a nearby corner and told me: "I was here in a village election a few years before. At that time, the villagers sat there, and they were given the ballots. Then someone walked among them and said, 'Let me fill the ballot for you.' And he collected many ballots from these villagers and did just that. No one cared." But this time, right behind us, an empty room with doors on two sides was used for voting booths. Inside, three desks were set up far apart. Voters went through the checkpoint, where their voter certification cards were inspected, after which they headed into the room through one door, walked to one of the desks alone, filled out the ballot, exited from the other door, and cast their ballots on the way out. Only members of the township government work team were permitted to stand at the doors or inside the voting room, checking voting certification cards, directing traffic, and helping illiterate voters fill out ballots.

Another indicator of election success is the high, voluntary participation of villagers. Except for migrant workers who were away from the village, most eligible voters came out to vote. In the decollectivization era, villagers attend to their own land and engage in informal social interactions. Seldom does one observe such a large public gathering in the village. The high turnout rate was largely due to the candidates' mobilization efforts, reflecting the competitiveness of the elections. Even in villages where candidates were not seriously challenged, they still pushed for a high turnout rate to solidify their basis of legitimacy. I recall one scene in which, as a middle-aged woman walked to the voting booth, she half-jokingly mocked the slogans on the wall and said: "Now it is time for me to exercise my own right in democracy." In another scene, an elderly woman was carried into the voting site in order to cast her vote. Through these substantive as well as symbolic processes, the villagers gained a sense of collective power and found their voice in village governance.

Perhaps the most notable element of village election success is the changing role of the township government in the electoral process. The township government clearly made great efforts to assist its favorite candidates, but in almost all cases, as far as I could tell, their candidates were elected (or reelected) not because of government manipulation, but because of their own record or standing in the village. In several instances, as the episode in Bao Village illustrated, despite the township government's great efforts to foment resentment against the current village head, villagers defied government meddling and stubbornly voted their own candidates into office. In another village, the villagers simply refused to participate in the election before the village cadres' alleged wrongdoing was investigated. The township government's repeated appeals and efforts were met with silent noncooperation. In the end, this was the only village in FS Township where elections did not take place. In the absence of a newly elected village committee, the previous one still operated, though with diminished legitimacy and effectiveness.

This is not to say that the elections in FS Township were flawless. There were cases of confrontation, bribery, kinship-based voting, false accusations in the mobilization and voting processes, and even physical fights.[10] On several occasions, township officials and villagers both commented that those being elected were *not* the best or the most able; a few elected cadres quit their positions shortly after elections. Overall, however, this was the most successful election cycle since village elections were instituted in FS Township in the late 1980s. And it was certainly one of the brightest moments in my participatory research experience during the two years I studied this township.

Village Elections as a Microcosm of Institutional Change

The episodes above provide a glimpse into the complexities and dynamics of village elections. Treating these episodes as a microcosm of larger institutional change, and with the benefit of hindsight, I will now endeavor to explain the processes and mechanisms that have contributed to the evolution of the *institution* of village elections.

Of the many processes that shaped the patterns of the 2006 village elections in FS Township, the changing role of local governments is the most important one. This is also an arena in which we have significant gaps in knowledge. Previous studies have primarily focused on the implementation of formal processes and election activities at the village level. The vital role of township government is acknowledged but treated more or less as a black box, partly due, I suspect, to the difficulty of gaining access to township governments' inner workings. As I show later, the shift of the local government from the role of manipulating election processes to that of safeguarding them was key to the successful 2006 elections in FS Township. This is not to suggest that other processes are unimportant; rather, because all other processes intersect intensively with the roles of the township government, a focus on the latter allows us to weave the threads of these interrelated processes into the broader scene of institutional change.

In the sections that follow, I provide an organizational analysis of the changing role of the township government. At the core of my arguments is the proposition that such changes can be best understood by examining both the evolving relationships between the township government and its environment and the changing incentive structure within the Chinese bureaucracy. A large number of studies have examined the interactions among organizations and the way they respond to constraints imposed by their environments.[11] Recent studies of organizations in economics have also highlighted the importance of incentives in inducing corresponding organizational behaviors.[12] These theoretical ideas direct our attention to those aspects of organizational environments that may not correlate to village elections. Nevertheless, broad changes in the Chinese bureaucracy and in organizational environments (such as conflicting task environments, the withdrawal of the government from household farming decisions, the dwindling efforts of state taxation in rural areas, and the greater flow of migrant labor) have prompted profound changes in the local governments and their relationships to villages and village cadres. These developments have shaped the evolution of the village election as an emergent institution.

I begin by spotlighting the township government. The township government in this region has been and remains the central player in the village election process. As the lowest level of government, the township is responsible for directly administering village elections. It implements the directives from higher levels of government, dictates the timing and sequencing of elections across villages, and sends in work teams of office staff to safeguard—and often directly organize—election processes. The township government officials also strategize behind the scenes on helping their favored candidates get elected and, more importantly, on avoiding confrontations and disruptions in the process.

Township government officials move cautiously. Village elections are regarded as one of the most, if not *the* most, challenging tasks. Since the late 1990s, the situation in many rural areas has deteriorated—grievances and tensions are rife, the result of many years of excessive taxation, disastrous policies, and government neglect. Lacking other legitimate channels to voice their complaints, the village election cycle every three years provides villagers with their only opportunity to engage in legitimate, open confrontations, to settle scores, to voice their dissatisfaction, and to challenge the authority order.

Since the late 1980s, village elections have been ritually carried out every three years in rural China. In recent years, however, the township government has largely controlled these elections—they handpicked the candidates, conducted the ceremonies, and set up the processes, all with predictable outcomes. Even as the elections grew more competitive in the recent cycles, the township government still influenced, often decisively, the outcomes through manipulation and tactical maneuvers. Government officials to whom I spoke were fond of recounting the plots they used—controlling crowds, miscounting ballots, and discrediting opponents—to achieve the desired result. Indeed, the winners of village elections were determined as much in township government meeting rooms as they were in the voting booths at village centers.

Gradually the dynamics changed, and the township government shifted from being an active participant to a more neutral guardian of procedures.

178

Township governments did not embrace this shift voluntarily; rather, it came about through profound changes in the organizational environments to which local governments must respond. Let us first consider local governments' task environment. The township government faces multiple, inconsistent demands in implementing village election procedures. Its behavior—especially the behavior of the leading officials—can be understood from the perspective of multiple goals, constraints, and incentives. In the case of village elections, the township government's primary goal is, to put it simply, to get the job done—to implement the designated election tasks and carry out elections in all villages under its jurisdiction. This would seem to be a rudimentary task, but it is by no means a sure thing. As has happened in the past, confrontations among villagers could disrupt and stall election proceedings, leaving the township government looking embarrassed and incompetent. A second and related goal is to choose favored candidates and get them elected. Even though the township government–village relationship has become tenuous, the government must still interact with village cadres from time to time, in order to implement policies and to resolve local problems. Having their preferred, competent village cadres in place facilitates interactions. A third goal is to "maintain social stability"—a coded term that means preventing social protests or petitions from extending beyond one's administrative jurisdiction. This issue is especially sensitive in FS Township because it is less than a three-hour drive from Beijing.

These goals are by no means congruent, and the pursuit of one may make it difficult to reach another. For example, efforts to select a favorite candidate may lead to manipulations that cause resentment and confrontations in the village, jeopardizing the goal of social stability. Therefore, prioritizing and balancing these goals present a critical challenge to the local governments. To those local cadres, the priority is clear. Foremost among these goals is that of maintaining social stability—senior officials state this priority unequivocally and emphatically and ensure that it is enforced with visible discipline at the most basic government levels. Over the years, social stability has become *the* paramount concern of government at all levels. To this end, a policy of "veto by one item" (一票否决) was implemented, which dictates that problems on the social stability front negate good government performance in *every* other arena. Officials whose jurisdictions experience serious problems in this area are considered weak, incompetent, and lacking leadership; their careers stall or even end. Hence, even though the township government wants to see its favored candidates elected to ensure smooth interactions in the future, this goal is far less important than the imperative of safeguarding social stability, the failure of which often leads to an immediate threat to one's bureaucratic career. This imperative is best captured in the slogan "Stability takes precedence over all other matters!" (稳定压倒一切!), which is seen everywhere in big letters, followed by an exclamation mark, screaming for attention.

Other fundamental changes in the institutional environment have reinforced the changing roles of local governments. Since the mid-1990s, the

179

central government's recentralization efforts have drastically diminished local governments' resources, especially at the township government level, and many are now heavily in debt.[13] With resources thus dwindling, the township government cannot sustain traditional clientelist ties with village leaders. Nor are such clientelist ties as important as in the past. The state's gradual withdrawal from the rural areas, especially via its abolition of agricultural taxation in 2005, has weakened the already tenuous link between the township government and villages. No longer does the township government depend on village cadres to accomplish the demanding tasks of collecting taxes and fees from the village households. Exacerbating this trend are the rotation policies that require leading cadres of local governments to move across regions every few years. In FS Township, the average tenure of key officials in township governments is only about three years, which means these key decision-makers care more about short-term achievements than long-term clientelistic relationships.[14] Over the years, this sequence of events has profoundly altered relationships between local governments and villages, and simultaneously changed local officials' attitudes about village elections. Playing with the wording of the village elections' three main criteria—openness, fairness, and justice (公开, 公平, 公正), as advocated by the official documents—a top township government official remarked, "As long as the procedure is fair, we don't care who is elected. If the villagers elect a pig, so be it. All we can do is to be open and fair. Whether it is justice or not depends on the choice of the villagers." Clearly, the township government has become less interested in the outcomes of village elections than in ensuring that the election process occurs smoothly, with no social protests, unrest, or other complications.

Moreover, focusing only on the government side provides an incomplete picture. To be sure, state policies and government behaviors have evolved over time in response to increasing political pressures—riots, protests, and demands for participation in village governance—bubbling up from the grassroots level. When elections first came to this region in the late 1980s, the villagers were not surprised. Symbolic voting had been in place since the establishment of the PRC, and even in the most chaotic years of the Cultural Revolution, the team leaders and village (brigade) leaders were nominally voted into office by their fellow villagers. No one was surprised at the village election, therefore; yet at the same time no one took it seriously. Under the dense ties of kinship and social bonding, it is difficult to openly challenge the leaders in power. Moreover, the role of the village committee was more symbolic in the early days and the party secretary had the ultimate authority. Above all, the township government played a critical—often decisive—role in handpicking its candidates and getting them elected.

With time, however, villagers learned to exercise their rights and to not only play by the rules but also to use the rules to challenge the township government's attempts at manipulation, to check the behavior of local cadres, and to strive for their own interests. The local cadres' reactions toward the villagers reflect these changes. Government officials to whom I spoke recalled many occasions in which some villagers held up the handbook of government regulations on elections to challenge the manipulative arrangements by local cadres. As one government official put it, "These villagers often know more about election regulations than we cadres. They can challenge you if you are not careful about what you say or do." On several occasions in the 2006 election season, villagers demanded that the village committee open its books on revenues and expenditures and account for irregular spending before an election took place. Other village governments learned quickly—some took a proactive role and opened the collective accounts for public review at the beginning of the election meeting. Other learning processes developed as well, as candidates across villages imitated strategies from one another. In one case, a recently elected village head invited the head of another village, who was well known for his contentious relationship with his own party secretary, to dinner. A quick learner, soon after that dinner the recently elected village head mobilized his supporters and had himself elected into the party secretary position, defying the prior arrangement by the township government.

Ironically, amid these large processes of institutional change, the township government insisted on procedural fairness as a strategies choice to ensure social stability and to keep potential explosions in check. In other words, the township government used the banner of protecting procedural integrity as its most lethal weapon in deterring potential disruptions to village elections. Aware that any procedural violation could potentially trigger social protests or petitions, the township government made sure that procedures were followed to the letter, both to eliminate any excuse for such actions and to protect itself in the event that protests did arise and investigations ensued. Township governments enforced these procedures even at the risk of electing "undesirable" candidates. The case of Bao Village, mentioned earlier, illustrates that in the face of confrontations and potential disruptions, work teams ensure the completion of the voting process even at the expense of their favored candidate.

The villagers recognized and accepted the township government's role shift. I witnessed one election committee meeting in a village in which the members from different cliques contended the election arrangements, but all sides agreed to let the township government work team take charge of election procedures—checking voter certificates, distributing ballots, and assisting illiterate voters in filling out the ballots. This gave the township government the legitimized opportunity to get involved and play an active role in village elections.

The township government was indeed active and involved every step of the way, deploying many strategies at its disposal—some subtle, others little more than naked displays of intimidation—to ensure that elections operated smoothly. In some cases, as in Bao Village, intimidation was evident, with police cars and uniformed police personnel present, and video cameras recording. In other cases, the handling was more subtle—government staff members were carefully selected and dispatched to those villages where they had close ties or could exert the strongest influence to put a lid on potential explosions.

I witnessed an episode that neatly illustrates the latter strategy. One early morning, I was boarding a small truck with a work team to witness a village election when I was ushered to a car nearby. It turned out that the car—one of only two owned by the township government (the other one being used exclusively by the party secretary)—belonged to the township bureau of water management, whose head, Mr. Wu, was appointed to take charge of this village's election. Although I had stayed in the township government frequently for the past two years, I seldom saw Mr. Wu. His office was only partly under the township government's administration and he rarely showed up in the government courtyard. Why was he appointed to head the work team overseeing this village? The reason soon became apparent. The former head of this village, who was most likely to cause disruption, had been involved in some water-related projects that depended on the water-management office. Mr. Wu's presence in this village effectively checked the former village head's behavior. Indeed, the former village head was there at the village center, making complaints and trying (through his relatives) to disrupt voting, but Mr. Wu engaged him in personal and informal conversations, and neutralized his opposition for the remainder of the election process.

The relatively smooth operations in the recent election cycle were also facilitated by other processes in apparently unrelated areas, which nevertheless played a significant role in reducing the intensity of competition in elections. For example, the dwindling benefits enjoyed by village cadres, coupled with the expanding outside opportunities made village office less attractive, a theme that Oi and Rozelle have explored.[15] Over the years, collective assets in most villages have drastically diminished. Many village governments are heavily in debt, and tensions are mounting in villages as villagers find themselves in debt to the collective, and vice versa. These factors make cadre positions less attractive, especially in smaller, poorer villages. At the same time, the "exit" option has gradually become more open and appealing. The presence of outside opportunities—becoming a migrant worker or engaging in entrepreneurial activities—has made it easier for those who lose elections to seek other employment outside their villages, thereby reducing potential complications in the aftermath of a defeat. In the case of the Bao Village, where the party secretary lost a contentious election, instead of continuing the fight on other fronts, he simply packed his belongings and left, as his predecessor had done. In another village, the party secretary did not win a seat in the village committee and was pushed aside by the elected village head. Within a year, he resigned from his party secretary position and went on to profit from operating a transport business using his own vehicle.

In sum, local governments have played a critical role in the evolution of village elections as an institution. The significant, recent changes in FS Township were largely due to organizational responses by the township government, both to changing organizational environments and to changing incentives within the Chinese bureaucracy. These changes in turn reflect larger-scale institutional transformations in China that have weakened the organizational capacities and resource bases of township governments and village authorities.

Making Sense of Village Elections: The Significance of Political Change

A Chinese proverb—"A falling leaf can tell the coming of autumn"—came to mind as I reflected on my observations of village elections in FS Township. I do not necessarily think the FS Township experience is applicable to other parts of rural China. Indeed, as we have seen, even within FS Township, there are considerable variations across villages, which have evolved over time. On the one hand, it would be absurd to extrapolate from the experience in this small agricultural town and assume that it applies to other towns, regions, or the whole country. On the other hand, I would suggest that the events in this small corner of rural China are by no means isolated; rather, they are part of the sea changes sweeping through rural China. What we learned from this small town has important implications for understanding the monumental changes now underway in China's societal transformation.

What is the significance of village elections for rural governance? One lasting effect of the village election is that it has established an alternative, legitimate basis of authority in rural governance. Village elections bring to the fore tensions between two distinct lines of authority in the village. One is the traditional party authority, with the party secretary selected by the party members in the village and formally appointed by the township government. The other is the authority bestowed on the village committee, with the head of the committee becoming the village head. These two lines of authority have distinct bases of legitimacy, the former based on top-down appointment by the township government, and the latter on bottom-up, popular (or kinship-based) support from the villagers. The relationship between the two lines is subtle and evolving. Formally, the Organic Law of Village Committees dictates a model of so-called village self-governance under the leadership of the Communist Party, which—as many frustrated village and township cadres are fond of pointing out—is a contradiction in terms. This model of governance puts the party secretary at higher authority. In reality, however, this authority structure is undermined by the power of village elections, which allows village leaders to be elected independent of (and even, at times, in defiance of) party nomination.

Over time, even those who have held the dual posts of both party secretary and village head come to recognize that the village head position has special appeal because it represents the legitimacy granted by the villagers. The village party secretary can be removed directly by the township government, but legally the village head can be removed only by village election. In many instances, the legitimacy based on popular support allows the village head to gain an upper hand in his dealings with the party secretary. As one village head put it:

Here is how I think about this. Why do you want to be a party secretary? What is the use, right? I am now the village head elected by the villagers, there is nothing you [the township government] can do about it. I got five to six hundred votes. As a party secretary, the township government can dismiss you at any time. But as a village head, I cannot be removed without the villagers' approval. As a village party secretary, if your work is good, the township party secretary praises you; but if your work has problems the next day he will not recognize you and will simply dismiss you right away. If he is on good terms with you, he will notify you ahead of time and ask you to resign. If you two are not on good terms, he would directly dismiss you. If I am promoted by the township party secretary, I have to follow his instructions. But if I am elected by the villagers, then it is a different story; we go our separate ways.

Another village head, who was also the village party secretary, reflected on his dual roles in his dealings with the township government:

My position as the village head was elected by the villagers. The township government can only provide "guidance" but not "administrative order" to me in this position. There was one instance a few years ago when a township official asked us to provide free labor for a government project. I made the arrangements for two days. But he bullied us and demanded free labor for one more day. I was outraged and refused to do it. I yelled at him: "You don't have authority to remove me from my position; and I don't have any money if you want to fine me." At that time, I did not say that I was the party secretary, but that I was the village head, elected by the villagers, and he had no authority to remove me from my position.

This is a major breakthrough in governance structure in rural China. Since the inception of the PRC in 1949, village governance derived its legitimacy from a top-down approach, as village leaders were formally appointed and often directly selected by the governments above.[16] Now, for the first time, village elections provide an alternative basis—popular support—for village leadership. The differences were hardly discernible at first, while traditional party leaders still exerted their control. Gradually but surely, however, the center of gravity in village authority shifted to the elected officials. I often heard village cadres comment that they now needed to get more involved in the village committee rather than the party committee.

The institution of village election thus subtly introduced a profound dynamic, the impact of which has been felt only many years later. Village elections not only provide a legitimate vehicle for the rise of collective action but also sets the stage for dialogue between the ruling party and the villagers, and between the township government and village leaders. Village elections also provide a basis for institutional innovation, giving villages opportunities to address their own problems and to search for their own solutions. For example, in one village in FS Township, one villager (a formal cadre) formed his own "cabinet," which ran for election as a team. This contrasts sharply with the conventional practice by which individuals run on their own and the resulting village committee comprises the three candidates who have received the highest votes. Seen in this light, village elections represent a major institutional innovation, opening up the possibility of a significant departure from the present political order in rural China.

In sum, let us step back from the local settings described in this chapter and draw some lessons about the larger processes at work. The FS Township experience offers a microscope through which to view the complexities and subtleties of the instutional change process. As we have seen, an interesting feature of these episodes is that their dynamics seemed mysterious and surprising even to those who were closest to them. This is largely because the outcomes of village elections result from the interaction of independent streams of events, involving long processes, often across large areas, and their unanticipated consequences.

First, institutional change takes time, and time is an important dimension for understanding the processes of institutional change. Take the village elections in this region as an example. According to the anecdotal evidence I have gathered in my fieldwork, for a long time since the late 1980s, village elections were largely symbolic and subject to the manipulation of the township government. Changes in several important processes—the shifting role of the township government, the learning process among the villagers, the loosening of the link between the township government and villages—have evolved and have finally reached a stage, in recent years, at which qualitative changes in electoral behaviors have become visible and significant. In other words, the path of change is not continuous or linear or monotonic; as such, it defies predictions based on simplistic models. This observation implies that, if we insert our research probes at different points over these long processes, we are likely to draw different lessons and arrive at different conclusions—perhaps prematurely disappointing or exuberant by turns—about the prospects of institutional change in this area.

Second, institutional change involves multiple, often disparate, processes. For example, the shifting role of the local government depends on several key processes that took place in other areas, some of which took more than a decade to evolve. The fiscal reform in the late 1990s was a part of the central government's effort to recentralize resource allocation. By depriving local governments of resources, it had the unintended consequence of loosening the grip of local governments in rural areas. Over time, this has meant that local governments play a more disinterested role in village elections. More recently, the abolition of agricultural taxation—again motivated by considerations unrelated to village elections—has to a large extent freed the township government from its clientelistic relationships with villages and village cadres. The flow of migrant workers between urban and rural areas, together with the presence of business opportunities in the nearby areas—expanded over long periods of economic development—has increased the attractiveness of the "exit" option for aspiring villagers. All these processes are distinct and separate, evolving in their own realms, with no direct link to the institution of village elections. However, their intersections at specific axes of time and place may have generated the conditions necessary to facilitate the evolution of the institution of village elections.

Finally, significant institutional change is often not born of rational design; rather, it develops from interactions among multifarious, disparate processes and their unintended consequences. To be sure, bureaucratic obligations and blame avoidance dominated the township governments' concerns and behavior more than any desire to advance the agenda of political reform. Nevertheless, the consequences of these behaviors, as I have sought to demonstrate in this chapter, contributed significantly to fundamental institutional changes underway in China. For example, in the policy design of village elections, self-governance under the party leadership was clearly the official intention. However, the village election has evolved to such an extent that the center of gravity has shifted to the elected village cadres and undermined the traditional authority of the ruling party. Because of the confluences of multiple and disparate processes, the outcomes are likely to surprise even those close to or deeply involved in these processes.

These considerations raise questions about approaches to understanding institutional changes in transitional economies. First, one needs to take a *process* view of the phenomena under investigation. This cautions us to be patient in drawing conclusions about ongoing institutional change. Second, one needs to go beyond traditional analytical tools and conduct substantive institutional analysis through close observation. Third, although causal models are virtuous, the actual processes are likely to be messy, due to the confluence of several processes and their unanticipated consequences. An interpretive approach may be especially informative in dissecting the complexities and subtleties involved in these processes.

In my view, the institutionalization of village elections is likely to become a major launch pad for China's political change. In contemporary China, rural areas have often been catalysts for social change. The strategy of the "countryside encircling cities" and the emphasis on the rural bases eventually led the Chinese Communist Party to drive out the Nationalist Party and come to power in 1949. In the late 1970s, land reform in the rural areas ushered in China's economic reform. The successful institutionalization of village elections may well provide positive feedback to the central government, inducing further experimentation in democratization. Further, the loose coupling of rural governance and the state administrative order could expand public space independent of state intervention, thereby leading to the decentralization of political pressures and risks, the potential reduction of unorganized collective action, and the development of future political reform, both in other arenas and in urban areas.[17]

Of course, not everyone applauds village elections. Those least in favor were the local cadres whose lives and careers were affected most by the new institution. As one complained bitterly, "The urbanites are more educated and knowledgeable, but the government does not allow them to vote for their local leaders. Peasants are the least educated, yet the government gives them the most important voting right. This is ridiculous." Indeed, as peasants—who constitute two-thirds of China's total population—have become accustomed to exercising their rights to select their leaders, it is only logical that those living in urban areas and other arenas may do likewise sooner or later. However, unlike a Trojan horse that smuggles alien forces into the fortress, village elections as an institution will continue to evolve, as multiple and disparate processes and distant events—shaped by recombinant historical contingencies and institutional contexts[18]—interact with one another. The village election episodes in FS Township show that we should be open-minded, patient, and willing to embrace elements of surprise in China's great transformation.

Notes

[1] An earlier version of this chapter was presented at the conference titled "Growing Pains: Tensions and Opportunity in China's Transformations" Shorenstein APARC, Stanford University, November 2–3, 2007. I thank the participants of the conference, especially Jean C. Oi, Scott Rozelle, and Andrew Walder for their helpful comments. All names of the township, villages, and individuals in this chapter have been changed to ensure the anonymity of the sources.

[2] Kevin J. O'Brien and Lianjiang Li, "Accommodating 'Democracy' in a One-Party State: Introducing Village Elections in China," *China Quarterly* 162 (June 2000): 465–89; Robert A. Pastor and Qingshan Tan, "The Meaning of China's Village Elections," *China Quarterly* 162 (June 2000): 490–512.

[3] See Lin Nan, "Local Market Socialism: Local Corporatism in Action in Rural China," *Theory and Society* 24 (1995): 301–54.; Victor Nee, "A Theory of Market Transition: From Redistribution to Markets in State Socialism," *American Sociological Review* 54 (1989): 663–81; Victor Nee, "Social Inequality in Reforming State Socialism: Between Redistribution and Markets in State Socialism," *American Sociological Review* 54 (1991): 663–81; Jean C. Oi, *State and Peasant in Contemporary China: The Political Economy of Village Government*, (Berkeley, CA: Univ. of California Press, 1989); Jean C. Oi, *Rural China Takes Off: Institutional Foundations of Economic Reform*, (Berkeley, CA: Univ. of California Press, 1999); Yusheng Peng, "Kinship Networks and Entrepreneurs in China's Transitional Economy," *American Journal of Sociology* 109 (2004): 1045–74; Andrew G. Walder, "Local Governments as Industrial Firms: An Organizational Analysis of China's Transitional Economy," *American Journal of Sociology* 101 (1995): 263–301; and Andrew G. Walder, "Markets and Income Inequality in Rural China: Political Advantage in an Expanding Economy," *American Sociological Review* 67 (2002): 231–53.

[4] Special issue, "Elections and Democracy in Greater China," *China Quarterly* 162 (June 2000).

[5] For a review, see Gunter Schubert, "Village Elections in the PRC: A Trojan Horse of Democracy," unpublished manuscript, Institute for East Asian Studies/East Asian Politics, Gerhard-Mercator-University Duisburg, Germany (2002).

[6] See Fenfu Luo, Linxiu Zhang, Jikun Huang, and Scott Rozelle, "Elections, Fiscal Reform and Public Goods Provision in Rural China," *Journal of Comparative Economics*

35 (2007): 583–611; Melanie Manion, "The Electoral Connection in the Chinese Countryside," *American Political Science Review* 90 (1996): 736–48; Kevin J. O'Brien, "Villagers, Elections, and Citizenship in Contemporary China," *Modern China* 27 (2001): 407–35; Jean C. Oi and Scott Rozelle, "Elections and Power: The Locus of Decision-Making in Chinese Villages," *China Quarterly* 162 (2000): 513–39; and Tianjian Shi, "Village Committee Elections in China: Institutionalist Tactics for Democracy," *World Politics* 51 (1999): 385–412.

[7] See Anita Chan, Richard Madsen, and Jonathan Unger, *Chen Village under Mao and Deng* (Berkeley, CA: Univ. of California Press, 1999); Edward Friedman, Paul G. Pickowicz, and Mark Selden, *Chinese Village, Socialist State* (New Haven, CT: Yale Univ. Press, 1991); William L. Parish and Martin King Whyte, *Village and Family in Contemporary China* (Chicago, IL: Univ. of Chicago Press, 1978); Vivienne Shue, *The Reach of the State: Sketches of the Chinese Body Politic* (Stanford, CA: Stanford Univ. Press, 1988).

[8] O'Brien and Li, "Accommodating 'Democracy' in a One-Party State."

[9] There appeared to be no official voting hours on election day. The minimum requirement of "at least fifty percent of the eligible voters" is often used as the rule of thumb in deciding when to close the voting booth. Village elections usually took place in the early spring before the busy farming season began. Most villagers attended the voting event as soon as the voting booth was open, and voting activities usually ended in the early afternoons. If the election was contentious or lacked participation, the voting process could last late into the night, as local cadres or contenders struggled to mobilize for more votes.

[10] In one village, large posters appeared the day before an election, charging the incumbent village head with corruption and womanizing. Unfazed by the accusation, he took to the loudspeakers to read the accusations to the entire village, challenging the anonymous accuser to come forward with evidence. He was reelected into office the next day.

[11] See W. Richard Scott, *Organizations: Rational, Natural, and Open Systems*, 5th edn. (Englewood Cliffs, NJ: Prentice Hall, 2003); James Q. Wilson, *Bureaucracy: What Government Agencies Do and Why They Do It* (New York: Basic Books, 1989).

[12] Paul Milgrom and John Roberts, *Economics, Organization and Management* (Englewood Cliffs, NJ: Prentice Hall, 1992).

[13] Jean C. Oi and Shukai Zhao, "Fiscal Crisis in China's Townships: Causes and Consequences," in M. Goldman and E. Perry, eds., *Grassroots Political Reform in Contemporary China* (Cambridge, MA: Harvard Univ. Press, 2007), 75–96.

[14] Xueguang Zhou, "Inverted Soft Budget Constraint: An Organizational Analysis of Government Extra-Budgetary Seeking Behavior [逆向软预算约束: 一个政府行为的组织分析]," *Social Science in China* [中国社会科学] 2 (2005): 132–43 (in Chinese).

[15] See Oi and Rozelle, "Elections and Power."

[16] Chan, Madsen, and Unger, *Chen Village under Mao and Deng*; Friedman, Pickowicz, and Selden, *Chinese Village, Socialist State*.

[17] Xueguang Zhou, "Unorganized Interests and Collective Action in Communist China," *American Sociological Review* 58 (1993): 54–73.

[18] David Stark, "Recombinant Property in East European Capitalism," *American Journal of Sociology* 101 (1996): 993–1027.

Family Planning Enforcement in Rural China: Enduring State-Society Conflict?

Ethan Michelson[1]

China's family planning policies have been both celebrated and vilified. They have received widespread praise for staving off Malthusian apocalypse and for bringing economic and environmental benefits to the world's most populous country. At the same time, they have been intensely unpopular both among those people whose family size is subject to their control and among outside observers who criticize official enforcement practices. Even their most ardent proponents recognize that the policies have contributed to some of China's growing pains, most notably a gender ratio unbalanced by millions of "missing girls." While much is already known about the policies' demographic costs, in this chapter I consider their costs in state-society friction. Findings I present from the first large-scale survey on the topic suggest that, over time, the policies and their painful consequences will become increasingly irrelevant as fertility levels continue to drop for socioeconomic reasons unrelated to family planning enforcement.

I have two goals in this chapter. First, I attempt to quantify the volume of conflict spawned by the policies and, in particular, the degree to which they prompted popular discontent with the local political leaders charged with their enforcement. While qualitative accounts and case studies abound, I use unique survey data to measure the extent and consequences of top-down policy enforcement and bottom-up policy resistance in rural China. I aim to fill a conspicuous gap in the scholarship both on rural Chinese society and on China's family planning policies by assessing the prevalence of family planning conflict in these areas and the extent to which it damages state-society relations. The survey data paint a vivid portrait of local governments devoting enormous energy to family planning enforcement, in ways that have been often contested and have significantly eroded popular trust in local government.

Second, I aim to assess the extent to which sustained economic development has affected this dynamic. We will see that the decline in fertility rates accompanying ongoing economic development in rural China will continue to alleviate this important source of state-society conflict in the future. I conclude by arguing that a series of rural socioeconomic policies introduced several years after the completion of the survey on which this chapter is based have likely decreased family planning conflict. Family planning enforcement practices are a transitional feature of rural China that are rapidly being outgrown.

Family Planning Policies

China's current family planning policies date back to 1979, although similar policies had been attempted in earlier years.[2] The popular "one-child policy" moniker is misleading in two important respects. First, there is no unified, monolithic policy, but rather a wide array of local policies exhibiting tremendous regional variation.[3] Second, although the policies encourage couples to limit their fertility to one child, they also provide many opportunities for rural couples to have two (or more) children.

Policy Properties

Only in urban—and in some highly developed suburban—areas is the limit to a single child per couple a general rule.[4] Although family planning policies vary by region, most in the countryside include conditions under which it is acceptable to have two children. For example, miners, owing to their significantly higher mortality rates, and couples who live in low-population-density locales are often permitted to have two children.[5] Members of officially recognized ethnic minorities are likewise typically permitted to have two children, sometimes even three if they live in remote border areas. But by far the most salient exception to the one-child rule applies to rural couples whose first child is a girl.[6] According to Gu et al.,[7] in the late 1990s this particular exception applied to 664 million people, over half of China's total population.[8]

Because "fertility policy" (*zhengce shengyu*) translates to 1.5 children in most parts of rural China, here the so-called "one-child policy" should be called the "one-son-or-two-child policy"[9] or "1.5-child policy."[10] This policy represents the official recognition that social security in rural areas is provided not by the government but by the family. More specifically, it reflects the paramount importance of sons in ensuring both old-age support and the continuity of the family line.[11] Assuming no exemptions to the general 1.5-child rule, the following two situations would constitute policy noncompliance, known idiomatically as "excess births," "above-quota births," or "out-of-plan births" (*chao sheng*): (1) giving birth to a second child after a firstborn son and (2) giving birth to more than two children. Let us consider policy implications.

Policy Benefits

By many accounts, the policies have been highly successful in realizing their overriding goal of slowed population growth. Fanfare surrounds reports that, since their inception in the early 1970s, these policies have prevented anywhere from 250–300 million[12] to 400 million births.[13] If these claims are true, the policies have undoubtedly helped China avert potentially calamitous population growth. Family planning policies have long been viewed as a source of economic benefits for poor, developing countries in general[14] and for China in particular.[15] According to Potts, family planning in China "was a source of great pain for one generation, but a generation later it began to yield important economic benefits."[16] Beyond their alleged economic benefits, the policies have also been attributed with making contributions to environmental protection: "Prevention of unwanted births today by family planning might be one of the most cost-effective ways to preserve the planet's environment for the future."[17] According to some estimates, the prevention of 300 million births in China translates into "1.3 billion metric tons of avoided carbon dioxide emissions."[18]

Policy Costs

Instead of crediting the policies with easing China's growing pains, however, other observers have blamed the policies for aggravating them. The well-documented social and political costs of the policies include a yawning childhood gender imbalance; coercive and sometimes violent official enforcement; popular noncompliance, resistance, and conflict with state agents; and popular discontent with local governments.

Gender imbalance

No different from other parts of Asia,[19] the preference for a son in China has deep historical roots and persists owing to enduring cultural values and immediate practical necessity.[20] Only 5 percent of China's rural elderly have retirement pensions.[21] In the absence of a comprehensive social security system in rural China, the vast majority of the elderly rely on family for old-age support.[22] A study funded by the United Nations Development Programme (UNDP) found that the most important source of old-age support was children, followed by personal savings.[23] Because daughters in China tend to marry out of their natal villages, sons and their wives are expected to assume responsibility for supporting and caring for elderly parents. China's family planning policies allow, in most instances, a maximum of two attempts to bear a son. "The 1.5-child policy in fact implicitly tells peasants that one boy is sufficient for family welfare but one girl is not and that they need to have another child."[24] By creating enormous pressure to produce a son in the first or second attempt, the family planning policies have contributed to a grave gender imbalance.[25] With only two chances to produce a boy, the most important perceived source of old-age security in rural China, many couples do not leave the gender of their offspring to fate.

The most important proximate mechanisms of the gender imbalance are gender-selective abortion and female infanticide and neglect.[26] Over time the former mechanism has eclipsed the latter thanks to the diffusion of ultrasound technology widely accessible to ordinary villagers,[27] even though fetal gender testing has been outlawed since 1994.[28] Zeng estimates that the proportion of couples whose first child was a boy and who "underwent prenatal sex determination and sex-selective abortion to have a boy as a second child" was more than four times higher in 1.5-child policy areas than in 2-child policy areas (19.1 percent versus 4.6 percent).[29]

The demographic consequences of these motives and mechanisms have been thoroughly documented. According to government census data, the gender ratio at birth in 1980, 1990, and 2000 was 107, 111, and 120 boys per 100 girls, respectively, for the country as a whole.[30] The gender imbalance was not only far greater in rural areas than in urban areas,[31] but was also far greater among second- and thirdborn children than among firstborn.[32] Census data show that China's skewed gender ratio is almost entirely an artifact of the 1.5-child policy: in areas with a 1.5-child policy, the gender ratio is 125 boys per 100 girls at birth—far higher than the ratio of 112:100 in places with a strict 1-child policy and 109:100 in places with a 2-child policy.[33]

The gender imbalance and the conditions that have spawned it were publicly acknowledged by President Hu Jintao as early as 2004,[34] and remain a major priority of his administration. According to census data, boys under the age of fifteen outnumbered girls in the same age group by over eighteen million in the year 2000.[35] This demographic problem carries severe social implications. In a speech at the 10th National People's Congress in 2004, a high-ranking official of the Chinese People's Political Consultative Conference predicted that the current widespread use of prenatal gender tests, by creating as many as forty million bachelors unable to find wives by the year 2020, will "trigger such crimes and social problems as mercenary marriage, abduction of women and prostitution."[36] Indeed, some scholars have grimly predicted intensifying crime and violence within China, and even of an increasingly ominous Chinese military presence beyond its borders, caused by the growing population of unmarried men.[37]

Family planning enforcement

The state family planning administration reaches as far as the township (which averages about twenty thousand people), but extends into the village (which averages about one thousand people) in a significant but less formal capacity.[38] The performance of local cadres is evaluated to an important measure by their success in meeting birth targets.[39] In order to keep local fertility levels within these fixed targets, couples wishing to have a child are required to apply for a birth permit. Birth permits are issued only to applicants who satisfy policy conditions—if the local birth quota for the year has not been reached. In other words, every birth is supposed to be authorized, or "on the plan."[40] In reality, however, not every couple applies for authorization before having a child.[41] While some unauthorized births are registered retroactively, many births escape detection.[42]

From the late 1970s through the early 1980s, the policies were zealously enforced through the birth-permit system, mandatory birth control, induced abortions to terminate unauthorized pregnancies, and a series of infamous "shock attack" sterilization campaigns.[43] Policy violators were often punished by hefty fines and property confiscation.[44] When targets of enforcement fled the village, their homes were sometimes nailed shut[45] or dismantled.[46] Unauthorized children (known as "black children," or *hei haizi*) were sometimes deprived of state benefits, such as collective land distribution.[47] In addition to these forms of punishments policy violators were often required to undergo sterilization surgery—women far more often than men.[48]

Policy noncompliance

To say that villagers did not easily acquiesce to policy enforcement practices is an understatement: unauthorized births as a proportion of all births remained above 30 percent into the mid-1990s. Indeed, the policies have created a population of "excess-birth guerrillas" (*chaosheng youji dui*) who give birth in hiding outside their home villages.[49]

Family planning disputes

When policy noncompliance was discovered by local state officials, they had at least two options. One was to collude with violators.[50] Another—and far more common—option was to confront violators in an effort to enforce the policies. In the rural Chinese context, popular resistance against official family planning demands has been an enduring source of disputes.

Discontent with local government

In the mid-1980s, one village party secretary characterized popular sentiment toward the "new policy" in this way: "To be honest with you, all the villagers hate it."[51] Yet, despite the seemingly universal unpopularity of the policies in rural China, local state cadres, on the whole, have strived to implement and enforce them faithfully. Failing to meet birth quotas would put a big dent into, or entirely eliminate, a cadre's annual bonus, and possibly even put an end to his or her political career.[52] From the beginning, villagers have blamed and attacked the primary policy messengers and enforcers—rural cadres.[53] Because "the enforcement of state regulations on family planning and cremation fell on the shoulders of village cadres, these cadres bore the brunt of peasant dissatisfaction."[54] Indeed, family planning cadres have been subject to harassment, violent physical attacks, and even murder, as well as theft and property damage.[55] Some hapless victims were guilty of no more than loyal fulfillment of their duty. In other cases, assailants were reacting to "the excessive zeal and the intolerable abuses" of rural cadres.[56] Suffice it to say that local cadres found themselves caught between an unbending state above and angry peasants below.

Subsequent developments

Reports of coercive enforcement and violent resistance continued into the 1990s and 2000s. For example, the news media reported a violent protest in Guangdong Province in 1997 that involved perhaps a thousand participants.[57]

In 2006 a blind legal activist received widespread media coverage for trying to mobilize scores of villagers in the countryside surrounding Shandong Province's city of Linyi in order to mount a legal challenge against local policy enforcement practices.[58] Such media reports notwithstanding,[59] the more general trend has been policy relaxation. The national campaigns of the 1980s have since been downsized, shortened, and localized, and policy enforcement methods have become less coercive.[60] Indeed, a debate has emerged about whether family planning policies should be scrapped altogether.[61]

The move away from campaign-style enforcement is at least in part due to natural fertility decline.[62] As depicted in figure 8.1, between 1979 and 2005, the proportion of the total population residing in rural areas declined from over 80 percent to 57 percent, and the proportion of the rural labor force employed in industry and construction (the census definition of "secondary industry") rose from little more than 0 percent to almost 20 percent. Meanwhile, the proportion of the rural labor force working in off-farm jobs increased from a little more than 0 percent to over 40 percent.[63] These changes, perhaps more than any other, have diminished the everyday salience of China's family planning policies.

Economic forces appear to have been at least as decisive as policy enforcement in China's fertility decline.[64] If it has not done so already, the effect of economic development will soon eclipse the effect of policy enforcement on both fertility levels and policy noncompliance for at least two reasons. First, the exodus of labor out of agriculture has lessened the imperative to bear children. Rural nonfarm employment rates, which rose even faster for women than for men in the 1990s,[65] have delayed and reduced fertility.[66] Research suggests that rural migrants, who have grown in number from almost zero to over two hundred million, and a growing proportion of whom are women, have lower fertility levels than nonmigrant villagers.[67] Second, marketization and labor mobility have weakened the local state's grip on the lives of villagers. The earlier family planning campaigns were virtually inescapable owing to the legacy of Mao-era organized dependence.[68] Since then, the authority of village government and its ability to enforce state policy have weakened as household farming replaced collective agriculture and as markets supplemented and supplanted state procurement.[69]

Thus, economic development and labor-market transformation have proven to be double-edged swords for family planning policy enforcement. Cutting one way, they have reduced family planning policy evasion by lowering fertility. Cutting the other way, they have also facilitated policy evasion by loosening restrictions on geographic mobility, making noncompliance harder to detect and punish. Despite a greater ability to evade detection, evidence from fertility surveys suggests that policy noncompliance (unauthorized births as a proportion of all births) dropped from almost 50 percent in 1980 to 30 percent in the mid-1990s.[70]

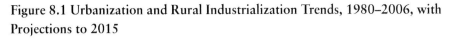

Figure 8.1 Urbanization and Rural Industrialization Trends, 1980–2006, with Projections to 2015

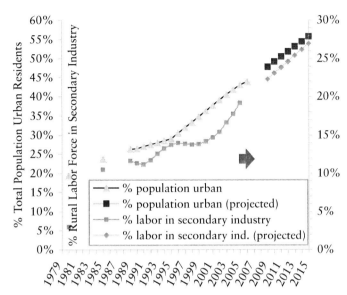

Source: SSA 2007, tables 4–1 and 13–4.
Note: Projections are based on trends beginning in 1998: a 0.78 annual percentage-point increase in urbanization and a 1.32 annual percentage-point increase in rural industrialization.

New policy developments have also helped mitigate family planning disputes. In response to mounting social and political challenges posed by skewed gender ratios, China's central government has introduced new policy initiatives and public awareness campaigns.[71] As part of the official "Care for Girls" campaign (Guan'ai Nühai Xingdong)[72] family planning authorities announced a shift away from the use of negative sanctions toward the use of positive financial incentives in efforts to encourage families to stop trying for a son after giving birth to a girl. The rewards include old-age pensions for those in compliance with family planning regulations,[73] as well as cash, free schooling, and better housing for families with daughters.[74]

Do family planning disputes remain a salient source of conflict in contemporary rural China? Do local governments continue to devote a substantial share of their total efforts to family planning policy administration and enforcement? Do family planning conflicts significantly damage state-society relations? I now attempt to answer these questions.

Plan of Analysis

I use unique household survey data to assess the amount of pain—that is, the amount of state-society conflict and friction—produced by the policies and their enforcement. I divide this assessment into three steps:

1. My first step is to use census data to explore the *determinants* of high fertility and skewed gender ratios. Although I could also use my household survey data to complete this step, I use census data for two reasons. First, because census data provide comprehensive coverage of China's population, they are more credible than my household survey as a source of information about household fertility. Second, replicating this step of the analysis using my household survey data will enhance our confidence in the results reported in steps two and three.

2. I then use my household survey data to explore the determinants of policy noncompliance, policy enforcement effort, policy disputes, and policy-produced discontent with village government. In this step I use my survey data to identify the *consequences* of high fertility and skewed gender ratios.

3. My third and final step is to consider how continued fertility declines might alter the landscape of policy conflict by weakening the conditions that prompt policy noncompliance in the first place.

In all three steps of my analysis I use aggregated data; I aggregate my household survey data because the census data are aggregated to county-level administrative units.

Data and Measures

Together with sociologists at Renmin University of China, I designed and organized the first large-scale survey on real-life grievances and real-life disputing behavior in rural China. In January and early February of 2002, our survey team completed usable interviews of almost three thousand rural households in one county in each of five provinces (Henan, Hunan, Jiangsu, Shaanxi, and Shandong) and one centrally administered city (Chongqing). The 2,902 households included in my analyses are distributed across thirty-seven villages in six provinces: ten villages in Shandong; six villages each in Henan and Hunan; and five villages each in Shaanxi, Jiangsu, and Chongqing. Our original target was five villages per county and a hundred interviews per village, or three thousand households in total. The survey sites were selected not randomly but purposively. The six counties[75] in which the survey was carried out capture enormous socioeconomic and regional diversity, including relatively prosperous coastal areas. Indeed, one survey site is in the heart of the spectacularly developed Sunan region of southern Jiangsu Province, not far from Shanghai, in which average household incomes approach those of Beijing. At the other end of the spectrum are relatively poor, interior areas in Henan and Hunan. Because the six survey sites were selected with the goal of maximizing regional and economic variation, the households interviewed are not intended to be representative of rural China as a whole but only of the six counties from which they were sampled. Although we did not select the survey sites randomly, we trained and instructed survey interviewers to select households randomly within villages and to select respondents randomly within households. Information on refusals was not recorded. But all indications suggest that this is a representative sample. Age, education, income, and occupational distributions in the sample closely match official statistics and published findings from nationally representative samples.

The survey questionnaire recorded information on household composition and several dimensions of state-society friction. I used (1) information on household members to estimate village-level fertility and gender ratios, and (2) information on disputes and general attitudes, as communicated by survey respondents, to estimate village-level official enforcement efforts, noncompliance, conflict, and discontent.

Fertility and Gender Ratios

Whereas most studies on family planning policy noncompliance and gender ratios take pregnancies and births as the units of analysis, our survey collected no information on pregnancies, and only seventy-five households (or less than 3 percent of the sample) reported an infant baby (aged one year or less). The survey was designed to collect information on all "household members with whom the respondent shares common life." That is, the survey enumerated and recorded information about all household members. On the basis of this detailed information, I identified households with children born within the past five years (i.e., with children under age six).

Thus, my measure of *fertility* is the number of children (variously under age fifteen and under age six) per household. Census data confirm that this measure is a reasonable proxy for fertility: among all 2,870 county-level administrative units in the 2000 census, the mean number of children under age five per household is correlated with the crude fertility rate at $R=0.88$.[76] My measure of *gender imbalance* is the ratio of boys to girls (multiplied by 100) under the age of five years in the census data and under the age of six years in the survey data.[77]

Policy Enforcement

The survey questionnaire asked respondents to report whether or not they approached their villagers' committee for a variety of reasons, including applying for a birth permit (literally "planned birth quota," or *jihua shengyu zhibiao*). The following is the complete list, presented to respondents, of nine reasons they may have approached the villagers' committee: (1) to pay or discuss the costs of agricultural burdens; (2) to discuss a welfare benefit (such as a minimum living allowance or some kind of emergency aid); (3) to obtain or certify a document

197

for themselves or someone else; (4) to report or discuss a crime; (5) to report or discuss a collective problem (such as water or road infrastructure); (6) to obtain a birth permit; (7) to purchase or obtain emergency goods; (8) to report a neighbor dispute; and (9) to report a family dispute (such as a dispute between a mother-in-law and daughter-in-law). My measure of *policy enforcement effort* is thus calculated as the number of birth permits requested from villagers' committees as a proportion of all reported encounters with these committees. This measure provides an estimate—however rough and imperfect—of the share of the workload of villagers' committees devoted to the administration and enforcement of family planning policies.

Noncompliance

From the subsample of households containing at least one child under age six, I identified households that appear to have violated family planning policies between late 1997 and early 2002. The reason for limiting the operational definition of *policy noncompliance* to this subset of households is that, as we will see below, the operational definition of a family planning dispute is likewise limited to the previous five years. Fifteen percent of respondents reported at least one child under the age of six in the family. Of the families with at least one child under age six, 28 percent reported two, and 2 percent reported three. No families containing at least one child under age six reported more than three children.

Of the six provinces included in our survey, four permitted couples to have a second child if the first was a girl: Henan, Hunan, Shaanxi, and Shandong provinces. But nowhere in the areas surveyed were couples permitted to have three children.[78] According to census data from the year 2000, over 99 percent of the total population in all six counties was Han.[79] Thus, although the survey did not collect information on ethnicity, it is fairly safe to assume that no families in the sample qualified for an exemption on the basis of minority status. For the purposes of my analyses, therefore, I infer policy noncompliance (between 1997 and 2002) from the following criteria: (1) the presence of two boys, (2) the presence of a firstborn boy and a secondborn girl, or (3) the presence of three or more children among households containing at least one child under age six. There are several obvious reasons why this operational definition may undercount the true extent of noncompliance.

Family Planning Disputes

The survey questionnaire also contains a battery of questions on everyday disputes: (1) housing land ownership; (2) water use; (3) debt collection; (4) family planning; (5) a major consumer purchase; (6) divorce; (7) neighbor issues; (8) collecting wages; (9) responsibility land (farmland contracted from the village) or township and village enterprise contracting; (10) agricultural taxes and fees; (11) intrafamily issues (for example, elderly care or property division); (12) dealings with a government agency; (13) personal injury (complainant); (14)

property damage or loss; (15) personal injury or property damage (accused); (16) children's education; and (17) other (open ended). The original wording of the question regarding a family planning dispute is: "In the past five years, did a family planning conflict (*maodun*) emerge between you or another family member and village cadres or someone else?" Because the remaining dispute questions were also bound by a five-year time frame, I am able to use this dispute information to estimate the proportion of households experiencing family planning disputes between 1997 and 2002. Thus, my measure of *family planning disputes* is the proportion of households that reported one.

Discontent with Local Government

Finally, I develop a measure of local political discontent using responses to questions about satisfaction with village government. I calculate a "scale of discontent with the villagers' committee" as the sum of the following two items: First, "Overall, are you satisfied with the villagers' committee? (1) very satisfied; (2) somewhat satisfied; (3) neutral; (4) somewhat dissatisfied; or (5) very dissatisfied." Second, "Overall, people's attitude toward villagers' committee cadres is one of (1) great respect; (2) some respect; (3) neutral; (4) some disrespect; or (5) great disrespect." This scale has nine values, ranging from two to ten. The two items are correlated at $R=0.67$ with a Cronbach's alpha of 0.79, meaning they can be combined (with high internal consistency) into a single scale of discontent with the villagers' committee. In order to facilitate the interpretation of the results, I collapsed the full scale into a simplified three-point scale. In this simplified three-point scale, "content" is defined as a value of two to five on the full scale, "discontent" is defined as a value of seven to ten on the full scale, and "neither content nor discontent" is defined as a value of six on the full scale.[80] Thus, my measure of *discontent with the village government* is the proportion of households reporting "discontent" on this three-point scale.

Additional Independent Variables

To help explain the foregoing policy outcomes, I include in my analyses measures of industrialization, urbanization, Han ethnicity, and education. In the census data, *industrialization* is measured as the proportion of the labor force in secondary industry (manufacturing and construction). In my survey data, industrialization is measured as the proportion of the labor force employed in enterprises. In the census data, *urbanization* is measured as the proportion of the population residing in cities. In the census data, *Han ethnicity* is the Han population as a proportion of the total population. In both sources of data, *education* is measured as the average number of years of education among the population aged six and older. Because my analyses were constrained by measures included in the census, I do not include a measure of income. But since any measures of industrialization and income are highly correlated, industrialization is a reasonable proxy for income. Moreover, industrialization may be more theoretically relevant than income, given that nonfarm work is an important mechanism of fertility decline.

Step One: Findings on Causes of Fertility and Gender Ratios

The 2000 census recorded 37.6 million boys and 31.3 million girls under age five, representing a gender ratio of 120 boys to 100 girls.[81] Assuming a natural gender ratio of 105 boys to 100 girls, this translates into 4.5 million "nominally missing" girls under age five.[82] My household survey data contain 307 boys and 253 girls under age six, representing a gender ratio of 121 boys to 100 girls.

Figure 8.2 summarizes results from a series of regression analyses of census data on determinants of fertility and child gender ratios. By eroding the imperative to produce children for family agricultural labor and old-age security, economic development is a key component of many theoretical explanations of fertility decline. Thus, figure 8.2 is consistent with decades of research on the role of urbanization and industrialization in demographic transitions throughout history and around the world.[83]

Figure 8.2 Path Model of Causes of Fertility and Child Gender Imbalance, All County-level Administrative Units, 2000 (standardized OLS regression coefficients)

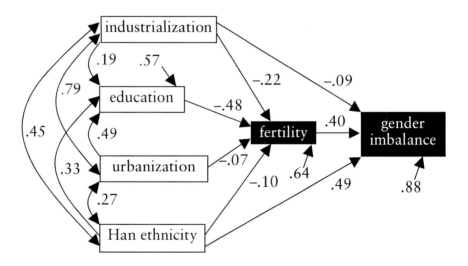

Source: SSA 2003a.
Note: All coefficients statistically significant at $p \leq .001$, two-tailed tests. N=2,870 county-level administrative units. Complete regression results on which this figure is based are in the appendix, table A3 (models 1 and 3). Descriptive characteristics of variables in this analysis are presented in the appendix, tables A1 and A2.

At the same time, figure 8.2 also reveals the unmistakable hallmarks of China-specific state policy on fertility. China's policy-induced demographic transition is reflected in the following two patterns. First, net of controls, Han ethnicity is negatively associated with fertility. Insofar as the policies target Han Chinese, the effect of ethnicity on fertility is a direct artifact of the policies. Second, net of controls, fertility and Han ethnicity have both contributed to China's child gender imbalance. Recall that because the 1.5-child policy imposes pressure on Han couples to produce a son within two attempts, secondborn children are far more likely to be boys than girls, meaning that the incremental addition of children incrementally skews the gender ratio. Thus, positive associations between fertility and child gender ratios and between Han ethnicity and child gender ratios are also direct artifacts of state policy.

The scatterplots in figure 8.3 serve two purposes. First, they provide a more detailed view of the relationships between industrialization and fertility (figure 8.3a) and between fertility and child gender ratios (figure 8.3b). Second, insofar as these associations also emerge from my household survey data (figures 8.3c and 8.3d), the census data lend credibility to step two of my analytical strategy. To be sure, gender ratios well below one hundred and well above one hundred and fifty in several of the survey sites reflect volatility unavoidable in small sample sizes. Nonetheless, not only do the relationships in my survey data closely mirror those in the census data, but the county survey sites (labeled by their provinces) are similarly arranged. In both the census and my survey, Jiangsu's Taicang County emerges as an extreme case of low fertility and a low boy/girl gender ratio. At the same time, in both sources of data, Shaanxi's Hengshan County and Henan's Ru'nan County appear on the high end of the fertility and gender imbalance distributions. Also, in support of step three (in which I will generalize from the survey data), figures 8.3a and 8.3b show that the six county survey sites span China's full economic and fertility spectra.

Step Two: Findings on Consequences of Fertility and Gender Ratios

Now we move to policy consequences, step two of my three-step plan of analysis. Whereas the path model in figure 8.2 ended with fertility and gender imbalance, the path model in figure 8.4 extends to their consequences. In other words, figure 8.4 picks up where figure 8.2 leaves off. Figure 8.4 replicates the negative effect of industrialization on both fertility and child gender imbalance, the negative effect of education on fertility, and the positive effect of fertility on child gender imbalance. It also shows that fertility exerted strong and positive effects on policy noncompliance, policy enforcement effort, and family planning disputes, and a positive indirect effect on discontent with village government. Let us consider each policy outcome in turn.

Figure 8.3 Scatterplots of Causes of Fertility and Child Gender Imbalance, Six Counties, Rural China, 2002, and All County-level Administrative Units, China, 2000

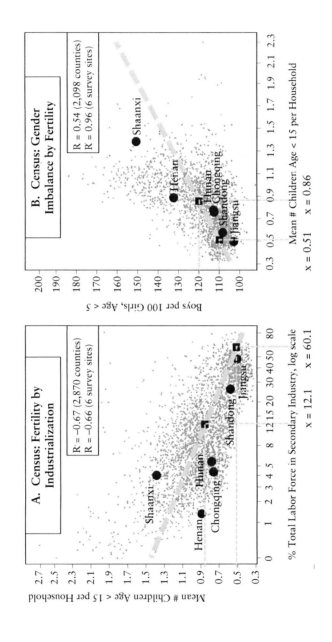

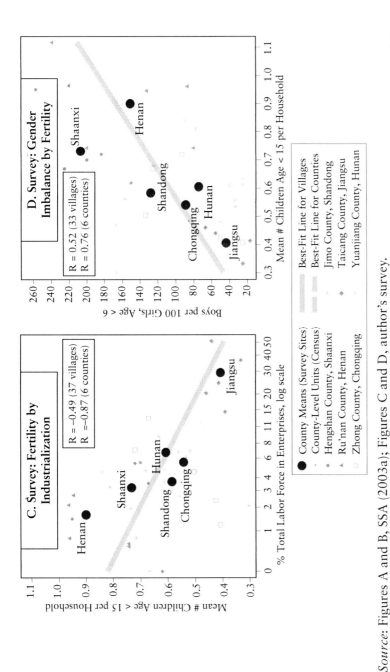

Source: Figures A and B, SSA (2003a); Figures C and D, author's survey.

Note: All correlations are statistically significant at $p \le 0.01$. Four of the thirty-seven village samples contain no children under age six. Figure B is limited to county-level units with Han populations accounting for more than 90 percent of the total.

Figure 8.4 Path Model of Consequences of Fertility and Child Gender Imbalance, Six Counties, Rural China, 2002 (standardized OLS regression coefficients)

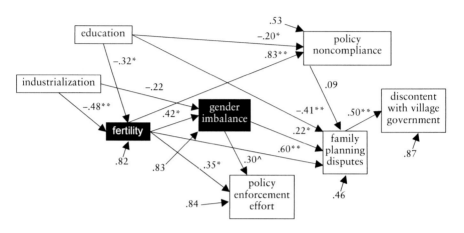

Source: Author's survey.
Note: ^ $p \leq 0.10$, * $p \leq 0.05$, ** $p \leq 0.01$, two-tailed tests. N=33 villages. Four of the thirty-seven village samples contain no children under age six. Complete regression results on which this figure is based are in the appendix, table A6 (models 1 and 4), table A7 (model 4), table A8 (model 2), and table A9 (models 1 and 4). Descriptive characteristics of variables in this analysis are presented in the appendix, tables A4 and A5.

Policy Enforcement

Overall, 28.3 percent of the surveyed households reported approaching villagers' committees for birth permits. But the likelihood of requesting a birth permit varied greatly according to the composition of children within households. Among households with no children under age six, among households with one child under age six, and among households with at least one child under age six and a total of at least two children, 24.0 percent, 46.9 percent, and 65.9 percent, respectively, reported approaching a villagers' committee for a birth permit.

In terms of policy enforcement efforts, processing birth permits comprised a nontrivial part of the work of the local government. Overall, birth-permit applications accounted for 13.8 percent of all reported instances of approaching villagers' committees. But in the high-fertility Shaanxi and Henan sites, birth permits accounted for 20.3 percent and 17.8 percent, respectively, of all reported encounters with villagers' committees.

Policy Noncompliance

According to my definition of policy noncompliance, 2.1 percent of all households, 14.7 percent of households with at least one child under age six, and 48.1 percent of all households with more than one child (at least one of whom was under age six) were presumed noncompliant. Figure 8.5a displays the close association between policy noncompliance and fertility. In the high-fertility Shaanxi and Henan sites, 3.0 percent and 7.6 percent of all households (figure 8.5a), 24.2 percent and 26.2 percent of all households with at least one child under age six, and 57.7 percent and 61.3 percent of households with more than one child (at least one of whom was under age six), respectively, were presumed noncompliant.

Family Planning Disputes

Disputes are another important means by which people encounter the state. Precisely 10 percent of all households in the survey reported family planning disputes. Among all households with at least one child under age six, 24.2 percent reported family planning disputes. And among all households with more than one child (at least one of whom was under age six), 51.1 percent reported family planning disputes. As before, the Shaanxi and Henan sites stand out as hotbeds of family planning conflict. In the Shaanxi samples, 12.4 percent of all households, 21.0 percent of all households with at least one child under age six, and 26.9 percent of all households with more than one child (at least one of whom was under age six), respectively, reported family planning disputes. Meanwhile, in the Henan samples, 28.9 percent of all households, 50.3 percent of all households with at least one child under age six, and 83.9 percent of all households with more than one child (at least one of whom was under age six), respectively, reported family planning disputes.

Figure 8.5b displays the close association between family planning disputes and policy noncompliance. However, the effect of policy noncompliance on family planning disputes is explained entirely by fertility. That is, the effect of policy noncompliance disappears when these variables are introduced into the analysis (see figure 8.4 and the appendix table A7). As we can see in figure 8.5c, the areas with the highest fertility levels are those with the highest incidence of family planning disputes.

If we consider birth-permit applications *and* family planning disputes together, the full extent to which policy enforcement put people in contact with the local state becomes even more apparent. Almost exactly one-third (32.5 percent) of all households reported one or both types of encounters with the local state over family planning disputes. In the high-fertility sites of Shaanxi and Henan, almost half (42.4 percent) and over half (53.3 percent), respectively, of all households reported one or both types of encounters.

Figure 8.5 Scatterplots of Consequences of Fertility, Six Counties, Rural China, 2002

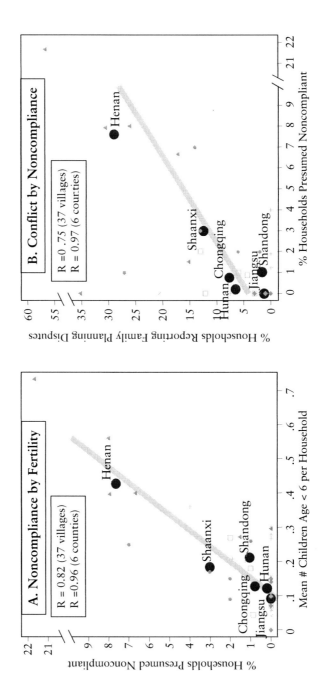

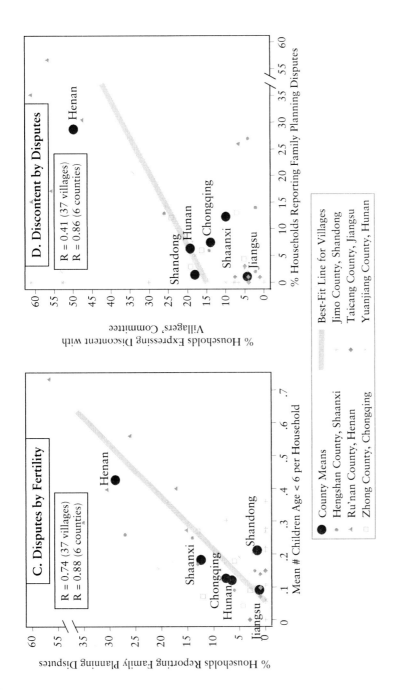

C. Disputes by Fertility

R = 0.74 (37 villages)
R = 0.88 (6 counties)

% Households Reporting Family Planning Disputes

Mean # Children Age < 6 per Household

Henan

Shaanxi

Chongqing
Hunan

Shandong

Jiangsu

D. Discontent by Disputes

R = 0.41 (37 villages)
R = 0.86 (6 counties)

% Households Expressing Discontent with Villagers' Committee

% Households Reporting Family Planning Disputes

Henan

Shandong
Hunan

Chongqing

Shaanxi

Jiangsu

County Means

Hengshan County, Shaanxi

Ru'nan County, Henan

Zhong County, Chongqing

Best-Fit Line for Villages

Jimo County, Shandong

Taicang County, Jiangsu

Yuanjiang County, Hunan

Source: Author's survey.

Note: Best-fit lines calculated before breaking axes. All correlations are statistically significant at $p \leq .01$.

Discontent with Local Government

The data also reveal that encounters with the local state in the context of family planning policy enforcement were often abrasive and antagonistic. Overall, 19.3 percent of respondents reported discontent with village government. Family planning disputes dramatically increased the probability of reporting such discontent. Respondents who reported family planning disputes were exactly two times more likely than respondents who did not report family planning disputes (35.3 percent versus 17.6 percent) to express discontent with the performance of the villagers' committee.

Figure 8.5d displays the correlation between planning disputes and discontent with the village government. Note that this relationship persists in household-level regression models that control for every other type of dispute, for life satisfaction (another dimension of discontent), for social connections to village leaders, and for other variables that could potentially explain it away. In other words, the strong relationship between family planning disputes and discontent with village government is robust to controls (details not reported). The Shaanxi survey sites appear anomalous. Despite their relatively high prevalence of family planning disputes, the Shaanxi samples were relatively upbeat about the village government. Perhaps the mere existence of a family planning dispute is not a sufficient condition of discontent with village government. Perhaps the manner in which village leaders handle such disputes—about which the survey collected no information—is also an important determinant of discontent.

Step Three: Discussion of Findings

In the final step of my analysis, I consider the prospects of future declines in policy enforcement efforts, policy noncompliance, family planning disputes, and discontent with village government even if the policies themselves do not change. This extrapolation exercise may be a "fool's errand" given that (1) the six county survey sites were not randomly selected and were therefore not intended to be representative of rural China as a whole, (2) there are well-known limitations of using cross-sectional data to project the future, and (3) there are imperfections of key measures (such as policy noncompliance) and obvious modeling limitations (including the possibility of endogeneity and unobserved correlates). Although the point estimates I report in this final step of my analysis are far less important than the strength and direction of the relationships I reported in steps one and two, I nonetheless venture this extrapolation exercise in order to establish a baseline for future research. My starting premise in this unorthodox exercise is that fertility will continue to decline in rural China.

Gender Imbalance

In 2000, had China's gender ratio been 110 boys instead of the observed 120 boys per 100 girls under age five, the population of "missing" girls would be

1.7 million less.[84] What would it take to reduce the gender ratio this much? According to the bivariate relationship depicted in figure 8.3b, a decline in fertility from 0.86 children to 0.51 children under age fifteen per household could produce such a gender ratio decline of 120 to 110 boys per 100 girls under age five. What would it take to reduce fertility from 0.86 children to 0.51 children under age 15 per household? According to the bivariate relationship depicted in figure 8.3a, an increase from 12.1 percent to 60.1 percent in the proportion of the labor force in manufacturing and construction could produce such a fertility drop. Of course such dramatic growth in the industrial labor force is unrealistic. Table 8.1a contains more realistic scenarios of change based on multiple regression models. If educational change is also factored in (an average increase from 8.0 to 10.5 years), then the proportion of the labor force in secondary industry need only increase to 27.0 percent in order to lower fertility by the same amount.

Turning to the number of children under age five per household, table 8.1b also shows that a decline from 0.21 to 0.08 could also lead to a gender ratio decline of 120 to 110 boys per 100 girls under age five. With respect to the conditions necessary for such a fertility drop, the census data suggest that rising average education (from 8.0 years to 11.2 years) and rising industrialization (from 2.4 percent to 37.0 percent of the labor force in secondary industry) could produce such a fertility decline. While such changes are probably beyond the realm of possibility in the near term, they are not far beyond reach. As we saw in figure 8.1, assuming rural industrialization proceeds according to recent trends, the proportion of the rural labor force in manufacturing or construction could approach 30 percent by 2015. In the remainder of this section I consider the consequences of a drop in fertility from 0.21 to 0.08 children under age five per household.

Policy Enforcement

By reducing policy noncompliance, continued fertility decline could reduce policy-enforcement efforts. Table 8.1c shows that a decline in the number of children under age five per household from 0.21 to 0.08 corresponds to a -19.6 percent change in policy enforcement efforts (that is, a decline in the number of birth-permit applications as a proportion of all reported encounters with villagers' committees from 13.8 percent to 11.1 percent).

Policy Noncompliance

If we draw straight vertical lines on figure 8.5a, connecting 0.21 and 0.08 on the x-axis to the best-fit regression line, we can see that such a fertility decline is associated with a drop in policy noncompliance from 2.2 percent to less than 0 percent. In other words, fertility decline could completely eliminate policy noncompliance. Table 8.1d confirms this self-evident implication of continued fertility decline.

Table 8.1 Estimated Causes and Consequences of Fertility Change

A. Causes of fertility change (Children under age 15 per household)

Source	Δ years of education from	to		Δ industrialization from	to		Δ kids/hh (age < 15) from	to		Δ boys per 100 girls from	to
Fig. 3B							.86	.51	=	120	110
Tab. A3, M3				−0.4%	13.0%	+	.86	.51	=	120	110
Tab. A3, M1	8.0	10.5	+	6.5%	27.0%	=	.86	.51			

B. Causes of fertility change (Children under age 5 per household)

Source	Δ years of education from	to		Δ industrialization from	to		Δ kids/hh (age < 5) from	to		Δ boys per 100 girls from	to
omitted							.21	.08	=	120	110
Tab. A3, M4				3.7%	32.9%	+	.21	.08	=	120	110
Tab. A3, M2	8.0	11.2	+	2.4%	37.0%	=	.21	.08			

C. Effect of fertility change (and concomitant changes) on policy enforcement effort

Source	Δ kids/hh (age < 6) from	to		Δ boys per 100 girls from	to		Δ enforcement efforts from	to
Tab. A6, M1	.21	.08	+	120	110	=	13.8%	11.1%

D. Effect of fertility change (and concomitant changes) on policy noncompliance

Source	Δ kids/hh (age<6) from	to		Δ boys per 100 girls from	to		Δ years of education from	to		Δ households noncompliant from	to
Fig. 5A	.21	.08	=							2.2%	-0.6%
Tab. A6, M3	.21	.08	+	120	110	=				2.1%	-0.8%
Tab. A6, M4	.21	.08	+				7.0	8.0	=	2.5%	-1.9%

E. Effect of fertility change (and concomitant changes) on family planning disputes

Source	Δ kids/hh (age <6) from	to		Δ boys per 100 girls from	to		Δ households noncompliant from	to		Δ family planning disputes from	to
Fig. 5B							2.5%	0.0%	=	10.1%	4.2%
Fig. 5C	.21	.08							=	9.6%	1.6%
Tab. A7, M4	.21	.08	+	120	110		2.5%	0.0%	=	9.7%	1.9%

F. Effect of fertility change (and concomitant changes) on discontent with villagers' committee

Source	Δ kids/hh (age <6) from	to		Δ family planning disputes from	to		Δ discontent with villagers' committee from	to
Fig. 5D			+	9.7%	1.9%	=	22.2%	16.8%
Tab. A8, M3	.21	.08		9.7%	1.9%	=	20.7%	13.7%

Source: Author's compilation.

Note: Calculated using postestimation procedures on linear regression models listed in the column labeled "source." Where unspecified, variable values are set to means presented in the appendix, tables A1 and A4.

Family Planning Disputes

The same exercise shows the possibility of a precipitous decline in the volume of family planning disputes. Assuming the above-derived changes in fertility, gender ratios, and policy noncompliance, the probability of experiencing a family planning dispute could change by as much as -80 percent. According to the best-fit regression line in figure 8.5b, values of 2.5 and 0.0 on the x-axis (policy noncompliance) correspond to values of 10.1 percent and 4.2 percent on the y-axis (family planning disputes). Likewise, in figure 8.5c, values of 0.21 and 0.08 on the x-axis (children under age five per household) correspond to values of 9.6 percent and 1.6 percent on the x-axis (family planning disputes).[85]

Discontent with Local Government

Finally, all the foregoing changes could culminate in dramatically lower levels of popular discontent with village government. The best-fit regression line in figure 8.5d shows that a decline from 9.7 percent to 1.9 percent in the incidence of family planning disputes is associated with a change of -24.3 percent in the incidence of expressing discontent with villagers' committees (from 22.2 percent to 16.8 percent). Table 8.1f, shows that, after adding fertility to the model, a change in the prevalence of discontent could be even greater (-33.8 percent, or from 20.7 percent to 13.7 percent).

Implications and Conclusions

The survey findings I have presented in this chapter suggest that, in 2002, the enforcement of family planning policies preoccupied local cadres in rural China to a great extent. A substantial share of their time and effort was devoted to processing birth permits and to rooting out and punishing policy violators. The family planning policies were a key state-society friction point, and among the most important reasons why villagers made contact with local government leaders. A significant share of state-society interaction was policy-induced and conflict-ridden. My findings reveal heavy policy costs in the form of administrative workloads strained by processing birth-permit requests and by punishing couples who give birth outside local quotas, and in the form of popular discontent with villagers' committees spawned by family planning disputes. In short, in 2002, more than twenty years after the family planning policies were first introduced to rural China, they were still sapping government efforts and energies and exacting a heavy toll on popular satisfaction with local government performance.

Given China's vast rural population, the sometimes modest percentages reported in this chapter translate into an enormous population. If the survey estimate of a 28.3 percent incidence of seeking the villagers' committee for a birth permit is accurate, then, conservatively speaking, fifty million Han households containing almost two hundred million people in rural China experienced such an encounter. Likewise, consider the survey estimate that 13.8 percent of all instances of seeking the villagers' committees were for birth-permit applications. Given the fact that there were 640,000 villagers' committees in China in 2005,[86] processing birth permits consumed a colossal amount of time and resources by any standard. A policy noncompliance rate of 2.1 percent between 1997 and 2002 conservatively translates into four million households containing fourteen million individuals. But our measure of noncompliance captures only a small portion of households at risk of coming into direct contact—including direct conflict—with the state because of family planning policy enforcement efforts. Given our estimate that 10 percent of rural Han households experienced family planning disputes, perhaps twenty million households and their sixty-eight million members in rural China were affected by such conflicts between 1997 and 2002. Finally, given that 19.3 percent of respondents were discontent with villagers' committees, perhaps as many as 131 million people in 35 million households were either themselves discontent with the villagers' committee or were living with other individuals who were discontent—in large part because of family planning policy enforcement.[87]

On the one hand, the foregoing extrapolations suggest that state-society conflicts stemming from family planning policy enforcement remain palpable and continue to foment popular discontent in rural China into the new millennium. On the other hand, however, the conditions demanding policy enforcement may be waning—hence recent debates and discussions among scholars and policymakers about the very necessity of the policies in their current form.[88] What would happen if the policies were rescinded? First, pressure to have a son in the first two attempts would be alleviated and the gender ratio at birth might begin to even out. Second, one of the most important sources of state-society friction and conflict in rural China would be eliminated. Third, family planning disputes would disappear altogether; tens of millions of individuals would be saved from experiencing family planning disputes. Finally, villagers' committees would experience a major boost in popularity as a major source of discontent with their performance would be eliminated.

If the nationwide abolishment of agricultural taxes in 2006 set a policy precedent, a similar move with family planning is not beyond the realm of possibility.[89] But even if the policies are not scrapped, this source of state-society conflict may still fade away by other means. As China continues to develop economically, farming will continue to diminish in importance relative to urban manufacturing and service-sector jobs. The labor-force changes depicted in figure 8.1 will continue to lower fertility in rural China, which in turn will alleviate family planning conflict. My survey data suggest that the fertility decline accompanying such changes[90] could reduce state-society conflict over family planning policy to a tiny fraction of its original volume, even in the absence of a family planning policy shift. Survey data collected after my 2002 survey support these predictions. In one study, villagers and cadres were asked to assess the amount of energy cadres devoted to different official tasks in 1997

213

and 2005. In rankings of official tasks according to time and effort spent by cadres, family planning dropped from first place to third place between these two points in time.[91]

Socioeconomic policies introduced since 2006 under the banners of "building a new socialist countryside" and "constructing a harmonious society," will likely accelerate the diminishing relevance of the family planning policies by strengthening rural social security and in so doing further weakening the importance of having a son for old-age support. Such policies include not only tax relief but also grain subsidies, the expansion of rural health insurance, the elimination of tuition and fees for basic-level education, the introduction of minimum living allowances for the childless elderly, and massive investments in medical and other infrastructure.[92]

In sum, if the findings I have presented in this chapter are at all accurate, family planning conflict will prove to be a growing pain. Socioeconomic change in rural China, by reducing fertility and—by extension—family planning disputes and discontent with village government, will reduce state-society friction and conflict regardless of whether or not the family planning policies are retooled or abandoned.

Notes

[1] The survey data on which this chapter is based were collected with the generous financial support of the Ford Foundation's Beijing office; for this I owe a special thanks to Phyllis Chang and Titi Liu. I would also like to thank Feng Shizheng, Guo Xinghua, Han Heng, Li Lulu, Liu Jingming, Lu Yilong, Shen Weiwei, Wang Ping, and Wang Xiaobei for administering the survey. This chapter has further benefited from the comments and suggestions of Laurel Bossen, Scott Rozelle, Leah VanWey, and Martin King Whyte.

[2] See John F. May, "Population Policy," in Dudley L. Poston and Michael Micklin, eds., *Handbook of Population* (New York: Kluwer Academic/Plenum, 2005), 827–52; and Tyrene White, *China's Longest Campaign: Birth Planning in the People's Republic, 1949–2005* (Ithaca and London: Cornell Univ. Press, 2006), 59.

[3] See Thomas Scharping, *Birth Control in China 1949–2000: Population Policy and Demographic Development* (London and New York: RoutledgeCurzon, 2003); Gu Baochang, Wang Feng, Guo Zhigang, and Zhang Erli, "China's Local and National Fertility Policies at the End of the Twentieth Century," *Population and Development Review* 33, no. 1 (2007): 129–48; and Susan E. Short and Zhai Fengying "Looking Locally at China's One-Child Policy," *Studies in Family Planning* 29, no. 4 (1998): 373–87.

[4] See Sulamith Heins Potter and Jack M. Potter, *China's Peasants: The Anthropology of a Revolution* (Cambridge and New York: Cambridge Univ. Press, 1990), 232.

[5] See Huang Shu-min, *The Spiral Road: Change in a Chinese Village through the Eyes of a Communist Party Leader* (Boulder, CO: Westview Press, 1989), 179–80.

[6] See Ma Rong, "Population Growth and Urbanization," in Robert E. Gamer, ed., *Understanding Contemporary China* (Boulder, CO and London: Lynne Rienner Publishers, 1999), 216; and Peng Xizhe, "Is it Time to Change China's Population Policy?" *China: An International Journal* 2, no. 1 (2004): 136.

[7] Gu et al., "China's Local and National Fertility Policies," 138.

[8] For a more thorough treatment of all the many exceptions to the one-child rule, see Yanzhong Huang and Dali L. Yang, "Population Control and State Coercion in China," in Barry Naughton and Dali L. Yang, eds., *Holding China Together: Diversity and National Integration in the Post-Deng Era* (Cambridge and New York: Cambridge Univ. Press, 2004), 193–225; Gu et al., "China's Local and National Fertility Policies"; and Short and Fengying, "Looking Locally at China's One-Child Policy," 373–87.

[9] See Chu Junhong "Prenatal Sex Determination and Sex-Selective Abortion in Rural Central China," *Population and Development Review* 27, no. 2 (2001): 264.

[10] See Gu et al., "China's Local and National Fertility Policies"; and Zeng Yi, "Options for Fertility Policy Transition in China," *Population and Development Review* 33, no. 2 (2007): 215–46.

[11] See Delia Davin, "The Single-Child Family Policy in the Countryside," in Elizabeth J. Croll, Delina Davin, and Penny Kane, eds., *China's One-Child Family Policy* (New York: St. Martin's Press, 1985), 66–8; Deborah Davis-Friedmann, "Old Age Security and the One-Child Campaign," in Croll, Davin, and Kane, eds., *China's One-Child Family Policy*, 149–61; Laurel Bossen, *Chinese Women and Rural Development: Sixty Years of Change in Lu Village, Yunnan* (Lanham, MD: Rowman & Littlefield, 2002), chapter 8; Rong, "Population Growth and Urbanization," 215; Potter and Potter, *China's Peasants*, 227–30; Gale D. Johnson, "Population and Economic Development," *China Economic Review* 10 (1999): 13; Lu Mai and Mingliang Feng, "Reforming the Welfare System in the People's Republic of China," *Asian Development Review* 25, no. 1/2 (2007): 65.

[12] Therese Hesketh, Li Lu, and Zhu Wei Xing, "The Effect of China's One-Child Family Policy after 25 Years," *New England Journal of Medicine* 353, no. 11 (2005): 1172.

[13] *Herald Sun*, "Less Growing Pains," March 23, 2006, 42.

[14] Julian L. Simon, "Family Planning Prospects in Less-Developed Countries, and a Cost-Benefit Analysis of Various Alternatives," *The Economic Journal* 80, no. 317 (1970): 58–71; Julian L. Simon, "On Aggregate Empirical Studies Relating Population Variables to Economic Development," *Population and Economic Development* 15, no. 2 (1989): 323–32; Ismail Sirageldin and Samuel Hopkins, "Family Planning Programs: An Economic Approach," *Studies in Family Planning* 3, no. 2 (1972): 17–24.

[15] Li Hongbin and Junsen Zhang, "Do High Birth Rates Hamper Economic Growth?" *The Review of Economics and Statistics* 89, no. 1 (2007): 110–17.

[16] Malcolm Potts, "China's One Child Policy: The Policy that Changed the World," *British Medical Journal* 333, no. 7564 (2006): 361.

[17] John Cleland, Stan Bernstein, Alex Ezeh, Anibal Faundes, Anna Glasier, and Jolene Innis, "Family Planning: The Unfinished Agenda," *The Lancet* 368, no. 9549 (2006): 1814.

[18] Darren Samuelsohn, "Bush-Led Talks Spark Diplomats' Debate over Post-Kyoto," *Environment and Energy Daily*, September 27, 2007; also see Debra Kahn, "Chinese Bid to Cast One-Child Policy as Emissions Curb Raises Eyebrows," *Greenwire*, October 4, 2007.

[19] Kenneth Hill and Dawn M. Upchurch, "Gender Differences in Child Health: Evidence from the Demographic and Health Surveys," *Population and Development Review* 21, no. 1 (1995): 127–51; Elizabeth Croll, *Endangered Daughters: Discrimination and Development in Asia* (New York: Routledge, 2000).

[20] Elizabeth Perry, *Challenging the Mandate of Heaven: Social Protest and State Power in China* (Armonk, NY: M.E. Sharpe, 2001), 5–6; Zeng, "Options for Fertility Policy," 230.

[21] Wu Jiao, "Elderly Becoming Increasingly Isolated," *China Daily*, December 18, 2007, www.chinadaily.com.cn/china/2007-12/18/content_6328105.htm.

[22] Wang Dewen, "China's Urban and Rural Old Age Security System: Challenges and Options," *China & World Economy* 14, no. 1 (2006): 109–10.

[23] UNDP (United Nations Development Programme), *Study on the Rural Social Security System in China*, Report prepared jointly by China's National Social Security Institute and the Ministry of Labour and Social Security: 33 (2007), www.undp.org.cn/monitordocs/56779.pdf.

[24] See Zeng, "Options for Fertility Policy," 230.

[25] Li Shuzhuo, "Imbalanced Sex Ratio at Birth and Comprehensive Intervention in China," Paper presented at Fourth Asia Pacific Conference on Reproductive and Sexual Health and Rights, October 29–31, 2007, Hyderabad, India.

[26] Ansley J. Coale and Judith Banister, "Five Decades of Missing Females in China," *Demography* 31, no. 3 (1994): 459–79; Judith Banister, "Shortage of Girls in China Today," *Journal of Population Research* 21, no. 1 (2004): 19–45; Wu Juan and Carol S. Walther, "The Impact of Sex Preference on Induced Abortion," in Dudley L. Poston, Jr., Che-Fu Lee, Chiung-Fang Chang, Sherry L. McKibben, and Carol S. Walther, eds., *Fertility, Family Planning, and Population Policy in China* (London and New York: Routledge, 2006); Yong Cai and William Lavely, "China's Missing Girls: Numerical Estimates and Effects on Population Growth," *The China Review* 3, no. 2 (2003): 13–29; Wu Zhuochun, Kirsi Viisainen, and Elina Hemminki, "Determinants of High Sex Ratio among Newborns: A Cohort Study from Rural Anhui Province, China," *Reproductive Health Matters* 14, no. 27 (2006): 172–80.

[27] Zeng Yi, Tu Ping, Gu Baochang, Xu Yi, Li Bohua, and Li Yongpiing, "Causes and Implications of the Recent Increase in the Reported Sex Ratio at Birth in China," *Population and Development Review* 19, no. 2 (1993): 283–302; Qian Zhenchao, "Progression to Second Birth in China: A Study of Four Rural Counties," *Population Studies* 5, no. 12 (1997): 221–8; Chu, "Prenatal Sex Determination," 259–81; Croll, *Endangered Daughters*, chapter 1, 71–74; Bossen, *Chinese Women and Rural Development*, 289–90; and Laurel Bossen, "Forty Million Missing Girls: Land, Population Controls and Sex Imbalance in Rural China," *ZNET* 7 (October 2005), www.zmag.org/content/print_article.cfm?itemID=8891&sectionID=1; *Current Events*, "Boy Troubles: Will Too Many Males Spell Disaster for China?" 104, no. 6 (2004): 1–3; Rachel Murphy, "Fertility and Distorted Sex Ratios in a Rural Chinese County: Culture, State, and Policy," *Population and Development Review* 29, no. 4 (2003): 595–626; Kay Ann Johnson, *Wanting a Daughter, Needing a Son: Abandonment, Adoption, and Orphanage Care in China* (St. Paul, MN: Yeong & Yeong Book Company, 2004); Robert Marquand, "China Faces Future as Land of Boys," *Christian Science Monitor*, September 3, 2004: 1; Peng, "Is it Time to Change China's Population Policy?" 135–49; Hesketh, Li, and Zhu, "The Effect of China's One-Child Family Policy," 1171–6; Yanzhong Huang and Dali L. Yang, "China's Unbalanced Sex Ratios: Politics and Policy Response," *The Chinese Historical Review* 13, no. 1 (2006): 1–15; Dudley L. Poston Jr. and Karen S. Glover, "Too Many Males: Marriage Market Implications of Gender Imbalances in China," *Genus* 61, no. 2 (2005): 119–40; Dudley L. Poston Jr., and Karen S. Glover, "The Managed Fertility Transition in Rural China and Implications for the Future of China's Population," in Poston et al., *Fertility, Family Planning, and Population Policy in China*, 172–86; Wu, Viisainen, and Hemminki, "Determinants of High Sex Ratio among Newborns," 172–80; and Li, "Imbalanced Sex Ratio at Birth."

[28] *Current Events*, "Boy Troubles," 1–3; Yu Da, "A Shortage of Girls: Traditional Views that Say that Men are Superior to Women Still Prevail, Leading to a Gender

Imbalance in Births," *Beijing Review* 47, no. 27 (2004): 29; Chu, "Prenatal Sex Determination," 259–81; Bossen, "Forty Million Missing Girls."

[29] See Zeng, "Options for Fertility Policy," 230.

[30] Yu, "A Shortage of Girls," 28.

[31] Liu Hongyan, "Analysis of Sex Ratio at Birth in China," *China Population Today* (October 2004): 32–6.

[32] Qian, "Progression to Second Birth in China," 221–8; Coale and Banister, "Five Decades of Missing Females in China"; Yu, "A Shortage of Girls," 28; Wu, Viisainen, and Hemminki, "Determinants of High Sex Ratio among Newborns," 176; Chu, "Prenatal Sex Determination," 271–2; Li, "Imbalanced Sex Ratio."

[33] Zeng, "Options for Fertility Policy," 229.

[34] Yu, "A Shortage of Girls," 29; Marquand, "China Faces Future as Land of Boys," 1.

[35] Yu, "A Shortage of Girls," 28.

[36] BBC (British Broadcasting Corporation), "CPPCC Official Warns Gender Screening 'Threat' to Society," BBC Monitoring Service, reported March 8, citing the Xinhua News Agency, March 7, 2004.

[37] Andrea den Boer and Valerie M. Hudson, "The Security Threat of Asia's Sex Ratios," *SAIS Review* 24, no. 2 (2004): 27–43; Huang and Yang, "China's Unbalanced Sex Ratios," 7–8; Lena Edlund, Hongbin Li, Junjian Yi, and Junsen Zhang, "Sex Ratios and Crime: Evidence from China's One-Child Policy," IZA Discussion Paper No. 3214 (2007), ftp://repec.iza.org/RePEc/Discussionpaper/dp3214.pdf.

[38] Merli, Qian, and Smith, "Adaptation of a Political Bureaucracy," 242–43; Wu, Viisainen, and Hemminki, "Determinants of High Sex Ratio among Newborns," 173, 177; and Potter and Potter, *China's Peasants*, 233–34.

[39] Maria Edin, "State Capacity and Local Agent Control in China: CCP Cadre Management from a Township Perspective," *The China Quarterly* 173 (2003): 35–52; Giovanna M. Merli, Zhenchao Qian, and Herbert L. Smith, "Adaptation of a Political Bureaucracy to Economic and Institutional Change Under Socialism: The Chinese State Family Planning System," *Politics & Society* 32, no. 2 (2004): 231–56; Huang and Yang, "Population Control and State Coercion in China," 206.

[40] Li Jiali, "China's One-Child Policy: How and How Well has it Worked? A Case Study of Hebei Province, 1979–88," *Population and Development Review* 21, no. 3 (1995): 563–85; Scharping, *Birth Control in China*, 94–104.

[41] Li, "China's One-Child Policy,"

[42] Wu, Viisainen, and Hemminki, "Determinants of High Sex Ratio among Newborns."

[43] Tyrene White, "Domination, Resistance and Accommodation in China's One-Child Campaign," 183–203, in Elizabeth J. Perry and Mark Selden, eds., *Chinese Society: Change, Conflict and Resistance, Second Edition* (London and New York: Routledge Curzon, 2003), 134–48; Potter and Potter, *China's Peasants*, 234–44.

[44] Lucien Bianco and Hua Chang-ming, "Implementation and Resistance: The Single-Child Family Policy," in Stephan Feuchtwang, Athar Hussein, and Thierry Pairault, eds., *Transforming China's Economy in the Eighties, vol. 1: The Rural Sector, Welfare and Employment* (Boulder, CO: Westview Press, 1988), 147–68.

[45] Potter and Potter, *China's Peasants*, 242.

[46] Huang, *The Spiral Road*, 182.

[47] Susan Greenhalgh and Edwin A. Winckler, *Governing China's Population: From Leninist to Neoliberal Biopolitics* (Stanford, CA: Stanford Univ. Press, 2005),

208; Huang, *The Spiral Road*, 181; Huang and Yang, "Population Control and State Coercion in China"; Margery Wolf, *Revolution Postponed: Women in Contemporary China* (Stanford, CA: Stanford Univ. Press, 1985), 258–9.

[48] Huang, *The Spiral Road*, 181; Huang and Yang "Population Control and State Coercion in China"; Wolf, *Revolution Postponed*, 258–9.

[49] John S. Aird, *Slaughter of the Innocents: Coercive Birth Control in China* (Washington, D.C.: The AIE Press, 1990), 17; Greenhalgh and Winckler, *Governing China's Population*, 206; Nancy E. Riley, "China's Population: New Trends and Challenges," *Population Bulletin* 59, no. 2 (2004): 19.

[50] White, "Domination, Resistance and Accommodation," 177–83.

[51] Huang, *The Spiral Road*, 179.

[52] Davin, "The Single-Child Family Policy in the Countryside," 72; Huang and Yang, "Population Control and State Coercion in China," 208.

[53] White, *China's Longest Campaign*, 193–6; Huang, *The Spiral Road*.

[54] Dali L. Yang, *Calamity and Reform in China: State, Rural Society, and Institutional Change since the Great Leap Famine* (Stanford, CA: Stanford Univ. Press, 1996), 192.

[55] Davin, "The Single-Child Family Policy in the Countryside," 71; White, "Domination, Resistance and Accommodation," 257; Scharping, *Birth Control in China*, 225; Huang and Yang, "Population Control and State Coercion in China," 218; Jeffrey Wasserstrom, "Resistance to the One-Child Family," *Modern China* 10, no. 3 (1984): 257; Riley, "China's Population," 19.

[56] Bianco and Hua, "Implementation and Resistance," 149.

[57] Scharping, *Birth Control in China*, 226.

[58] Kevin J. O'Brien and Lianjiang Li, *Rightful Resistance in Rural China* (Cambridge and New York: Cambridge Univ. Press, 2006), 8n6; White, *China's Longest Campaign*, 198.

[59] Also see Jonathan Watts, "Villagers Riot as China Enforces Birth Limit: Official Beaten by Crowd in South-Western Province," *The Guardian*, May 22, 2007, 22; and Clarissa Oon, "Anger in China's Villages: Residents Strike Out in Violence against Harsh Family Planning Campaign," *The Straits Times*, June 4, 2007.

[60] White, *China's Longest Campaign*, 164–9.

[61] Peng, "Is it Time to Change China's Population Policy?" 135–49; Hesketh, Li, and Zhu, "The Effect of China's One-Child Family Policy"; Zeng "Options for Fertility Policy"; Ching-Ching Ni, "Questions Raised over Future of China's One-Child Policy," *Los Angeles Times*, March 4, 2008, A6; Jane MacArtney, "Bring on the Girls: China Offers Hope of Sisters for Generation of Only Children," *The Times*, February 29, 2008, 35.

[62] John Wong, "China's Sharply Declining Fertility: Implications for its Population Policy," *Issues & Studies* 37, no. 3 (2001): 68–86; Scharping, *Birth Control in China*, 249–87.

[63] SSA (State Statistical Administration), *2006 Zhongguo Tongji Nianjian* [2006 China Statistical Yearbook)] (Beijing: Guojia Tongji Chubanshe, 2007), table 13-4.

[64] Johnson, "Population and Economic Development"; Dudley L. Poston, "Social and Economic Development and the Fertility Transitions in Mainland China," *Population and Development Review* 26 (2000) (Supplement: Population and Economic Change in East Asia): 40–60; Paresh Kumar Narayan and Xiujian Peng, "An Econometric Analysis of the Determinants of Fertility for China, 1952–2000," *Journal of Chinese Economic and Business Studies* 4, no. 2 (2006): 165–83.

[65] Alan deBrauw, Jikun Huang, and Scott Rozelle, "The Sequencing of Reforms in China's Agricultural Transition," *Economics of Transition* 12, no. 3 (2004): 235–6.

[66] Poston, "Social and Economic Development"; Narayan and Peng, "An Econometric Analysis of the Determinants of Fertility"; Zeng "Options for Fertility Policy"; Zhang Hong, "From Resisting to 'Embracing?' the One-Child Rule: Understanding New Fertility Trends in a Central China Village," *The China Quarterly* 192 (2007): 855–75.

[67] Alice Goldstein, Michael White, and Sidney Goldstein, "Migration, Fertility, and State Policy in Hubei Province, China," *Demography* 34, no. 4 (1997): 481–91; You Xiuhong and Dudley L. Poston, Jr., "The Effect of Floating Migration on Fertility," in Poston et al., *Fertility, Family Planning, and Population Policy in China*, 127–44.

[68] Jean C. Oi, *State and Peasant in Contemporary China: The Political Economy of Village Government* (Berkeley, CA: Univ. of California Press, 1989).

[69] See Merli, Qian, and Smith "Adaptation of a Political Bureaucracy," 237; but for recent trends also see Kim Singer, Scott Rozelle, Jean Oi, Lixiu Zhang, and Renfu Luo, "The Forgotten Side of the China Development Model: How is China Sustaining the Countryside in an Industry-First Development Strategy?" Paper presented to the Sixth International Symposium of the Center for China-US Cooperation, "Washington Consensus' Versus 'Beijing Consensus': Sustainability of China's Development Model, May 30–31, 2008, Denver, Colorado.

[70] Scharping, *Birth Control in China*, 221–3.

[71] Greenhalgh and Winckler, *Governing China's Population*, 172–6.

[72] Li, "Imbalanced Sex Ratio at Birth."

[73] Alice Yan, "One-Child Policy Adherents Rewarded," *South China Morning Post*, August 9, 2004, 5

[74] BBC (British Broadcast Corporation), "Chinese Given Perks to Have Girls: A Pilot Programme in Rural China is Offering Cash and Other Incentives to Families Who Have Daughters," BBC News, August 12, 2004; Jim Yardley, "Fearing Future, China Starts to Give Girls Their Due" *The New York Times*, January 31, 2005, A3.

[75] Throughout this chapter I refer to the six survey sites as counties even though, from an administrative standpoint, three are municipalities.

[76] SSA, *2000 Nian Renkou Pucha Fenxian Ziliao* [2000 Population Census Material Disaggregated by County], Electronic Edition (Beijing: Guojia Tongji Chubanshe, 2003).

[77] Census data permit me to aggregate children into an age <5 category (by using the age <1 and age 1–4 categories). I aggregate my household survey data into an age <6 category because, given that not a single baby recorded by the survey was reported as zero years old, I suspect many if not most survey respondents reported nominal age (*xu sui*, adding a year at birth and adding a year at each subsequent lunar New Year) as opposed to calendar age (*zheng sui*).

[78] Huang and Yang, "Population Control and State Coercion in China"; Gu et al., "China's Local and National Fertility Policies," 129–48.

[79] According to the 2000 census data, only 0.6 percent of the total population in the surveyed counties was non-Han. (Most of the non-Han people in these counties belong to the Shui nationality and were concentrated in Chongqing's Zhong County.)

[80] More specifically, "content" is defined as a response of "somewhat satisfied" or "very satisfied" to the first item *or* a response of "some respect" or "great respect" to the second item. "Discontent" is defined as an answer of either "somewhat dissatisfied" or "very dissatisfied" to the first item *or* an answer of either "some disrespect" or "great disrespect" to the second item. "Neither content nor discontent" is defined as providing this response to both items (the only possible way to avoid falling into the "discontent" and "content" categories) or as providing contradictory responses to the two items

(which happened in only 6 percent of all interviews).

[81] SSA, *2000 Nian Renkou Pucha Fenxian Ziliao.*

[82] Cai and Lavely ("China's Missing Girls") estimate that about two-thirds of "nominally missing" girls are "truly missing." The difference is accounted for by girls who are concealed by their families and unreported in the census. Because male mortality rates are greater than female mortality rates (Poston and Glover, "Too Many Males," 123), I use 105 as the "natural" gender ratio at age 0 to 5 instead of Cai and Lavely's ("China's Missing Girls," 16) value of 106 at birth.

[83] For example, John Bongaarts and Susan Cotts Watkins, "Social Interactions and Contemporary Fertility Transitions," *Population and Development Review* 22, no. 4 (1996): 639–82; Griffith Feeney, "Fertility Decline in East Asia," *Science* 266, no. 5190 (1994): 1518–23; Karen Oppenheim Mason, "Explaining Fertility Transitions," *Demography* 34, no. 4 (1997): 443–54.

[84] Assuming the number of boys under age five remained constant at 37.6 million, a ratio of 110 boys to 100 girls would have meant 34.2 million girls instead of the observed 31.3 million girls. Meanwhile, as we saw earlier, had the gender ratio been the "natural" 105 boys per 100 girls, the population of girls under age five would have been 35.9 million.

[85] Table 8.1e, shows that these patterns persist in multiple regression models.

[86] SSA, *2006 Zhongguo Tongji Nianjian*, table 13-1.

[87] The above population extrapolations assume that 181.2 million Han rural households and their 678.8 individual members were at risk. I limit the population at risk to the Han rural population because the survey data on which the estimates are based were collected in areas of rural China that are almost exclusively Han. According to the 2000 census tabulations, 91.5 percent of the total population was Han, and 63.1 percent of the total population resided in rural areas. To ensure my estimates are conservative, I assume that the entire non-Han population resides in rural areas. Subtracting the non-Han population from the total rural population yields an estimated 86.6 percent Han population in rural China. Multiplying 86.6 percent by the actual total rural population of 783.8 million individuals in 209.2 million households (in the year 2000) yields my conservative estimates of the number of Han individuals and households at risk. Owing to the fact that non-Han households are, on average, larger than Han households, my estimated number of households at risk (181.2 million) is even more conservative (that is, *ceteris paribus*, a Han population will be distributed among more households than a non-Han population of the same size).

[88] Peng, "Is it Time to Change China's Population Policy?"; Hesketh, Li, and Lu, "The Effect of China's One-Child Family Policy"; Zeng, "Options for Fertility Policy"; Ni, "Questions Raised over Future of China's One-Child Policy"; MacArtney, "Bring on the Girls."

[89] Edward Cody, "In Face of Rural Unrest, China Rolls Out Reforms," *Washington Post*, January 28, A01; Kennedy, "From the Fee-for-Tax Reform to the Abolition of Agricultural Taxes."

[90] Also see White, "Domination, Resistance and Accommodation," 165–7; and Wong, "China's Sharply Declining Fertility," 80.

[91] I thank Scott Rozelle for allowing me to cite this unpublished finding.

[92] Cheng Chu-Yuan, "China's New Development Plan: Strategy, Agenda, and Prospects," *Asian Affairs: An American Review* 34, no. 1 (2007): 47–59; Lu and Feng, "Reforming the Welfare System, 58–80.

Statistical Appendix

Table 8.A1 Descriptive Characteristics of Variables, All County-level Administrative Units, China, 2000

	Mean	St. Dev.	Min.	Max.
Fertility				
Mean # children (age<15) per household	0.884	0.320	0.325	2.660
Mean # children (age<5) per household	0.222	0.100	0.056	0.892
Gender imbalance				
Boys per 100 girls (age<5)	116.633	13.770	89.666	197.291
Education				
Mean years of education (age>6)	7.432	1.514	0.634	11.848
Industrialization				
% Total labor force in secondary industry	16.793	15.931	0.000	81.180
% Total labor force in secondary industry (log)	2.470	0.939	0.000	4.409
% Population Han				
% Total population Han	83.835	28.979	0.219	100.000
Urbanization				
% Total population urban residents	38.430	31.685	0.000	100.000

Source: SSA 2003a.
Note: N=2,870 county-level administrative units.

Table 8.A2 Correlation Matrix of Variables, All County-level Administrative Units, China, 2000

	A	B	C	D	E	F	G
A. Mean # children (age<15) per household	1.00						
B. Mean # children (age<5) per household	0.90	1.00					
C. Boys per 100 girls (age<5)	0.23	0.02	1.00				
D. Mean years of education (age>6)	-0.74	-0.73	0.00	1.00			
E. % Total labor force in secondary industry (log)	-0.67	-0.57	-0.14	0.73	1.00		
F. % Total population Han	-0.48	-0.59	0.25	0.55	0.45	1.00	
G. % Total population urban residents	-0.62	-0.48	-0.19	0.73	0.79	0.27	1.00

Source: SSA 2003a.
Note: N=2,870 county-level administrative units.

Table 8.A3 Determinants of Fertility and Gender Imbalance, All County-level Administrative Units, China, 2000 (unstandardized OLS regression coefficients)

| | Fertility (kids/hh) (×100) | | Gender imbalance | |
| | (Age<15) | (Age<5) | | |
	Model 1	Model 2	Model 3	Model 4
% Total population Han	-0.115**	-0.090**	0.232**	0.213**
	(0.017)	(0.005)	(0.009)	(0.010)
% Total population urban residents	-0.071*			
	(0.022)			
% Total labor force in secondary industry (log)	-7.468**	-0.651**	-1.285**	-3.880**
	(0.729)	(0.186)	(0.330)	(0.312)
Mean years of education (age>6)	-1.081**	-3.571**		
	(0.445)	(0.124)		
Mean # children (age<15) per household			17.334**	
			(0.987)	
Mean # children (age<5) per household				17.893**
				(3.247)
Constant	194.097**	57.895**	85.055**	104.370**
	(2.355)	(0.624)	(1.731)	(1.648)
R^2	0.595	0.585	0.226	0.152
Adjusted R^2	0.594	0.585	0.226	0.151

Source: SSA 2003a.
Note: * $p \leq 0.01$, ** $p \leq 0.001$, two-tailed tests. Standard errors in parentheses. N=2,870 county-level administrative units. "Fertility" is measured as the mean number of children per household. "Gender imbalance" is measured as the number of boys per hundred girls under age five. Urbanization removed from model 2 owing to multicollinearity (causing the effect to flip direction from negative in a bivariate model to positive in a multivariate model).

Table 8.A4 Descriptive Characteristics of Variables, Six Counties, Rural China, 2002

	Mean	St. Dev.	Min.	Max.
Discontent with village government				
% Households expressing discontent with villagers' committee	20.967	20.590	1.042	61.111
Family planning disputes				
% Households reporting family planning dispute	9.903	12.976	0.000	56.667
Policy enforcement effort				
% Reported encounters with villagers' committee for birth permit applications	13.873	8.000	2.837	33.784
Policy noncompliance				
% Households presumed policy violators	2.243	4.233	0.000	21.667
Fertility				
Mean # children per household (age<15)	0.646	0.199	0.304	1.117
Mean # children per household (age<6)	0.219	0.150	0.040	0.733
Gender imbalance				
Boys per 100 girls (age<6)	115.740	77.000	16.667	266.667
Education				
Mean years of education (age>6)	7.348	0.614	6.212	8.706
Industrialization				
% Total labor force in enterprises	7.756	10.891	0.000	50.970
% Total labor force in enterprises (log)	1.700	.926	0.000	3.951

Source: Author's survey.
Note: N=33 villages. Four of the thirty-seven village samples contain no children under age six.

Table 8.A5 Correlation Matrix of Variables, Six Counties, Rural China, 2002

	A	B	C	D	E	F	G	H
A. Mean # children (age<15) per household	1.00							
B. Mean # children (age<6) per household	0.75	1.00						
C. Boys per 100 girls (age<6)	0.52	0.41	1.00					
D. Mean years of education (age>6)	-0.30	0.05	-0.07	1.00				
E. % total labor force in enterprises (log)	-0.48	-0.38	-0.42	-0.02	1.00			
F. Policy noncompliance	0.68	0.82	0.47	-0.15	-0.33	1.00		
G. Policy enforcement effort	0.49	0.48	0.44	0.03	-0.17	0.53	1.00	
H. Family planning disputes	0.71	0.73	0.53	-0.41	-0.31	0.74	0.31	1.00
I. Discontent with villagers' committee	0.46	0.41	0.21	-0.34	-0.29	0.31	0.13	0.50

Source: Author's survey.
Note: N=33 villages. Four of the thirty-seven village samples contain no children under age six.

Table 8.A6 Determinants of Family Planning Policy Noncompliance and Enforcement Effort, Six Counties, Rural China, 2002 (unstandardized OLS regression coefficients)

	Policy enforcement effort	% Policy noncompliance		
	Model 1	Model 2	Model 3	Model 4
Boys per 100 girls (age<6)	0.031^	0.026**	0.009	
	(0.017)	(0.009)	(0.006)	
Mean # children (age<6) per household	18.919*		21.466***	23.602***
	(8.926)		(3.088)	(2.747)
Mean years of education (age>6)				-1.351*
				(.700)
Constant	6.130*	-.745	-3.479***	7.012
	(2.470)	(1.206)	(0.855)	(4.942)
R^2	0.301	0.221	0.701	0.718
Adjusted R^2	0.255	0.195	.682	0.699

Source: Author's survey.
Note: ^ $p \leq 0.10$, * $p \leq 0.05$, ** $p \leq 0.01$, *** $p \leq 0.001$, two-tailed tests. Standard errors in parentheses. N=33 villages. Four of the thirty-seven village samples contain no children under age six.

Table 8.A7 Determinants of Family Planning Disputes, Six Counties, Rural China, 2002 (unstandardized OLS regression coefficients)

	Model 1	Model 2	Model 3	Model 4
% Households presumed noncompliant	2.277***	1.317*	1.027	0.263
	(0.369)	(0.627)	(0.627)	(0.519)
Mean # children (age<6) per household		32.965^	31.825^	51.652***
		(17.733)	(17.146)	(14.112)
Boys per 100 girls (age<6)			0.038^	0.037*
			(0.021)	(0.017)
Mean years of education (age>6)				-8.719***
				(1.969)
Constant	4.795**	-0.258	-3.737	57.821***
	(1.745)	(3.196)	(3.659)	(14.193)
R^2	0.552	0.598	0.637	0.787
Adjusted R^2	0.537	0.571	0.600	0.756

Source: Author's survey.
Note: ^ $p \leq 0.10$, * $p \leq 0.05$, ** $p \leq 0.01$, *** $p \leq 0.001$, two-tailed tests. Standard errors in parentheses. $N=33$ villages. Four of the thirty-seven village samples contain no children under age six. Dependent variable is "% households reporting family planning disputes."

Table 8.A8 Determinants of Discontent with Village Government, Six Counties, Rural China, 2002 (unstandardized OLS regression coefficients)

	Model 1	Model 2	Model 3
Mean # children per household (age<6)	56.255*		13.086
	(22.556)		(32.019)
Family planning dispute in past 5 years		0.789**	0.678^
		(0.247)	(0.369)
Constant	8.666	13.155**	11.391^
	(5.947)	(3.998)	(5.921)
R^2	0.167	0.247	0.251
Adjusted R^2	0.140	0.223	0.201

Source: Author's survey.
Note: ^ $p \leq 0.10$ * $p \leq 0.05$ ** $p \leq 0.01$, two-tailed tests. Standard errors in parentheses. $N=33$ villages. Four of the thirty-seven village samples contain no children under age six. Dependent variable is "% households expressing discontent with villagers' committee."

Table 8.A9 Determinants of Fertility and Gender Imbalance, Six Counties, Rural China, 2002 (unstandardized OLS regression coefficients)

	Fertility (Kids/HH)		Gender Imbalance		
	Age<15	Age<6			
	Model 1	Model 2	Model 3	Model 4	Model 5
% Total labor force in enterprises (log)	-0.104**	-0.061*	-34.582*	-18.076	-25.490^
	(0.032)	(0.027)	(13.579)	(14.370)	(14.232)
Mean years of education (age>6)	-0.101*	0.011			
	(0.049)	(0.041)			
Mean # children (age<15) per household				161.210*	
				(66.873)	
Mean # children (age<6) per household					149.505^
					(88.092)
Constant	1.566***	0.244	174.540***	42.356	126.389**
	(0.364)	(0.308)	(26.200)	(6.006)	(38.107)
R²	0.325	0.144	0.173	0.307	0.246
Adjusted R²	0.280	0.087	0.146	0.261	0.195

Source: Author's survey.
Note: * $p \le$ -0.05 ** $p \le 0.01$ *** $p \le 0.001$, two-tailed tests. Standard errors in parentheses. N=33 villages. Four of the thirty-seven village samples contain no children under age six. Education omitted from "gender imbalance" models owing to multicollinearity (causing the effect to flip direction from negative in a bivariate model to positive in a multivariate model).

PUBLIC GOODS AND CITIZEN REACTION

KAN BING NAN, KAN BING GUI: CHALLENGES FOR CHINA'S HEALTH-CARE SYSTEM THIRTY YEARS INTO REFORM

Karen Eggleston[1]

Virtually all recent research and commentary on China's health-care system—both in China and abroad—opens with some reference to *kan bing nan, kan bing gui,* the ubiquitous lament among patients in the People's Republic of China (PRC). Translated as "getting medical care is difficult and expensive," this phrase appears prominently both in the PRC's outline of the Eleventh Five-year Plan for national economic and social development and in the 2009 national health system reform plan.[2] According to the Implementation Plan for 2009–2011, "the implementation of the five priority reform programs aims at effectively solving the problem of 'difficult and costly access to health care services,' which arouses intense public concerns."[3] In a national poll of more than three thousand people in 2005, the top five problems reported were health care (*kan bing nan, kan bing gui*) (75 percent), followed by income inequalities (67 percent), corruption (62 percent), educational expenses (58 percent), and social security (48 percent). Polls in 2008 reflected a similar emphasis on health care.[4] In fact, in 2005 a research institute under the state council issued a report stating that China's health-care reforms had been "basically a failure"—earning these reforms the dubious distinction of being the only major policy labeled a failure by a government agency.[5]

Outside views of China's health-system reforms, including systems for assuring food and product safety, have been equally unflattering, evoking concern about a crisis or collapse that threatens both China's social fabric and the health of global consumers.[6] The severe acute respiratory syndrome (SARS) epidemic in 2003 in particular focused an international spotlight on problems in China's health sector. More recent outbreaks of avian influenza have done little to quell fears of China spawning "superbugs" that threaten global public health.[7] The head of China's State Food and Drug Administration (SFDA) was sentenced to death for corruption in 2007. Numerous product recalls have alarmed consumers. If China is to maintain the enhanced international profile it earned as host of the 2008 Summer Olympics and safeguard the reputation of the "Made in China" label, it must address the problems plaguing its health system.

Health-care systems around the world are confronting challenges of improving quality, maintaining or extending access, and controlling costs, even while new technologies inexorably increase the capabilities of medicine.

Among industrial and traditionally market-based economies, experiments with more market-based incentives in the health sector constitute a "third wave" of international medical-care reforms, according to Cutler.[8] China's experiences provide some insight into the broader debate about the appropriate roles of governments and markets in the health sector. Several studies ably document China's health and health-care-system reforms.[9] But both the media coverage and the academic literature give conflicting appraisals of China's reality: Is health care expensive and difficult to access in contemporary China, or is it just perceived as such? Have reforms "marketizing" health care undermined progress in assuring affordable access for all? If so, should these reforms be rolled back, and the government's role in financing, delivering, and regulating health services be strengthened? Analysts and policy advisers have engaged in a sometimes acrimonious debate on these issues. Some champion a government-led system like Britain's National Health Service (NHS), while others passionately argue that market forces should play a greater role.[10] What are the prospects for China's current reform efforts, including its impressive expansion of government-subsidized health insurance coverage for both the rural and urban populations (through the New Cooperative Medical System [NCMS], urban residents' insurance program, and other medical aid programs)?

In social policy, as in medicine, the success of an intervention depends on the accuracy of the diagnosis. In this chapter, I examine China's health-system reforms since the 1980s, when the transition from a centrally planned economy to a "socialist market economy" began in earnest. The first several sections focus on positive analysis: How has China's health system evolved over the past quarter century? What have been the drivers of that change? How do China's health outcomes and health-care-system reforms compare to those of other countries, including other developing and transitional economies? What has been the political economy of developing the reform plan, and what specifically do the 2009 reforms entail? The last section returns to the normative question, Are the problems plaguing China's health system "growing pains" that the envisioned reforms will effectively address, or are they signs of a deeper crisis—a ticking time bomb that may derail China's social and economic development?

The core of the argument is straightforward. Effectively expanding China's health-care coverage and redressing problems in service delivery will require difficult and thorough restructuring of the distorted incentives embedded in the current system, which arose early in the reform era and remain a key challenge for the 2009 health reform plan. Following the success of dual-track reforms in other sectors of its economy, China enacted health policies intended to protect a "plan track" of access to basic health care even for the poorest patients while at the same time encouraging a "market track" for providers offering new, high-tech, more discretionary services to patients able to pay for them. The plan for basic access was neither defined nor protected in terms of risk pooling, so when organized financing (insurance) for health care largely collapsed (because it was linked to agricultural communes and soft-budget constraints for state-owned enterprises before the 1980s), little was put in its place until recently (see table 9.1). Only in the early years of the twenty-first century, almost thirty years into China's reforms, did the political economy of the SARS crisis and other links to social instability drive policymakers to reassess the problems in China's health-care system as a whole. As emphasized by prominent Chinese health economist Shanlian Hu of Fudan University, China's *kan bing nan, kan bing gui* problem is a "systemic disease" (*zhiduxing jibing*), stemming mainly from the confluence of three factors: lack of insurance, inadequate government financing, and distorted payment incentives.[11] While the 2009 health-system-reform plan clearly addresses the first two points—with about $124 billion in committed government financing and a goal of universal coverage—exactly how China will address the last crucial point about the incentive structure is less clear. The articulated goals for 2009–2011 are extending basic health insurance coverage to 90 percent of the population, expanding the public health service benefit package, strengthening primary care, implementing an essential drug list for all grassroots service providers, separating prescribing and dispensing, and reforming government-owned hospitals. The reform plan acknowledges that implementation of these policies represents "an arduous and long-term task."[12] As I will argue in this chapter, effectively restructuring incentives will be the key to whether government financing and universal coverage achieve the intended goals of ameliorating the *kan bing nan, kan bing gui* problem.

The chapter proceeds as follows. The next section presents an overview of population health trends in China and the changing burden of disease. The relative stagnation in health improvement during rapid economic development presents a puzzle, and links between the risk factors for burden of disease and provider incentives provide a clue regarding the fundamental argument, that dysfunctional system incentives for health-care providers are at the root of the problem. The chapter then turns to an analysis of China's medical care system and its challenges, with a conceptual framework based on dual-track reform.[13] The chapter proceeds to delve deeper into the causes behind the *kan bing nan, kan bing gui* problem, highlighting the collapse in organized financing and the distortions in provider incentives. China's experience with rising inequality is then placed in international context. Later we discuss the political economy behind China's recent significant reforms, from the response to the 2003 SARS epidemic (which profoundly raised the political profile of health-care reform) to the 2009 national reform announcement. The chapter concludes by returning to the question of whether or not the problems in China's health-care system should be understood as growing pains and what challenges lie ahead in making China's new commitment to universal coverage sustainable.

Table 9.1 Percent of Chinese Residents with Health Insurance Coverage in Urban and Rural Areas, 1993–2008 (National Health Surveys)

	National				Urban				Rural			
	1993	1998	2003	2008	1993	1998	2003	2008	1993	1998	2003	2008
Urban Employee BMI	n/a	n/a	8.9	12.7	n/a	n/a	30.4	44.2	n/a	n/a	1.5	1.5
GIS	5.8	4.9	1.2	1.0	18.2	16.0	4.0	3.0	1.6	1.2	0.2	0.3
LIS	9.7	6.2	1.3	n/a	35.3	22.9	4.6		1.1	0.5	0.1	n/a
CMS (and New CMS)	7.7	5.6	8.8	68.7	1.6	2.7	6.6	9.5	9.8	6.6	9.5	89.7
Urban resident BMI	n/a	n/a	n/a	3.8	n/a	n/a	n/a	12.5	n/a	n/a	n/a	0.7
Other social insurance	6.6	5.0	2.0	n/a	17.4	10.9	4.0	n/a	3.1	3.0	1.3	n/a
Commercial insurance	0.3	1.9	7.6	n/a	0.3	3.3	5.6	n/a	0.3	1.4	8.3	n/a
Uninsured	69.9	76.4	77.9	12.9	27.3	44.1	50.4	28.1	84.1	87.3	87.3	7.5

Sources: Ministry of Health, Center for Health Statistics and Information, *Zhongguo Weisheng Fuwu Diaocha Yanjiu: Disanci Guojia Weisheng Fuwu Diaocha Fenxi Baogao* (Analysis Report of National Health Services Survey in 2003), p.16; data for 2008 from Ministry of Health, National Health Services Survey 2009. BMI denotes urban basic medical insurance, which includes Octarate municipality-level risk pooling for urban employees and for nonemployed urban residents. GIS and LIS stand for the original government and labor insurance systems, respectively. CMS denotes cooperative medical schemes in rural areas; in 2003 and 2008 this reflects enrollment in the new CMS. Some forms of insurance are overlapping (e.g., commercial insurance may be supplementary coverage for someone whose primary coverage is through one of the social insurance programs).

Demographic and Epidemiological Transitions and China's Burden of Disease

China was famous for infectious disease control and expanded primary care through "barefoot doctors" during the early decades of the PRC.[14] In fact, between 1950 and 1980 China was host to the largest sustained mortality decline in documented global history, despite the disastrous Great Leap Famine. Some have questioned the accuracy of the statistics showing dramatic health improvement during China's "classical socialist" period because of the strong incentives for data distortion under such a system.[15] However, careful reanalysis of censuses and surveys largely confirms the story, with life expectancy estimated to have jumped from about 60 in the 1960s to over 71 by 2000.[16] A recent study[17] highlights the importance of nonmedical determinants of the Mao-era longevity gains, especially enhanced education and its interaction with public health measures like improved sanitation, immunizations, and campaigns against malnutrition.

After 1980, improvements in health outcomes slowed relative to China's breakneck economic growth. China began the reform era as an international outlier, with health indicators significantly better than would be expected given the nation's income level. Since then, China has "regressed to the mean," matching for most health indicators what would be expected given its per capita income.[18] While in principle this pattern need not signal failure—certainly the previous health improvements helped to fuel rapid economic gains, which in turn may be just as valuable as increased health improvements—it does pose a challenge to those who assume that economic growth is the key to longer, healthier lives. Why did China make such dramatic health gains when it was relatively poor and then stop making gains during a period of rapidly rising income? This unexpected finding suggests that the problems China faces in the health sector—or in addressing the social determinants of health that go far beyond the health sector *per se*—may be more than mere growing pains.

Demographic and Epidemiological Transitions

Understanding patterns of health change in China requires understanding China's demographic and epidemiological transitions. Demographically, China benefited from a relatively young population, with a growing fraction of residents at prime working age, helping to fuel economic growth in the reform era. According to Wang and Mason, this "first demographic dividend" accounted for about 15 percent of China's growth in output per capita between 1982 and 2000.[19] The controversial one-child policy does not appear to be responsible for the onset of the demographic transition nor for significantly greater human capital investments per child; rigorous analysis using twins suggests that "the contribution of the one-child policy in China to the development of its human capital was modest."[20] China's steady deceleration in population growth beginning around 1970 predates the one-child policy and has had its largest

233

impact in terms of decreasing the proportion of children and increasing the share of working-age adults in the population.[21] As a result, the dependency ratio has fallen and is likely to continue to do so for a few more years despite the significant aging of the population. In fact, population aging has the potential to yield a "second demographic dividend" that would increase savings and capital investment, further fueling increases in output per worker.[22] Several scholars have highlighted the importance of these demographic changes for social and economic development in China and throughout East Asia.[23]

Just as important, China's burden of disease is changing from that of a low-income country to that of a higher-income country, especially in urban areas. Noncommunicable diseases accounted for more than 70 percent of China's disease burden by 2001, up from 50 percent in 1990.[24] Among the ten most prevalent diseases in China are cardiovascular diseases, chronic obstructive pulmonary disease (COPD)—traceable to rampant male smoking and poor air quality from coal use and other air pollutants—and cancers. Depression, road-traffic accidents, and age-related vision disorders are other noninfectious conditions among the top ten causes of disease burden in China (table 9.2). Rapid urbanization, income growth, more sedentary lifestyles, and large dietary shifts (toward edible oils, animal-derived foods, and energy-dense diets) have contributed to making more than one in five Chinese adults overweight.[25]

Yet in poorer areas, particularly in rural and inland China, malnutrition and infectious diseases such as tuberculosis remain health concerns. Pulmonary tuberculosis was still among the top ten leading causes of death in China's rural areas in 2005, although the overall list of diseases contributing to mortality in rural China is growing more similar to that of urban areas (see table 9.3). Infectious diseases continue to pose a risk in both urban and rural areas, especially human immunodeficiency virus (HIV) or acquired immunodeficiency syndrome (AIDS), which could spread from high-risk groups such as intravenous drug users to the general population—though to the government's credit, new policies have begun to address that threat.

Like many developing and transitional economies, China has a large burden of disease from mental health disorders as well.[26] According to China's statistics, mental conditions are among the top ten leading causes of death for both men and women in both urban and rural areas (tables 9.3a and 9.3b).

In sum, China now faces a "double burden" of diseases, including those common in both developing and industrialized economies. Reducing behaviors that lead to chronic disease—including smoking, unhealthy diets, and sedentary lifestyles—will be key to reducing the burdens of future morbidity and mortality.

Table 9.2 Ten Leading Causes of Diseases Burden, China, and Low- and Middle-Income Countries, 2001

	China			Low- and middle-income countries (including China)	
	Cause	Percent of total DALYs		Cause	Percent of total DALYs
1	Cerebrovascular disease	9.7	1	Perinatal conditions	6.4
2	Chronic obstructive pulmonary disease	6.4	2	Lower respiratory infections	6.0
3	Perinatal conditions	4.9	3	Ischaemic heart disease	5.2
4	Unipolar depressive disorders	4.5	4	HIV/AIDS	5.1
5	Ischaemic heart disease	3.4	5	Cerebrovascular disease	4.5
6	Road-traffic accidents	3.1	6	Diarrhoeal diseases	4.2
7	Age-related vision disorders	2.6	7	Unipolar depressive disorders	3.1
8	Self-inflicted injuries	2.6	8	Malaria	2.9
9	Stomach cancer	2.5	9	Tuberculosis	2.6
10	Lower respiratory infections	2.5	10	Chronic obstructive pulmonary disease	2.4

Source: Disease Control Priorities Project 2006, www.dcp2.org.
Note: DALY = disability-adjusted life year.

Table 9.3 Ten Leading Causes of Death in China's Rural and Urban Areas: Totals, and for Men and Women Separately, 2007

A. In Rural Areas

No.	Cause of death	Percentage of total deaths
	Total	93.19
1	Malignant tumor	24.8
2	Cerebrovascular disease	20.59
3	Diseases of the respiratory system	17.24
4	Heart diseases	14.8
5	Trauma and toxicosis	8.96
6	Diseases of the digestive system	2.69
7	Endocrine, nutritional, and metabolic diseases	1.52
8	Disease of the genitourinary system	1.22
9	Disease of the nervous system	0.77
10	Mental disorders	0.6
	Male total	93.66
1	Malignant tumor	28.05
2	Cerebrovascular disease	19.64
3	Diseases of the respiratory system	15.83
4	Heart diseases	13.28
5	Trauma and toxicosis	10.33
6	Diseases of the digestive system	2.96
7	Disease of the genitourinary system	1.27
8	Endocrine, nutritional, and metabolic diseases	1.16
9	Disease of the nervous system	0.67
10	Mental disorders	0.47
	Female total	92.55
1	Cerebrovascular disease	21.92
2	Malignant tumor	20.26
3	Diseases of the respiratory system	19.22
4	Heart diseases	16.92
5	Trauma and toxicosis	7.05
6	Diseases of the digestive system	2.31
7	Disease of the genitourinary system	2.02
8	Endocrine, nutritional, and metabolic diseases	1.17
9	Disease of the nervous system	0.9
10	Mental disorders	0.78

Source: China Statistical Yearbook 2008, www.chinadataonline.org.
Note: Statistics in the table cover all the counties under the jurisdiction of city governments in Beijing and Tianjin, and 80 counties (cities at county level) in 14 provinces (or province-level municipalities) such as Jiangsu.

B. In Urban Areas

No.	Cause of death	Percentage of total deaths
	Total	91.28
1	Malignant tumor	28.53
2	CerebrovaculardDisease	18.04
3	Heart diseases	16.29
4	Diseases of the respiratory system	13.1
5	Trauma and toxicosis	6.09
6	Endocrine, nutritional, and metabolic diseases	3.3
7	Diseases of the digestive system	2.83
8	Disease of the genitourinary system	1.28
9	Disease of the nervous system	0.95
10	Mental disorders	0.87
	Male Total	92.33
1	Malignant tumor	32.04
2	Cerebrovascular disease	16.82
3	Heart diseases	14.91
4	Diseases of the respiratory system	13.5
5	Trauma and toxicosis	6.68
6	Diseases of the digestive system	2.93
7	Endocrine, nutritional, and metabolic diseases	2.6
8	Disease of the genitourinary system	1.25
9	Disease of the nervous system	0.92
10	Mental disorders	0.68
	Female Total	91.85
1	Malignant tumor	25.04
2	Cerebrovascular disease	20.17
3	Heart diseases	19.53
4	Diseases of the respiratory system	11.37
5	Endocrine, nutritional, and metabolic diseases	4.93
6	Trauma and toxicosis	4.61
7	Diseases of the digestive system	2.83
8	Disease of the genitourinary system	1.37
9	Disease of the Nervous System	1.08
10	Mental Disorders	0.92

Source: China Statistical Yearbook 2008, www.chinadataonline.org.

The disease burden is exacerbated by perverse incentives in the health-care delivery system, such as the practice of financially rewarding invasive procedures over lower-tech methods that are often far safer and more cost-effective.[27] For example, contaminated injections were responsible for 2 percent of China's total disease burden in 2001, making it the tenth leading risk factor for China's burden of disease.[28] Improving the incentives facing health-care providers will no doubt be central to achieving health gains in the coming years for China's population of more than one billion. The next section turns to how and why these dysfunctional health-care-system incentives arose during China's transition and how recent reforms address the problem.

A Conceptual Framework

China's economic reforms, beginning with agriculture in the 1980s, have achieved unprecedented success in lifting average incomes and bringing millions out of poverty.[29] Yet the same approach to reform that worked so dramatically for other sectors of the economy did not give rise to a coherent and sustainable system for health-care financing and delivery.

China's economy was dominated by state control at the onset of reforms, but in the years since, it has seen a higher growth rate of the nonstate sector than the state sector, thus "growing out of the plan."[30] Figure 9.1 illustrates this trend, showing China's total and state-controlled GDP from 1980 to 2005 in internationally comparable dollars, taking into account the effects of inflation.[31] State-controlled GDP has grown in absolute and real terms, but the nonstate share of the economy has outpaced that growth significantly. As a result, state-controlled output makes up a steadily declining share of China's economy.[32]

Economic theory can explain China's dual-track reforms by focusing on how China continued to enforce a planning "track" through regulated prices and/or production quotas, while allowing market-based incentives to govern firms' production decisions on the margin (such as through sales of above-quota production at market-based prices). The resulting market-based signals for resource allocation spurred economic growth and allowed the planned share of the economy to shrink in relative terms as China's economy "grew out of the plan."

The following section summarizes the theory of dual-track reforms and discusses why the distinctive features of the health sector made applying such reforms to health care problematic.

The Economic Theory of Dual-track Reforms

In "Reform Without Losers: An Interpretation of China's Dual-Track Approach to Transition," Lau, Qian, and Roland suggest that China's use of dual tracks—continued central planning in addition to a market track—enabled economic reform to be simultaneously efficient and Pareto-improving (making everyone better off).[33] Enforcing a central plan prevented disorganization of the production process as firms struggled to secure new market-based contracts for procuring all inputs and selling all outputs.[34] Such disorganization has become a leading theory for why all transition economies except China and Vietnam experienced transformational recessions.[35]

238

Figure 9.1 "Growing Out of the Plan" in China: Relative Growth of the Nonstate Sector

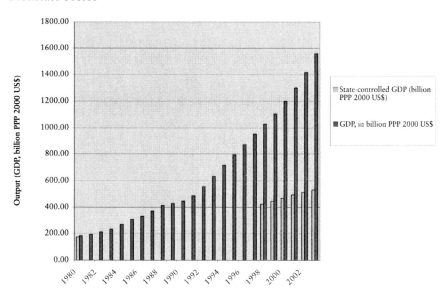

Sources: The GDP data are in 2000 U.S. dollars at purchasing power parity (PPP), drawn from the World Development Indicator (WDI) database (World Bank, http://wwwr.worldbank.org/data). The estimates of the state-controlled share of the economy (1998 to 2003) come from Garnaut et al. (2005, 10).

One key feature of China's dual-track system was the emphasis on "grandfathering" the old system: those who benefited from plan-based prices and allocations could continue to enjoy those benefits (or economic rents). Under the dual-track system, those plan benefits constituted inframarginal lump-sum transfers from producing to consuming firms or vice versa, depending on whether the plan price was set below or above the market price. These benefits were "inframarginal" in the sense that they did not govern firms' behavior on the margin, since decisions about expanding or contracting investment and production would be based on market prices. Lau, Qian, and Roland show that the dual-track system works even if the efficient quantity is less than the planned quantity, so that transition to markets would entail contractions in production, as long as the government enforces the plan in terms of rents rather than physical quantities.[36] Importantly, such a dual-track system also benefits from using existing planning institutions rather than relying on the rapid development of new coordinating institutions.[37] Evidence corroborates this story of "growing out of the plan," at least through the early transition years before production quotas were phased out for many goods and services.

Such a dual-track system works most readily along the chain of production for industrial goods, with firms as both the "planned suppliers" and "rationed users." The framework applies less smoothly to goods sold directly to consumers and even worse for services that cannot be traded such as medical care. (The ability to retrade products sold on one track in another is critical to the efficiency properties of "full market liberalization," allowing firms to purchase on the market to fulfill plan production quotas.)[38]

The Problems of Defining a Dual Track for Health Care

Multiple features of health care complicate a dual-track approach, ultimately rendering such a reform neither efficient nor Pareto-improving. Despite these complications, I submit that China in a real sense did apply a dual-track approach to the health sector, broadly in parallel with reforms in other sectors of the economy. Loosely interpreted, the dual-track approach meant guaranteeing access to some basic amount of a good or service under "old system rules," while allowing market-based incentives to govern expansion or newer goods and services. This principle could be applied to health—and I argue that it was. Central to the dual track was enforcing "the plan" in terms of regulated prices for the services commonly available to patients at the outset of reforms. Allowing market-based prices or regulated prices with a profit margin for newer services (and for pharmaceuticals) seemed consistent with market-track reforms for most other sectors in China.

Unfortunately, "the plan" was not defined in terms of insurance or risk pooling, but rather in terms of specific services. China's population experienced a precipitous decline in effective health-insurance coverage that arose from agricultural decollectivization and the breakdown of the "iron rice bowl" policy for urban formal-sector employees.[39] Moreover, planners apparently underestimated the supply-side response to distortions in regulated prices. In fact, these two policies are linked: lack of third-party payers in China (see table 9.1) meant that the price that consumers paid was the same as the price suppliers received, and a low price to guarantee patient access implied a low incentive for suppliers to invest or produce.[40]

As health economists are wont to point out, the characteristics of health care are not individually unique, but when taken in combination, they make health care distinctive and prone to market failures.[41] Most prominent among these characteristics is the value attached to health. While medical care is not the most significant determinant of an individual's health—lifestyle choices and other factors, as Victor Fuchs states in his classic book *Who Shall Live?*, are often more important health determinants—timely and appropriate medical care nevertheless can often be a matter of life or death.[42] Hence allocating access to health care is a controversial exercise in "pricing the priceless."[43]

Related to the seminal value of health is a "norm of equal access"; in many societies, a majority of people feel that everyone has a right to basic health care.

This norm is sometimes expressed as "specific egalitarianism," or supporting the equal distribution of specific goods and services considered necessities.[44] People may view a system in which rich people can buy better health care for their families than poor people as more inequitable than a system with differences in income, housing, or education.

Other key characteristics of health care include uncertainty and the demand for insurance, and asymmetry of information. Insurance, or risk pooling, is a vital component of any health-care system, introducing an important institutional feature of the health sector—a third-party payer between the consumer and the provider. The consumer, the insurer, and the provider each possess different information (about the current and future state of health, propensity to use medical care, appropriate treatment for a given medical condition, and so on), a situation that gives rise to problems of adverse selection (the sick are more likely to buy insurance) and risk selection (as when insurers or providers "cherry-pick" healthy patients). Moreover, when individuals are insured, they tend to overuse services because they do not bear the full cost of those services, a behavior called moral hazard. When patients as a group overuse medical services because these services appear to be free or close to it, the cost of supplying insurance coverage rises. Deterring moral hazard usually requires making the patient pay some of the cost of care at time of use. But deductibles and coinsurance reimpose financial risk on consumers and may decrease their access to medical care. Health insurance thus involves a fundamental trade-off between spreading risk and giving appropriate incentives for efficient use of medical care.

The health sector also confronts challenges from the relative defenselessness and desperation of the patient, and potentially misaligned incentives among the three main players—patient, provider, and payer/insurer—and the three key goals of access, quality, and reasonable cost. For example, health service providers have an incentive and an opportunity to exploit asymmetry of information to overprovide profitable services and underprovide unprofitable services, especially (but not only) when there is clinical ambiguity about the appropriate treatment.

These characteristics illustrate how difficult it is to define and implement a successful dual-track reform in the health sector. The central challenge is how to define the plan and the market for health care. Except perhaps for some population health services such as childhood immunizations or screening for certain diseases, no government agency can define and enforce a plan for delivering a specific quantity of services to specific patients: health care requires the mediation of a health-care provider to match services to patient need, or effective demand. Thus, for health care, "plan quantities" would not be contractible. The government would have to enforce the plan according to rents instead of quantities, even if efficiency required expansion of output. But the government cannot enforce the plan in terms of rents either, because planners do not know the consumer's "true demand"—asymmetric information, moral hazard, individual heterogeneity, and the potential for supplier-induced demand make it difficult, if not impossible, to "grandfather" access to certain health-care services, while allowing markets to allocate other health-care services. Government could try to enforce access in terms of entitlements to "basic care" rather than quantities of specific services, but this further begs the question of how to define "basic" medical services.

According to this conceptual framework, then, the *kan bing nan, kan bing gui* problem has two major and related causes: first, risk-pooling institutions (including tax-based financing) for health care deteriorated, as seen by the decreasing share of government financing for health and concomitant reliance on patient out-of-pocket expenditures. This collapse was in turn linked to problems with local governance and a transformational decline in central government revenues during the early period of economic reform. Second, distortions in the system of incentives for providers, intended as a substitute for risk pooling, in fact exacerbated the problems of access by financially penalizing population health services such as immunizations and low-cost interventions, while financially rewarding the oversupply of high-tech interventions and dispensing medications. These factors, together with the increasing capabilities of medicine, made getting medical treatment increasingly difficult and costly for patients (*kan bing nan, kan bing gui*) and are the topic of a more detailed discussion in the next section.

Kan Bing Nan, Kan Bing Gui: In Search of the Causes

Collapse of Risk Pooling

Has the health sector "grown out of the plan" as other sectors of the economy have done? Figure 9.2 shows that in terms of expenditures on health, China has indeed seen a parallel pattern since 1980. The vertical axis plots total and government expenditures on health, expressed in 2000 U.S. purchasing power parity (PPP) dollars.[45] According to this figure, government expenditures on health has grown in absolute terms but has shrunk as a fraction of total expenditures on health (TEH) in China. Government expenditures on health declined from 79 percent of TEH in 1980 to only 36 percent in 2001, though they have rebounded since then. Beginning in the mid-1990s, private financing has constituted a larger share of total health spending than government financing. Note that government expenditures include social insurance, as is standard for national health accounting. Thus, the government spending figures include government financing flowing both to the demand side (social insurance) and to the supply side (through government-owned providers), with some shift between the two (see figure 9.3). The precipitous decline of government financing as a share of total health expenditures parallels the broader fiscal erosion China experienced during the first period of economic reforms. Between 1978 and 1995, China's budgetary revenues declined from 33 percent of GDP to only 10.8 percent.[46]

Figure 9.2 Total and Government Expenditures on Health, 1980–2007

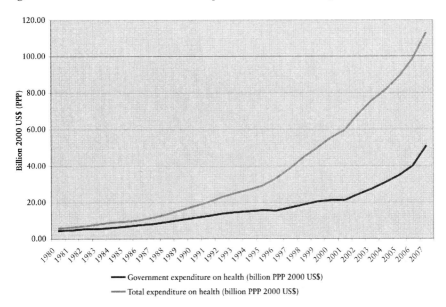

Sources: World Health Organization (WHO) national health accounts (www.who.int/nha/en/) and China National Health Accounts Report (Ministry of Health 2004).

Since tax-based financing inherently cross-subsidizes people and regions, depending on tax progressivity and other features of the tax system, government financing represents a form of risk pooling. This form of risk pooling shrank as a share of total health spending during the reform era. The striking parallel between figures 9.1 and 9.2 provides some *prima facie* evidence that China's "crossing the river by feeling for the stones" approach to the health sector approximated dual-track reform.

In short, as China's economy grew, health spending also grew rapidly, with the vast majority of that growth coming from private financing. Without more information about the type of private financing, one cannot say much about the welfare implications of this trend.[47] Private financing can in principle include commercial insurance and other risk-pooling mechanisms that protect patients from risk and enable access to services when needed. This has not been the case in China, where the vast majority of the private financing takes the form of out-of-pocket payments—namely, households paying when they need health care (figure 9.4 and table 9.1). Before 1996 estimates of China's national health accounts suggest that China's private health-care spending was entirely out of pocket—the most regressive form of payment. Since then, prepaid and risk-pooling plans have grown somewhat, but they still account for no more than 10 percent of private spending.

Figure 9.3 The Structure of Health-care Financing in China, 1980–2007

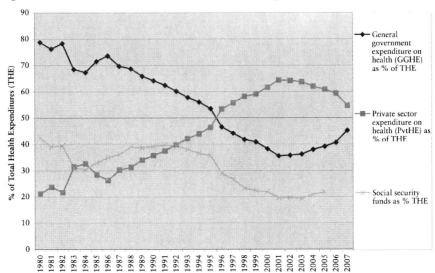

Source: World Health Organization (WHO) national health accounts (www. who.int/nha/en/) and China National Health Accounts Report (Ministry of Health 2004).

Thus, China at the dawn of the twenty-first century financed the majority of health-care services with a "tax on the sick." This means that the majority of health spending in China did not involve any risk pooling, either through social health insurance or tax-based financing. Such a lack of risk pooling is not only inequitable but also inefficient: the poor are most vulnerable to risk, and all uninsured are denied an efficient mechanism to transfer wealth from times when it is needed less (when healthy) to times when it is needed more (upon becoming sick or injured). Those with large expenses such as hospitalizations are especially disadvantaged. Dollar notes that the problem of unaffordable hospital care in China reflects both lack of insurance and costly care, as measured by inpatient episode spending as a percent of household consumption per capita.[48] Average medical expenses per inpatient grew from an already high 29 percent of per capita GDP in 1990 to 33 percent of per capita GDP in 2005.[49] For a family with below-average income, a hospitalization of above-average expense could wipe out annual income and savings. Unsurprisingly, then, affordability of health care ranked among Chinese citizens' top concerns.[50]

Figure 9.4 China's Private Health Spending, Out-Of-Pocket and Commercial Insurance

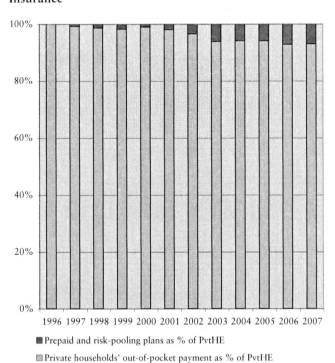

■ Prepaid and risk-pooling plans as % of PvtHE
▩ Private households' out-of-pocket payment as % of PvtHE

Source: World Health Organization (WHO) national health accounts (www. who.int/nha/en/).

System Incentives and Provider Behavior

One hypothesis that might explain why medical care is expensive and difficult to obtain is that supply has not kept up with demand from a growing, urbanizing, and aging population.[51] Although a relative disequilibrium between physical supply and effective demand may be part of the story, it appears unlikely to be the whole story. For example, China's supply of physicians and inpatient beds per capita approximates international norms for China's income level. China has more physicians per capita than wealthier Malaysia and Thailand, and not many fewer than some significantly higher per capita income countries like Singapore and South Korea. The total supply of hospital beds per thousand people in China increased from 2.02 in 1980 to 2.45 in 2005, more than in Mexico or Malaysia.

Perhaps more tellingly, occupancy rates fell during much of the reform era, from already low levels at township hospitals, suggesting an oversupply in some regions even as undersupply remains a significant barrier for the poorest parts of China. Between 1985 and 2005, occupancy rates at township-level hospitals decreased from 46 percent to 37.7 percent (a rebound after a low of 31.3 percent in 2001); over the same period occupancy rates in general-acute hospitals fell from an average of 87 percent to 76.6 percent.[52] But neither oversupply nor undersupply of doctors and hospitals convincingly explains the *kan bing nan* problem nationally.

Another hypothesis, frequently heard in the policy debate in and about China, is that the current ills of the system all stem from privatization run amok. According to this view, commercialization of the health-care sector turned the whole system over to a flawed "market track" and thus precipitated innumerable market failures that reduced quality and access while fueling expenditure growth.

While there are some elements of truth in such an account, other elements are exaggerated, oversimplified, and simply not consistent with the facts. A review of empirical evidence on determinants of provider performance in both the Chinese and English literature suggests that privatization of health-care delivery is neither the main culprit of China's health-system woes nor the magic pill for their improvement.[53]

The health-care delivery system in China before the 1980s was 100 percent government-controlled and organized according to three tiers: village clinics, township health centers (THCs), and county hospitals in rural areas; and street clinics, district hospitals, and city hospitals in cities. The most complex cases could be referred to provincial and national hospitals for more specialized care. The ownership structure of delivery evolved in a pattern somewhat parallel to that of health-care financing. By the turn of the twenty-first century, half of China's health-care organizations were private, for-profit organizations; however, most of those organizations were small, ambulatory care providers, such as rural clinics. Larger organizations—especially urban secondary and tertiary hospitals, the "commanding heights" of health-care delivery—remained under government control. Consistent with the general state-owned-enterprise policy of "grasping the large and letting go of the small," private-sector entry and (limited) privatization have transformed the ownership structure of providers such as clinics, village doctors, and some health centers, while keeping key providers, particularly hospitals, under government ownership.

Indeed, it was only in mid-2000 that China developed an official policy for the organizational transformation of hospitals and similar provider organizations, by requiring them to declare for-profit or nonprofit status. Nonprofit firms were subject to price regulation and exempt from taxes, with government-owned nonprofits continuing to be entitled to some (relatively small) government subsidies. In contrast, for-profit firms have to pay taxes and can set their own prices.[54] In urban areas, some private providers also began to serve the expatriate markets and, gradually, the Chinese population that was able to afford health-care services at high-income-country prices.[55]

By 2006 the market share of private, for-profit providers remained in the single digits overall (for example, 3.6 percent of total visits and 2.8 percent of hospitalizations) but was higher for specialty hospitals (where for-profits accounted for 14 percent of inpatients) and especially for outpatient departments (50 percent of patients). Unfortunately, there are few good data on private, not-for-profit providers, an important—often dominant—category in many countries' health-care systems.

Moreover, during the reform era, government ownership ceased to imply government financing of care. As discussed above, China's health-care financing became much more reliant on out-of-pocket spending by patients, despite the continued presence of government delivery for most hospital services (and outpatient care). What happened? Government hospitals received a shrinking share of their revenues from government subsidies (on average less than 10 percent), and these funds were largely devoted to supporting retirees and some basic salaries for staff. The vast majority of government hospital incomes began to come from patient fees (user charges) for diagnostics, treatment, and dispensing pharmaceuticals.[56]

Patients in China therefore do not choose between getting government-subsidized services and paying for private services, as is the case in many developing countries; instead, Chinese patients pay for their services from both public and private providers.

China's rural majority visit village doctors and other providers who charge fees for services—in other words, private, for-profit providers serving a population that was uninsured or underinsured (albeit less so with the expansion of NCMS over the past five years). Furthermore, even government-owned providers tend to act as "net-revenue maximizers," receiving minimal direct governmental support and deriving most revenue from user charges. Those user charges in turn systematically diverge from the true social net benefit of services, sending highly distorted signals to providers.[57] It is this combination of lack of insurance and distorted incentives facing both public and private providers, and not private-sector ownership *per se*, that most plausibly explains the *kan bing nan, kan bing gui* problem.

The evidence regarding distorted payment incentives is especially striking. Fee-for-service (FFS) payment is widely recognized to contain perverse incentives to over- and underprovide services according to profitability; studies of payment reforms in China corroborate the growing international evidence on this point.[58] To cite another example, price regulation allows providers a substantial markup over wholesale prices when dispensing drugs. It is therefore unsurprising that even after years of effort to reduce hospitals' reliance on drug sales, drugs accounted for 42 percent of total revenues in Chinese hospitals in 2008. Drug expenditures represented 52.8 percent of expenditure per inpatient episode and 64.2 percent of expenditure per outpatient visit in 1995, with mild decreases since then (see table 9.4).

Distorted payment incentives also make it difficult to improve the quality of care. For example, an expert group studying a sample of township health centers and village clinics in Chongqing (a province-level municipality) and Gansu Province determined that less than 2 percent of prescriptions were "rational" (consistent with best practices, given the clinical indications). Antibiotics constituted 70 percent of prescriptions in Henan village clinics and township health centers.[59] Evidence suggests that provider payment reforms—toward bundled payment and "pay for performance"—hold promise for controlling expenditure growth and improving quality without sacrificing equity goals, although careful monitoring is required.[60]

Table 9.4 Pharmaceutical Expenditures as a Percentage of Expenditure per Inpatient Episode or Outpatient Visit, All Hospitals

	Inpatient episode	Outpatient visit
1995	52.8	64.2
2000	46.1	58.6
2005	43.9	52.1
2008	43.9	50.5

Source: China Statistical Yearbook 2008, www.chinadataonline.org.

China's Health Policy Reform Challenges in Comparative Perspective

Economic System Transition

China's overall spending on health is roughly what one would expect for its economic level and demographic structure (figure 9.5), although the heavy reliance on out-of-pocket spending exceeds international norms (figure 9.6). One might expect to see an increase in the private share of health spending—in particular, in under-the-table payments for health care[61]—in an economy transitioning from central planning to markets, but how does China's "growing out of the plan" in the health sector compare to that of other transitional economies? This section addresses that question.

Figure 9.5 Total Health Expenditure as Percentage of Gross Domestic Product, 2006

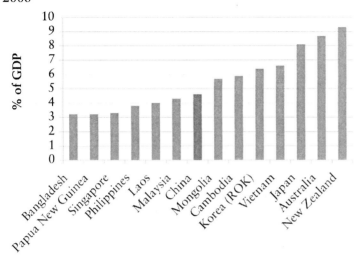

Source: WHOSIS (World Health Organization Statistical Information System, www.who.int/whosis/en/).

Figure 9.6 Out-of-Pocket Spending as Percentage of Total Health Expenditure, 2006

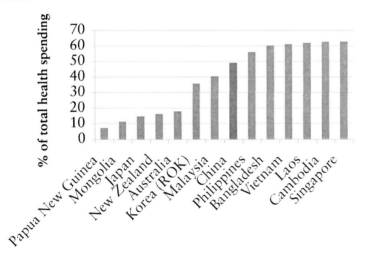

Source: WHOSIS (World Health Organization Statistical Information System, www.who.int/whosis/en/).

China and Vietnam are the only transitional economies that did not experience "transformational recessions"—large falls in per capita income associated with shifting to a market-based economy.[62] Ironically, one factor may explain not only why macroeconomic transition in China (and Vietnam) was easier than for all other transition economies but also why achieving universal health-care coverage in a market-based economy is so difficult. That factor: a large agricultural-based population.[63] The "disorganization" effects of systemic transition were stronger in more urban and industrialized economies than in rural ones, but risk-pooling institutions were also more resilient. In other words, it has proved easier to maintain near-universal health coverage during transition in urban, higher-income economies than in poor rural ones. The contrast with Central and Eastern Europe (CEE) is striking: CEE managed to keep universal coverage despite transformational recession, whereas China had a majority without insurance (table 9.1) until recently, despite rapid economic growth.[64]

Reasons for this irony abound. Countries throughout the world find it difficult to extend coverage to the self-employed and informal sectors. To oversimplify, establishing social insurance based on payroll taxes is difficult when the majority of the population is not on a payroll. In China, experiments throughout the 1990s with reestablishing community financing in rural areas finally culminated in the rapid expansion of NCMS nationwide over the past five years. In that effort, as elsewhere, the difficulties in collecting premiums from households have led many to believe that tax financing would be a more efficient method for financing coverage of the informal sector (which cannot be covered by payroll deductions).

Inequality

Income inequality has increased significantly in almost all transition economies, in some cases to very high levels (with Gini coefficients over 47 in the Ukraine and over 51 in Russia in the 1990s).[65] China's estimated Gini coefficient increased from 36 in the mid-1980s to 41.4 a decade later.[66] To some extent, increasing inequality is an almost inevitable part of moving from central planning to markets. Some forms of inequality may even be desirable: for example, returns to education have increased significantly. In a paper published in 2005, Z. Liu points out that since low educational attainment among rural residents and low rewards to education in rural employment contribute to China's wide urban-rural gap, the *hukou* (residential permit) system restricting urbanization is a major contributing factor to rural-urban inequality.[67] Dollar identifies three additional policy features that exacerbate China's inequalities: restrictions on selling rural land, the decentralized fiscal system, and the large trade surplus. According to some estimates, the rise of inequality in China was the most significant contributor to growing regional inequality in East Asia.[68]

Several studies have explored the health and health-care implications of China's growing income inequalities.[69] For example, Adams and Hannum use the 1989, 1993, and 1997 waves of the China Health and Nutrition Survey (CHNS) to examine school enrollment, grade-for-age in school, and children's access to health insurance.[70] They find that all three measures improved and that socioeconomic disparities, though wide, were not increasing. Community resources and their unequal distribution in China did appear to matter for social services, a finding consistent with much of the literature. Indeed, "where you live does matter" is the subtitle of Chen, Eastwood, and Yen's 2007 study of childhood malnutrition patterns in China. Across provinces, the ratio of maximum to minimum provincial average life expectancy was 1.26 in 1990, falling slightly to 1.21 in 2000.[71] In 2000 regional life expectancies ranged from a low of 62.5 for men in Tibet to a high of 80 for women in Shanghai.[72]

As these statistics reveal, health disparities compound income disparities, leading to even wider gaps in "full income" (life expectancy multiplied by per capita income) across regions (table 9.5) and between urban and rural areas. Accounting for risk further widens urban-rural disparities for several reasons: higher income volatility in rural areas increases the effective urban-rural income gap; higher health-care spending risk in rural China also increases the effective urban-rural gap in well-being; and rural residents are more likely to suffer the death of a child or a wife and mother in childbirth.[73]

These risks—and lack of risk pooling—exacerbate poverty and relative deprivation. Those who suffer catastrophic health events often spend family savings and assets to pay for health care, while simultaneously losing the income of a wage earner for a nontrivial time period. Gan, Xu, and Yao estimate that a household suffering a major health shock on average falls short of its normal income trajectory by 11.8 percent over fifteen years, and does not recover for nineteen years.[74] A study using the 1998 CHNS data revealed that out-of-pocket medical spending increased the number of rural households living below the poverty line by 44.3 percent and the poverty gap by 146 percent.[75] According to Liu and Rao, this large impact of medical spending on poverty proved to be one of the key points convincing top policymakers to establish government-subsidized health insurance in rural areas.[76]

Table 9.5 Regional Inequalities in Urban "Full Income" (life expectancy* urban per capita disposable income), 1990 and 2000

		Region's full income relative to the national average	
		1990	2000
北 京	Beijing	1.32	1.74
天 津	Tianjin	1.20	1.35
河 北	Hebei	1.00	0.91
山 西	Shanxi	0.90	0.75
内蒙古	Inner Mongolia	0.77	0.79
辽 宁	Liaoning	1.11	0.87
吉 林	Jilin	0.78	0.78
黑龙江	Heilongjiang	0.82	0.79
上 海	Shanghai	1.66	2.02
江 苏	Jiangsu	1.06	1.11
浙 江	Zhejiang	1.41	1.53
安 徽	Anhui	0.96	0.84
福 建	Fujian	1.22	1.19
江 西	Jiangxi	0.80	0.78
山 东	Shandong	1.05	1.06
河 南	Henan	0.82	0.75
湖 北	Hubei	0.97	0.87
湖 南	Hunan	1.08	0.97
广 东	Guangdong	1.70	1.58
广 西	Guangxi	1.01	0.92
海 南	Hainan	1.17	0.86
重 庆	Chongqing	part of Sichuan	1.00
四 川	Sichuan	1.00	0.93
贵 州	Guizhou	0.91	0.75
云 南	Yunnan	0.98	0.92
西 藏	Tibet	1.02	1.06
陕 西	Shaanxi	0.94	0.79
甘 肃	Gansu	0.82	0.73
青 海	Qinghai	0.69	0.75
宁 夏	Ningxia	0.97	0.76
新 疆	Xinjiang	0.86	0.84
	Minimum	0.69	0.73
	Maximum	1.70	2.02
	Ratio max/min	2.46	2.76

Source: Author's calculations based on data from *China Statistical Yearbook* 2008, www.chinadataonline.org.

The Political Economy of Reform

Health-care reformers must not only answer difficult technical questions about appropriate policy and regulation but also confront a complicated web of interest groups, each advocating for reforms that support its interests. The former problems of content can make the latter problems of political economy all the more delicate and intransigent. Even when virtually all stakeholders are discontent with the current system, conflicts of interest can conflate with and exacerbate contrary views on appropriate policy reforms. Evidence is open to interpretation, and limited evidence on some policy questions leaves ample scope for recommendations to be driven by the recommenders' beliefs and values. As Victor Fuchs concluded from a survey of experts in the United States, many policy questions have questions of fact embedded in them, and when the questions of fact lack a conclusive evidence base, experts tend to let their values drive their policy recommendations.[77]

Unlike pension reform, health-care reform has to deal with a large supply side of entrenched interests among health-service providers. Like education, personal health-care services are largely private goods (investment in individual human capital), albeit sometimes with large externalities, and allocating access involves problems of provider incentives and selection from choice (or competition). But unlike education, health care involves insurance, so the market structure of financing and delivery are arguably more complex. And perhaps most important, health systems are deeply embedded in a country's history and culture. To mention just one example, physician dispensing of medication has been an accepted institution in most of East Asia, and China has much to learn from the controversial reforms separating prescribing and dispensing in Korea, Japan, and Taiwan.[78] Integration of prescribing and dispensing survived from premodern China through socialist governance during the Mao era to today's socialist market economy. Understanding why physician dispensing persisted across China's economic system transformations of 1949 and 1979, but then became one of the central targets of China's 2009 health-reform plan, can shed light on how and why institutions change.[79]

For all of these reasons, although the specific policy context varies across countries, implementing evidence-based and carefully evaluated health-policy reforms is a challenge everywhere.

In China, the odyssey of major health-system reform dates back at least to the 2003 SARS crisis.[80] China's new political leadership, General Secretary and President Hu Jintao and Premier Wen Jiabao, officially took office just as the crisis was peaking in March 2003. As Saich notes, "before they could develop an effective profile of their own, they were knocked off course, but SARS may have provided them with an unprecedented opportunity to establish themselves as modern leaders concerned with the welfare of the people."[81] After months of cover-up, official policy shifted course in April 2003. The leaders dismissed Minister of Health Zhang Wenkang and Beijing mayor Meng Xuenong, and placed Vice Premier Wu Yi in charge of the Ministry of Health (MOH) and anti-SARS efforts, with a central command center under the state council. By the end of the episode more than one hundred and twenty dismissals of local officials were linked to the SARS crisis. China established a new emergency management organization and enhanced transparency and accountability in the public health reporting and political systems.[82] The SARS crisis focused international attention on the weaknesses in China's health sector. As a direct result, health-sector reforms became a national priority.[83]

One of the first programs to benefit from this newfound attention to health reform was the NCMS in China's vast rural areas, launched in late 2002.[84] The government had announced that rural coverage should rely on community financing back in 1996. However, as Liu and Rao suggest, the government was reluctant to subsidize rural insurance, hoping instead that rising incomes would lead to demand for private organized financing, with an appropriate supply-side response.[85] Unfortunately, and perhaps unsurprisingly, pilot programs throughout the 1990s did not lead to a groundswell of increasing coverage. Some commercial insurance did penetrate into rural areas—as shown in table 9.1, the percent of rural residents nationally who reported having commercial health insurance increased from 1.4 in 1998 to 8.3 in 2003. However, such policies appeared to primarily target limited and favorable risk pools (such as schoolchildren) and failed to provide comprehensive coverage even to the small fraction of rural residents who purchased them.

It was not until a couple of years into the new millennium that China announced a government-subsidized program for rural health insurance.[86] Unlike the reforms of the 1990s, this time the central government committed substantial resources to subsidizing voluntary enrollment. The original financing scheme called for 10 yuan each from the central government, the local government, and rural households; this later was increased to 20/20/10 and in December 2007 to 40/40/20, reflecting significant increases in government subsidization. The low initial financing necessitated relatively shallow coverage, with high deductibles and coinsurance rates, and low caps on insurance reimbursement. As a result, even insured rural residents continued to face significant health-care financing risk, with large regional variations. Nevertheless, the NCMS puts in place a national institution for risk pooling (at the county level) that can be gradually expanded to cover more services. Early evaluations (although complicated by the endogenous placement of the NCMS pilots and lack of comparable control groups) indicate that the NCMS has improved access to care, especially increasing inpatient utilization rates; although adverse selection exists—enrollment is higher among the chronically sick—it has not derailed risk pooling.[87]

Yet the design of the NCMS, which emphasizes reimbursement for inpatient expenses, sidestepped the crucial issue of reforming provider incentives. The recognition that risk pooling alone would not solve the *kan bing nan, kan bing gui* problem arguably prompted the broader inquiry into how to restructure

254

the health-care system as a whole. Premier Wen Jiabao referred to the NCMS and the larger reform plan in the "Report on the Work of the Government" that he delivered at the first session of the Eleventh National People's Congress on March 5, 2008:

> We will fully implement the new type of rural cooperative medical care system in all rural areas. Within two years, we will raise the standard for financing from 50 yuan to 100 yuan per person per year, with central and local government contributions to be raised from 40 yuan to 80 yuan per person. . . . The state council commissioned a study of the issue of how to deepen reform of the system of pharmaceuticals and health care. A preliminary plan has been produced and will soon be publicized to solicit opinions from the general public. The basic goal of the reform is to maintain the public service nature of public medical and health-care services and set up a basic medical and health-care system to provide people with basic medical and health-care services that are safe, effective, convenient, and affordable. We must resolutely carry out this reform to provide everyone with access to basic medical and health services and improve their health.

As Premier Wen mentions, the state council in late 2006 decided that a high-level interministerial commission should be assigned the challenge of developing a blueprint for China's health system. Thus the National Commission on Health System Reform was born. The commission included originally ten government agencies (this was later raised to fourteen), cochaired by the National Development and Reform Commission (NDRC) and the MOH. Leadership by the powerful NDRC is expected to help broker compromise among the many disparate ministries with jurisdictions overlapping in the health sector, each with its own interests and point of view. For example, the MOH, as manager of the current delivery system, generally favors supply-side subsidies, while the Ministry of Labor and Social Security clearly favors a separate insurance purchaser role. Statements by the leadership of the China Insurance Regulatory Commission (CIRC) make it no secret that the CIRC strongly supports promoting commercial health insurance, at least as a supplementary system of coverage in urban areas, and perhaps rural ones as well.[88]

As part of this mediation and brainstorming process, the National Commission on Health System Reform took the interesting and somewhat unusual step of soliciting about ten reform proposals from independent research organizations (including several Chinese universities, the World Health Organization, the World Bank, and the international consulting firm McKinsey).[89] Even at the outset, apparent consensus existed on two critical issues: the need for greater government financing for health care, and the goal of universal coverage (at a basic level). China piloted a new urban resident insurance program in 2007, supplementing the basic medical insurance for the urban employed introduced in the 1990s; introduced the NCMS in 2002–2003 for the self-employed rural majority; and initiated other new insurance and medical support programs for the poor.

Should the government subsidize the supply side directly, as is the case with a public-integrated model like the NHS, or should it subsidize the demand side, through a public-contract model offering social insurance? This was one of the key questions of reform design in China. As Docteur and Oxley note, the *public-integrated*, or Beveridge, model prevalent in the Nordic countries and the United Kingdom before the 1990s reforms, combines on-budget financing of health-care provision with hospital providers that are part of the government sector.[90] In contrast, under the *public-contract* model, public payers—such as social insurance funds—contract with private health-care providers, as in most continental European countries and Canada. Only the United States and Switzerland rely on a *private-insurance/private-provider* model, with insurance mandatory in Switzerland and voluntary in the United States. Many countries feature a mixture of systems. Even in the United States, for example, Medicare uses a public-contract model, the Veteran's Administration combines a public-integrated model with contracting, and community hospitals owned by local governments receive both direct government subsidies and commercial and social insurance payments. Most transitional economies, especially in central and eastern Europe and Central Asia, emphasized subsidizing the demand side by introducing (or reintroducing) Bismarckian social insurance, although often with public-hospital budgets for capital investment and some recurrent expenditure.[91] Thus, most countries feature some combination of demand-side and supply-side financing.

China's health-system-reform plan announcement was postponed multiple times, no doubt reflecting the complicated political economy of health-sector reform. A draft reform plan made available for public comments from October 14 through November 14, 2008, elicited some 35,260 comments.[92] In the event, China's leaders chose a combination of demand-side and supply-side financing for health care as the foundation of the 2009 health-system reform, to the details of which we now turn.

The 2009 Health Reform

In early 2009, China's top authorities approved the national-health-system-reform plan, and in April the plan was officially released. By September 2009, the government had issued 14 implementation documents and guidelines, including an action plan of targets for reform from 2009 through 2011 (April 2009) and a 307-item essential drug list (August 2009).

These reforms, laid out in broad strokes in the "Opinions of the CPC Central Committee and the State Council on Deepening the Health Care System Reform," focus on expanding coverage of basic medical care, combining social insurance (reportedly accounting for two-thirds of the new government financing) with direct government provision (the remaining one-third of funds).[93] "Estimates suggest that governmental investment (both central and local) of CNY850 billion (about $124 billion) will be injected into the health-care system in the coming 3 years, doubling the average annual governmental expenditure compared with 2008."[94]

The Implementation Plan for 2009–2011 articulates five priorities for policy through 2011 and makes clear that the reform aims to ameliorate if not fully eliminate the distorted incentives permeating China's service delivery. As the implementation plan document exhorts policymakers, "making the basic health care system as public goods to the general public and providing everyone with basic health care services is a major reform concept…"; the reforms should "reverse the profit-orientated behaviors of public health care institutions and drive them to resume their commonweal nature."[95]

More specifically, the three-year reform priorities cover five areas. The first is expanding basic medical insurance to 90 percent coverage. In urban areas in addition to the urban employee basic medical insurance, non-employees will be covered by urban resident basic medical insurance. Rural residents may voluntarily join the NCMS. And specially targeted programs (e.g., the medical aid program by the Ministry of Civil Affairs) subsidize coverage for the poor in both rural and urban areas. The reform explicitly calls for government funding for urban nonemployees and farmers to increase to 120 yuan per person by 2010.

The second reform priority is establishing a national essential drug system. Using a list of 307 medications (including 102 herbal medicines) as the basis for procurement and management of drugs for all grassroots service providers in urban and rural areas, these reforms aim to improve drug supply and affordability while forcing changes in manufacturing and distribution (i.e., "bring into full play the role of market forces in pushing forward merger and restructuring of pharmaceutical manufacturing and distributing enterprises").[96] The central government is to set "guiding retail prices" of essential medicines, and then provincial governments will set "unified purchasing prices" based on a bidding process, "with the distribution charge included in the purchasing price." The reform stipulates that "government-run health care institutions at grass-roots levels shall sell drugs with zero markup." Essential medicines will be insured, "with the reimbursing rate much higher than that of non-essential medicines."[97] Patients are also allowed to purchase drugs in retail pharmacies with a prescription.

Strengthening grassroots health services (i.e., primary care) is the third major reform priority. The government will construct around 2,000 county-level hospitals; build or renovate 3,700 urban community health centers and 11,000 community health stations; and train 360,000 health-care professionals for township health centers, 160,000 for urban community health institutions, and 1.37 million for village clinics in three years. The grassroots health service

257

organizations are required to sell pharmaceuticals on the essential drug list with no markup, one of the components of the reform plan designed to separate prescribing from dispensing.[98]

The fourth priority area is the "gradual equalization of basic public health services." This reform includes defining the basic public service benefit package; creating personal health records nationwide; providing regular health checkups for seniors and infants as well as prenatal care; and expanding health education, especially for the key chronic noncommunicable diseases of hypertension, diabetes, and mental disorders, as well as for HIV/AIDs and tuberculosis.[99] The reform plans calls for average per capita public health funding to be 20 yuan or more by 2011, and explicitly promises central government subsidies for poorer regions.

The final and arguably most difficult priority is conducting pilot programs for reforming government hospitals. The plan calls upon local governments to experiment with the restructuring of government hospitals to improve efficiency, quality, and responsiveness. Although the exact measures are left open, in one area the plan is quite explicit: prescribing and dispensing should be completely separated, removing hospitals' reliance on drug-dispensing revenues:

> The separation of health care services and drug sale should be promoted, gradually rescinding the drug price margin, and banning the acceptance of any drug procurement discount. The revenue reduction and losses incurred from the reform shall be resolved through introducing prescription fees, readjusting the charging criteria for some technical service, increasing government investment, and [other measures]. The prescription fees shall be integrated into the reimbursement scope of the basic medical insurance.[100]

The plan also states that "special needs [VIP] services" should be limited to no more than 10 percent of services provided at government hospitals. Finally, the reform plan encourages development of mixed-ownership delivery: "non-public investors are encouraged to sponsor non-profit hospitals. Non-public hospitals are entitled to the same treatment with their public-owned counterparts."[101]

The implementation plan also contains several clues about the longer-term direction of health-sector reforms. Under the "overall coordination and guidance" of the State Council Leading Group for Deepening the Health Care System Reform, China's authorities aim to explore ways of integrating China's disparate risk pools for employees, urban residents, and the rural self-employed, as well as extend successful public hospital reform pilots to other regions by 2011. The actual reform process will no doubt unfold over many years, as pilot programs related to all the reform priorities are evaluated and scaled up nationwide.

Conclusion

Innovation, Institutions, and Incentives

International medical care reforms in higher-income countries over the past half century came in three waves, according to Cutler. The first, after World War II, focused on establishing universal coverage and equal access.[102] Then, in the face of rapidly increasing health-care expenditures, a wave of reforms implemented controls, rationing, and expenditure caps. More recently, countries have begun to introduce incentives and competition into health-care systems to a greater extent than previously was the case. As the capabilities of medicine continue to expand, bringing new ways of saving and extending lives and increasing the quality of life, the expense of care rises as well. All societies face challenges in making the fruits of those innovations accessible and affordable to all.

China's health-system challenges need to be understood against this global backdrop of policy experimentation and difficult social trade-offs. The ultimate success or failure of China's health-system reform process lies not with the broad outlines of reform, as important as those are. Rather, "the devil is in the details," especially regarding governance and incentive structures. To truly resolve the *kan bing nan, kan bing gui* problem, policymakers must pay close attention to payment incentives (including provider reliance on drug-dispensing revenue, or *yi yao yang yi*), quality assurance, efficient insurance management, accountability, patient satisfaction, and responsiveness.

Increasing government financing and achieving risk pooling on a national scale, while tremendously important and laudable, are only half of the solution. Without reform of the payment and delivery system, the financing reforms will not be sustainable. In the 1980s and 1990s, patients' ability to pay out of pocket put some demand-side constraints on the system, but as insurance coverage expands, those constraints will loosen. The difficult task of constraining health expenditures will then fall to the organized payers: social insurance schemes and policymakers allocating tax financing. Simply exhorting providers to supply services "as public goods" and removing 40 percent of their revenues (from drug dispensing) will not ultimately prove effective unless those revenues and incentives are replaced, so that providing services that improve patient health at reasonable cost—enhancing "value"—becomes the key to financial security and professional status. At times the rhetoric in China tends to oversimplify and sometimes directly blame providers for exploiting asymmetric information to manipulate patients and thus inflate health-care expenditures. Just as it is wrong to say that providers are immune to economic incentives, it is equally misleading to allege that supplier-induced demand is the only factor driving health-care spending increases. China's access problems extend beyond the greed, incompetence, or malfeasance of some "bad apples"; analysts' and patients' ire would be better focused on systemwide incentive problems, though these are not easy to capture in media sound bites or policy statements.

259

The importance of system incentives is aptly captured by the title of a classic article in the management literature: "On the folly of rewarding A, while hoping for B."[103] Two such pairs of misaligned goals and rewards have strongly shaped China's health-care reforms since 1980. The first was the pattern of dysfunctional incentives for health-care providers. Policymakers were hoping to assure access through low "plan" prices for basic health-care services and cross-subsidization of unprofitable population health services such as immunizations from providers' revenues on curative care. However, policies actually rewarded providers for emphasizing profitable high-tech diagnostics, curative care, and dispensing drugs.

Local governance and China's political contract system created a second case of misaligned incentives. Performance contracts that must be signed by local governments and officials reward achieving "hard targets" on economic growth, social stability, and family planning. Policy statements suggest that the leadership was hoping for balanced attention to "soft goals" of social development, such as environmental protection and public health. Unfortunately, such a mismatch of incentives meant that it took a crisis like SARS to highlight the inadequacy of the public health and social protection systems, directly threatening social stability. As Saich has suggested, "if social development goals were written into these contracts and given more weight, this would be a major step forward in changing local government incentives."[104] With China's leadership openly acknowledging the need to create a more "harmonious society," social development goals may begin to garner the attention they deserve in the incentive structure for public servants.

"Growing Pains" in China's Health-care System?

So, are the problems plaguing China's health-care system "growing pains"? Not in the sense that these problems were an *inevitable* result of China's rapid growth and transition from plan to market. But they are indeed growing pains in the sense that China can and quite probably will grow out of them, and in fact already appears committed to doing so.[105]

Let me first elaborate on why the pervasive access problems in China's health-care system were not an inevitable offshoot of China's rapid economic growth. Many other transitional economies were able to maintain population coverage—at a weakened but nevertheless creditable level—despite collapsing economies during their transformation recessions. Thus it strains credulity to assert that China could not have put in place a program resembling the NCMS while growing rapidly during the beginning of the reform period. After all, China had pioneered broad coverage in the 1970s, and even shallow but consistent coverage would have been preferable to the collapse and then rebuilding of risk-pooling institutions. There are no major design features of the NCMS that would have precluded such a system from having been put in place much earlier. Between the collapse of the CMS and the implementation of the NCMS, China's rural majority faced a whole generation without health insurance (figure 9.7).

Two major obstacles account for China's inability to maintain insurance coverage without that gap: (1) strained government finances and (2) lack of trust in local governance. Despite economic growth and lack of a transformational recession, China did experience a "transformational" decline in central government revenues that squeezed resources precisely when new social protection mechanisms were needed. Fiscal decentralization accentuated the problem for poorer areas. Second, the association of CMS with the Cultural Revolution and collective economy combined with the lack of confidence in local government to create an institutional vacuum for pooling health-care risk in rural China. Farmers would rather stuff money in their mattresses than pay insurance premiums to someone they felt was likely to abscond with their funds.[106] This perspective of rural governance failure contrasts with the widely held view in the transitional economics literature that China succeeded where others failed precisely because China's government never collapsed and therefore was able to enforce dual-track reforms to "grow out of the plan."

Figure 9.7 Health Coverage for China's Rural Majority, 1978–2008

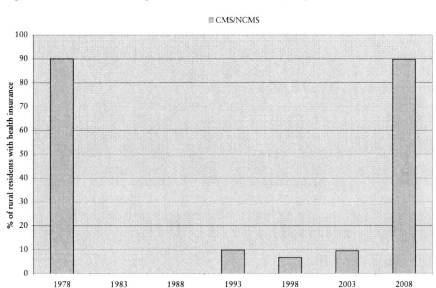

Source: National Health Surveys (1993, 1998, 2003, 2008) as reported on the Ministry of Health Web site, www.moh.gov.cn/publicfiles//business/htmlfiles/zwgkzt/pwstj/index.htm.

Note: Comparable national data not available for 1983 and 1988, though localized studies suggest CMS coverage collapsed in the early 1980s and was at 10 percent or less before the end of the 1980s.

In this sense, dual-track "reform without losers" in China, although viable for industrial and agricultural product markets, faced serious challenges in the realm of social services. The government could not credibly enforce the plan (access to basic services) because of the difficulties of defining entitlement and accountability for "basic health services" and because of corruption and lack of faith in village and township governance (to manage health insurance funds or directly supply services). Some of the elements of the 2009 health reforms —such as the essential drug list or directly limiting VIP services at government hospitals—resemble efforts to define a "plan track" of basic health services and directly regulate their delivery. These aspects of the reform must confront the same challenges as the earlier efforts to establish and defend a "plan track" for basic services. Arguably their success rests on "getting the incentives right" through effective implementation of the other aspects of China's reform plan, including extending risk pooling, strengthening primary care, and reengineering service delivery to better fit the needs of China's increasingly urban, affluent, and aging society.

It seems highly unlikely that China will implement mandatory coverage any time soon; the system in practice and envisioned in the reform plan is voluntary (albeit according to many observers "quasi-voluntary" because local governments are under heavy pressure to keep enrollment high and invest considerable resources in "persuading" households to join NCMS, for example). Voluntary enrollment does provide a limited "market signal" about whether the program is working and some protection for residents against failures of local governance or insurance management, because if their money disappears and they do not receive health-care benefits perceived as commensurate with their voluntary premiums, the people can "vote with their feet" by refusing to enroll in subsequent years. But voluntary enrollment has the disadvantage of limiting China's ability to reach the goal of universal coverage, leading to problems of adverse selection. As the father of health economics, Victor Fuchs, has pointed out, universal coverage requires subsidization and compulsion.[107] China has committed to subsidize insurance, but compulsion appears to be off the table. This commitment to choice (despite the complexity it presents for universal coverage) may come as a surprise to those who view China as a totalitarian state.

Achieving universal health-care coverage in China will not be easy for other institutional reasons as well. Guaranteeing basic health-care coverage for all citizens is rarely a simple process, typically requiring the coordination and expansion of multiple insurance funds over many years, as well as nontrivial government subsidies for the most vulnerable. Japan achieved universal health-care coverage in 1961, when GDP per capita (in constant 2000 U.S. dollars) was $7,883. South Korea achieved universal coverage in 1989 with GDP per capita of $6,130. Mexico, striving to achieve universal coverage by 2010, has GDP per capita of $6,387.[108] In contrast, China's current GDP per capita is only $1,595. (All GDP figures are excerpted from the World Bank's World

Development Indicators, WDI, online database.) Of course the country that spends the most per capita on health care—the United States—is still grappling with how to achieve universal coverage.

Despite the challenges of achieving it, universal coverage fits with China's social and macroeconomic goals—building a "harmonious society," addressing disparities, rebalancing economic growth toward domestic demand and the service sector, upgrading industrial structure, and promoting innovation.[109] Above all, resolving health-care affordability problems figures prominently in efforts to assure social stability.[110]

Policymakers' commitment to extending health insurance coverage arguably stems from the realization that social stability may prove a mirage without an effective social safety net.[111] China has dramatically expanded health insurance coverage for the population over the past five years. Once coverage for basic care is fully in place, policymakers in their role as payers cannot escape confronting the difficult social trade-offs associated with making health care accessible yet financially sustainable. China's health reforms of 2009 appear poised to go a long way towards achieving that goal, and represent a large social experiment that can provide lessons not only for China's future health system but also for other developing and transitional economies. Therefore, cautious optimism about China's health-care system reforms appears warranted.

Notes

[1] I am grateful to Xueguang Zhou and Martin K. Whyte for comments on a previous draft. This chapter is dedicated to the loving memory of Dr. Li Yishen, skilled surgeon and gentle soul; may he rest in peace.

[2] Section 10 of the outline, "Building a Socialist Harmonious Society," lists as a goal during the next five years "resolving the problem of limited health-care resources and expensive medical care" (*renzhen jiejue qunzhong kanbing nan kanbing gui wenti*); http://ghs.ndrc.gov.cn/15ghgy/W020060526575598075309.jpg.

[3] *Yiyaoweisheng tizhi gaige jinqi zhongdian shishi fang'an 2009-2011nian* 2009.

[4] Shanlian Hu, "Zhongguo weisheng gaige yu fazhan lantu de gouxiang" [A blueprint of China's health reform and development], *Zhongguo Weisheng Jingji* [*Chinese Health Economics*] 25, no. 8 (2006): 6; *Lianghui diaocha* (poll taken for the "two meetings"), http://poll.people.com/cn/286_ctdzb_001/2008lianghui_diaocha.php.

[5] Guowuyuan Fazhan Yanjiu Zhongxin Ketizu (Study Group from the Development Research Center of China's State Council). *Dui zhongguo yiliao weisheng tizhi gaige de pingjia yu jianyi (gaiyao yu zhongdian)*, 2005.

[6] See www.time.com/time/magazine/article/0,9171,501030519-451006,00.html, http://news.bbc.co.uk/2/hi/asia-pacific/4062523.stm, and www.cbsnews.com/stories/2007/01/02/asiaLetter/main2324841.shtml.

[7] Indeed, according to historical research, China may have been the source of the 1918–1919 influenza virus, which caused a deadly global pandemic. See Christopher Langford, "Did the 1918–19 Influenza Pandemic Originate in China?" *Population and Development Review* 31, no. 3 (September 2005): 473–505.

[8] David M. Cutler, "Equality, Efficiency, and Market Fundamentals: The Dynamics of International Medical-Care Reform," *Journal of Economic Literature* 40, no. 3 (2002): 881–906.

[9] William C. L. Hsiao, "The Chinese Health Care System: Lessons for Other Nations," *Social Science & Medicine* (1982) 41, no. 8 (October 1995): 1047–55; Gerald Bloom and Shenglan Tang, "Rural Health Prepayment Schemes in China: Towards a More Active Role for Government," *Social Science and Medicine (New York)* 7 (April 1999): 951–60; John S. Akin, William H. Dow, and Peter M. Lance, "Did the Distribution of Health Insurance in China Continue to Grow Less Equitable in the Nineties?" Results from a longitudinal survey, *Social Science and Medicine (Amsterdam)* 2 (January 2004): 293–304.

[10] See for example Gordon G. Liu, X. Wu, C. Peng, and A. Z. Fu, "Urbanization and Health Care in Rural China," *Contemporary Economic Policy (Huntington Beach, CA)* 21, no. 1 (January 2003): 11–24; Ling Li, "Zhongguo zhengfu ying caiqu zhengfu zhudaoxing de yiliao tizhi" [China's government should adopt a government-directed health-care system], *Zhongguo Yu Shijie Guancha* 1 (2005): 1–3; Qiren Zhou, "Huafei yu gonggei bufu: Zhe suan namenzi yiliao shichanghua," *Jingji Guancha Bao* (January 20, 2007); Ming Wu, "Woguo yiliao weisheng lingyu de shichanghua chengdu fenxi" [Analysis of the degree of marketization in China's health-care sector], *Zhongguo Weisheng Jingji (Chinese Health Economics)* 26, no. 8 (2007): 5–8.

[11] Hu, *Zhongguo weisheng gaige yu fazhan lantu de gouxiang.*

[12] *Zhonggong Zhongyang Guowuyuan Guanyu Shenhua Yiyao Weisheng Tizhi Gaige de Yijian* 2009.

[13] Barry J. Naughton, *Growing Out of the Plan: Chinese Economic Reform, 1978–1993* (Cambridge: Cambridge Univ. Press, 1995); L. J. Lau, Y. Qian, and G. Roland, "Reform Without Losers: An Interpretation of China's Dual-Track Approach to Transition," *Journal of Political Economy* 108, no. 1 (2000): 120.

[14] V. W. Sidel, "The Barefoot Doctors of the People's Republic of China," *The New England Journal of Medicine* 286, no. 24 (June 15, 1972): 1292–30; D. T. Jamison, China: *The Health Sector* (Washington D.C.: World Bank, 1994).

[15] Janos Kornai, *The Socialist System: The Political Economy of Communism* (Princeton, NJ: Princeton Univ. Press, 1992).

[16] Judith Banister and Kenneth Hill, "Mortality in China 1964–2000," *Population Studies* 58, no. 1 (March 2004): 55–75.

[17] Grant Miller, Karen Eggleston, and Qiong Zhang, "Explaining China's Mortality Decline under Mao," Working paper, Stanford University, September 2009.

[18] Christopher Grigoriou, Patrick Guillaumont, and Wenyan Yang, "Child Mortality under Chinese Reforms," *China Economic Review* 16, no. 4 (2005): 441–64. Grigoriou, Guillaumont, and Yang find that while China continued to outperform most countries in terms of infant survival, China's edge over these countries decreased during the reform period and the impact of household income on infant survival increased. See figure 1b and discussion in Karen Eggleston, Jian Wang, and Keqin Rao, "From Plan to Market in the Health Sector? China's Experience," *Journal of Asian Economics* 19: 400–12, http://dx.doi.org/10.1016/j.asieco.2008.09.002.

[19] Feng Wang and Andrew Mason, "The Demographic Factor in China's Transition," in Loren Brandt and Thomas G. Rawski, eds., *China's Great Economic Transformation* (Cambridge: Cambridge Univ. Press, 2008), 136–66.

[20] Mark Rosenzweig and Junsen Zhang, "Do Population Control Policies Induce More Human Capital Investment? Twins, Birth Weight and China's 'One-Child' Policy," *Review of Economic Studies* 76, no. 3 (2009): 1149–74.

[21] In Athar Hussain's "Social Welfare in China in the Context of Three Transitions," in Nicholas C. Hope, Dennis Tao Yang, and Mu Yang Li, eds., *How Far Across the River? Chinese Policy Reform at the Millennium* (Stanford, CA: Stanford Univ. Press, 2003), 273–312.

[22] Wang and Mason, "The Demographic Factor in China's Transition"; Andrew Mason and Ronald Lee, "Reform and Support Systems for the Elderly in Developing Countries: Capturing the Second Demographic Dividend," *Genus* 62, no. 2 (2006): 1–25.

[23] For examples, see Robert W. Fogel, "Forecasting the Demand for Health Care in OECD Nations and China," *Contemporary Economic Policy* 21, no. 1 (January 2003): 1–10; Peter S. Heller, "Is Asia Prepared for an Aging Population?" Working Paper 06/272, International Monetary Fund, 2006; Geoffrey McNicoll, "Policy Lessons of the East Asian Demographic Transition," *Population and Development Review* 32, no. 1 (March 2006): 1–25.

[24] Barry M. Popkin, "Will China's Nutrition Transition Overwhelm Its Health Care System and Slow Economic Growth?" *Health Affairs* 27, no. 4 (July/August 2008): 1064–76.

[25] The data are from the NIH/WB/WHO Disease Control Priorities Project; see Alan D. Lopez, Colin D. Mathers, Majid Ezzati, Dean T. Jamison, and Christopher J. L. Murray, "Global and Regional Burden of Disease and Risk Factors, 2001: Systematic Analysis of Population Health Data," *Lancet* 367, no. 9524 (May 27, 2006): 1747–57; and Disease Control Priorities Project, *Burden of Disease in China in 2001*, April 2006, www.dcp2. org. Also see Gonghuan Yang, Lingzhi Kong, Wenhua Zhao, Xia Wan, Yi Zhai, Lincoln C. Chen, and Jeffrey P. Koplan, "Emergence of Chronic Non-Communicable Diseases in China," *Lancet* 372 (2008): 1697–705.

[26] Arthur Kleinman and David Mechanic, "Mental Illness and Psycho-Social Aspects of Medical Problems in China," in Arthur Kleinman and Tsung-Yi Lin, eds., *Normal and Abnormal Behavior in Chinese Culture* (Boston, MA: D. Reidel, 1981), 331–56; Yu-cun Shen, "People's Republic of China [mental health policy]," in Donna R. Demp, ed., *International Handbook on Mental Health Policy* (Westport, CT, and London: Greenwood, 1993), 287–302; Rene Stockman, "Mental Health Care in Central Africa and China," *British Journal of Psychiatry (London)* 2 (August 1994): 145–8; Hsueh-Shih Chen, "Development of Mental Health Systems and Care in China: From the 1940s through the 1980s," in Tsung-Yi Lin, Wen-Shing Tseng, and Eng-Kung Yeh, eds., *Chinese Societies and Mental Health* (Oxford and New York: Oxford Univ. Press, 1995), xxiii, 315–25, 379; Ji Jianlin, "Advances in Mental Health Services in Shanghai, China," *International Journal of Mental Health* (Armonk, NY) 4 (Winter 1995): 90–7; Ji Jianlin, "The Application of Mental Health Economics Methods in the People's Republic of China," in M. Moscarelli, A. Rupp, and N. Sartorius, eds., *Schizophrenia* (Chichester, UK and New York: John Wiley, 1996), 546; Michael Philips, "The Transformation of China's Mental Health Services," *China Journal (Canberra)* 39 (January 1998): 1–36; Kam-Shing Yip, "An Historical Review of the Mental Health Services in the People's Republic of China," *International Journal of Social Psychiatry (London)* 2 (June 2005): 106–18.

[27] Shanlian Hu, Shenglan Tang, Yuanli Liu, Yuxin Zhao, Maria-Luisa Escobar, David de Ferranti, "Reform of How Health Care is Paid for in China: Challenges and Opportunities," *Lancet* 372 (2008): 1846–53.

[28] Such injections, commonly leading to hepatitis B or C transmission, receive generous reimbursement and have come to be viewed by many patients, particularly in rural areas, as a sign of quality care despite their track record for being unsafe.

[29] Justin Yifu Lin, "Rural Reforms and Agricultural Growth in China," *American Economic Review* 82, no. 1 (1992): 34–51. Also see Y. Qian, "The Process of China's Market Transition (1978–98): The Evolutionary, Historical, and Comparative Perspectives," *Journal of Institutional and Theoretical Economics* 156, no. 1 (2000): 151–71; Martin Ravallion and Shaohua Chen, "China's (Uneven) Progress Against Poverty," *Journal of Development Economics* 82, no. 1 (January 2007): 1–42.

[30] This term was coined by Barry Naughton in the 1980s and is the title of his 1995 book on China's reforms, *Growing Out of the Plan: Chinese Economic Reform, 1978–1993*.

[31] The GDP data in figure 9.1 are in 2000 U.S. dollars at purchasing power parity (PPP), drawn from the World Development Indicator (WDI) database (World Bank, www.worldbank.org/data). The estimates of the state-controlled share of the economy (1998 to 2003) come from Ross Garnaut, Ligang Song, Stoyan Tenev, and Yang Yao, *China's Ownership Transformation: Process, Outcomes, Prospects* (Washington, D.C.: International Finance Corporation and World Bank, 2005), 10.

[32] The share of the economy actually allocated according to "central planning" is considerably less, since the dual-track pricing system of the earlier reform period has gradually been phased out for most goods and services, so that state-controlled firms in China now largely operate in competitive markets.

[33] Lau, Qian, and Roland, "Reform Without Losers," 120.

[34] Oliver Blanchard and Michael Kremer, " Disorganization," *Quarterly Journal of Economics* 112, no. 4 (November 1997): 1091–126.

[35] N. F. Campos and F. Coricelli, "Growth in Transition: What We Know, What We Don't, and What We Should," *Journal of Economic Literature* 40, no. 3 (2002): 793–836.

[36] Lau, Qian, and Roland, "Reform Without Losers," 120.

[37] Ibid.

[38] Ibid.

[39] Karen Eggleston, Li Ling, Meng Qingyue, Magnus Lindelow, and Adam Wagstaff, "Health Service Delivery in China: A Literature Review," *Health Economics* 17 (2008): 149–65.

[40] For a discussion of why low prices for basic services failed to guarantee access in China, also see Karen Eggleston and Winnie Yip, "Hospital Competition under Regulated Prices: Application to Urban Health Sector Reforms in China," *International Journal of Health Care Finance and Economics* 4, no. 4 (December 2004): 343–68.

[41] See Victor R. Fuchs, *Who Shall Live? Health Economics and Social Choice* (New York: Basic Books, 1975); Cutler and Zeckhauser, "The Anatomy of Health Insurance," chapter 11; and Joseph P. Newhouse, *Pricing the Priceless: A Health Care Conundrum* (Cambridge, MA: MIT Press, 2002). This summary draws from Janos Kornai and Karen Eggleston, *Welfare, Choice, and Solidarity in Transition: Reforming the Health Sector in Eastern Europe* (Cambridge: Cambridge Univ. Press, 2001).

[42] Fuchs, *Who Shall Live?*

[43] Newhouse, *Pricing the Priceless.*

[44] For a review of the international literature on inequalities in health and health care, see A. Wagstaff and E. van Doorslaer, "Equity in Health Care Finance and Delivery," *Handbook of Health Economics* 1 (2000): 1803–62.

[45] The data come from the World Health Organization (WHO) national health accounts and from the Ministry of Health (MOH), Center for Health Statistics and Information, China National Health Accounts Report (Beijing, PRC, 2004).

[46] Barry Naughton, "A Political Economy of China's Economic Transition," in Loren Brandt and Thomas G. Rawski, eds., *China's Great Economic Transformation* (Cambridge: Cambridge Univ. Press), 108.

[47] Granted, China's increase in private financing during the two decades of rapid economic growth runs counter to much international experience: private financing tends to fall with economic development, since the income elasticity of public financing exceeds 1. See G. Schieber, and A. Maeda, "Health Care Financing and Delivery in Developing Countries," *Health Affairs* 18, no. 3 (May 1, 1999): 193–205. But the transition from central planning to a market-based economy would tend to suggest that private financing might increase in China, and indeed it has, and to a much greater extent than for most other transition economies, as will be discussed further below.

[48] David Dollar, "Poverty, Inequality, and Social Disparities during China's Economic Reform," Policy Research Working Paper Series: 4253, World Bank, 2007.

[49] Sources for these calculations are from the 2006 Health Statistics Yearbook, 659; the 1997 Health Statistics Yearbook, 423; and GDP per capita from China statistical yearbooks, as compiled in "China data online," http://chinadataonline.org/member/macroy/macroytshow.asp?code=A0101.

[50] Hu, *Zhongguo weisheng gaige yu fazhan lantu de gouxiang*, 5–7; Lianghui diaocha.

[51] Gregory Chow, "An Economic Analysis of Health Care in China," Working Paper 132, Princeton University, Department of Economics, Center for Economic Policy Studies, 2006.

[52] Data are from MOH Yearbook of Public Health, 1997 and 2006; the Almanac of China's Hospitals (*Zhongguo Yiyuan Nianjian* 2006).

[53] Eggleston et al., "Health Service Delivery in China."

[54] See discussion in Eggleston and Yip, "Hospital Competition under Regulated Prices"; Eggleston et al., "Health Service Delivery in China."

[55] As a manager of one private health-care organization said (discussion in July 2007), they benefit from the need for China's increasingly globally competitive firms to attract managerial talent—both Chinese and foreign—with benefit packages that include attractive health-care coverage, including access to medical services at U.S. or European standards.

[56] For more detailed analysis of hospital finances, see Y. Liu, P. Berman, W. Yip, H. Liang, Q. Meng, J. Qu, and Z. Li, "Health Care in China: The Role of Non-Government Providers," *Health Policy (Amsterdam, Netherlands)* 77, no. 2 (July 2006): 212; and Eggleston et al., "Health Service Delivery in China."

[57] See studies on price regulation reviewed in Eggleston et al., "Health Service Delivery in China."

[58] Newhouse, *Pricing the Priceless*; for example, Winnie Yip and Karen Eggleston, "Provider Payment Reform in China: The Case of Hospital Reimbursement in Hainan Province," *Health Economics* 10, no. 4 (2001): 325–39.

[59] Eggleston et al., "Health Service Delivery in China."

[60] See for example Yip and Eggleston, "Provider Payment Reform in China"; Eggleston and Yip, "Hospital Competition under Regulated Prices;" Karen Eggleston and Chee-Ruey Hsieh, "Healthcare Payment Incentives: A Comparative Analysis of Reforms in Taiwan, South Korea and China," *Applied Health Economics and Health Policy* 3, no. 1 (2004): 47–56.

[61] Maureen Lewis, "Informal Payments and the Financing of Health Care in Developing and Transition Countries," *Health Affairs* 26, no. 4 (July 1, 2007): 984–97.

[62] Janos Kornai, "Transformational Recession: The Main Causes," *Journal of Comparative Economics* 19, no. 1 (1994): 39–63.

[63] For more details about the agricultural sector in transition economies, see Scott Rozelle and J. F. M. Swinnen, "Success and Failure of Reform: Insights from the Transition of Agriculture," *Journal of Economic Literature* 42, no. 2 (1994): 404–56.

[64] See figure 9.2; for more on health-sector reforms in Central and Eastern Europe, see Kornai and Eggleston, *Welfare, Choice, and Solidarity in Transition*.

[65] Gerard Roland, *Transition and Economics: Politics, Markets, and Firms* (Cambridge, MA: MIT Press, 2000), 21.

[66] Ibid.

[67] The role of the *hukou* system in contributing to growing inequalities in China during much of the reform era is discussed in both Dollar, *Poverty, Inequality, and Social Disparities*, and Xiaogang Wu and Donald J. Treiman, "The Household Registration System and Social Stratification in China: 1955–1996," *Demography* 41, no. 2 (May 2004): 363–84.

[68] Dollar, *Poverty, Inequality, and Social Disparities*; Gaurav Datt and Thomas Walker, "Recent Evolution of Inequality in East Asia," *Applied Economics Letters* 11, no. 2 (February 2004): 75–9.

[69] Yuanli Liu, William C. Hsiao, and Karen Eggleston, "Equity in Health and Health Care: The Chinese Experience," *Social Science & Medicine* (1982) 49, no. 10 (November 1999): 1349–56.

[70] Jennifer Adams and Emily Hannum, "Children's Social Welfare in China, 1989–1997: Access to Health Insurance and Education," *China Quarterly* 181, no. 3 (2005): 100–21.

[71] Zhuo Chen, David B. Eastwood, and Steven T. Yen, "A Decade's Story of Childhood Malnutrition Inequality in China: Where You Live Does Matter," *China Economic Review* 18, no. 2 (2007): 139–54.

[72] *China Statistical Yearbook* 2008, www.chinadataonline.org.

[73] See John Whalley, and Ximing Yue, "Rural Income Volatility and Inequality in China," Working Paper 12779, National Bureau of Economics Research, December 2006.

Although the higher child mortality and maternal mortality rates in rural areas would be directly reflected in lower life expectancy compared with urban areas, the effects of such deaths on other family members are not directly quantified in any health statistics but surely take their toll in terms of rural well-being.

[74] Li Gan, Lixin Colin Xu, and Yang Yao, "Health Shocks, Village Elections, and Long-Term Income: Evidence from Rural China," Working Paper No. 12686, National Bureau of Economic Research, 2006.

[75] Yuanli Liu and Keqin Rao, "Providing Health Insurance in Rural China: From Research to Policy," *Journal of Health Politics, Policy and Law* 31, no. 1 (2006): 71–92.

[76] Ibid.

[77] Victor R. Fuchs, "Economics, Values, and Health Care Reform," *The American Economic Review* 86, no. 1 (March 1996): 1–24.

[78] See the numerous country-specific chapters in Karen Eggleston, ed., *Prescribing Cultures and Pharmaceutical Policy in the Asia-Pacific* (Stanford, CA: Shorenstein Asia-Pacific Research Center, 2009).

[79] Karen Eggleston, "Institutions and Health Policy: Explaining Physician Dispensing in East Asia," Working paper, Stanford University, September 2009.

[80] From the first recorded case in southern China in November 2002 to its global control by July 2003, SARS infected more than 8,000 people and was responsible for 916 deaths. See Arthur Kleinman and J. L. Watson, *SARS in China: Prelude to Pandemic?* (Stanford, CA: Stanford Univ. Press, 2006), 21. The majority of SARS victims were mainland Chinese.

[81] T. Saich, "Is SARS China's Chernobyl or Much Ado about Nothing?" in Kleinman and Watson, *SARS in China*, 71.

[82] Precisely how these steps have helped to contain SARS and other public health threats since then remains controversial and may not be clear until tested by future outbreaks of potential pandemic diseases. Those hoping that SARS might be "China's Chernobyl" or "China's Waterloo"—spurring fundamental political change or providing "an opportunity to show off its growing scientific prowess to the international community"—were disappointed. See Cong Cao, "SARS: 'Waterloo' of Chinese Science," *China: An International Journal* 2, no. 2 (September 2004): 262–86, and "Is SARS China's Chernobyl." Yet China's strong actions to contain the spread of H1N1 influenza in 2009 contrast favorably with the handling of the SARS crisis.

[83] For further writings about SARS, see for example Jane Duckett, "An Opportunity for China's Health System? [SARS may Stimulate Health Reform Hopes]," *China Review (London)* 25 (Summer 2003): 5–7; Gary W. Shannon and Jason Willoughby, "Severe Acute Respiratory Syndrome (SARS) in Asia: A Medical Geographic Perspective," *Eurasian Geography and Economics* 45, no. 5 (July–August 2004): 359–81; Alan Schnur, "The Role of the World Health Organization in Combating SARS, Focusing on the Efforts in China [includes a chronology of events related to the WHO's role]," in Kleinman and Watson, *SARS in China*, 31–52; Johnathan Schwartz and R. Gregory Evans, "Causes of Effective Policy Implementation: China's Public Health Response to SARS [includes a case study of Shaanxi province]," *Journal of Contemporary China (Abingdon, Oxfordshire, UK)* 51 (May 2007): 195–213.

[84] For background on CMS and NCMS, see Naisu Zhu, Z. H. Ling, J. Shen, J. M. Lane, S. L. Hu, "Factors Associated with the Decline of the Cooperative Medical System and Barefoot Doctors in Rural China," *Bulletin of the World Health Organization (Geneva)* 67 (1989): 431–41; Xiao-ming Chen, Teh-wei Hu, and Zihua Lin, "The Rise and Decline of the Cooperative Medical System in Rural China," *International Journal of Health Services (Amityville, NY)* 23 (2003): 731–42; Xingyuan Gu, G. Bloom, T. Shenglan, Zhu Yingya, Zhou Shouqi, and Chen Xingbao, "Financing Health Care in Rural China: Preliminary Report of a Nationwide Study, Social Science and Medicine (New York) 36, no. 4 (February 1993): 385–91; Xueshan Feng, S. Tang, G. Bloom, M. Segall, and Y. Gu, "Cooperative Medical Schemes in Contemporary Rural China," *Social Science and Medicine (New York)* 8 (October 1995): 1111–8; Guy Carrin, Aviva Ron, Yang Hui, Wang Hong, Zhang Tuohong, Zhang Licheng, Zhang Shuo, Ye Yide, Chen Jiaying, Jiang Qicheng, Zhang Zhaoyang, Yu Jun, and Li Xuesheng, "The Reform of the Rural Cooperative Medical System in the People's Republic of China: Interim Experience

in 14 Pilot Countries," *Social Science and Medicine (New York)* 7 (April 1999): 961–72; Yuanli Liu, "China's Public Health-Care System: Facing the Challenges," *Bulletin of the World Health Organization (Geneva)* 7 (July 2004): 532–8; Sukhan Jackson, Adrian C. Sleigh, Li Peng, and Xi-Li Liu, "Health Finance in Rural Henan: Low Premium Insurance Compared to the Out-Of-Pocket System," *China Quarterly* 181, no. 3 (2005): 137–57; and Liu and Rao, "Providing Health Insurance in Rural China."

[85] As suggested in Liu and Rao, "Providing Health Insurance in Rural China."

[86] In October 2002 the government promulgated the "Decision on Strengthening Rural Health Work" (*Guanyu Jinyibu Jiaqiang Nongcun Weisheng Gongzuo de Jueding*), which proposed a new cooperative medical system (*Xinxing Nongcun Hezuo Yiliao Zhidu, or NCMS, xin nong he*). NCMS has been highlighted in speeches by President Hu and Premier Wen; a task force headed by the vice premier oversaw the implementation, with experimental sites in select provinces later followed by more general expansion. The outline of the Eleventh Five-year Plan for National Economic and Social Development also listed expanding the NCMS enrollment as 1 of only 22 "major indicators of economic and social development in the eleventh five-year plan period" (http://ghs.ndrc.gov.cn/15ghgy/t20060526_70573.htm), and the 2009 reform plan prominently calls for expanding financing for the NCMS and keeping (voluntary) enrollment high enough to achieve virtually universal coverage by 2011.

[87] See for example Adam Wagstaff and Yu Shengchao, "Do Health Sector Reforms Have Their Intended Impacts? The World Bank's Health VIII Project in Gansu Province, China," *Journal of Health Economics* 26, no. 3 (May 2007): 505–35.

[88] Examples include the speeches by Meng Zhaoyi, director general, International Department, CIRC, and Fang Li, Deputy Director General, Life Insurance Department, CIRC, at the CIRC-NAIC Joint Seminar on Health Insurance, July 18–19, 2007, Yichang, Hubei, PRC.

[89] Although the proposals and the solicitation process were formally secret, the original list included Peking University, Fudan University, the State Council Development Research Center, the World Health Organization (WHO), the World Bank, and McKinsey, and was later expanded to include proposals from the Beijing Normal University, Tsinghua University, and People's University.

[90] E. Docteur and H. Oxley, "Health System Reform: Lessons from Experience," in *Towards High-Performing Health Systems* (Paris: OECD, 2003).

[91] Adam Wagstaff and Rodrigo Moreno-Serra, "Europe and Central Asia's Great Post-Communist Social Health Insurance Experiment: Aggregate Impacts on Health Sector Outcomes," *Journal of Health Economics* 28 (2009): 322–40.

[92] *Xin yigai fang'an gong zhengqiu 3.5wanyu yijian he jianyi*, November 15, 2008.

[93] *Zhonggong Zhongyang Guowuyuan Guanyu Shenhua Yiyao Weisheng Tizhi Gaige de Yijian* 2009.

[94] Chen 2009, 1322.

[95] *Yiyaoweisheng tizhi gaige jinqi zhongdian shishi fang'an 2009-2011nian* 2009.

[96] Ibid.

[97] Ibid.

[98] "The service charges of grass-roots health care institutions shall be set according to the costs after deduction of government subsidy. As long as drugs are sold at zero price margin, the revenue from drug sales will no longer be compensation sources for funding grass-roots health care institutions, and drug discount shall not be accepted." See *Yiyaoweisheng tizhi gaige jinqi zhongdian shishi fang'an 2009–2011nian* 2009, (Implementation Plan for

the Recent Priorities of the Health Care System Reform, 2009–2011) official translation, available at http://shs.ndrc.gov.cn/ygjd/ygwj/t20090408_271137.htm.

[99] Programs launched starting from 2009 include catch-up Hepatitis B vaccination for individuals under 15; eliminating the hazards of toxication by coal-burning fluorosis; providing supplementary intake of folic acid for rural women; cataract treatment for economically constrained patients; and improving water supply and toilet facilities in rural areas.

[100] *Yiyaoweisheng tizhi gaige jinqi zhongdian shishi fang'an 2009-2011nian* 2009.

[101] Ibid.

[102] Cutler, "Equality, Efficiency, and Market Fundamentals," 881–906.

[103] S. Kerr, "On the Folly of Rewarding A, While Hoping for B," *The Academy of Management Journal* 18, no. 4 (1975): 769–83.

[104] Saich, "Is SARS China's Chernobyl,"100.

[105] After all, if any country were to experience "growing pains," it would have to be China—no other country has had such a record of growth, sustained for 25 years.

[106] Although many scholars have studied China's rural economic growth and evolution of governance, research into the relationship between local governance and health-care effectiveness is rather limited. In an interesting 2006 paper, Gan, Xu, and Yao studied 48 Chinese villages between 1986 and 2002 and found that villages are more likely to establish a health-care coverage plan after introducing village elections. Their research linking village elections to health coverage is based on the logical and empirically defensible assumption that families suffering a health shock impose negative externalities on richer families by borrowing from them. One implication is that improvements in local governance will be crucial to sustain health-care reforms providing universal coverage. See Li Gan, Lixin Colin Xu, and Yang Yao, "Health Shocks, Village Elections, and Long-Term Income: Evidence from Rural China," NBER Working Paper 12686, National Bureau of Economic Research, Cambridge, MA.

[107] Fuchs, *Who Shall Live?*

[108] FeliciaMarie Knaul and Julio Frenk, "Health Insurance in Mexico: Achieving Universal Coverage through Structural Reform," *Health Affairs* 24, no. 6 (November 1, 2005): 1467–76.

[109] See Dollar, *Poverty, Inequality, and Social Disparities*. For example, biopharmaceuticals (*shengwu yiyao*) are listed among the seven high-tech industries for focused development during the current five-year plan, and innovative medicines and "prevention and control of key communicable diseases such as AIDS and viral hepatitis" are listed among the high-priority programs in science and technology (http://ghs.ndrc.gov.cn/15ghgy/t20060526_70573.htm).

[110] Indeed, building social stability, quelling corruption, and bolstering Chinese Communist Party legitimacy—not, as one might expect, awareness of the economic inefficiency of not enforcing the "plan" under dual-track reforms—were the driving forces behind "reform without losers" (see Lau, Qian, and Roland, "Reform Without Losers"). One of the most prominent slogans during the 1989 student protests was "down with guandao"—officials enriching themselves by turning access to plan-track goods into market-track profits. The harsh sentencing of selected corrupt officials, including the former head of the Chinese SFDA, can be interpreted in this light.

[111] China issued an official white paper on "China's Social Security and its Policy" in 2004. The first paragraph highlights and acknowledges the importance of assuring social stability as a motivation for reforming China's social security system: "Social security is one

of the most important socio-economic systems for a country in modern times. To establish and improve a social security system corresponding to the level of economic development is a logical requirement for coordinated economic and social development. It is also an important guarantee for the social stability and the long-term political stability of a country" (p. 1, italics added, http://english/gov/cn/official/2005-07/28/content_18024.htm).

ENVIRONMENTAL DEGRADATION AS A COST OF CHINA'S ECONOMIC GROWTH: TRANSITIONAL SETBACK OR IRREVERSIBLE CHANGE?

Leonard Ortolano[1]

Environmental degradation in China has elicited great international interest, for good reason. For decades it has been apparent that changes in China's environment, particularly those associated with air and water pollution (the main subjects of this chapter), can have far-reaching domestic and international ramifications.[2] For example, air-quality degradation has had an immediate effect on large numbers of China's people, and while often less evident, air pollution in China is causing significant problems for China's neighbors in East Asia.[3] Moreover, China's production of carbon dioxide (CO_2) and other emissions contributing to global climate change has severe consequences for all nations.[4]

China's environmental quality has deteriorated significantly during the past few decades. Whether those changes can be reversed in a matter of years—or even decades—instead of generations remains unclear. But the timetable for making notable improvements in environmental quality will no doubt affect the economic efficiency of China's growth trajectory: major investments in environmental infrastructure have been made, but huge monetary damages from pollution and land degradation continue to be incurred, and problems tied to increases in unregulated pollutants are mounting, thereby adding to costs of remediation efforts that may eventually be required.

For the first few decades following the initiation of reforms in 1978, China adopted a "grow now, clean later" approach to economic development.[5] In this sense, it seemed to be following the economic development approaches employed decades earlier in the United States, Japan, and other highly industrialized countries. However, since 2003 a new concept for development has been promoted by the administration of President Hu Jintao and Premier Wen Jiabao. The new strategy calls for using a "concept of scientific development" to construct a "harmonious socialist society."[6]

In his report at the 17th Congress of the Chinese Communist Party (CCP) in 2007, President Hu Jintao said the new development strategy was motivated by fundamental problems that had yet to be addressed, including China's relatively low capacity for innovation and low efficiency of resource use in production processes. In that report, the president was unequivocal: "We must give prominence to building a resource-conserving, environment-friendly society in our strategy for industrialization and modernization and get every organization and family to act accordingly."[7]

In this chapter, I contend that China will soon lift some key obstacles to regulatory enforcement and improved efficiency in resource use but that these changes will not yield major improvements in environmental quality anytime soon. Principal parts of the argument can be summarized as follows:

- China is facing a set of challenges that highly industrialized countries did not face when they were in their high-growth periods—namely, an enormous population, extraordinary gross domestic product (GDP) growth, and an unprecedented pace of urbanization accompanied by rapid increases in material consumption.
- The government has created many regulations to curtail air and water pollution, but compliance has been weak for several reasons, including the dependence of environmental protection bureaus (EPBs) on local leaders, who have incentives that prioritize GDP growth.
- Regulatory compliance and the efficiency of resource use will improve because of recent changes, such as market-related pressures on firms to boost environmental performance and criteria for evaluating local officials that rely on meeting energy efficiency improvement targets.
- But even if regulatory compliance improves, environmental quality cannot be expected to rapidly get better for these reasons: the size of China's population and its increasing material consumption; unprecedented rates of urbanization and economic growth; increased motor-vehicle use; the difficulty of reversing changes in land use made in response to rising vehicle use; and the presence of significant sources of unregulated pollution, such as runoff from farms and cities.

This chapter begins by summarizing the driving forces that underlie environmental change in China, as well as the consequences of those forces for environmental quality and natural resource use. The chapter then details government programs created in response to environmental degradation and the systemic challenges that have limited the extent of compliance with environmental rules. The final sections return to the question in the chapter's title, elaborating on how China is likely to deal with obstacles to environmental enforcement and why China's recent prioritization of resource conservation and environmental protection may not lead to rapid improvements in environmental quality.

Factors Underlying Environmental Degradation

China's environmental degradation is linked to the country's inability to keep pace with the unintended side effects of increasing economic development and the rapid urbanization that is lifting many Chinese out of poverty. This urbanization comes at a time when communications and mass marketing are encouraging the formation of a "consumer class," which, because of China's enormous population, has the potential to impose extraordinary stress on the environment. Each of these factors—population, economic development, urbanization, and the growing consumer culture—is examined below.

China's success in lifting millions out of poverty following the post-1978 reforms has been widely chronicled and justifiably celebrated. The reforms—which include decentralized economic decision-making and revenue allocation—have unleashed a flood of entrepreneurial activity and have yielded spectacular economic growth. Since 1979, China's average annual GDP growth has exceeded 9 percent.[8] In the Eleventh Five-year Plan, the government charted a course for continued rapid development, with a target of 7.5 percent annual economic growth through the end of 2010.

China's enormous population, officially estimated at about 1.3 billion in 2005, makes changes in economic output, as reflected in the increasing GDP per capita, particularly significant.[9] As shown in figure 10.1, the population has been leveling off as a result of the one-child-per-family policy, but demographic imbalances and other adverse consequences of the policy have led to minor modifications and pressure to relax the policy.[10] It is difficult to predict whether (and when) the one-child-per-family policy will be loosened further and how such changes would affect population growth.[11]

Figure 10.1 also illustrates China's sharply rising GDP per capita, a trend that is driven in part by the growth of cities. Many suffering from rural poverty move to cities in search of higher-paying employment opportunities, and they are migrating in uncountable numbers, as ambiguous references to the "floating population" make clear.[12] An analysis of China's 2000 census estimated the floating population to be seventy-nine million, but many think it is larger.[13]

The National Development and Reform Commission (NDRC) reported that the urban population constituted 43 percent of the total population in 2005.[14] The commission indicated that the size of the urban labor force was increasing at twenty million per year, with half the annual increase due to rural migrants moving to cities. Qiu Baoxing, vice minister of China's Ministry of Construction, has projected that 57 to 66 percent of China's projected 2020 population of 1.47 billion will be in urban areas.[15]

China's rapid urbanization and the attendant growth in industry, physical infrastructure, and building construction are placing extraordinary pressure on natural resources. For example, to satisfy skyrocketing electricity demands, China is building coal-fired power plants at a pace that is projected to make it responsible for about half the global use of coal by 2030.[16]

Figure 10.1 Growth of China's GDP and Population

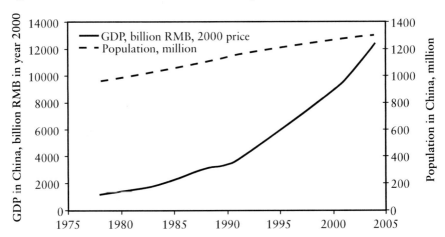

Source: Wang, et al. (2006, 11).

The country's urban and industrial expansion has also increased demand for aluminum, concrete, steel, and other building materials. In 2005 Qiu Baoxing reported that 40 percent of the world's annual construction was taking place in China.[17] And according to MIT professor John Fernandez, "annually, and for the foreseeable future, China builds roughly half of all new building volume in the world."[18] Finally, China accounts for about half of the global demand for concrete and is the world's leading producer of it.[19] These levels of consumption of building materials are expected to continue for decades and to have major impacts on global prices for materials and on total carbon emissions.[20]

The increasing affluence of China's urban residents has motivated the international business community to aggressively cultivate the growing "consumer class." The popular press has reported the following projections:

- Those migrating from rural areas to cities will eventually become members of the middle class. Andrew Grant, head of the consulting firm McKinsey & Co. in China, indicates that though their incomes—which he estimates at around $5,000 a year—will be modest to begin with, income in China buys a lifestyle that would cost four times as much in the United States. Grant expects seven hundred million Chinese to have joined the "consumer class" by 2020, up from fewer than one hundred million in 2007.

- Lifting millions of people out of poverty and into the middle class in such a brief time span is an extraordinary accomplishment, but one that has caused massive environmental degradation and resource depletion.[21]

Some of the most significant effects are tied to the fact that national leaders are relying on the motor-vehicle industry to be a pillar in the country's continued economic expansion, and China's growing middle and upper classes are purchasing cars in record numbers.[22]

- China is now the world's second-largest market for motor vehicles after the United States, and sales of new light vehicles have been projected to increase at a compound annual growth rate of 8 percent through 2013.[23] Researchers at Argonne National Laboratory have estimated that by the mid-2030s China will have more motor vehicles on its highways than the United States will in 2030.[24]

- More generally, increased consumption by affluent urban dwellers emulating the consumerist lifestyles of Western countries is contributing to more intensive resource use and higher solid-waste loads.[25] In China, urban dwellers consume 3.5 times the energy per capita as rural citizens, and this usage is expected to rise since it is still well below levels found in highly industrialized countries.[26]

Urbanites in China also use more water per capita for domestic purposes than rural residents do. Per capita usage rises as city dwellers increase their disposable income and purchase washing machines and move into apartments with flush toilets and individual showers.[27]

Indicators of Environmental Pollution

The list below, compiled by China's State Environmental Protection Administration (SEPA) in 2005, indicates what the SEPA considered to be the most significant environmental issues facing the nation.[28]

- Urban air pollution
- Water pollution
- Water shortages, particularly in northern China
- Hazardous and toxic solid waste in urban areas
- Soil erosion
- Loss of forests and grasslands
- Loss of biodiversity

The air quality in Chinese cities has become notoriously bad. Despite China's ambitious regulatory program, the World Bank and the SEPA reported that "between 2000 and 2005, air pollution emissions have remained constant or in some instances have increased."[29] And Chinese cities continue to rank among the world's most polluted.[30]

The situation in Beijing demonstrates how challenging it can be for Chinese cities to meet air-quality standards. In preparing for the 2008 Olympic Games, Beijing invested aggressively in emission-control measures to improve air quality, but the city still violated China's ambient air-quality standards in 2008. Air-quality-modeling studies demonstrate that even if "Beijing generates no man-made emissions, levels of fine PM [particulate matter] and ozone could still be high and could exceed healthful levels under unfavorable meteorological conditions."[31] Pollution from nearby Tianjin and from neighboring Hebei and Shandong provinces is particularly problematic in Beijing.

Improving China's water quality has also been challenging. In 2006 the SEPA found that more than 28 percent of the water in China's water-quality-monitoring program could not meet even the lowest level of the nation's five-tier system of water-quality standards; that is, it was suitable only for very limited purposes, such as industrial cooling.[32] An additional 10 percent of the water in China's monitoring network was at this bottom level (i.e., usable as cooling water only), and another 22 percent was one level up, or suitable for industrial purposes (in addition to cooling) and recreational uses (except for swimming). And water quality appears to be worsening: in 2000, 58 percent of the water in the seven large river systems was of a quality high enough to satisfy or exceed the third tier of China's system of water-quality standards, but the corresponding figure for 2006 was only 40 percent.[33]

Northern China bears special pollution burdens. Most of the areas with the highest per capita exposure to air pollution are in the north, as are many of the most severely polluted river basins. Moreover, northern China also suffers from severe water shortages, which are exacerbated by water pollution.

Reports on the cost of air and water pollution in China vary. A study by the World Bank and the SEPA estimated these costs in 2003 at between 2.68 percent and 5.78 percent of the GDP.[34] The range reflects the analysts' use of different methods to monetize the cost of health-related damages.

Solid-waste generation continues to rise in China, with the tonnage of industrial solid waste generated in 2006 representing a 13 percent increase over the previous year.[35] Because solid-waste generation is highly correlated with the GDP, solid-waste-disposal problems are expected to grow dramatically. A 2005 World Bank study highlighted three challenges for solid-waste management in China: an "unsurpassed rate of growth . . . , dramatically changing composition [of solid waste], and minimal waste reduction efforts."[36] The study also cited China's inability to keep up with the growing demand for solid-waste-disposal services and the lack of adequate environmental protection in waste-disposal operations.[37] In addition, the report emphasized the need for increased attention to "special wastes," such as batteries, construction demolition materials, and medical waste.

Increases in hazardous materials (for example, electronic components) in solid-waste streams stem from both domestic and imported sources. China regulates imported waste intended for recycling, but waste smugglers and challenges in tracking numerous small recycling operations have hampered efforts to control environmental damage.[38]

China's land resources are changing as a result of increased construction of infrastructure and buildings. Between 2005 and 2006, for example, the amount of land devoted to communications and transportation (for example, highways and parking lots) increased by 3.67 percent.[39] At the same time, the amount of arable land dropped by 0.25 percent.[40]

National programs to protect particular species of wild flora and fauna appear to be working: in 2005 sharp drops were recorded in the loss of more than a thousand species of rare and endangered wild flora and two hundred species of rare and endangered wild animals.[41] However, species not under national protection, especially those with high economic value, continue to be seriously threatened.

Organizations Created in Response to Environmental Degradation

In 1974 China created an Environmental Protection Office, with a staff of twenty. That modest start was the beginning of a process that led to the formation of the SEPA, a central environmental agency with a ministerial rank, in 1998. In March 2008, the SEPA became the Ministry of Environmental Protection (MEP). Given that the MEP is the official designation of the top environmental administrative body in China, that name will, with few exceptions, be used in the rest of this chapter. The exceptions concern references to documents issued by the SEPA.[42] Although the U.S. press has referred disparagingly to the SEPA's small staff size (fewer than three hundred people), such observations about the SEPA (and now the MEP) are misleading because China employs a highly decentralized approach to implementing national environmental policies and regulations.[43] Nearly all the government's environmental protection personnel are at subnational levels.

In keeping with the traditional organizational structure of ministries within China, each lower level of government (down to the county) has an EPB. These bureaus have both horizontal (or territorial) reporting relationships with leaders of local governments and vertical relationships to EPBs at higher levels of government; provincial-level EPBs report directly to the MEP. Thus, for example, the Jinan Municipal EPB is an arm of the Jinan Municipal People's Government, and it reports to both the Office of the Mayor of Jinan and the Shandong Provincial EPB.[44]

In addition to having their own staffs, the EPBs typically have affiliated organizations that carry out activities such as monitoring and research.[45] Each of these affiliated units can have hundreds of staff members. Collectively, China has about 170,000 government staff in the EPBs.[46]

The MEP works on environmental policy design, but it is not alone in this regard. Policy formulation, particularly the development of legislation, is also carried out by the Environment Protection and Resources Conservation Committee of the National People's Congress. However, the committee often relies heavily on the MEP's technical experts in carrying out its work.[47]

Counterparts to this legislative unit also exist as environmental protection committees under local people's congresses. In many jurisdictions, local people's congresses supervise the work of the EPBs and accept complaints by local citizens regarding environmental pollution.[48]

Since the early 1990s, Chinese environmental nongovernmental organizations (NGOs) have played an increasingly important role in implementing environmental policy, particularly in monitoring pollution and uncovering incidents in which local governments were lax in enforcing regulations.[49] The central government has seen advantages in encouraging such work, in part due to the inability of the MEP and "an over-strained and under-funded environmental protection bureaucracy" to deal with the challenges of monitoring environmental performance.[50]

Environmental NGOs have proliferated since the mid-1990s, but their enforcement work is constrained by their lack of access to both technical expertise and monitoring data. Moreover, they are careful to select activities that do not involve strong confrontations with the government. NGOs generally have a keen sense of how far they can push local governments that fail to enforce environmental rules, and their self-censorship has in most cases allowed them to continue operating without undue interference by the state.[51] Sometimes informal alliances develop among MEP staff members, NGOs, and the media in calling attention to local governments that have failed to enforce environmental regulations.[52]

Citizen action on the environment is not limited to protests by groups of citizens and campaigns organized by environmental NGOs. Individual citizens may register environmental complaints with EPBs and local governments via well-established channels; indeed, such complaints have increased rapidly since the late 1990s.[53] Citizens may also use the 1990 Administrative Litigation Law to sue EPBs that fail to implement environmental laws.[54] However, such reporting is not without risk: citizens (and NGOs) who expose violations may face reprisals if they report on enterprises protected by the local governments due to their profitability or ones whose leaders maintain *guanxi* relationships with government officials.[55]

Environmental Regulatory Programs

Beginning in the 1970s, China developed many laws and regulations to deal with its environmental problems, and its regulatory programs have often been innovative and sophisticated.[56] However, enforcement and compliance challenges have limited their overall effectiveness.

A number of the key programs can be characterized under the rubric "command and control" (see table 10.1). Under authority granted in the 1989 PRC Environmental Protection Law, the National Environmental Protection Agency (NEPA), the precursor to the SEPA, established ambient environmental-quality and waste-discharge standards.

Table 10.1 Principle Regulatory Programs

Command and control approaches
• Environmental standards
• Discharge permit system
• Vehicle emission standards
• "Three simultaneous steps"
Market-based strategies
• Pollution levies
• Experimental "cap and trade" activities
Information generation and disclosure programs
• Environmental impact assessment requirements
• Assessment of urban environmental quality
• Environmental (or ecological) model cities
• Cleaner production audit requirements
• Environmental labels
• "Greenwatch"
Performance evaluation programs
• Environmental responsibility system
• Green GDP

Soon after the standards were issued, the NEPA determined that water quality was continuing to deteriorate because discharge standards were given only in terms of pollutant concentrations. The NEPA then developed the discharge-permit system, in which waste dischargers are issued permits to constrain both concentrations and total mass of waste released per unit of time.

Pollutant-discharge standards also apply to motor vehicles. To register vehicles, owners must have them tested annually to ensure that emission standards are satisfied. Moreover, these standards, based on those used in the European Union (EU), are becoming increasingly stringent. Vehicles sold in China had to meet the equivalent of so-called Euro I standards by 2000 and Euro II standards by 2005. More stringent standards in the Euro series are being phased in, with the goal of having China eventually enforce the same vehicle-emission requirements as the EU.

The "three simultaneous steps" program is a Chinese innovation, and it works in tandem with the environmental impact assessment (EIA) rules. The latter require developers of industrial projects likely to have significant environmental impacts to prepare an environmental assessment, which must be approved by either the MEP or an EPB, depending on the significance of the proposed facility. The three simultaneous steps program is meant to ensure that the waste-management systems called for in an EIA are actually built. Under the first simultaneous step, pollution-control measures and the main elements of a proposed project are designed at the same time. The second simultaneous step requires that waste-management facilities be constructed when the proposed project is built. In the third simultaneous step, environmental authorities inspect waste-reduction systems when other agencies inspect the main project.

China's most significant effort at using market-based environmental policy tools involves the pollution levy system. This program requires stationary sources of pollution to pay fees based on the amount of waste they release. Revenues from levy collection are typically used to support the EPB staffs and operations and to subsidize waste-management facility construction.

Several cities in China have experimented with "cap and trade" programs as well.[57] In such programs an upper limit (or "cap") is set on the total amount of pollution that may be released in an area, and then a fixed number of discharge permits are issued. These permits may subsequently be bought and sold (or "traded"). The cap cannot be exceeded because dischargers are not allowed to release wastes without permits. However, as of late 2007, the approach had still not been widely adopted, even in the cities conducting experiments.[58]

Although the EIA requirements can be viewed as a command-and-control tool (since projects are not permitted to go forward without conducting such assessments), they can also be regarded as a means of information generation and disclosure. In 2003 China modified its EIA program to allow citizen participation in the EIA process.[59] It remains to be seen how effectively this change will be implemented, but for China it represents a major shift. Although earlier EIA procedures could accommodate citizen involvement, in typical cases only agency officials and invited experts reviewed the EIA documents.[60]

China has several other information-generation and disclosure programs:

- The Assessment of Urban Environmental Quality annually scores the environmental conditions in major cities and publishes the results;
- Environmental programs invite cities to apply for designation as "model cities" by submitting information on local environmental conditions to a specified agency;[61]
- The Cleaner Production Law requires that enterprises violating discharge-permit conditions conduct audits and research ways of improving resource use and minimizing waste generation in order to meet standards;
- Environmental labeling programs allow manufacturers that meet standards on the production and composition of their products to display a "China Environmental Label"; and
- "Greenwatch" rates the environmental performance of firms and publicizes results based on a color scheme indicating the degree of compliance with standards.

The last items in table 10.1 concern innovative approaches that China has used (or is considering using) to link the evaluation of local officials' performance to environmental measures. The environmental responsibility system involves officials signing contracts with their supervisors in which they agree that specific environment-related targets will be met. Contracts are reviewed annually to evaluate performance.

In 2004 China's top officials advocated that performance evaluations include the "Green GDP," which is calculated by adjusting the traditional GDP by the monetary value of estimated pollution damages, as well as ecosystem and natural resource changes.[62] The Green GDP was computed for 2004 and 2005, but the 2005 results were not published or used in evaluations because of disagreements over calculation procedures.[63] Government efforts to estimate the Green GDP stalled in 2007.

Systemic Challenges to Implementing Regulatory Programs

China has developed a robust set of environmental regulations, but implementation has been thwarted by systemic impediments, discussed below, in three categories:

- Priorities of local officials vis-à-vis environmental performance
- Dual reporting responsibilities of the EPBs, which report horizontally to local territorial leaders (for example, the mayor in the case of a municipal EPB) and vertically to higher-level environmental agencies
- Factors constraining the EPBs' ability to enforce requirements

Enforcement of environmental requirements often conflicts with the interests of local officials. Post-1978 reforms granted local leaders authority to obtain revenues through a variety of means, as well as giving them responsibility for financing a broad array of public services, such as public health and education.[64] Local governments have also been given authority over many state-owned enterprises, and this authority provides them with opportunities to impose fees that can be used to finance both government operations and public services.

Because fund transfers from the central government are often insufficient to finance centrally mandated local public services, local officials have strong incentives to raise funds. Promoting development gives officials greater ability to access fees from local firms. Thus, they have incentives to not enforce environmental rules strictly at economically important sites.

The tendency of local officials to privilege financial interests over environmental goals is reinforced by the central government. Even as top central government officials offer rhetorical support for prioritizing environmental protection, their message is diluted by criteria to evaluate the performance of local officials. Enhancing local GDP has long been among the top criteria used to evaluate and promote local officials, and thus local officials often allow economic growth to trump environmental concerns.[65]

Effects of the cadre-evaluation system on local environmental-protection efforts should not be underestimated. In describing this system, Harvard professor Tony Saich points to a number of perverse outcomes, including job performance criteria that reward meeting physical infrastructure targets by prescribed deadlines, but without accounting for infrastructure quality or sustainability.[66] Thus, while local officials have been increasingly willing to invest funds to meet central government environmental infrastructure mandates, they have not always allocated funds to operate and sustain these infrastructure systems. Examples of poor environmental infrastructure operations include a utilization rate of only 60 percent for more than a thousand wastewater treatment plants built between 2000 and 2006, with some plants not operating at all.[67] Two reasons for this have been identified: a lack of wastewater collection networks, and the fact that revenue collections for treatment services are being diverted to the general city budget, without subsequent transfers to service providers to cover plant operating costs.

The prominence of economic growth in the annual evaluations of local leaders also weakens the incentives of these leaders to prioritize their enforcement capabilities. Moreover, the EPBs must compete with other local bureaus for resources. As a consequence, the EPBs struggle with insufficient budgets, overextended staff, and inadequate monitoring equipment.

Conflicts between economic development and environmental protection at the local level are recognized by top officials in China. Pan Yue, executive vice minister of the MEP, has cited local governments' refusal to fulfill their environmental responsibilities and their interference with law enforcement as key reasons for China's persistent environmental problems.[68] Pan has also suggested a remedy: "Only by [including environmental protection criteria in performance evaluations for local officials] can we change the officials' 'economy-overriding-all' perspective."[69]

The second systemic challenge concerns EPBs' dual reporting responsibilities. Consider, for example, an EPB for a municipality. It reports vertically to the relevant provincial EPB and is supposed to show that applicable environmental regulations are being followed. Horizontally, the EPB is also part of the municipal government and reports to the mayor's office, which appoints top EPB officials, sets the EPB's' budget, and determines its allocation of permanent staff positions. Under the circumstances, the EPBs often privilege goals set by local leaders when conflicts arise between enforcing environmental rules and meeting local government objectives.[70]

The third problem involves weak EPB enforcement and the resulting poor compliance with environmental regulations. Key underlying causes have already been noted, including the economic development priorities of local officials and the grip these officials have over the EPB budgets and enforcement abilities. Among the other causes of weak enforcement are the discretionary powers of

EPB staff due to ambiguities in China's environmental laws and regulations. The ability to exercise discretion—combined with Chinese traditions that encourage negotiation to maintain harmonious relationships—frequently leads EPBs to negotiate with polluters rather than demand strict compliance. The EPBs typically avoid enforcement actions stronger than modest levies and financial penalties, except for major pollution incidents or when regulated parties show no signs of cooperating. Another reason for moderate penalties is that the EPBs cannot take tough action (for example, closing down a polluting factory) without explicit approval from local leaders.

Regulated parties caught breaking environmental rules typically bargain for waste-reduction targets they feel comfortable meeting, instead of agreeing to meet requirements fully. Moreover, EPB enforcement often centers on negotiating pollution-levy amounts rather than moving toward compliance with discharge standards. The original goal of the levy system was to motivate enterprises to cut pollution, but many EPBs operate the system to maximize funds collected as levies and penalties for late payments.[71] For a polluter, paying negotiated levies and penalties is often much cheaper than building waste-treatment facilities, and sometimes even cheaper than operating existing facilities.[72]

The EPBs face particular difficulties in obtaining the regulatory compliance of small enterprises.[73] Such enterprises are numerous and thus difficult to keep track of and are often located in the countryside far from EPB offices. In addition, a small enterprise facing stiff penalties (or closure orders) may be able to evade them by changing legal ownership or dismantling equipment and restarting operations elsewhere.

A study of environmental enforcement at small enterprises noted that an EPB may be motivated to intentionally underreport the number of small firms within its boundaries by not including all firms in its inventory of firms that are regulated and inspected routinely. Reporting a complete inventory could make an EPB's inspection records look bad; inadequate staffing makes it impossible for EPBs to inspect all of the thousands of small enterprises that may be within their jurisdictions.[74] Meanwhile, citizen complaints may lead EPBs to inspect enterprises not within their inventories, but depending on citizens to report violations is not a systematic approach to enforcement.

Recent Changes Should Enhance Regulatory Compliance and Resource Management

One possibility for China's future is that the status quo will continue without fundamental changes in industrial structure, energy efficiency, or environmental compliance. This scenario is unlikely. Top officials in China are aware of the losses revealed in the Green GDP calculations, and they know that continual environmental degradation and resource mismanagement will interfere with economic development, threaten China's security, and diminish the country's international standing. Moreover, further environmental degradation will almost certainly lead to more public protest, with consequent threats to social stability. The central government's concern for the nation's environment and natural resources is apparent in its calls for attaining a harmonious society by means of scientific development, that is, "economic growth that takes into consideration the welfare of disadvantaged people in regions as well as environmental concerns."[75]

The Eleventh Five-year Plan's goal of building a harmonious society is to be met by attaining specific targets, of which environment- and energy-related targets are notable because they are categorized as "restricted"—a term used for targets that will not be met by market forces alone. Instead, "governments at various levels are obliged to achieve" restricted targets.[76] For 2010 these targets include a 20 percent drop in energy consumption per unit of GDP, a 30 percent reduction in water consumption per unit of industrial value added, and a 10 percent cut in emissions of major pollutants. Opinions differ as to whether the plan's goal of a 7.5 percent annual GDP growth rate will dominate its aspirations for sustainable development. After noting that it is too early to assess plan implementation, Barry Naughton, a leading China scholar in the United States, argues that the plan contains "a rich and comprehensive vision of a sustainable development process in China, and a glimpse of the kind of governmental role that would be required by this development process."[77]

In addition to the environmental and resource management mandates in the Eleventh Five-year Plan, other actions indicate that environmental compliance and resource management are likely to improve as:

- The central government is changing performance-appraisal criteria used in evaluating local officials to emphasize environmental and energy-efficiency parameters
- The MEP is making efforts to loosen the grip that local officials have over environmental enforcement
- EPBs are relying more heavily on courts to help execute their enforcement penalties
- Firms are facing market pressures to improve environmental stewardship
- Citizens and NGOs are taking greater roles in enforcement

Officials have already discussed using environmental criteria, including the Green GDP, in the performance reviews of local officials. While Green GDP efforts stalled in 2007 amid challenges to calculation procedures, the Green GDP concept still remains an option for the future.

Meanwhile, other experiments are underway that seek to better integrate environmental-protection measures in cadre-appraisal systems. In 2006 Qinghai Province stopped using GDP growth to evaluate the performance of government officials in two prefectures. A recent article in *China Daily* said this signaled "a departure from the 'GDP cult,' which sees economic growth as the only yardstick for development."[78] In addition, a proposed national cadre-appraisal system that considers attainment of public service goals has been tested in Qingdao, Shandong Province.[79]

One key change in the national cadre-evaluation procedures has already been mandated. China's revised Energy Conservation Law, effective since April 2008, emphasizes energy efficiency in determining the job performance of local officials.[80] The influence of this change will depend on implementation details. Although doubts about the effectiveness of the revised law have been expressed, some experts are optimistic about its outcome.[81]

According to Xie and Liu, local governments have been making changes in response to China's Circular Economy Promotion Law, which became effective on January 1, 2009, because the law signals that "major indicators of the recycling economy will be included in assessments of local officials' performance."[82] They note that the governments of Shenzhen and Chongqing have already taken steps to provide subsidies and special funds that will encourage increases in the extent of recycling.

The central government is also trying to deal with problems created by EPBs' dependence on local leaders for staffs and budgets.[83] The MEP has considered two strategies. In one, sometimes referred to as "vertical administration," the MEP would have direct control over local environmental officials.[84] (A variation of this concept has also been considered in which a provincial EPB would select the head of a municipal EPB and set the budget and staff size.) Vertical administration has not been implemented because the MEP has not yet been granted the requisite authority.

An alternative strategy for strengthening the MEP's influence at the local level—and one that has already been implemented—involves the MEP creating regional "environmental protection supervision centers." In the past few years, six such centers have been created.[85] A MEP deputy director has referred to them as "regional environmental watchdogs" that constitute "an important step to remove local protectionism, a major obstacle in our law enforcement."[86] The centers, which serve largely to keep the MEP informed of important local problems, check on the regulatory compliance violations of local polluters. Centers submit most of the environmental complaints they receive to local EPBs, but report major, influential problems directly to the MEP.[87] Centers themselves have limited autonomy.[88] They have no monitoring capacity and rely on local EPBs for that. Moreover, a center cannot instruct an EPB to conduct work.

Many EPBs have developed their own strategy for enhancing leverage over polluters by making frequent use of China's 1990 Administrative Litigation Law. Article 66 allows EPBs to ask for court assistance in the collection of levies and penalties, and a study in Hubei Province showed that some EPBs have used this provision extensively.[89] EPBs throughout China are relying increasingly on courts to execute their orders.

Another indication that environmental compliance may improve is that enterprises now being offered financial incentives to behave in environmentally responsible ways. In 2007 the People's Bank of China and the China Banking Regulatory Commission issued a rule requiring commercial banks to stop making new loans (and to call in old ones) for firms on the SEPA's (now the MEP's) list of significant polluters.[90] This policy was implemented in many provinces, and resisted in others. Despite the resistance, the government is considering the use of mandates for environmental standards compliance in other financial transactions, such as those related to insurance and stock markets.[91]

Another notable change is the increasing adoption by multinationals and firms within China of ISO 14001, an international, voluntary environmental-management standard.[92] Compliance with ISO 14001 requires that, among other things, companies have:

- An environmental policy that sets out performance objectives and targets and includes a commitment to comply with environmental requirements and prevent pollution
- A documented, externally approved environmental-management system that provides the firm with a basis for meeting its environmental objectives and targets

Firms give many reasons for obtaining ISO 14001 certification, including cutting costs by minimizing waste and enhancing regulatory compliance. Significantly, firms that sell to other companies sometimes adopt the management standard because their customers insist on working with ISO 14001–certified suppliers; strong encouragement for supplier certification is common among multinational corporations (MNCs). A survey of one hundred and eighteen Chinese firms found them more likely to self-regulate and/or adopt ISO 14001 if they are owned by MNCs or are selling a large percentage of their outputs to the EU, to Japan, or to MNCs.[93] In this context, self-regulation implies meeting environmental requirements in the absence of strong enforcement by environmental authorities.

Further proof that Chinese enterprises are improving their environmental performance in response to market forces is the widespread adoption of the "China Environmental Label." The Xinhua Online News Service recently reported that during the past fifteen years, more than 1,600 enterprises (and more than 35,000 different product models) received China's Environmental Label.[94] This label allows firms to maintain (or increase) their market share of products sold to organizations abroad and within China (for example, the Chinese government) that have "green" procurement policies. As China increasingly engages with MNCs and competes in countries that favor environmentally responsible firms, the greening of Chinese firms will continue and there will be more attention to self-regulation and international norms, as reflected in the adoption of ISO 14001.

Meanwhile, China's 2002 Cleaner Production Law requires environmental audits for enterprises not in compliance with applicable environmental requirements. Were that law to be implemented more vigorously, Chinese factories would be forced to find ways of reducing waste—cutting production costs while satisfying waste-release restrictions in discharge permits.[95] Similarly, China's emphasis on creating eco-industrial parks—as part of a national effort to develop a "circular" economy in which energy use is minimized and water, solid waste, and wastewater are increasingly recycled—will also encourage firms to act in an environmentally responsible manner.[96] The effective use of eco-industrial parks might yield notable environmental gains, but implementation has thus far been stilted.[97]

Another promising sign is the strong encouragement that the MEP and top central government officials have given to environmental NGOs challenging local governments for failing to enforce environmental laws. In comparison to the situation in the mid-1990s, when environmental NGOs concentrated on noncontroversial activities, such as environmental education and bird watching, many NGOs are now engaged in court actions and confrontations with both polluters and local officials. [98]

The media are also playing an important role in the environmental movement by educating citizens on environmental issues and working with NGOs to publicize violations of environmental rules.[99] Recently, the MEP's Pan Yue enlisted the media to help inform citizens of the nation's environmental-impact-appraisal requirements and to bring attention to enterprises violating these requirements.[100]

Struggling with the Adverse Impacts of Rapid Development

During the past few years, the top leadership's embrace of scientific development to achieve a harmonious society has entered the public discourse and become a mandate for sustainable development. What will this mean for China's future in terms of environmental pollution and resource depletion? Assume that, as argued in the previous section, the status quo does not continue. Instead assume that China will make progress in cutting pollution and conserving resources based on targets in the Eleventh Five-year Plan.

Even these positive changes, however, will not lift the near future's major environmental challenges, many of which are related to the pace of urbanization and an increasing reliance on motor vehicles. China is showing few signs of slowing a rapid increase in motor vehicle ownership, and skyrocketing vehicle usage will increase pollution from nitrogen oxides, volatile organic compounds, ozone, and CO_2.[101] And although increasingly stringent vehicle-emission regulations and alternative fuel vehicles will help, they are unlikely to keep pace with the rapid increase expected in total miles driven in urban areas.[102] Until recently, the aforementioned pollutants were not problematic in many Chinese cities because motor vehicles were not widely used, but increasing concentrations have already been observed in Beijing and Shanghai, where vehicle populations have expanded rapidly. In addition to problems with conventional pollutants, increases in CO_2 and black carbon emissions from vehicles will reinforce China's position as the world's largest emitter of greenhouse gases.[103]

Traffic congestion will inevitably rise, and this will lead to more deaths and injuries from roadway accidents, as well as economic losses from time wasted in traffic. Moreover, congested roads involve lower vehicle speeds, which mean higher emissions per mile traveled. Many Chinese cities have responded to congestion by expanding highway networks and adding "ring roads." Cities have also tried to cut congestion by widening existing roadways, eliminating bicycle pathways, and cutting down roadside trees.[104] But experience in many countries has demonstrated that massive investments in roads frequently do not relieve congestion. Reduced congestion on a widened highway in an economically vibrant urban area often induces increased usage and only leads to more congestion.

In addition to traffic congestion and pollution, China's rapidly evolving car culture is tied to increasing demand for oil, which China began importing in 1993. In 2004 China became the world's second-largest consumer of petroleum products, trailing only the United States.[105] Rising consumption of imported fuels has obvious implications for China's long-term energy security.

China's embrace of motor vehicles has consequences for land utilization. Rising vehicle use has been associated with extensive conversions of farmland for urban development and the dedication of more surface area to roads and parking areas. In addition, increasing automobile ownership has allowed more people to move to the periphery of cities, where parking and larger living spaces are available. Increasingly, individuals commute to work in single-occupant vehicles.[106] Deliberately or not, China is in the process of committing to urban sprawl and automobile dependence, with all their attendant problems, including respiratory diseases and obesity.[107] Automobile dependence is not easily reversed. As MIT professor Edward Steinfeld observes, "[t]he substantial investments being made in the extensive supporting energy infrastructure for automobiles—petroleum distribution facilities, filling stations, and so forth—raise the costs of switching to alternative transportation fuels in the future. This extensive supporting infrastructure creates a variety of vested interests that also make it difficult to switch to . . . alternative modes of transportation."[108]

Related issues concern the energy, water, and materials it will take to sustain rapid urbanization and anticipated high levels of GDP growth. While many such issues have been mentioned above (for example, demand for petroleum and building materials), the upsurge in coal use deserves added emphasis. China is under enormous pressure to increase its electricity-generation capacity by taking advantage of its massive coal reserves.[109] While the country is attempting to expand its nuclear power plants and rely more on renewable energy sources, coal is expected to dominate electricity generation for the foreseeable future. Given skyrocketing coal use, China will continue to face major air pollution problems, such as suspended particulate matter, smog, and acid rain (from oxides of sulfur and nitrogen). Meanwhile, releases of CO_2 and black carbon will contribute to global climate change.

Chinese authorities have focused regulatory efforts on conventional pollutants (for example, chemical oxygen demand in wastewaters and sulphur dioxide, SO_2, and suspended particulates in air emissions). Much less attention has been given to toxic materials or to pollution from nonpoint sources, such as runoff from farms and city streets. Even if traditional contaminants from point sources are controlled, pollutants that are not receiving regulatory attention now will pose problems in the future. Analysts concerned with environmental quality in rural areas have already called for improvements in "quality standards for soil and water, as well as [measures to control] pollution from pesticides, fertilizers, industrial waste, agricultural waste, and garbage."[110] In addition to the problems of unregulated contaminants, per capita solid and hazardous waste (including more plastic and electronic waste) will rise with increased per capita GDP.[111]

Unseen environmental costs are accumulating in China because so-called legacy pollution problems continue to be created even as conventional air and water pollutants are brought under control. The most well-known legacy problem is posed by land disposal sites that are not properly designed or safely operated. The U.S. experience demonstrates the huge costs of remediating contaminated waste-disposal sites.[112]

In the future, water will pose special problems. Even as municipal and industrial effluents are controlled, water pollution will continue to be an issue as unregulated nonpoint sources grow.[113] Degraded water quality will compound existing water-shortage problems in northern cities. China's response to shortages has included massive water-development projects, with their attendant adverse social and environmental impacts, as well as the widespread mining of groundwater aquifers, with consequent drops in groundwater tables.[114] Groundwater depletion has caused many problems, including increased pumping costs, land subsidence and associated damages to bridges and buildings, and saltwater intrusion in coastal provinces.[115]

Future water shortages will also be affected by changing diets. As incomes rise, people will decrease reliance on grains and consume more animal protein, which will require enormous quantities of water to produce.[116] Moreover, as water shortages increase and China diverts water from agriculture to higher-value municipal and industrial uses, more grains will need to be imported, impacting world food prices.[117]

In the final analysis, two factors make China's environmental and resource challenges different from those of almost all other countries. One is the country's huge population. The significance of the population is reflected in the so-called "IPAT equation" introduced in the 1970s and recently reformulated in the context of "industrial ecology."[118] In this context, the IPAT equation is interpreted as follows: environmental impacts (I) in the future can be determined, at least conceptually, as the product of population (P); affluence (A), measured as GDP per capita; and technology (T), expressed as environmental impact per unit of per capita GDP.[119] Since population is difficult to reduce, and since increasing affluence is a widely held goal, improvements in technology are a key to offsetting the combined effects of increasing affluence and population.[120] Another key consists of the rigorous implementation of China's environmental laws and regulations. Whether the design and effective implementation of technologies and regulations to conserve resources and cut pollution will provide the needed counterbalance to China's large and increasingly affluent population is an open question. And even if such technologies are invented soon, it will take years to bring them on line.[121]

A second factor that makes China's situation unique is urbanization. Countries have urbanized rapidly in the past, but what makes China's case unusual, in addition to the pace, is that television, the Internet, and other forms of modern communication are shaping the tastes of newly affluent urban dwellers. Inevitably, those tastes change to mimic the contemporary lifestyles in highly industrialized countries, with the associated consequences of resource depletion and environmental pollution.[122] Had the current Chinese government not attempted to shift away from the earlier "grow now, clean later" approach and emphasized sustainable development, as reflected in the Eleventh Five-year Plan, China's future environmental challenges would be even worse.

A less disheartening future could be imagined if China were to rethink its current approach to motor vehicles and spatial planning, as advocated forcefully by Qiu Baoqing, vice minister of construction. Qiu is one of China's leading advocates for the implementation of well-structured and effectively implemented urban plans that rely on public transit, and for the careful renovation of rural areas including towns and villages. His 2007 book, *Harmony and Innovation: Problems, Dangers and Solutions in Dealing with Rapid Urbanization in China*, includes numerous lessons for China based on spatial planning in other countries and provides details on energy-efficient buildings and effective urban water management.

Qiu's ideas, as well as the central government's broad vision of a "circular economy" based on waste reduction, materials and water reuse, and energy efficiency have proven to be difficult to implement. But if implementation were improved, China would have a much brighter future than the one sketched in this chapter.

Notes

[1] A draft of this chapter was originally presented at "Growing Pains: Tensions and Opportunity in China's Transformation," a conference at Stanford University, November 1–3, 2007. I would like to thank conference participants for their comments, particularly Scott Rozelle, who offered a number of helpful suggestions afterward. In addition, I am grateful to David Nieh, Andrew Perlstein, Mara Warwick, and Xuehua Zhang for their comments on an earlier draft of the chapter.

[2] Several of China's environmental policies are not covered by this chapter, including afforestation, habitat and agricultural land conservation, and, more generally, protection of fragile ecosystems and endangered species.

[3] For example, Japan has been struggling for many years with the effects of acid deposition originating in China.

[4] For an overview of the international implications of China's environmental degradation, see Jianguo Liu and Jared Diamond, "China's Environment in a Globalizing World," *Nature* 30 (June 2005): 1183–85.

[5] For more on the "grow now, clean later" approach employed in China, see Peter Ho, "Trajectories for Greening in China: Theory and Practice," *Development and Change* 37, no. 1 (2006): 3–28.

[6] For a discussion of this shift to scientific development, see C. Cindy Fan, "China's Eleventh Five-Year Plan (2006–2010): From 'Getting Rich First' to 'Common Prosperity,'" *Eurasian Geography and Economics* 47, no. 6 (2006): 709–11. The new approach is detailed in "Hu Jintao's Report at 17th Party Congress" (2007), *China Daily*, www.chinadaily.com.cn/china/2007-10/25/content_6204667.htm.

[7] *China Daily*, "Hu Jintao's Report at 17th Party Congress."

[8] "China's gross domestic product (GDP) grew an annual average of 9.67 percent from 1978 to 2006," stated Ma Kai, the minister of the National Development and Reform Commission. See Embassy of the People's Republic of China in the United States, www.china-embassy.org/eng/xw/t316811.htm.

[9] National Development and Reform Commission (NDRC), *China's National Climate Change Programme* (Beijing: NDRC, June 2007).

[10] For information on side effects of the policy, see, for example, "Report: China's One-child Policy Has Prevented 400 Million Births," *International Herald Tribune, Asia-Pacific*, www.iht.com/articles/ap/2006/11/09/asia/AS_GEN_China_One_Child_Policy.php. Recent changes are illustrated by shifts in policy within Shanghai. See "Shanghai Makes It Easier to Have a Second Child," *China Daily*, November 7, 2003, www.chinadaily.com.cn/en/doc/2003-11/07/content_279307.htm.

[11] China's minister of the National Population and Family Planning Commission recently indicated the country would delay any major changes to its family-planning policy until about 2018. See Jim Yardley, "China Sticking with One-Child Policy," *New York Times*, March 11, 2008, www.nytimes.com/2008/03/11/world/asia/11china.html?_r=1&scp=1&sq=China+Says+One-Child+Policy+Will+Stay+&st=nyt&oref=slogin.

[12] China's 1.3 billon population (as of 2005) does not include the so-called floating population. Kenneth Roberts clarifies the term as follows: "For China we must first distinguish between 'migration' (*qianyi*), which is a move that is officially documented by a permanent change in an individual's place of household registration, and temporary population movement, whose participants are called the 'floating population' (*liudong renkou*). Because of the difficulty of transferring household registration, the first group is . . . much less numerous than the second." Roberts also notes: "The floating population includes not only rural migrant laborers but also people traveling for business, education, tourism, and to visit relatives—that is, all people who are in a city at a particular time but who are not permanent residents of that city." Kenneth D. Roberts, "China's Tidal Wave of Migrant Labor: What Can We Learn from Mexican Undocumented Migration to the United States?" *International Migration Review* 31, no. 2 (1997): 252.

[13] Liang Zai and Ma Zhongdong, "China's Floating Population: New Evidence from the 2000 Census," *Population and Development Review* 30, no. 3 (2004): 472. The absence of credible data on the floating population makes it difficult to accurately characterize China's rural-urban migration.

[14] NDRC, *China's National Climate Change Programme*, 15.

[15] Qiu Baoxing, *Harmony and Innovation: Problems, Dangers and Solutions in Dealing with Rapid Urbanization in China* (Milan, Italy: l'Arca Edizioni, 2007), 17.

[16] This projection is by the U.S. government's official source of energy statistics, the Energy Information Administration (EIA). EIA, *International Energy Outlook*, Report No. DOE/OIA 0484 (Washington, D.C.: EIA, U.S. Department of Energy 2007), 7.

[17] Qiu, *Harmony and Innovation*, 465.

[18] John E. Fernandez, "Resource Consumption of New Urban Construction in China," *Journal of Industrial Ecology* 11, no. 2 (2007): 100.

[19] Fernandez, "Resource Consumption of New Urban Construction in China," 103. In addition, China's annual steel consumption in the early 2000s represented 20 to 30 percent of the world's total. For other estimates of China's steel consumption, see Anon., 2004, "China's Steel Consumption Not to Peak Before 2010, Experts," www.chinadaily. com.cn/en/doc/2004-01/25/content_300957.htm. See also W. Chandler and H. Gwin, "China's Energy and Emissions: A Turning Point?" Report No. PNWD-SA-6548, Pacific Northwest laboratories, Richland Washington, www.pnl.gov/aisu/pubs/chandgwin.pdf.

[20] Fernandez (2007, 105) cites studies indicating that "global concrete production accounts for 3 percent to 8 percent of total anthropogenic carbon emissions." See, also, Edward S. Steinfeld, "Energy Policy," in Shahid Yusuf and Tony Saich, eds., China *Urbanizes: Consequences, Strategies and Policies* (Washington, D.C.: World Bank, 2008), 127.

[21] On the environmental issues tied to the rise of the middle and upper classes in China, see Norman Myers and Jennifer Kent, *The New Consumers: The Influence of Affluence on the Environment* (Washington, D.C.: Island Press, 2004). On environmental destruction in China, see Elizabeth C. Economy, *The River Runs Black: The Environmental Challenge to China's Future* (Ithaca, NY: Cornell University Press, 2004).

[22] Steinfeld, "Energy Policy," 137. Lower-income classes are shifting from bicycles to two-wheeled motorized vehicles because, in many Chinese cities, distances to workplaces have increased and public transit is inadequate.

[23] Steinfeld, "Energy Policy," 138; and CSM Worldwide, as quoted in Heather Timmons, "In India, a $2,500 Pace Car," *New York Times*, October 12, 2007, www. nytimes.com/2007/10/12/business/worldbusiness/12cars.html?scp=1&sq=Timmons+CS M+Worldwide+China&st=nyt.

[24] Micheal Q. Wang, Hong Huo, Larry Johnson, and He Dongquan, "Projection of Chinese Motor Vehicle Growth, Oil Demand, and CO_2 Emissions through 2050," Report ANL/LES/06-6 (2006), Argonne National Laboratory, Argonne, IL. The authors projected the total number of motor vehicles by extrapolating from past trends and assuming no change in China's policies regarding vehicle ownership and use.

[25] On this emulation of Western lifestyles, see Fritz Reusswig, Hermann Lotze-Campen, and Katrin Gerlinger, "Changing Global Lifestyle and Consumption Patterns: The Case of Energy and Food," paper presented at the PERN Workshop on Population, Consumption and the Environment, October 19, 2003, Montreal, Canada, www. populationenvironmentresearch.org/workshops.jsp.

[26] Steinfeld (2008) characterizes the increased intensity of energy usage by those living in high-density, multistory urban dwellings in terms of energy-intensive climate-control systems; extensive lighting usage; and demand for energy-intensive appliances, automobiles, and long-distance transport networks needed to deliver goods to urban markets. He also points to the generation of "demands for entirely new, and decidedly energy intensive, production systems, such as the refrigerated food supply chain, from upstream industrial-scale preparation to supermarket retailing," 126.

[27] For example, domestic household water consumption per capita in the Beijing-Tianjin region rose by almost a factor of ten between 1949 and 2000, from 28 to 240 liters per day per person. See the University of British Columbia's 3x3 Beijing Tianjin Water Resources Management Project Web site, www.chs.ubc.ca/china/introbeijing.htm.

[28] Based on State Environmental Protection Administration (SEPA), *Report on the State of the Environment in China in 2005* (Beijing: SEPA, 2005).

[29] World Bank and SEPA, *Cost of Pollution in China: Economic Estimates of Physical Damages* (Washington, D.C.: World Bank, 2007), xi.

[30] For example, according to press accounts in 2005, the "World Bank has warned [that China] is home to 16 of the planet's 20 most air-polluted cities." J. Watts, "Satellite Data Reveals Beijing as Air Pollution Capital of World," *The Guardian*, October 25, 2005, www.guardian.co.uk/news/2005/oct/31/china.pollution.

[31] David G. Streets, Joshua S. Fu, Carey J. Jang, Jiming Hao, Kebin He, Xiaoyan Tang, Yuanhang Zhang, Zifa Wang, Zuopan Li, Qiang Zhang, Litao Wang, Binyu Wang, Carolyne Yu, "Air Quality during the 2008 Beijing Olympic Games," *Atmospheric Environment* 41, no. 3 (2007): 490.

[32] SEPA, *Report on the State of the Environment in China in 2006* (Beijing), http://english.sepa.gov.cn/standards_reports/soe/SOE2006/.

[33] SEPA, *Report on the State of the Environment in China in 2000* (Beijing); and SEPA, *Report on the State of the Environment in China in 2006*.

[34] World Bank and SEPA, "Cost of Pollution in China," xvii.

[35] SEPA, *Report on the State of the Environment in China in 2006*.

[36] World Bank, "Waste Management in China: Issues and Recommendations," Urban Development Working Paper No. 9, East Asia Infrastructure Department, World Bank, Washington, D.C., 2005, 1–3.

[37] Ibid. The rapidly changing composition of solid waste in China is illustrated in Wuhan, where the quantities of glass, plastics, and paper in its municipal solid waste more than doubled between 1984 and 1994. World Bank, "Waste Management in China," 10.

[38] Scott Tong, "Our E-waste Comes Back to Haunt Us," *Marketplace*, American Public Media, November 14, 2007, http://marketplace.publicradio.org/display/web/2007/11/14/consumed5_pm_1/#.

[39] SEPA, *Report on the State of the Environment in China in 2006*.

[40] As a result of afforestation efforts, however, forest lands increased by 0.16 percent. SEPA, *Report on the State of the Environment in China in 2006*.

[41] SEPA, *Report on the State of the Environment in China in 2006*, 75.

[42] For more on the new ministry, see: Xin Qui and Honglin Li, "China's Environmental Super Ministry Reform: Background, Challenges, and the Future," *Environmental Law Reporter, News & Analysis* 39, no. 2 (2007): 10152–63; and Anon., "China's Environment Ministry 'lacks local powers,'" *Reuters*, March 13, 2008, www.reuters.com/article/environmentNews/idUSPEK283666200803 13?feedType=RSS&feedName=

environmentNews.

[43] See, for example, Joseph Kahn and Jim Yardley, "Choking on Growth: As China Roars, Pollution Reaches Deadly Extremes," New York Times, August 26, 2007, www.nytimes.com/2007/08/26/world/asia/26china.html?pagewanted=1. They report: "The environmental agency [SEPA] still has only about 200 full-time employees, compared with 18,000 at the Environmental Protection Agency in the United States." After the SEPA became the MEP, the staff size at the headquarters was augmented to 311; this is according to an official notice dated July 10, 2008 on the MEP Web site (in Chinese), www.sepa.gov.cn/law/fg/gwyw/200808/t20080801_126885.htm. Elsewhere on the Ministry Web site (in Chinese, www.mep.gov.cn/dept/jgznjj), it indicates that the MEP also includes a number of entities that are "direct subsidiary" agencies. These include organizations such as the "environmental central monitoring station," the "environmental service center," and the "environmental science research institute." They also include the MEP's six regional "environmental protection supervision centers," which were created in an effort to more directly track events outside of Beijing. Pacific Environment (2008) "China Intensifies Regional Environmental Supervision," www.pacificenvironment.org/article.php?id=2943. As noted below, taken together, the MEP headquarters plus the subsidiaries have a staff size estimated to be less than 3,000.

A July 17, 2008 account (on the World Resources Institute [WRI] Web site) of the staff size after the SEPA became the MEP is no less disparaging on the subject of staffing than the aforementioned New York Times article by Joseph Kahn and Jim Yardley. In the WRI account, Gang He argues as follows:

> In a country of 350 million people, the U.S. Environmental Protection Agency has more than 17,000 employees, not including outside contractors. China, a country with four times the population and significantly more pollution per capita, has only about 300 workers at the MEP in Beijing and perhaps 30 people in each of the five regional inspection offices. Including affiliate agencies and institutes, the total number of personnel can perhaps reach 2,600. Some important support comes from the affiliated research institutions, but the ministry remains weak, lacking the decision-making capacity and financial resources of many other agencies.

(From Gang He, "China's New Ministry of Environmental Protection Begins to Bark, but Still Lacks in Bite," July 17, 2008, http://earthtrends.wri.org/updates/node/321.)

[44] Typically, the local reporting line for an EPB is to the vice mayor in charge of environmental protection.

[45] For example, the Beijing EPB has several affiliated units, including the Beijing Environmental Protection Monitoring Center, the Beijing Environmental Protection Science Research Institute, and the Beijing Environmental Information Center.

[46] The 170,000 figure is from the SEPA, Bulletin of China's Environmental Statistics (in Chinese) (2006), www.zhb.gov.cn/plan/hjtj/qghjtjgb/200709/t20070924_109497.htm; relevant information translated by Xuehua Zhang.

[47] Maohong Bao, "The Evolution of Environmental Policy and Its Impact in the People's Republic of China," Conservation and Society 4, no. 1 (2006): 49

[48] Ma Xiaoying and Leonard Ortolano, Environmental Regulation in China: Institutions, Enforcement, and Compliance (Boulder, CO: Rowman & Littlefield, 2000), 58–59.

[49] Since the late 1980s, NGOs in China have had the opportunity to follow

registration procedures established by the Ministry of Civil Affairs (MOCA) and thereby to become legally recognized as "social organizations" (*shehui tuanti*). This is significant because it provides NGOs with some practical advantages, such as the ability to open bank accounts. More broadly, it establishes NGOs as legitimate entities in the eyes of the government.

[50] Jonathan Schwartz, "Environmental NGOs in China: Roles and Limits," *Pacific Affairs* 77, no. 1 (2004): 45–46.

[51] For more on NGO self-censorship, see Ru Jiang and Leonard Ortolano, "Corporatist Control of Environmental Non-Governmental Organizations: A State Perspective," in Peter Ho and Richard Edmonds, eds., *Embedded Environmentalism: Opportunities and Constraints of a Social Movement in China* (Oxford: Routledge, 2008), 63. An example of government interference involves a case in which the Yunnan government "launched a thorough investigation [of Green Watershed, an NGO working to protect the Nu River], restricted its activities and barred its director from traveling abroad." For details of the case, see Lu Yiyi, "Environmental Civil Society and Governance in China," *International Journal of Environmental Studies* 64, no. 1 (2007): 59–69.

[52] For a well-documented example of NGO actions against local interests, see the description of the Nu River case in Lu (2007). The case also demonstrates the effective use by environmental NGOs of the Internet, traditional media, and alternative media such as newsletters, CDs, and DVDs: see Yang Guobin and Craig Calhoun, "Media, Civil Society, and the Rise of a Green Public Sphere in China," in Ho and Edmonds, *Embedded Environmentalism*, 81–85.

[53] Anna Brettell, "Channeling Dissent: The Institutionalization of Environmental Complaint Resolution," in Ho and Edmonds, *Embedded Environmentalism*, 113–17.

[54] For the full text of the law, sometimes referred to as the Administrative Procedure Law, see the Web site of the Congressional-Executive Commission on China, www.cecc.gov/pages/newLaws/adminLitigationENG.php?PHPSESSID=faee93ad641f31b454f84c7503892c7b.

[55] Citizens who have described violations have reportedly been penalized—sometimes with jail sentences based on allegedly trumped-up charges. See, for example, Joseph Kahn, "In China, a Lake's Champion Imperils Himself," *New York Times*, October 14, 2007, www.nytimes.com/2007/10/14/world/asia/14china.html.

[56] On the innovative nature of environmental regulatory programs in China, see Economy, *The River Runs Black: The Environmental Challenge to China's Future*. For details on individual programs, see Ma and Ortolano, *Environmental Regulation in China*.

[57] Richard D. Morgenstern, Piya Abeygunawardena, Alan Krupnick, Robert Anderson, Ruth Greenspan Bell, and Jeremy Schreifels, "Emissions Trading to Improve Air Quality in an Industrial City in the People's Republic of China," in K. A. Day, ed., *China's Environment and the Challenge of Sustainable Development* (New York: M.E. Sharpe, Armonk, 2005), 150–79.

[58] Jeremy Schreifels, U.S. Environmental Protection Agency, Washington, D.C., personal communication, September 17, 2007.

[59] This was accomplished with the passage of the 2003 Environmental Impact Assessment Law. This law also expands the EIA program by requiring EIAs for government plans as well as the construction projects covered by previous versions of environmental impact assessment regulations. For details, see Jesse L. Moorman and Ge Zhang, "Promoting and Strengthening Public Participation in China's Environmental

Impact Assessment Process: Comparing China's EIA Law and the U.S. NEPA," *Vermont Journal of Environmental Law* 8, no. 2 (2007): 281–335.

[60] For more on citizen engagement in the EIA process in China, see Wang Yan, Rickhard K. Morgan, and Mat. Cashmore, "Environmental Impact Assessment of Projects in the People's Republic of China: New Law, Old Problems," *Environmental Impact Assessment Review* 23, no. 5 (2003): 543–79.

[61] An illustration of the types of environment-oriented model cities programs is given by Dalian, which had received the following designations as of 1997: "The 10 Excellent Cities for Environment Comprehensive Treatment in China," "China Sanitary Cities," "China Afforestation Advanced Cities," "National Garden Cities," and "National Environment Protection Model Cities." From the ESCAP Virtual Conference Web site, www.unescap.org/DRPAD/VC/CONFERENCE/ex_cn_14_dee.htm.

[62] For an indication of challenges in calculating Green GDP, see James W. Boyd, "Nonmarket Benefits of Nature: What Should be Counted in Green GDP?" *Ecological Economics* 61, no. 4 (2007): 716–23.

[63] Anon., "China Plans to Set Up Green GDP system in 3–5 years," *China Daily*, March 12, 2004, www.chinadaily.com.cn/english/doc/2004-03/12/content_314332. htm. For more on internal conflicts over the GDP calculation procedures, see R. Spencer, "China's Green GDP audit put on hold," Telegraph.co.uk, July 23, 2007, www.telegraph. co.uk/earth/main.jhtml?xml=/earth/2007/07/23/eachina123.xml.

[64] According to Tony Saich, "The central authorities have transferred a much larger percentage of expenditure responsibilities to local government than is normally the case. . . . [And] local governments are excessively reliant on central transfers, supplemented by off budget revenues." Tony Saich, "The Changing Role of Urban Government," in Yusuf and Saich, *China Urbanizes: Consequences, Strategies and Policies*, 183. Although the growing tax intake has allowed for greater transfers of funds from the central government, local governments are still often short of funds to meet their public service provision obligations, especially in the less prosperous central and western provinces. For more on local funding challenges, see World Bank, "China: Public Services for Building the New Socialist Countryside," Report No. 40221-CN, East Asia and Pacific region, World Bank, Washington, D.C., 2007.

[65] According to SEPA (now MEP) vice minister Pan Yue:

> [China] needs a new mechanism for evaluating official performance that no longer enshrines local GDP growth at the expense of all else, and which stresses environmental protection efforts. As long as the GDP-centered evaluation system is in place, officials will blindly seek economic growth often at the cost of local environment and ecology, ignoring the teachings of the central leadership on the "scientific concept" of development.

(Pan Yue as quoted by Wang Jiaquan, "China's Economic Engine Forced to Face Environmental Deficit," July 26, 2007, World Watch Institute, www.worldwatch.org/ node/5259.)

[66] Saich, "The Changing Role of Urban Government," 187.

[67] Information in the remainder of this paragraph is from Zmarak Shalizi, "Water and Urbanization," in Yusuf and Saich, *China Urbanizes: Consequences, Strategies and Policies*, 172. See also, Qiu, *Harmony and Innovation*, 166, which cites a ministry of

construction survey delineating 40 cities in which wastewater network systems were incomplete, funds for operations were inadequate, and overall performance was poor.

[68] Pan's remarks on local government interference with environmental enforcement are discussed in Anon., "SEPA to Launch 3 More Watchdogs," http://en.chinagate.com. cn/english/environment/50251.htm. Chinagate.com was originally developed by the Chinese government in cooperation with a foundation.

[69] Pan Yue as quoted in *BizChina* (ChinaDaily.com.cn), January 18, 2007.

[70] It is not uncommon for top local officials to force an EPB to call off an enforcement action at a polluting enterprise that is a source of local employment or revenue. In some instances, the motivation for blocking the EPB enforcement is a personal relationship (*guanxi*) between a top official and enterprise leaders.

[71] This point has been made frequently. See for example, Ma and Ortolano, *Environmental Regulation in China*, 126–29. As they point out, levies provide an important source of revenues for EPBs. Ma and Ortolano also note that many EPB staff members believe the way to bring most enterprises into compliance is by developing mutual understanding, providing technical and financial assistance, and negotiating reasonable compliance deadlines.

[72] Abigail J. Jahiel, reported on an interview with a municipal EPB official who indicated: "Discharge fees are only about 50 percent of the operating costs of machinery for pollution control. As a result, many firms would still prefer not to use their own equipment and pay the fee instead." See Abigail J. Jahiel, "Implementation through Organizational Learning: The Case of Water Pollution Control in China's Reforming Socialistic System," Ph. D. dissertation, University of Michigan, 1994, 237.

[73] See Mara K. Warwick, "Environmental Information Collection and Enforcement at Small-Scale Enterprises in Shanghai: The Role of the Bureaucracy, Legislatures and Citizens," Ph. D. dissertation, Stanford University, Stanford, California, 2003, for a study on township and village enterprises (TVEs), which numbered in the millions at the time of her study.

[74] Inspection records are used in evaluating performance of environmental work units. See Warwick, "Environmental Information Collection." Because TVEs were so numerous, the Shanghai district EPBs studied by Warwick included fewer than 30 percent of the TVEs within their jurisdictions in their official industry databases. Failing to have a complete inventory is tantamount to not imposing environmental restrictions on small enterprises excluded from the records.

[75] Willy Lam, "China's 11th Five-Year Plan: A Roadmap for China's 'Harmonious Society'?" *China Brief* 5, no. 22 (October 25, 2005).

[76] Fan, "China's Eleventh Five-Year Plan," 711.

[77] Barry Naughton, "The New Common Economic Program: China's 11th Five Year Plan and What It Means," *China Leadership Monitor* 16, no. 10 (Fall 2005): 9.

[78] Lei Xiong, "Saying Farewell to the GDP growth Cult," *China Daily*, February 4, 2008, www.chinadaily.com.cn/opinion/2008-02/04/content_6440091.htm .

[79] Saich, "The Changing Role of Urban Government," 187.

[80] Siobhan Devine, "Analysis: China Conservation Doubts Remain," *United Press International*, February 22, 2008, www.upi.com/International_Security/Energy/Analysis/2008/02/22/analysis_china_conservation_doubts_remain/8492/.

[81] Wang Mingyuan of the Center for Environmental, Natural Resources and Energy Law at Tsinghua University, as quoted by Devine, "Analysis: China Conservation Doubts Remain."

[82] Melinda Xie and Chang Liu, "Round and Round, China is Aiming for a Circular Society with the New Recycling Economy Promotion Law," *EuroBiz*, January 2009, 35.

[83] This paragraph is based on personal communication via e-mail with Xuehua Zhang (February 28, 2008) and Xuehua Zhang, "Institutional Constraints on China's Environmental Enforcement: The Perspective of Local Environmental Protection Bureau (EPB) Personnel," Master's degree thesis, Western Washington University, Bellingham, 2001.

[84] Anon., "China's Environment Ministry 'Lacks Local Powers.'"

[85] MEP Web site, "Environmental Protection Supervision Centers of SEPA," http://english.sepa.gov.cn/About_SEPA/Regional_offices/200708/t20070814_107907.htm.

[86] The deputy director's remarks quoted in this paragraph are from Anon., "SEPA to Launch 3 More Watchdogs."

[87] Information on activities of these centers is from an interview conducted by Xuehua Zhang with a senior official at the SEPA's Southwest Environmental Supervision Center, Chengdu, Sichuan Province, August 15, 2007.

[88] Centers only conduct full investigations in cases approved by the MEP; in such cases, they report investigation results to the MEP, which decides how those cases are handled.

[89] Article 66 is general and applies to all agencies: "If a citizen, a legal person or any other organization, during the period prescribed by law, neither initiates an action nor carries out the specific administrative act, the administrative organ may apply to a people's court for compulsory execution, or proceeds with compulsory execution according to law." See Congressional-Executive Commission on China, www.cecc.gov/pages/newLaws/adminLitigationENG.php?PHPSESSID=faee93ad641f31b454f84e7503892c7b. The Hubei study is by Xuehua Zhang "Agencies, Citizens, and Courts: Environmental Enforcement and Administrative Litigation Law in Hubei Province, China," Ph.D. dissertation, Stanford University, Stanford, California, 2008.

[90] Anon., "Green Credit: To Fight Pollution, China Takes the Capitalist Route," *International Herald Tribune*, July 30, 2007, www.iht.com/articles/2007/07/30/business/pollute.php.

[91] A SEPA press release, "SEPA Makes Public the Stage-based Progress in Green Credit Policy," February 13, 2008, http://english.sepa.gov.cn/News_service/news_release/200803/t20080310_119113.htm.

[92] ISO 14,001 standards are voluntary and devised by firms under the auspices of the ISO's guidelines for environmental management systems; see, for example, Dennis Rondinelli and Gyula Vastag, "Panacea, Common Sense, or Just a Label?: The Value of ISO 14001 Environmental Management Systems," *European Management Journal* 18, no. 5 (2000): 499–510.

[93] Petra Christmann and Glen Taylor, "Globalization and the Environment: Determinants of Firm Self-Regulation in China," *Journal of International Business Studies* 32, no. 3 (2001): 439–58. In contrast, Zhu, Sarkis, and Geng (2005) found that Chinese firms had increased their awareness of environmental factors due to market pressures and regulations, but increased environmental awareness had not yet been translated into strong adoption of green supply-chain management practices. Zhu Qinghua, Joseph Sarkis, and Geng Yong, "Green Supply Chain Management in China: Pressures, Practices and Performance," *International Journal of Operations & Production Management* 25, no. 5 (2005): 449–68.

[94] "'China Environmental Labeling,' fifteen years witnessed the promulgation of China's environmental protection process," October 16, 2009. Available at SourceJuice.com, the

online news service of Xinhua News Agency, www.sourcejuice.com/1265791/2009/10/16/ China-Environmental-Labeling-years-witnessed-promulgation-China-environmental-protection.

[95] For difficulties faced by local governments in implementing requirements for cleaner production audits, see He Hongyan and Leonard Ortolano, "Implementing Cleaner Production Programmes in Changzhou and Nantong, Jiangsu," *Development and Change* 37, no. 1 (2006): 99–120.

[96] Yuan Zengwei, Bi Jun, and Yuichi Moriguichi, "The Circular Economy: A New Development Strategy in China," *Journal of Industrial Ecology* 10, nos. 1–2 (2007): 4–8.

[97] Barriers to implementing eco-industrial parks are detailed by Geng Yong, Murray Haight, and Qinghua Zhu, "Empirical Analysis of Eco-Industrial Development in China," *Sustainable Development* 15, no. 2 (2007): 121–33.

[98] Under the Administrative Litigation Law, citizens and NGOs can sue administrative agencies that fail to carry out laws properly, and many cases against the EPBs are brought each year. NGOs have also assisted pollution victims in lawsuits demanding compensation from polluters. On the increasingly active role of citizens in implementing environmental laws, see the special issue of the Vermont Journal of Environmental Law: China in Transition (volume 8, issue 2, Spring 2007).

[99] Lu, "Environmental Civil Society and Governance in China." See, also, Jim Yardley, "Seeking a Public Voice on China's 'Angry River,'" *New York Times*, December 26, 2005, www.nytimes.com/2005/12/26/international/asia/26china.html?_r=1&pagewanted=print&oref=slogin.

[100] Elizabeth C. Economy, "China's Environmental Movement," Testimony before the Congressional Executive Commission on China Roundtable on Environmental NGOs in China: Encouraging Action and Addressing Public Grievances, February 7, 2005, www.cfr.org/publication/7770. The media often refer to such actions by Pan Yue as "environmental protection storms." For more on these, see "At the Center of China's Environmental Storm; Interview with 'Hurricane Pan,'" reported in *Southern Weekend* and presented by the China Business Council for Sustainable Development, http://english.cbcsd.org.cn/news/news/5022.shtml. That interview documents the SEPA's growing influence and its effective use of the media.

[101] On various taxes and standards that could affect demand for vehicles, see Congressional Budget Office (CBO), "China's Growing Demand for Oil and its Impact on U.S. Petroleum Markets," CBO, Congress of the United States, Washington, D.C., 2006, 13–15.

[102] Innovative vehicles relying on alternative fuels will not lead to rapid turnovers in vehicle fleet composition; that will take place gradually as vehicles are replaced. Also, vehicle emission control devices capable of operating effectively over long time periods are not a current reality. For example, Chang in his 2006 Ph.D. dissertation showed that, compared with other countries, a high fraction of vehicles in Beijing in 2002 could not pass annual vehicle emission tests on the first try. C. Chang, "Automobile Pollution Control in China: Enforcement of and Compliance with Vehicle Emission Standards," Ph. D. dissertation, Stanford University, Stanford, California, 2006.

[103] David G. Streets, Shalini Gupta, Stephanie T. Waldhoff, Michael Q. Wang, Tami C. Bond, and Bo Yiyun, "Black Carbon Emissions in China," *Atmospheric Environment* 35, no. 25 (2001): 4281–96. Black carbon is an elemental carbonaceous component of particulate matter; it is formed by incomplete combustion of organic material and contributes to global climate change. According to Streets et al. (2001), the leading source

of black carbon in China is coal and biofuels, especially as used in residential heating. With expected advances in technology and use of coal briquettes in residential heating, as well as the increased use of diesel vehicles, black carbon from the transport sector will become a more significant fraction of the total.

[104] Qiu, *Harmony and Innovation,* 472.

[105] Steinfeld, "Energy Policy," 135.

[106] Consequences of China's increased reliance on motor vehicles are described by Steinfeld, "Energy Policy," 135–39; see also, David O'Connor, "Grow Now/Clean later, or the Pursuit of Sustainable Development?" Working Paper No. 111, OECD Development Centre, OECD, Paris, 1996, 32.

[107] On automobile dependence, see Peter Newman and Jeffery Kenworthy, *Sustainability and Cities: Overcoming Automobile Dependence* (Washington, D.C.: Island Press, 1999). On links between increased vehicle use and health problems (including obesity), see Howard Frumkin, Lawrence Frank, and Richard Jackson, *Urban Sprawl and Public Health* (Washington, D.C.: Island Press, 2004).

[108] Steinfeld, "Energy Policy," 138.

[109] According to Warwick McKibbin, "China produces roughly 28 percent of global production of coal and consumes 26 percent of global production." See Warwick J. McKibben, "Environmental Consequences of Rising Energy Use in China," *Asian Economy Policy Review* 1, no. 1 (2006): 157–74.

[110] Li Zhiping, "Protection of Peasants Environmental Rights During Social Transition: Rural Regions in Guangdong Province," *Vermont Journal of Environmental Law* 8, no. 2 (2007): 353.

[111] Marian R. Chertow, "The IPAT Equation and its Variants," *Journal of Industrial Ecology* 4, no. 4 (2001): 23.

[112] This U.S. experience has demonstrated that sizeable costs can also be involved in determining who is legally responsible for the cleanup of legacy pollution problems.

[113] For details on the progress China has been making in treating municipal wastewater and the challenges that remain in that domain, see Greg J. Browder, Shiqing Xie, Yoonhee Kim, Lixin Gu, Mingyuan Fan, and David Ehrhardt, *Stepping up: Improving the Performance of China's Urban Water Utilities* (Washington, D.C.: World Bank, 2007).

[114] In this context, "mining" means removing more water from the groundwater annually than is replenished by recharge. As a result of mining, for example, groundwater levels in parts of Beijing have dropped between 100 and 300 meters. See Shalizi, "Water and Urbanization," 162. An example of a massive water resources development project is the South-North Water Transfer Scheme, which is planned for completion in about 2050, and will eventually divert nearly 45 billion m³ of water annually from southern China to population centers of the drier north. The transfer will link four rivers —the Yangtze, Yellow, Huaihe, and Haihe—via three major diversion routes, stretching south-to-north across the eastern, central, and western parts of the country. For details, see watertechnology.net at http://www.water-technology.net/projects/south_north/.

[115] Shalizi, "Water and Urbanization," 161–62.

[116] According to the USAID, "[t]he world's 1.3 billion cattle are . . . a significant component of the water-for-food budget, requiring 7 kg of grain for every 1 kg of live weight. (As a rule of thumb, 1,000 tons of water is required to produce 1 ton of grain.)" USAID Environment, "Food Security and the Global Water Crisis," www.usaid.gov/our_work/environment/water/food_security.html. See, also, Editorial, "Priced Out of

the Market," *New York Times*, March 3, 2008, http://www.nytimes.com/2008/03/03/opinion/03mon1.html?scp=1&sq=China+grain+shortages++&st=nyt.

[117] See Lester Brown and Brian Halweil, "China's Water Shortage Could Shake World Grain Markets," April 22, 1998, Worldwatch Institute, www.worldwatch.org/node/1621. On recent increases in world food prices, see D. Streitfeld, "A Global Need for Grain That Farms Can't Fill," *New York Times*, March 9, 2008, www.nytimes.com/2008/03/09/business/worldbusiness/09crop.html?scp=2&sq=grain+prices+increase&st=nyt.

[118] Chertow, "The IPAT Equation," 21.

[119] Ibid.

[120] Another option is to adopt less resource-intensive consumption patterns. However, intense corporate advertising (via traditional media and the Internet) urging consumption that follows models in highly industrialized countries makes this a daunting proposition.

[121] For an alternative view of the ability of technologies to solve China's environmental problems, see Rawski, "Urban Air Quality in China," and others who have embraced the logic of the "Environmental Kuznets Curve" (EKC). Thomas G. Rawski, "Urban Air Quality in China: Historical and Comparative Perspectives," unpublished (2006) (to appear in a volume edited by Nazrul Islam), http://ideas.repec.org/p/pit/wpaper/282.html. Note, however, that the rationale for and existence of the EKC have often been challenged; see, William T. Harbaugh, Arik Levinson, and David Molloy Wilson, "Reexamining the Empirical Evidence for an Environmental Kuznets Curve," *Review of Economics and Statistics* 84, no. 3 (2002): 541–51.

[122] For more on this point, see Steinfeld, "Energy Policy," 133.

FAIR VERSUS UNFAIR:
HOW DO CHINESE CITIZENS VIEW
CURRENT INEQUALITIES?

Martin K. Whyte

Since the country's post-1978 reforms, China has experienced sweeping changes in the principles of remuneration and distribution of benefits and opportunities. These changes have brought about corresponding—and generally increased—inequalities among the citizenry. The fact of these inequalities is not in dispute. But how do ordinary Chinese citizens view them? What do they think of the country's current structures of inequality and mobility opportunities? Do they accept them, or do they feel they are unfair? To what extent does China's population resent and resist these changes or even harbor nostalgia for the now officially rejected and discarded distributional principles of the planned socialism era (roughly from 1955 to 1978)?

Many recent analyses of Chinese society, by both Chinese and foreign observers, claim that the increased inequality generated by China's reforms has inspired anger among ordinary Chinese. Indeed, popular anger is often portrayed as a major force behind the wave of protest incidents that has buffeted China in recent years.[1] This kind of analysis places China on the edge of what I would describe as a "social volcano" from which political instability and system breakdown might erupt at any moment. For example, the Central Party School polled senior officials in 2004 and concluded that the income gap was China's most serious social problem, far ahead of crime and corruption, which were ranked two and three, respectively.[2] Similarly, a summary of the 2006 "Blue Book" (an annual assessment of the state of Chinese society published by the Chinese Academy of Social Sciences) stated, "The Gini coefficient, an indicator of income disparities, reached 0.53 last year, far higher than a dangerous level of 0.4."[3] But are these alarmist messages correct? Is there evidence of popular anger in China about inequality and distributive justice issues?

This chapter seeks to provide answers to these questions. To present a general descriptive overview of contemporary popular attitudes on these issues, I rely on responses to the 2004 National China Inequality and Distributive Justice Survey.[4] In examining the patterns of response to a wide range of questions used in our survey—questions dealing with both competing principles of distribution and perceptions of actual current patterns of inequality and social mobility—I seek to determine which inequality principles and patterns are seen as fair and which are seen as unfair.

Too Much Income Inequality?

In the survey, in response to a question about whether current national income differences are too large, somewhat too large, about right, somewhat too small, or too small, a substantial majority of respondents (71.7 percent) answered that the gaps are to some degree excessive—see row 1 in table 11.1a. However, when we asked respondents their opinions about income differences within their own work units and the neighborhoods in which they live, a much smaller proportion said that local income differences were excessive—only 39.6 percent and 31.8 percent, respectively. In fact, for these latter two questions, the most common response was that income differences within the work unit and the neighborhood were about right. Among other responses, however, more people said that local income differences were too large. So these responses contain mixed messages. Clearly most Chinese feel that income differences in the entire nation are larger than they should be, but when you ask them about people in their local environment—those whom they could realistically use as comparative reference groups—then only about one respondent in three says that current income differences are excessive.

Table 11.1a Popular Views on the Extent of Inequality (% of respondents)

	Too small	Somewhat small	About right	Somewhat large	Too large	N
National income gap	1.4	4.4	22.5	31.6	40.1	3,254
Work unit income	1.6	8.9	49.9	27.1	12.5	2,107
Neighborhood income	1.9	10.2	56.1	26.6	5.2	3,264

Table 11.1b Expected Change in Size of Poor and Rich (% of respondents)

	Decrease	Stays the same	Increase	N
% of poor	43.2	30.7	26.1	3,266
% of rich	6.9	32.1	61.1	3,265

Table 11.1c Attitudes on Current Income Gaps (% of respondents)

	Strongly disagree	Disagree	Neutral	Agree	Strongly agree	N
Rich get richer, poor get poorer	3.8	15.3	20.9	34.3	25.8	3,258
Inequality benefits rich	3.8	15.0	30.2	37.3	13.6	3,263
Income gaps threaten stability	2.9	12.5	33.5	36.4	14.8	3,262
Income gaps versus socialism	5.3	18.6	48.2	21.4	6.5	3,255

Source: All tables in this chapter based on *China Inequality and Distributive Justice Survey,* 2004.
Note: Here and in later tables, N=number of responses (out of 3,267 respondents).

The survey team asked a number of additional questions to gain more perspective on how Chinese citizens perceive current inequalities and inequality trends. Two questions concerned whether respondents thought the proportions of poor people to rich people in China would increase, stay about the same, or decrease in the next five years.[5] As we can see in table 11.1b, the most common response was that the number of poor will decrease while the number of rich will increase. In other words, there is a predominantly optimistic expectation that the rising tide of economic development will lift all boats, even if not at the same pace. However, we should not ignore the 26.1 percent of respondents who expect China's poor population to increase during the next five years.

A different impression is generated by another question, which asked respondents to register varying degrees of agreement or disagreement with the statement, "In the last few years, the rich people in our society have gotten richer, while the poor people have gotten poorer." The pattern of responses to this question, shown in table 11.1c, reveals that around 60 percent of all respondents agree or strongly agree with this statement, which seems puzzling in contrast to the optimism about the proportion of China's poor declining in the future. The second row in table 11.1c displays a similarly jaundiced view. When presented with the statement, "The reason why social inequalities persist is because they benefit the rich and the powerful," 50.9 percent agreed while only 18.8 percent disagreed. These responses suggest a popular suspicion that in the country at large, those at the very top of the inequality pyramid are manipulating the system to their own advantage.

Two other questions asked respondents to evaluate current inequalities in terms of whether they pose a threat to social stability and whether they violate the principles of socialism. As shown in table 11.1c, about 51 percent agreed about the threat to social stability, but substantially fewer, only about 28 percent, agreed that the principles of socialism are being violated.[6] These responses raise the possibility that many respondents see current inequalities as excessive not so much because such large gaps are inherently unjust, but because the disparities involved threaten the desirable goal of an orderly and harmonious society.[7] As we examine the responses to other questions below, we will have further opportunities to probe the importance of social injustice sentiments versus other types of negative reactions to current inequalities.

To sum up, these initial questions about the size of inequality gaps yield mixed impressions. It is clear that the wide income differences that now exist in China nationally are seen as unfair or undesirable by a large majority of Chinese citizens. Many citizens are particularly concerned that such gaps could undermine social stability. Perhaps they also are suspicious that those at the very top of the social hierarchy are manipulating the system to their private advantage. However, they are much less likely to see the income inequalities in their local communities and firms as excessive, and most do not expect that the widened income gaps fostered by the reforms will translate into an increase in poverty in the immediate future.

The Attribution of Poverty and Wealth

In judging the fairness or unfairness of inequalities in any society, it is not enough merely to decide whether current gaps are too large, about right, or too small. What matters more is identifying who is perceived to be at the bottom and at the top of the inequality hierarchy and how they are assumed to have ended up where they are. It makes a difference whether most rich people are perceived as enjoying "ill-gotten gains" versus "well-deserved fruits." Similarly, if people who are poor are perceived primarily as victims of discrimination and blocked opportunities, this will be seen as much more unfair than if the poor are seen as shiftless and incompetent. We thus enter the realm of the popular attribution of poverty versus wealth. Following the model of questions used in the International Social Justice Project, we asked each of our survey respondents to state how much they thought various listed traits influence why a person in China today is poor—to a very large degree, a large degree, to some degree, a small degree, or not at all. We followed this up with similar questions about why people in China are rich. Each list mixes attributes based on individual worthiness and merit with other factors related to external or structural causes.[8] The assumption underlying these questions is that if current inequalities are mainly attributed to variations in individual merit factors (such as talent, educational attainment, and hard work), they will tend to be seen as fair, whereas inequalities mainly attributed to external factors (such as unequal opportunities and discrimination) will tend to be seen as unjust. The resulting weighted marginal distributions are displayed in tables 11.2a and 11.2b.

Table 11.2a Attribution of Why People in China are Poor (% of respondents)

	Not at all	Small influence	Some influence	Large influence	Very large influence	N	Rank order
Lack of ability	2.2	4.5	32	43.5	17.8	3,265	1
Bad luck	9.1	18.1	45.9	21.7	5.2	3,265	6
Poor character	8.4	19.6	40.8	22.6	8.6	3,261	4
Lack of effort	3.2	7.2	35.6	43.9	10.1	3,257	3
Discrim-ination	7.2	18.8	52.8	16.9	4.3	3,261	7
Unequal opportunity	4.3	15.2	53.1	22.3	5.2	3,261	5
Unfair economic system	5.4	11.8	61.8	16.1	4.9	3,258	8
Low education	3	8.6	34	37.8	16.6	3,239	2

Table 11.2b Attribution of Why People in China are Rich (% of respondents)

	Not at all	Small influence	Some influence	Large influence	Very large influence	N	Rank order
Ability and talent	1.8	3.8	25	46.3	23.2	3,265	1
Good luck	7	13.4	40.5	29.8	9.3	3,264	6
Dis-honesty	13.3	26.7	42.6	12.8	4.6	3259	8
Hard work	1.5	5.7	31.1	49.5	12.3	3,261	2
Connec-tions	1.4	6.3	32.3	41	19	3,261	4
Better oppor-tunities	1.9	8.5	44.4	34.9	10.4	3,262	5
Unfair economic system	3.6	14.4	56	19.5	6.5	3,258	7
High education	2.3	6.2	30.9	39.5	21.1	3,240	3

By scanning tables 11.2a and 11.2b, it becomes clear that for most respondents, variations in individual merit factors—much more than external and structural causes—explain why some people in China today are poor while others are rich. The top three attributions of poverty in China today, in order, are lack of ability or talent, low education, and lack of effort. For wealth, the same three traits emerge as the most important, although in slightly different sequence, with ability and talent followed by hard work and then high educational level. However, one "negative" trait, variations in personal connections, was a close fourth in popular explanations of why some people in China are rich.[9] Notably, traits such as dishonesty, discrimination, and unfairness in the current economic system came out near the bottom in the rank ordering of reasons why some people are poor while others are rich.

These responses do not indicate that the dominant tendency in China today is for citizens to attribute the current patterning of wealth versus poverty to social injustice. Rather, while perhaps one-quarter of our respondents ranked external or structural "unfair" sources as important or very important in explaining why some people are rich while others are poor, the majority of respondents identified individual merit, and variations therein, as the primary driver.[10] As such, the dominant tendency is to see current inequalities as fair rather than unfair.[11]

How can these responses be squared with the fact that a large majority of respondents feel that there is too much income inequality in China today and that inequality exists because it benefits the rich and powerful? Two considerations may explain this apparent paradox. First, as suggested above, national inequality may be seen as excessive not because income gaps are inherently unjust but because they may threaten social stability. Second, it seems likely that when people responded to our series of questions about the explanations for why some people are poor while others are rich, they tended to focus on the rich and poor people in their own immediate environment, rather than on invisible or dimly perceived rich and poor people in other parts of China. If that is the case, then as we saw in table 11.1a, most respondents did not view such local inequalities as particularly excessive or unjustly derived. If we can assume that, as in other societies, what matters most to individuals is how they see themselves compared to various local reference groups, rather than the entire nation, then it would appear that most respondents consider the inequalities around them to be acceptable—even fair. They do not harbor strong resentment or feel that current inequalities are unjust, even if they worry about income disparities in the larger society.[12]

In short, the majority sentiment that current inequalities in China are too large cannot be interpreted as a general rejection of the current social order as unjust. Rather, there is a broad consensus that, at least in terms of the inequalities citizens see in their immediate environment, market reforms have produced new inequality patterns that are acceptable. Our survey results indicate that many Chinese citizens attribute these patterns to variations in individual merit rather than fundamental injustices in the social order.

Views on Egalitarian Distribution and Redistribution

Since many Chinese citizens object to the size of current inequalities, it is worth considering how they would feel about a more equal distribution of income and other resources and about government redistribution as a way to achieve that result. Table 11.3 contains several questions relating to these issues. First, we have responses to the statement, "Distributing wealth and income equally among people is the most fair method." As we can see from the first row of table 11.3, opinions are divided on this issue, but more respondents disagree than agree with this statement. Evidently most Chinese do not desire a strictly egalitarian distribution.[13] Nor is a need-based redistribution very popular, as seen in the similar pattern of reactions to the second question shown in table 11.3: "There should be redistribution from the rich to the poor in order to satisfy everyone's needs." Judging from the third row in the table, however, there is much more popular approval of affirmative action to help the poor; 61.9 percent of respondents agreed with the statement, "It is fair to give people from lower social strata extra help so they can enjoy more equal opportunities."

Table 11.3 Attitudes toward Egalitarian Distribution and Redistribution (% of respondents)

	Strongly disagree	Disagree	Neutral	Agree	Strongly agree	N
Equal distribution is most fair	10.6	34.1	26.3	22.9	6.2	3,262
Redistribute to meet needs	8.1	29.8	32.5	24.2	5.3	3,259
Extra help to poor is fair	1	6.8	30.2	45.6	16.3	3,252
Government to limit top income	7.9	26.8	31.5	24	9.8	3,262
Government to reduce rich-poor gap	1.8	10.3	30.6	34.2	23.1	3,260
Government to guarantee jobs	0.5	3.9	20	45.6	30.1	3,261
Government to guarantee minimum living standard	0.5	2.7	16.1	39.4	41.4	3,263

The next four questions all inquire whether the government should take additional measures to reduce inequality. It is apparent that most Chinese do not favor limits on the maximum income individuals should be able to earn (see row 4 in table 11.3), and the pattern of responses is similar to that of the table's first two questions. However, there is much more support for three other possible government actions, with 57.3 percent approving of government efforts to reduce the gap between high and low incomes, 75.7 percent favoring government guarantees of jobs for everyone willing to work, and 80.8 percent advocating government guarantees of a minimum standard of living for everyone. Taken together, these responses suggest that according to most Chinese citizens, the ideal pattern of inequality would differ from current patterns, mainly by eliminating poverty through government-sponsored job and income guarantees, but without setting limits on the income and wealth of the rich or redistributing from the rich to the poor. (Respondents were not asked to explain how the government could help the poor without extracting more from the rich.) This appears to be a formula for a market-oriented welfare state, rather than a socialist society.[14] Moreover, there is relatively little evidence here that most citizens resent China's newly emerging class of entrepreneurs, millionaires, and, yes, capitalists.

Is It All Right to Enjoy the Fruits of Success?

Attitudes about what forms of inequality are fair and unfair can be probed further by considering the questions we asked about those who are successful and prosperous. These responses are displayed in table 11.4. Close to half of all respondents (48.8 percent) agreed that it is fair for some occupations to receive more respect than others (see row 1 in table 11.4), and sizable majorities of our sample agreed with statements that it is fair for the rich to pay for superior education for their children (64.2 percent) and to obtain superior housing (58 percent). They were less certain that it is fair for the rich to obtain superior medical care (47.2 percent expressed approval and 27.6 percent disapproved). Also, a large majority agreed with the statement that rich people should be able to keep what they earn, even if this generates gaps between the rich and the poor (62.8 percent). Most respondents (61.2 percent) also said that inequality would be acceptable if China had equality of opportunity. However, a single question about elite status based on power rather than wealth generated a very different pattern of responses (see the final row in table 11.4). When presented with the statement, "It is fair for people in power to enjoy a certain amount of special treatment," 55.8 percent disagreed; only 21.4 percent expressed agreement. Evidently using acquired wealth to enjoy a better life than others is acceptable, but translating political power into a better life is not, even though the latter is just as common in China today—perhaps more so—as the former.[15]

Table 11.4 Attitudes toward the Rich Enjoying Advantages (% of respondents)

	Strongly disagree	Disagree	Neutral	Agree	Strongly agree	N
Fair, some jobs deserve more respect	3.4	15.5	32.3	40.6	8.2	3,260
Fair, rich kids receive better education	2.7	11.5	21.5	44.1	20.1	3,257
Fair, rich buy better housing	3	13.1	25.8	42.8	15.2	3,254
Fair, rich receive better health care	8.5	19.1	25.3	35.2	12	3,246
OK to keep earnings, even unequal	1	5.3	30.9	46.3	16.5	3,244
Inequality OK if opportunity is equal	1.8	9.5	27.5	48.2	13	3,259
Fair, powerful receive special treatment	26.3	29.5	22.9	16.4	5	3,256

Discrimination Against those with Rural Origins

We have just seen that there is considerable acceptance of the rich and their families enjoying the fruits of their success. Now we shift our attention to look at popular attitudes toward an important disadvantaged group—China's rural citizens. In one of the major ironies of China's socialist revolution after 1949, a leadership that had strong roots in the countryside and declared itself determined to eliminate "feudalism" and foster social equality produced something akin to "socialist serfdom" in actual practice. Those born into rural families were effectively bound to the soil in all but rare circumstances. Even after this bondage ended in the reform era and rural residents could migrate elsewhere and seek jobs in the cities, institutionalized discrimination against rural migrants—members of China's "floating population" who possess agricultural residential permits (*hukou*) no matter how long they may have lived in the city—has remained severe.[16] In our questionnaire we included questions to tap into popular attitudes about those with rural origins. Table 11.5 shows the distribution of responses.

Table 11.5 Attitudes toward Urban Bias (% of respondents)

	Strongly disagree	Disagree	Neutral	Agree	Strongly agree	N
Fair, urban households have more opportunities	12.2	32.8	29.9	19.4	5.8	3,236
Fair, deny migrants urban registration	24.3	34.9	26.2	11.8	2.8	3,249
Fair, bar migrant kids from schooling	40	36.8	15.8	5.5	2	3,257
Fair, bar migrants from some jobs	35.5	35.1	20.4	7.3	1.7	3,256
Equal job rights for rural/urban dwellers	2	5.8	19.7	44.5	28	3,254
Fair, migrants receive no urban benefits	34	32.9	24	7.4	1.8	3,260
Urbanites receive too much benefit	3.6	17.4	31.6	39.5	7.9	3,258
Urbanites contribute more to development	9.5	35.9	32.9	19.5	2.2	3,256

The numbers in table 11.5 differ significantly from those we reviewed earlier. In every instance, respondents affirmed that the various disadvantages suffered by rural people and migrants to the city are unjust. In the first row of the table we see that 45 percent of all respondents felt it was unfair for urban residents to enjoy greater opportunities than rural ones; only 25 percent saw this as fair. An even larger 59 percent of respondents believed it was unfair to deny urban household registrations to migrants from rural areas, while only 15 percent considered it fair. The sense of injustice becomes stronger still regarding rules that prevent migrant children from attending urban public schools unless they pay special high fees, and the regulations, common among city administrations, that forbid the hiring of migrants for a whole range of urban jobs. Here the consensus that these practices are unfair rather than fair is 77 percent versus 8 percent for the school exclusion and 71 percent versus 9 percent for the jobs exclusion. The figures in the fifth row of table 11.5 confirm the same pattern, with the jobs question asked the other way around. Overall, 73 percent of respondents felt that rural and urban citizens should have equal rights to jobs, while only 8 percent disagreed. The exclusion of urban migrants from welfare benefits enjoyed by China's urban residents is almost as unpopular: 67 percent of respondents viewed it as unfair while only 9 percent disagreed. The final two questions shown in the table concern not specific discriminatory practices but possible explanations for the higher income and other advantages that urban residents enjoy. Here the patterns are less lopsided, but they still show greater rejection than acceptance of the idea that urbanites deserve the advantages they enjoy. When asked whether urban residents have enjoyed more of the benefits of the reforms than they deserve, 47 percent agreed compared with 21 percent who disagreed. When asked whether the advantages enjoyed by urbanites were due to the fact they contribute more to the country and its development than do rural residents, only 22 percent agreed while 45 percent disagreed. In sum, throughout this set of questions we see the first clear-cut case of overall popular rejection of a current pattern of inequality.

Although we do not show the details in this chapter, these patterns are not solely driven by the resentment of rural-origin respondents. Even urban respondents generally recognize the unfairness of current institutionalized discrimination against those with rural *hukou*, although migrant respondents tended to express their opposition more strongly.[17] As may be obvious, the institutionalized discrimination against those of rural origin in China during the reform era contradicts the promarket ideology that China's leaders are now trying to persuade their citizens to accept. That ideology says that the ideal society offers equal opportunity, and that the differences between the rich and successful and the poor and unsuccessful should reflect variations in talent, effort, and other nonascribed characteristics. The leadership's success in promoting these ideas, as we have seen earlier (particularly in table 11.2), almost requires the population to reject the notion that it is fair to discriminate against individuals simply because they were born into rural families.

The Beneficial Effects of Incentives and Income Differences

Even if most Chinese citizens feel that it is acceptable for the rich to enjoy a better life than others (see table 11.4), are they willing to go further and agree that the incentive effect provided by current inequalities actually benefits society? When Deng Xiaoping contravened years of Maoist slogans that extolled asceticism and egalitarianism and instead proclaimed that "it is good for some to get rich first," did he persuade most Chinese? The abstract idea that inequalities are not simply tolerable, but may actually be desirable or even necessary because they benefit society (by increasing motivation, innovation, responsibility, and other desirable qualities), is central to the "functionalist theory of stratification."[18] That said, this idea flies in the face of the Maoist condemnation of material incentives as the "sugar-coated bullets of the bourgeoisie." How successful have Chinese reformers been since 1978 in legitimating current inequalities by claiming that they are actually beneficial?[19] We examine this issue by scanning the pattern of responses to questions in our survey that address the role of incentives and market competition, as displayed in table 11.6.

Table 11.6 Attitudes toward Benefits of Markets, Competition, and Incentives (% of respondents)

	Strongly disagree	Disagree	Neutral	Agree	Strongly agree	N
Market competition inspires	0.5	4.5	32.4	45.7	16.8	3,262
Free market crucial for development	0.8	4.6	40.8	41.4	12.4	3,261
Self-interest benefits society	1.9	11.9	43.6	34.5	8.1	3,245
Business profits benefit society	4.1	22.4	36	32	5.6	3,255
Competition brings out bad side of humans	8.3	30.2	38.6	18.9	3.9	3,262
Income gap fosters hard work	2.8	16.7	30.1	39.1	11.3	3,263
Need rewards to take on responsibility	2.8	14.7	32.5	39.2	10.8	3,264
Income gaps aid national wealth	15.9	27.6	36.9	16.3	3.3	3,259
Widen coast-interior gap for development	5.9	22	44.8	22.9	4.4	3,261
Fair to lay off state-owned enterprise workers	13.8	24.6	39.5	17.6	4.5	3,251

In the first row of table 11.6, we see responses to the statement, "The good thing about market competition is that it inspires people to work hard and be creative." A solid majority of respondents (62.5 percent) expressed agreement with this statement; only 5 percent disagreed. A more vague statement, "A free market economy is crucial to the economic development of our country," was also endorsed by a majority of respondents (53.8 percent), whereas only 5.4 percent disapproved. No other statement shown in the table elicits such broad approval. A related statement meant to convey Adam Smith's central justification for markets—"When every person can freely pursue his own interests, society as a whole will also benefit"—elicited more approval than disapproval (42.6 percent versus 13.8 percent). However, the most common response to this claim was a neutral view (43.6 percent). A similar pattern of responses emerges to provide another version of the same idea, but one that focuses specifically on the pursuit of profits by businessmen: "It is acceptable for businessmen to make profits because in the end everyone benefits." Again there was more agreement than disagreement with this statement (by a smaller margin than was the case with the prior question, 37.6 percent versus 26.5 percent), but the most common response was neutrality. A statement intended as roughly the opposite attitude to those just discussed, "Competition is harmful because it brings out the bad side of human nature," not surprisingly found more respondents disagreeing than agreeing, but again the most common response was neutrality. Clearly, Chinese citizens support market competition and incentives in the abstract, but they also harbor considerable misgivings and uncertainty about claims that the pursuit of self-interest and profit will benefit society in general.

The remaining statements in table 11.6 were designed to assess views on versions of the claim that incentive carrots and disincentive sticks are needed to motivate individuals to behave in desirable ways so that society will benefit. These statements elicited even more divided reactions than did the statements in the top two rows. Half (50.4 percent and 50 percent) agreed with the first two statements, "Only when income differences are large enough will individuals have the incentive to work hard," and "Unless there are greater rewards, people will not be willing to take on greater responsibilities at work." The remainder of the sample disagreed or took a neutral view. When the same idea was expressed at the level of societal income gaps rather than individual incentives—as in the statements, "For the prosperity of the country, there must be large differentials in incomes," and "To develop our country's economy, it is necessary to increase the income gap between coastal and inland regions"—respondents disagreed as much or even more strongly than they agreed, although in both cases the most common response was, once again, to take a neutral position. Finally, in the last row of table 11.6 we show responses to the one statement that dealt directly with the stick rather than the carrot side of incentives: "In order to reform state-owned enterprises, it is fair to lay off large numbers of individuals." In this case as well opinions were divided and the most common response was a neutral one, but more respondents disagreed with this statement (38.4 percent) than agreed (22.1 percent).

In general, based on the questions in table 11.6, we conclude that China's reformers have only partially succeeded in gaining popular acceptance of the idea that market competition, material incentives, and income differentials are necessary and beneficial for Chinese society. To be sure, these responses show that

Mao Zedong's doctrine—that material incentives and the pursuit of profits and economic betterment are inherently evil—has few champions today. However, uneasiness and uncertainty about the benefits of incentives and inequality are almost as common as approval of these ideas.

Optimism versus Pessimism about Social Mobility and Social Justice

The last set of questions from our survey concerns expressions of optimism versus pessimism about the chances for individuals and families to get ahead and to live in a more just society. Table 11.7 displays a variety of statements related to these questions. The first row is an assessment of whether respondents predicted that, five years from the time of the survey, their family's economic situation would be much worse than at present, somewhat worse, about the same, somewhat better, or much better. As we can see, the dominant mood was optimism, with 63.1 percent estimating that their families would be doing better in five years and only 7.5 percent predicting that their families would be doing worse. When presented with a more generic statement of optimism about mobility opportunities in China today, "Based upon the current situation in the country, the opportunities for someone like you to raise their living standard are still great," again the dominant response was to express agreement (61.1 percent) and thus optimism about upward mobility opportunities. However, the next several attitude statements reveal that most Chinese recognize that equal opportunity does not exist in China any more than it does in other societies. The statement, "Currently, the opportunities to be successful are the same for all people," elicited about as much disagreement as agreement. When the opposite view was stated, "People of different family backgrounds encounter different opportunities in society," almost 60 percent of respondents expressed agreement and only about 10 percent disagreed. Despite this recognition of the inequality of mobility opportunities, when presented with the statement, "In our country, hard work is always rewarded," again most respondents struck an optimistic note, with more than 61 percent agreeing and only about 15 percent disagreeing.

Table 11.7 Optimism versus Pessimism about Social Mobility and Social Justice (% of respondents)

	Strongly agree	Disagree	Neutral	Agree	Strongly agree	N
Family living standard in 5 years*	1.8	5.7	29.3	51.1	12	3,266
Great opportunity to raise standard of living	4.3	15.3	23.5	43.3	17.8	3,262
Equal opportunity exists to succeed	6.8	24.1	31.6	27.5	10	3,260
Family origin affects opportunities	1.4	8.9	30.1	43.2	16.3	3,246
Hard work always rewarded	2	13.4	23.5	43.3	17.8	3,258
Social justice talk has no meaning	6.1	23	36.5	27.5	6.9	3,261
Hard to say what is just	6	20.2	35.7	28.5	9.6	3,261
Officials don't care	4.5	16.5	28.9	31.2	18.9	3,260

Note: *Actual response categories were much worse, somewhat worse, no change, somewhat better, much better.

Taken together, the responses to these questions indicate that while most Chinese recognize that there is no level playing field that offers the same chances to all, they do not think that the social order is so unfair as to be stacked against ordinary people, preventing them from getting ahead. We see echoes here of the pattern of responses to explanations of why some people are rich and others are poor (see table 11.2). There appears to be a strong belief that diligent pursuit of social mobility through schooling, talent, and hard work will lead to social and economic betterment. Factors such as unequal opportunities and personal connections are also perceived to help some undeserving individuals to succeed, but not to the extent that deserving ordinary people are blocked from getting ahead. The responses to another question substantiate this view of the world. Respondents were asked which of two statements they agreed with more: "Some people getting rich first will reduce the chances for others to get rich," and "Some people getting rich first will increase the opportunities for others to get rich." Many more respondents favored the second option (by 48.6 percent to 11.1 percent), although a sizable 40.3 percent responded that it was hard to say or they didn't know. Evidently, most Chinese do not see the pursuit of wealth as a zero-sum game, and many seem to accept Deng's view that it is good for some people to get rich first.

The final three rows in table 11.7 display responses to three statements designed to explore feelings of injustice and pessimism about achieving social justice: (1) "Since we are unable to change the status quo, discussing social justice is meaningless"; (2) "Looking at things as they are now, it is very difficult to distinguish what is just and what is unjust"; and (3) "Government officials really don't care about what common people like me think." Opinions were divided on all three statements. For the first two, disagreement was almost as likely as agreement, with the most common response being a neutral answer. With respect to the third statement, a bare majority (50.1 percent) expressed agreement, compared to 21 percent who disagreed. Although the response patterns to these last three questions are somewhat mixed or negative, considered in conjunction with the other responses in table 11.7, it appears that Chinese citizens, at least at the time of our survey in 2004, felt neither anger at the fundamental injustice of current patterns of inequality nor pessimism about their ability to benefit from the current system.

Variations in Attitudes toward Inequality and Distributive Injustice

There is not sufficient space in this chapter to discuss in detail two additional research questions the China Inequality and Distributive Justice project has been analyzing. The first is how do popular Chinese attitudes about inequality and distributive injustice issues compare with those of citizens in other societies, particularly other postsocialist transition societies in Eastern Europe? Second, within China, which social groups display the most anger about inequality and distributive injustice, and, on the other hand, which groups are the most satisfied with current patterns? Even though we cannot do justice here to our project's complex findings on these issues, a few general patterns are worth noting.

Chinese Attitudes in Comparative Perspective

Since many of the questions used in our 2004 China national survey replicated questions asked in the International Social Justice Project (ISJP) surveys in the 1990s, we can compare the responses of Chinese to replicated questions.[20] To summarize the results of our comparison, Chinese citizens are often less critical of current inequalities and more optimistic about the opportunities for ordinary people to get ahead. Their responses to some survey questions show that the Chinese are even more accepting and optimistic than are citizens in advanced capitalist societies where market competition are familiar and less controversial.

A few examples convey the patterns we find. For instance, 71.7 percent of respondents in our China survey (see table 11.1a) found national income gaps to be too large. Notably, citizens in the United States (65.2 percent), Poland (69.7 percent), West Germany (70.8 percent), East Germany (72.1 percent), Japan (72.6 percent), and the United Kingdom (75 percent) hold similar views. The opinions of respondents in the other Eastern European surveys we examined are even more critical; in these instances, the proportion of those who deplored national income gaps as excessive ranged from 78.6 percent in the Czech Republic to a staggering 95.6 percent in Bulgaria.

The contrasts in assessments of what underlies poverty and wealth tend to be even more dramatic. While 61.3 percent of Chinese surveyed in 2004 thought that lack of ability had a large or very large influence on why some people are poor (see table 11.2a, first row), in all the other countries we compared, whether East European or advanced capitalist, fewer than 40 percent of those surveyed responded that way. For example, only 28 percent of Russians in 1996 and 25.7 percent of Japanese in 1991 thought that lack of ability had a large or very large influence on why some people are poor. To look at the other side of the ledger, a mere 26 percent of Chinese surveyed in 2004 thought that an unfair economic structure had a large or very large influence in explaining why certain people in China today are rich (see table 11.2b, second-to-last row). Among our research set, only one other country yielded a similar level (West Germany in 1991, with 25.1 percent). In every other country we analyzed, citizens believed that an unfair economic structure played a significant role in explaining who is rich, ranging from 39.4 percent of Americans to 77.5 percent of Bulgarians.

To present one final example, in our China survey 50.1 percent of respondents expressed agreement or strong agreement with the statement that officials do not care what ordinary people think (see table 11.7, final row). However, that turns out to be a *lower* level of agreement than in any of the other countries for which we have comparative data. For example, 64 percent of Americans, 69.7 percent of Russians, 72.3 percent of Poles, and 74.7 percent of Japanese surveyed felt that officials do not care about the opinions of ordinary citizens. This is quite a dramatic contrast, especially since Chinese cannot use ballots to challenge and replace the officials who rule over them, whereas citizens in the other surveyed countries can.

Chinese citizens are not always more accepting of current inequalities than their counterparts in the other countries. That said, they are hardly ever more *critical* of current inequalities; when contrasts do emerge with the patterns in other societies, these generally involve Chinese having more *favorable* attitudes. So a comparative perspective with other countries reinforces this chapter's earlier conclusion: Chinese citizens do not express a strong sense of distributive injustice that could pose a threat to China's political and social stability.

Variations in Chinese Attitudes toward Distributive Injustice

Again, limited space prevents us from making a detailed analysis of which social groups within China are most angry about inequality issues.[21] The conventional wisdom is that disadvantaged groups—such as farmers, urban migrants, the poorly educated, and residents of western provinces—are particularly likely to express anger about current inequalities and distributive injustice. According to our survey data, however, this conventional wisdom is mostly wrong. The large variety of survey questions summarized in this chapter provide multiple, relatively differentiated measures of various aspects of inequality attitudes, and no single pattern of variation across social groups and locations within China fits all of them. However, China's farmers, who remain at the bottom of the social status pyramid and who are often depicted as seething with anger, tend by many measures in our survey to be more accepting and less critical of current inequalities than other occupational and residence groups.[22] Migrants and residents of interior provinces are less consistent than farmers, but according to some attitude measures they also tend to view current inequalities in a relatively favorable light. In fact, the most critical attitudes toward inequality and distributive injustice tend to be expressed by residents of cities, especially those who are well educated, middle-aged, or are manual workers or unemployed.[23]

Survey figures help to illustrate how farmers differ from the rest of our sample in their views on the importance of "nonindividual merit" reasons for why some people in China today are rich and others are poor (see tables 11.2a and 2b). Overall, 15.6 percent of the farmers in our sample felt that discrimination has a large or very large influence on why some people are poor; in contrast, 25.9 percent of the remainder of the sample gave this response. Similarly, 20.8 percent of farmers said that lack of equal opportunity is an important or very important influence on why some people are poor, compared to 33.5 percent of the rest of the sample. Among farmers, 14.2 percent attributed poverty to problems in the economic structure, whereas 28.6 percent of the remainder of the sample gave this response. In explaining why some people are rich, 54.1 percent of farmers said that having connections is an important influence, but 64.3 percent of the rest of the sample gave this response. Among farmers, 36.6 percent agreed that unequal opportunities have an important influence on some people being rich, compared to 52.4 percent of the rest of the sample; and 18.9 percent of farmers said that unfairness in the economic structure is important in explaining who is rich, in contrast to 31.3 percent of the remaining sample. All of these differences are statistically significant. When we controlled for a wide variety of other possible influences on these attitudes, using multivariate statistical models, generally the net influence of being a farmer was still to express significantly more *favorable* attitudes toward current inequalities—again, versus the conventional wisdom.

Why is it the case that some low-status and disadvantaged groups, which logically ought to be angry, are in many instances *less* angry than other groups? This is a complex question that we explore in other writings from this project.[24] In general, we contend that past personal and family history, comparative reference groups, relative expectations, and other subjective factors intervene to affect attitudes toward inequality and distributive injustice issues as much or more than respondents' objective status characteristics, such as their income or educational attainment. To state the case simplistically, China's farmers, even though they remain at the bottom of the status hierarchy, have been released from near-feudal subjugation and may feel that they have nowhere to go but up. Likewise, they will generally be aware of many rural people who have become better off in recent decades, while at the same time recognizing that the chances of doing so are by no means equally distributed.[25] In contrast, former state workers and the urban unemployed do not feel that they have nowhere to go but up; instead, they may believe that their standards of living are threatened or have declined even as they see around them people who have become fabulously wealthy. Viewed in this admittedly somewhat oversimplified fashion, it is not surprising that Chinese farmers may view current inequalities more favorably than do the middle-aged, workers, and the unemployed who live in booming cities. In general, then, where a respondent stands within the income or other objective status hierarchies of contemporary China is not a reliable predictor of how that individual feels about inequality and distributive injustice issues.

Conclusion

Having reviewed the pattern of responses to attitude questions about inequality and distributive injustice, can we summarize how Chinese citizens feel about these issues? Which aspects of current inequalities in China do they accept and view as fair and which do they consider basically unjust? Our survey results indicate that the majority of respondents view most parts of the unequal, market-based society in which they now live as basically fair. Our data reveal scant evidence of strong feelings of distributive injustice, active rejection of the current system, or nostalgia for the distributional policies of the planned socialist era. In that sense ongoing debates about these issues should be regarded as another manifestation of the "growing pains" precipitated by market reforms, rather than harbingers of imminent political instability or social collapse.

Let us begin this summary by stating the principles of an *ideal* social order, according to the average Chinese citizen, that emerge from our survey results:

- There should be government-sponsored efforts to provide job and income guarantees to the poor and affirmative action policies to provide the disadvantaged with increased opportunities to succeed.

- There should be abundant opportunities for individuals and families to improve their livelihoods and social status and to enjoy the fruits of their success.
- As far as possible, there should be equal opportunity to succeed and prosper.
- Material advancement and success should be determined by merit factors, such as educational attainment, knowledge and skills, individual talent, and hard work, and not by nonmerit factors (not only external factors, such as prejudice, unequal opportunities, and personal connections, but also age, gender, family size, and household registration status).
- The pronounced divide between China's rural and urban citizens and the institutionalized discrimination against villagers and urban migrants are very unfair.
- Since individuals and families vary in their talents, diligence, and their cultivation and deployment of merit-based strategies for success, they will have unequal amounts of money and other resources. As long as such differences are based upon equal opportunity and merit-based pursuit of upward mobility, they are acceptable.
- There should not be any upper limit set on the incomes or other advantages that the upwardly mobile can enjoy, nor should there be a systematic government program to redistribute wealth from the rich to the poor (again, so long as wealth was obtained through equal, merit-based competition).
- It is acceptable for the rich to use their advantages to provide better lives for their families.
- However, those who hold positions of political power should not be entitled to special privileges or be able to use their positions to provide better lives for their families. Furthermore, they should be more concerned than they are now about the views of ordinary citizens on distributive justice issues.
- Despite the general acceptance of current inequalities, it is desirable not to allow income and other gaps to become too large nationally, as this could increase the likelihood of social instability.

As noted earlier, this summary of the views of Chinese citizens on the ideal social order differs greatly from the principles mandated during China's socialist era. Instead, it seems a generic formula for a market society supplemented by welfare-state guarantees for the poor and disadvantaged. An American or European citizen probably would agree with most of these same principles.[26]

At the same time, our survey reveals that to most respondents, the society in which they actually live differs from these ideals in several important ways. In particular, there is no adequate safety net of government-provided subsistence guarantees for the poor,[27] opportunities for social mobility are unequal, nonmerit factors play an important even if secondary role in access to opportunities, the politically powerful continue to enjoy privileges and special treatment, and no effective mechanism exists to prevent national income disparities from widening and provoking social turbulence.

However, this is the "glass-half-empty" version of the story, and we must also emphasize the ways in which the distributive glass is half-full in the eyes of most survey respondents. Upward mobility opportunities are seen as plentiful, individual merit factors are thought to play the dominant role in enabling individuals and families to better themselves, and no meaningful limits are perceived on upper incomes or on the ability of the rich to enjoy the rewards of their economic success. This mixed but generally upbeat picture provides the basis for our conclusion that most survey respondents see the gap between the ideal and the reality as acceptable and that they therefore consider the overall pattern of current inequalities to be more fair than unfair.

We temper this conclusion with three qualifications. First, the Chinese authorities' attempt to convince their citizens that current income gaps and competition for rewards are necessary and beneficial to society because they stimulate economic productivity has not been all that successful. As table 11.6 shows, some questions along these lines elicited almost as much disagreement as agreement, and many respondents who were uncertain settled for a neutral response. While the authorities have successfully counteracted the Maoist message that the pursuit of material success, upward mobility, and consumer goods is evil and socially harmful, they have had less luck in justifying and gaining popular acceptance of specific contemporary incentives and inequalities as means to productivity and economic growth. Because the latter claims inspire skepticism in the citizenry, China's leaders cannot count on public acceptance that specific current incentives and disparities are necessary and beneficial; in some instances they may even confront suspicion and anger, as in the cases of the privileges enjoyed by political elites and the mass layoffs of employees from state-owned enterprises.

The second qualification is that a majority of the population believes that a few specific features of current inequality patterns are unjust. The primary example is that most Chinese citizens feel that the current structures of discrimination against rural residents and urban migrants are unfair (see table 11.5). Even though urban migrants are generally the most vocal in condemning discrimination based upon China's *hukou* system, it is striking that even urbanites do not defend these practices. China's rural-urban divide, arguably the most important and extreme axis of inequality that currently exists in that society, is widely seen as fundamentally unjust.[28]

The third qualification to our conclusion that Chinese citizens broadly accept current patterns of inequality stems from the fact that we focus throughout this chapter on modal tendencies and majority responses to our survey questions. While the majority of survey respondents appeared to accept the status quo and to lack strong feelings of distributive injustice, it is also the case that for most of our attitude questions there was a sizable minority of respondents—generally 15–35 percent—who responded otherwise. So, for example, we can point to the following cases in which survey respondents expressed negative views on current inequalities:

- 26.1 percent of survey respondents predicted that the proportion of China's poor would increase in the coming five years
- 27.9 percent said that current inequalities conflicted with socialist principles
- 17.4 percent felt that dishonesty had a large or very large influence on who is rich in China
- 26 percent considered the unfair economic structure to have a large or very large influence on who is rich
- 29.1 percent said that it would be most fair to distribute income and wealth equally
- 33.8 percent thought the government should place upper limits on how much people could earn
- 27.6 percent believed it was unfair for the rich to obtain better health care for their families
- 26.5 percent did not agree that society benefits when business people are allowed to pursue profits
- 19.6 percent disagreed with the statement that great opportunities currently exist for ordinary people to improve their standards of living
- 34.4 percent said that talking about social justice was meaningless because the current system cannot be challenged or changed

To be sure, we cannot tell from these figures whether critical responses to a variety of specific questions cohere or not. Is it the same roughly 25 percent of our respondents, plus or minus, who see the current system as unjust across the board, or are these minority responses the product of shifting groups of respondents who offered critical views on certain specific questions and joined the majority in voicing positive responses to most other questions?

Regardless of the degree of coherence of such critical attitudes within our sample, these minority response patterns still give pause. If on most specific questions about distributive justice and injustice one-quarter or more of China's citizens see the current system as more unfair than fair, that is a sizable number of potentially angry and alienated individuals with which the government will have to contend. Since we are not talking of building an electoral majority in a still highly authoritarian China, and since the social protest activity that is seen as destabilizing does not originate from, or require, majority local sentiment, there are clearly more than enough disgruntled people in China to pose a potential threat to that stability. Mao Zedong himself observed in 1930 that "a single spark can start a prairie fire." So while it appears that a majority of Chinese citizens accept most aspects of current inequalities and are not outraged by the gaps between current realities and an ideal social order, majority sentiment by no means ensures that China will remain politically stable in the years to come.

How can we explain the apparent contradiction between the generally positive assessment our survey provides of Chinese popular attitudes toward inequality and distributive injustice issues and the prevailing view that China is becoming a social volcano? I would not claim that this is a simple matter of everyone else being wrong and our survey results being right. However, I do think that the social volcano scenario is dead wrong in certain respects. There is no basis for the claim that if income inequality rises above a certain level, this translates automatically into popular anger and the potential for social turmoil and political instability. What matters to people, both in China and in other societies, is not inequality per se but *inequity*—the sense that existing patterns of inequality that people observe in society and in their daily lives depart sharply from what they feel is deserved and fair. As our survey results show, a majority of Chinese citizens—but by no means all—feel that most elements (but again not all) of the current patterns of inequality and social mobility are basically fair. But if that is the case, how do we explain the rise in popular protests in recent years?

I believe that distributive injustice issues are only one possible source of popular discontent and probably not the most important. Some of the best recent studies of such popular protests do not contradict our survey results.[29] In most instances, local protests by workers, farmers, and others are touched off by unfair and abusive treatment by local officials, managers, and other authorities. These are not primarily distributive injustice issues, but matters of procedural injustice—people protest when they are treated badly by those in power locally and when they feel they cannot obtain redress through normal channels. In fact, such protest incidents may serve as testaments to the success of China's reformers and their ideology of meritocratic competition in a market-based system. Chinese protesters may feel that they should be able to improve their lot and achieve a better future in that system, but that greedy and corrupt local power-holders are blocking their way. Indeed, most such protests provide another kind of evidence of how ordinary Chinese broadly accept the current system, since protesters commonly appeal to higher levels of authority and the media in the expectation that interventions from above may provide redress. China's leaders are understandably only too eager to encourage this "if the emperor only knew . . ." syndrome—such an orientation reinforces both the central leadership's authority and the popular legitimacy of current patterns of inequality that they seek to promote.

Our survey leads us to conclude that there is broad general acceptance of the reformed, market-oriented, and increasingly unequal society that is China today, but this should not be interpreted as a Pollyanna view that everyone in China is satisfied with their lives or that China's leaders can relax and cease to worry about inequality and distributive injustice. There are numerous sources of popular discontent in China today, and many owe little or nothing to a rising Gini coefficient. Widespread social unrest and instability appear unlikely at present, but disgruntled individuals and groups abound, all battling a political structure that often responds poorly to popular concerns. In the years ahead, this combination may not produce a social volcano, but China will continue to be characterized more by "rocky stability" than by the harmony that its leaders seek to promote.

Notes

[1] To cite one example, in a 2006 article in *The New York Times* (October 12), China correspondent Joseph Kahn stated, "Because many people believe that wealth flows from access to power more than it does from talent or risk-taking, the wealth gap has incited outrage and is viewed as at least partly responsible for tens of thousands of mass protests around the country in recent years."

[2] Xinhua, "Survey of Chinese Officials' Opinions on Reform: Beijing Daily," *Xinhua News Bulletin,* November 29, 2004.

[3] Josephine Ma, "Wealth Gap Fueling Instability, Studies Warn," *South China Morning Post*, December 22, 2005.

[4] The 2004 survey was a collaborative effort in which I served as principal investigator and collaborated with Shen Mingming and Yang Ming at the Beijing University Research Center for Contemporary China. My research team included Albert Park (then at the University of Michigan), Wang Feng (University of California, Irvine), Jieming Chen (Texas A&M University, Kingsville), and Pierre Landry (Yale University), with assistance provided by Chunping Han, then a doctoral student at Harvard University. Using spatial probability sampling methods (see Pierre Landry and Mingming Shen, "Reaching Migrants in Survey Research: The Use of the Global Positioning System to Reduce Coverage Bias in China," *Political Analysis* 13 [2005]: 1–22), a nationally representative sample of 3,267 adults between ages 18 and 70 were interviewed in fall 2004. Since the sampling design involved stratification intended to increase the number of urban residents in the final sample, the descriptive figures presented in this chapter have been weighted to correct for urban oversampling and render figures that are representative of all Chinese adults. Many of the questions in our survey replicated those used to study attitudes toward inequality and distributive injustice in other societies, particularly the International Social Justice Project (ISJP) Surveys carried out in the 1990s in several transitional societies in Eastern Europe. See James Kluegel, David Mason, and Bernd Wegener, *Social Justice and Political Change*, (New York: Academic Press, 1995); and David Mason and James Kluegel, *Marketing Democracy: Changing Opinion about Inequality and Politics in East Central Europe*, (Lanham, MD: Rowman & Littlefield, 2000).

[5] Poor people were defined in the question as "those who cannot support basic living conditions like food, clothing, and housing," while rich people were defined as "those who can pretty much buy anything for themselves."

[6] Here our question relates to a debate that cannot be openly expressed in China under current conditions: Have the economic reforms since 1978 transformed China into a capitalist society, or should it still be considered a (market) socialist state? Clearly the Chinese authorities want to foster the impression that they are developing a form of market socialism, not restoring capitalism. The pattern of responses to this question suggests that the majority of Chinese citizens are willing to give the authorities the benefit of the doubt on this score.

[7] There is a logical link missing from this statement, since presumably current inequalities would not undermine social stability unless the poor and disadvantaged feel their treatment is unjust and are therefore inclined to join protests and other potentially disruptive activities. However, our respondents did not have to feel personally that current inequalities are inherently unjust in order to recognize that others might view them as such. On that basis, our respondents may have concluded that current inequalities are excessive and undesirable, more on the grounds of social instability than social injustice.

[8] In each list there is one trait (bad luck, good luck) that cannot be easily characterized as conveying either individual merit or external influences. It turns out that in their pattern of responses, our interviewees treated the luck questions as reflecting more external attribution than individual merit. To be precise, it might also be noted that two traits in the list of attributions for wealth (dishonesty and having personal connections) might be seen as reflecting the "negative merit" of individuals, rather than simply the unfairness of the external environment.

[9] The two lists of traits are not exact parallels, so we don't know how respondents would have ranked an *absence* of personal connections as an explanation of current poverty.

[10] A somewhat similar view is conveyed by the pattern of responses to another question (not displayed in the table) in which respondents were asked to give their views on the statement, "Whether a person gets rich or suffers poverty is his/her own responsibility." Responses varied, but 46.3 percent expressed varying degrees of agreement with this statement, while only 28.9 percent expressed disagreement.

[11] We posed another set of questions related to the fairness versus unfairness of current inequalities. Respondents were asked to say how much influence each of a list of thirteen traits *should* have on a person's salary, and then how much influence they thought each of those same thirteen traits *actually* has in determining a person's salary. The thirteen traits were educational level, adverse working conditions, individual effort, size of family, job responsibilities, seniority, being male, contributions to the work unit, ties with superiors, having personal connections (*renshi ren, you luzi*), having urban household registration, age, and having specialized technical skills. The traits that respondents thought *should* have most influence on a person's salary were (1) technical skills, (2) educational level, (3) individual effort, (4) having personal connections, (5) contributions to the work unit, and (6) job responsibilities. In terms of their *actual* influence on a person's salary, respondents identified (1) having personal connections, (2) technical skills, (3) educational level, (4) ties with superiors, (5) individual effort, (6) contributions to work unit, and (7) job responsibilities. In other words, the main difference perceived between what should and what actually does determine individual salaries is that the two *guanxi* traits (having personal connections, ties with superiors) received more influence than they should and thereby rose to the top of the rank ordering. All of the other traits, which involve individual merit factors, had very similar rankings in the "should" and "actual" responses (details not shown here). In other words, respondents felt that for the most part, the traits that ought to inform individual salaries are in fact emphasized. The major exceptions were that

connections with superiors and the ability to use personal relationships play a larger role than they should, with the latter viewed more favorably than the former.

[12] Our questionnaire included a series of questions that asked respondents to compare their current standards of living with a range of reference groups, including relatives, former classmates, coworkers, and neighbors, as well as more distant comparison groups—in the local city or county, in the province, and in the entire nation. Generally, about 60 percent responded that they had about the same living standard as their immediate reference groups, while about 25 percent said they were below that level, and about 15 percent above. Not surprisingly, in the more distant comparisons, between 50 and 60 percent said they were worse off, only about 35 percent said they were at about the same level, and less than 10 percent reported that they were better off.

[13] These opinions are congruent with the fact that when asked what traits should influence how much salary an employee is paid, respondents ranked family size last out of the thirteen traits listed in endnote 11.

[14] It should be noted that the egalitarianism of the Mao era, particularly during the Cultural Revolution, consisted primarily of measures to limit the incomes, bonuses, and other advantages of intellectuals, officials, and other advantaged groups, rather than to provide income and job guarantees for the poor. See Martin K. Whyte, "Destratification and Restratification in China," in G. Berreman, ed., *Social Inequality: Comparative and Developmental Approaches*, (New York: Academic Press, 1981).

[15] In the socialist era, of course, those with higher incomes could not readily translate this advantage into better housing, education, or medical care for their families, whereas those with high ranks and important political positions received systematic advantages for themselves and their families. Evidently the legacy of the political elite's special privileges under socialism remains a sore point for many Chinese.

[16] A substantial literature documents the institutionalized discrimination that China's rural *hukou* holders have experienced, both under Mao and in the reform era. See, for example, Kam Wing Chan, *Cities with Invisible Walls*, (New York: Oxford Univ. Press, 1994); Dorothy Solinger, *Contesting Citizenship in Urban China: Peasant Migrants, the State, and the Logic of the Market*, (Berkeley, CA: Univ. of California Press, 1999); Li Zhang, *Strangers in the City: Reconfigurations of Space, Power, and Social Networks within China's Floating Population*, (Stanford, CA: Stanford Univ. Press, 2001); Fei-ling Wang , *Organizing through Division and Exclusion: China's Hukou System*, (Stanford, CA: Stanford Univ. Press, 2005); and Martin K. Whyte, ed. *One Country, Two Societies: Rural-Urban Inequality in Contemporary China*, (Cambridge, MA: Harvard Univ. Press, 2010).

[17] See Feng Wang, "Boundaries of Inequality: Perceptions of Distributive Justice among Urbanites, Migrants, and Peasants," in Whyte, *One Country, Two Societies,*, an analysis based on the same survey data. Generally the responses of rural and urban residents are similar, with migrants adopting a slightly more critical perspective (details not shown here).

[18] See Kingsley Davis and Wilbert Moore, "Some Principles of Stratification," *American Sociological Review* 10 (1945): 242–49; Kingsley Davis, "Some Principles of Stratification: A Critical Analysis: Reply," *American Sociological Review* 18 (1953): 394–97.

[19] The notion that differential rewards serve a positive function is not unique to market-based or capitalist societies. In most socialist societies as well, the characterization of socialist distribution as involving rewards "to each according to his contributions" was used to justify a wide range of material incentives and hierarchically graded benefits and privileges from the time of Lenin onward. Indeed, Polish sociologists in the 1980s argued

that socialist societies were more meritocratic than capitalist societies, since salaries and other rewards could be more tightly calibrated to individual training, responsibility, and contributions without the complicating factors of private property ownership and inherited wealth. See Wlodzimierz Wesolowski and Tadeusz Krauze, "Socialist Society and the Meritocratic Principle of Remuneration," in Gerald D. Berreman, ed., *Social Inequality: Comparative and Developmental Approaches*, (New York: Academic Press, 1981). However, after the collapse of socialism in Eastern Europe, Weselowski acknowledged that socialist societies such as his own, Poland, were more meritocratic in theory than in reality. See Wlodzimierz Weselowski and E. Wnuk-Lipinski, "Transformation of Social Order and Legitimation of Inequalities," in W. Connor, ed., *The Polish Road from Socialism: The Economics, Sociology, and Politics of Transition*, (Armonk, NY: M. E. Sharpe, 1992). It was precisely this "functionalist" thinking that led Mao to condemn the Soviet Union and its East European satellite regimes as "revisionist" and to his attempt to curtail the use of material incentives throughout Chinese society between 1966 and 1976.

Given this legacy, Deng and his reformist colleagues had to overcome condemnation of material incentives in order to justify their official approval of incentives and income differentials. See Whyte, "Destratification and Restratification in China." In the process of market reforms, of course, they went beyond the "rewards proportional to contributions" formula of socialist societies, since increasingly China's income differentials are the product of competition in revived markets and even the power of privately owned property and not simply the result of differentiated wage and benefit scales supervised by the bureaucrats of a socialist planned economy. Ivan Szelenyi contended that in the context of a centrally planned socialist society, allowing secondary distribution via markets could actually *reduce* the considerable inequalities generated by bureaucratic allocation. However, once markets replace bureaucratic allocation as the basic distributive mechanism, as they have in China since the 1980s, they seem to lose this counterbalancing and equalizing role. See Ivan Szelenyi, "Social Inequalities in State Socialist Redistributive Economies," *International Journal of Comparative Sociology* 19 (1978): 63–87; and Ivan Szelenyi, *Urban Inequalities under State Socialism*, (New York: Oxford Univ. Press, 1983). Some would even argue that China today displays the "worst of both worlds" (capitalism and socialism) by enabling both the rich *and* the powerful to convert their advantages and resources into privileged lives for their families.

[20] The ISJP surveys were conducted in 1991 in Bulgaria, the Czech Republic, Estonia, Germany (East and West), Hungary, Japan, the Netherlands, Poland, Russia, Slovenia, the United Kingdom, and the United States. The follow-up round of the ISJP surveys was conducted in 1996, but only in five East European postsocialist locales: the former East Germany, Hungary, Russia, Bulgaria, and the Czech Republic. In our comparative analyses we have focused on the 1996 surveys in Russia, Bulgaria, Hungary, the Czech Republic, and the former East Germany, and on the 1991 surveys in Poland, the United States, West Germany, the United Kingdom, and Japan. The ISJP data are publicly available at www. butler.edu/isjp, and I thank David Mason, the principal investigator of the ISJP surveys, for his assistance in interpreting the ISJP archived data. The detailed results of these comparisons are reported in chapter 4 of Martin K. Whyte, *Myth of the Social Volcano: Perceptions of Inequality and Distributive Injustice in Contemporary China*. (Stanford, CA: Stanford Univ. Press, 2010).

[21] See Whyte, *Myth of the Social Volcano*, chapters 5–9.

[22] See the evidence reviewed in Chunping Han, "Rural-Urban Cleavages in Perceptions

of Inequality in Contemporary China," (Ph.D diss., Department of Sociology, Harvard University, 2009).

[23] See Chunping Han and Martin K. Whyte, "Social Contours of Distributive Injustice Feelings in Contemporary China," in D. Davis and Feng Wang, eds., *Creating Wealth and Poverty in Post-Socialist China*, (Stanford, CA: Stanford Univ. Press, 2009).

[24] See Han, "Rural-Urban Cleavages;" Han and Whyte, "Social Contours of Distributive Injustice Feelings;" and Wang, "Boundaries of Inequality."

[25] In addition, the household responsibility system divisions of village land after 1978 and, in many villages, subsequent local land redistributions (the latter in direct violation of state policy) have fostered relatively equal property stakes across families within any particular village. This differs dramatically from the way reforms in urban areas have sharply differentiated families' property endowments (mainly in the form of housing, not land), according to the industries and work units with which they were affiliated. If farmers consider inequalities on the local rather than the national scale, their tendency to see rural property endowments and mobility opportunities as more equal and fair than do urbanites has some objective basis in fact.

[26] James Kluegel and Eliot Smith, *Beliefs about Inequality: Americans' Views of What Is and What Ought to Be*, (New York: Aldine de Gruyter, 1986).

[27] In recent years a new system of minimum income subsidies (*dibao*) has been introduced in Chinese cities. But even this system does not provide guaranteed jobs, nor is it clear if the incomes provided are sufficient to reliably meet basic subsistence needs of recipient families. In any case the majority of the population—migrants and those living in the countryside—have not been similarly covered. In early 2008, however, Chinese media reported an effort underway to begin to implement a rural *dibao* system.

[28] The general consensus is that *hukou*-based discrimination is unjust, but it is questionable whether this particular injustice can serve as the basis for protest activity and political instability. The durability of *hukou*-based discrimination, despite increasing public recognition of its unfairness, is one of the puzzles explored in Whyte, *One Country, Two Societies*.

[29] See Thomas Bernstein and Xiaobo Lu, *Taxation without Representation in Contemporary China* (Cambridge: Cambridge Univ. Press, 2003); Ching Kwan Lee, *Against the Law: Labor Protests in China's Rustbelt and Sunbelt*, (Berkeley, CA: Univ. of California Press, 2007); and Kevin O'Brien and Lianjiang Li, *Rightful Resistance in Rural China*, (Cambridge: Cambridge Univ. Press, 2006).

INDEX

government officials, 117
antibiotics, overprescribing of, 248
anticorruption campaigns. *See*
 corruption
Anti-Rightist Campaign, 1957, 136
Assessment of Urban Environmental
 Quality program, 281, 282
asset stripping, 15–17
Australia, labor costs, 41
avian influenza, 229

B

bankruptcy
 impact on workers, 11
 state-supported, 19, 25n56
banks, state, 20
Bao Village, election process, 173–75,
 177, 181–82
"barefoot doctors," 233
basic health-care services, 258, 262
Beijing, Beijing area
 agricultural markets, early 1980s,
  60
 air pollution in, 277–78, 290
 corruption among government
  officials, 117
 environmental protection policies,
  296n45
 agricultural markets, 62–63,
  72–74, 76, 80
 intervention in land-use decisions,
  94
 private rice wholesalers, 71
 soybean price trends, 70–71
 See also urban areas; urbanization
Bi, X., 79
birth-permit applications (*jihua
 shengyu zhibiao*), 197–98, 204
black carbon emissions, 301n103
"black children" (*hei haizi*), 193
Boulevard Village, election process,
 172–73
Brandt, Loren, 44, 46
Brazil, labor costs, 41
bribery cases, prosecution of, 122,
 139–40n30. *See also* corruption

C

cadres, local
 changing power of, 186
 as constraint on corporate
  restructuring, 9
 environmental regulations
  enforcement, 287
 family planning policy
  enforcement, 212
 participation in village elections,
  148–49, 153–56, 170
 pressures on for economic growth,
  17–18
 responsiveness to villager
  demands, 180–81
Cai, Yongshun, 10, 12, 41–42
Canada, public-contract model of
 health-care financing, 256
cancer rates, 234–37
"cap and trade" activities, 281–82
capital
 corporate restructuring in, 9
 human, 106, 109, 233–34, 253
 and industrial development
  strategies, 34
 limited, alternatives to, xviii, 110
 private, sources of, 7, 14–15
capital punishment, for corruption
 trends over time, 120
 Zheng Xiaoyu, 117
carbon dioxide (CO_2) emissions, 273
cardiovascular disease rates, 234–37
Carter, Michael, 100–101, 103
Center for Chinese Agricultural
 Policy
 fertilizer procurement survey, 74
 land reallocation study, 91–93
Central and Eastern Europe (CEE),
 health-care system reforms, 250
central government
 control over restructuring process, 8
 corruption trends, 117, 122–23
 influence over local land
  reallocations, 91–92
 limits of, for addressing health and
  environmental needs, xxiii
 and market reforms

soybean price trends, 67–68
Jin, Songqing
on agricultural efficiency and
rental markets, 107
analysis by, overview, xviii
on land-reallocation patterns, 92
on measuring productive
efficiency, 90
job creation. *See* employment
joint ventures, and worker layoffs, 11
judicial system, legal system
corruption trials, 119–21
criminal code, 120, 128, 136
Criminal Procedure Law, 139n27
data from caseloads, 127–28
jurisdictional limits, 121
reconstruction and reforms of, xiv,
136
sentencing guidelines, 124
See also corruption

K
Kelliher, Daniel, 143
Kelon Electrical Holdings, Co., Ltd., 6
Korea, South, labor costs, 12, 41
medical care, 245

L
labeling laws, 282
labor force
annual surveys, 28
commitment to retaining, 13–14
demographic factors, 34–36
growth in, 207–8, 213–14
impact of economic reforms on,
10–13
and job-creation efforts, xvii, 34
job losses, 11–12, 18, 23–24n34
participation rates, 31–34
productivity, 41
rural, inefficient uses of, 100
shareholding by, 14–15, 17–18
social insurance programs, 28,
49–53
surplus labor supply
debates about, xvii
estimates of size of, 24n50
and labor shortages, 27

older workers, 42
relationship to labor markets,
19
in rural areas, 38, 41–42
and wage growth, 35–42
young, access to social insurance
programs, 50
See also employment; layoffs;
unemployment
Labor Law, 1994, 50–51
labor markets
impact of market reforms on,
10–11, 28–29, 34
impact of rural to urban
migration, 35
impact of unskilled and surplus
labor supply, xvii, 19
integration of, 43–48
and labor costs, regional
comparisons, 40–41
relationship to land markets, 108,
110–11
land markets, farm land rental
and agricultural productivity/
efficiency, 100–102, 107–11
analysis of, data sources and
methods, 89–90
household head participation in,
105
impact of decollectivization,
xviii–xix
impact on farm incomes, 87, 109
labor markets and, 110–11
land-reallocation patterns, 100
land-use decisions, 94–96, 109
quota requirements and, 111n10
rental market characteristics, xviii,
87, 96–98, 107
tenure security and, 89–93, 101–5,
108–10
transaction costs, 101
wages and labor shortages, 27
See also land policies
land policies
and agricultural productivity/
efficiency, 87
analysis of, data sources and
methods, 88–89

debates about property rights,
xviii–xix
heterogeneous sources for, 99
and income inequality, 332n25
land seizures, 170
land-transfer rights, 88–89, 96,
99, 108
and motor vehicle use, 289–90
Lang Xianping, 5, 6
Lau, L. J., 238–40
Law Yearbook, 127
layoffs
and dual-track reform approach,
11–12
internal retirement and, 10–11
use of severance packages/buyout
schemes for, 18
by state-owned enterprises, 23–
24n34
Lee, C. K., 10
legal system. *See* judicial system, legal
system
Leninist political systems and market
reforms, xiii–xvi
Lewisian curve, and labor shortages,
27
Liaoning Province
corruption-related tips from,
140n32
crop selection and land-use
restrictions, 94–95
household investment behavior
and land tenure in, 101–3
land policy and management,
88–89
land reallocations, 91
maize price trends, 64–65, 69–70
Li Lulu, 145
Lin, Justin Yifu, 77
Li Rongrong, 19–20
Liu, Yuanli, 251, 254
Liu, Z., 250
livestock production, 79
local elections. *See* elections, village
local government
Circular Economy Promotion Law
(2009), 287
control over land use and

allocations, 94–95, 109
control over SOEs, 15–17
environmental regulations
enforcement, 280, 283–84, 299n70
family planning policy
enforcement, 205, 207–8, 211–
12, 219n79
financing and expenditures for
social insurance programs, 51
growing legitimacy of, xxi
handling of dissent by, 9
health-related incentives for, 260
incentives for promoting
privatization, 9
performance evaluations, 17–18,
284, 286–87
role in corporate restructuring
process, 8
social insurance responsibilities, 49

M

maize
from Dailan, 83n39
market integration, 64–71
state procurement system for, 61
male children, preference for, 191–92
malfeasance, prosecution for, 122
malnutrition
among children, 251
in rural areas, 234
managers
buyouts by, 14–15
share ownership
and commitment to retaining
workers, 13–14
corruption and windfall profits,
xvi, 14
Manion, Melanie, 135–36
manufacturing sector
and benefits received under, 9–10
drug manufacture, 257
industrialization and, 199
labor costs
cross-country comparisons,
40–41
wages and education level, 47
labor-force participation rates,
209, 213

intervention in village elections, 170, 173–75, 177
land policies enforcement responsibility, 91, 99
social stability as priority of, 179
township health centers (THCs), 246
township hospitals
enhanced government support for, 257
occupancy rates, 245–46
traders, private, and agricultural competitiveness, 60–62, 71
transaction costs
and agricultural competitiveness, 76
inflation and, 83n34
for land-rental markets, 101
transformational recessions, 250
Transparency International (TI), on corruption levels in China, 117–18, 134
transportation, use of land for, 279
transportation gradients
agricultural markets, 67, 76
analyzing, data and approaches, 64, 84n40
and market efficiency, 70–71
trials. See judicial system, legal system
Tsai, Lily, xx–xxi

U

unauthorized births, 192–93
unemployment
causes of, 28–29
education and, 32–34
estimating, data sources for, 29
gender/age and, 31–32
hidden, from surplus labor supply, 19
internal retirement and, 10–11
and job creation efforts, 29
Park's analysis of, overview, xvi–xvii
in urban areas, 27, 29–31
and urban poverty, 49
unemployment insurance programs
inequities in access to, 28
rates of participation in, 49–50

United Kingdom
attitudes toward income gaps, 321
National Health Service (NHS), 230
United Nations Development Programme (UNDP), 191
United States
attitudes toward income gaps, 321
corruption in
comparison with China, 134
punishment for, 125, 139n28
sentencing for, 141n42
Environmental Protection Agency, 296n43
Federal Bureau of Investigation, 125
health-care financing in, 256
labor costs, 41
transportation gradients, 70–71
universal coverage, as goal of health reform, 262–63
unskilled workers
and industrial development strategies, 34
wage increases, 37–38
urban areas
agricultural prices, 60, 61
"consumer class" in, 276–77, 294n25
as democratization, 43–44
gender imbalance in, 192
health-care services, 246
health insurance coverage, 256, 257
informal employment, 52
migration rates, 46, 48
minimum living standards subsidies, 55n36
population growth, 275
social insurance programs, 49–51
unemployment and poverty in, 29–31, 49
urbanization
energy use, 294–95n26
environmental degradation and, xxiii, 274, 275, 292
and fertility declines, 200–204
and health status changes, 234

About the Contributors

Fang Cai, professor and director of the Institute for Population and Labor Economics of the Chinese Academy of Social Sciences, is well known as a leading expert on labor issues in China and has advised China's top leaders on labor policy. He is a member of the Standing Committee of the 11th National People's Congress of China. He has published widely in international and Chinese journals on China's labor-market development. His institute is frequently called upon to conduct analyses and make policy recommendations to government policymakers, especially those in the Ministry of Labor, as well as international organizations such as the World Bank and the International Labour Organization.

Klaus Deininger is a lead economist in the rural development group of the Development Economics Group, an integral part of Louis Berger International, one of the largest multidisciplinary consulting organizations in the world. His areas of research focus on income and asset inequality and their relationship to poverty reduction and growth; access to land; land markets and land reform and their impact on household welfare and agricultural productivity; land tenure and its impact on investment, including environmental sustainability; and capacity-building (including the use of quantitative and qualitative methods) for policy analysis and evaluation, mainly in Africa, Central America, and East and South Asia.

Yang Du is professor and director of the Division of Labor and Human Capital at the Institute of Population and Labor Economics, Chinese Academy of Social Sciences. He is a labor economist whose research focuses on labor-market issues, poverty, and human capital in China. He has published widely in both domestic and international journals and consulted for international organizations, including the World Bank, the Organisation for Economic Co-operation and Development, and the United Nations Development Programme.

Karen Eggleston joined the Walter H. Shorenstein Asia-Pacific Research Center in the summer of 2007 to lead the center's Asia Health Policy Program. She is also a fellow at the Stanford Center for Health Policy. She holds a B.A. in Asian studies from Dartmouth College, an M.A. in economics and another in Asian studies from the University of Hawaii, and a Ph.D. in public policy from Harvard University (completed in 1999). Eggleston studied in China for two years and was a Fulbright scholar in South Korea. In 2004 she was a consultant to the World Bank on health-service delivery in China. Eggleston has been a research associate at the China Academy of Health Policy at Peking University, Beijing, since 2003, and an adjunct professor at Xi'an Jiaotong University, Xi'an, since 2008.

Jikun Huang is the founder and director of the Center for Chinese Agricultural Policy (CCAP) of the Chinese Academy of Sciences, and a professor at the Institute of Geographical Sciences and Natural Resources Research. He is also vice president of the Chinese Association of Agricultural Economics and the Chinese Association of Agro-Technology Economics, and serves as a member of International Policy Council and a member of Global Agenda Council on Food Security (World Economic Forum). Huang received his B.S. degree from Nanjing Agricultural University in 1984 and his Ph.D. in economics from the University of the Philippines at Los Banos in 1990. His research covers a wide range of issues on China's agricultural and rural development, including agricultural R&D policy, water resource economics, price and marketing, food consumption, poverty, and trade policy. He has received the Outstanding Scientific Progress Award from the Ministry of Agriculture four times. He was honored as one of China's top ten outstanding youth scientists in 2002, and received the Outstanding Achievement Award for Overseas Returning Chinese in 2003, as well as the Outstanding Contribution Award on Management Science. He has published more than 120 papers in refereed international journals, including 2 research reports in *Science* and 1 paper in *Nature*, and about 160 papers in Chinese journals. He is the coauthor of fourteen books.

Songqing Jin is an assistant professor in the Department of Agricultural, Food, and Resource Economics at Michigan State University (MSU). A significant portion of his research is concerned with rural land-tenure, land-market, and land-reform issues, mainly in East and South Asia, and East and South Africa. His other research interests concern issues related to agricultural R&D and agricultural technology, rural nonfarm development, rural labor migration, and the economics of gender inequality in informal labor markets and political positions. Before joining the MSU faculty in fall 2007, he was a research economist at the World Bank. Jin received his Ph.D. in agricultural and resource economics from the University of California, Davis, and his B.S. degree from Zhejiang Agricultural University.

Ethan Michelson is associate professor of sociology and East Asian Languages and cultures, and associate professor of sociology and law at Indiana University–Bloomington. Born in Toronto, he received his B.A. in East Asian studies and sociology from McGill University. He holds an M.A. and Ph.D. in sociology from the University of Chicago. His research on Chinese lawyers and social conflict in rural China has been published in a variety of disciplinary and area studies journals, including the *American Sociological Review*, the *American Journal of Sociology*, the *China Quarterly*, *Law & Society Review*, *Social Problems*, and the *Journal of Conflict Resolution*. His research has been funded by the Ford Foundation, the National Science Foundation, the Social Science Research Council, the U.S. Department of Education (Fulbright-Hays), the American Bar Foundation, and the Hopkins-Nanjing Center.

360

Jean C. Oi is the William Haas Professor in Chinese Politics and a senior fellow at the Freeman Spogli Institute for International Studies at Stanford University. She also directs the Stanford China Program at the Walter H. Shorenstein Asia-Pacific Research Center. Her work focuses on comparative politics, with special expertise on Chinese political economy. Oi's books include *State and Peasant in Contemporary China: The Political Economy of Village Government* (1989); *Rural China Takes Off: Institutional Foundations of Economic Reform* (1999); *Property Rights and Economic Reform in China* (1999, coedited with Andrew Walder); and *At the Crossroads of Empires: Middlemen, Social Networks and State-building in Republican Shanghai* (2007, coedited with Nara Dillon). Currently, Oi is writing a book on the role and evolution of the state in China's corporate restructuring and continuing her research on rural China, especially finance and governance.

Leonard Ortolano is UPS Foundation Professor of Civil Engineering at Stanford University. He is a specialist in environmental and water resources planning, with a focus on the design and implementation of environmental policies and programs in the United States and developing countries. He and his students have been doing research on environmental policy implementation in China for more than two decades. One reflection of that work is the monograph, coauthored with Xiaoying Ma, *Environmental Regulation in China: Institutions, Enforcement, and Compliance*. His textbook on *Environmental Regulation and Impact Assessment* has been translated into Mandarin and is used in Chinese universities.

Albert Park is a reader in economics at the University of Oxford; previously he was associate professor in the department of economics at the University of Michigan. He is a development economist who has published widely on China's labor-market and poverty issues. He has codirected several large-scale household survey projects—including the China Urban Labor Survey (3 waves), the Gansu Survey of Children and Families (3 waves), and the China Health and Retirement Longitudinal Study—and has consulted frequently for the World Bank, where he has served as lead international consultant for the most recent World Bank China Poverty Assessment Report.

Scott Rozelle holds the Helen Farnsworth Endowed Professorship at Stanford University and is senior fellow and professor in the Food Security and Environment Program and the Walter H. Shorenstein Asia-Pacific Research Center at the Freeman Spogli Institute for International Studies. Rozelle received his B.S. from the University of California, Berkeley, and his M.S. and Ph.D. from Cornell University. Before arriving at Stanford, Rozelle was a professor at the University of California (1998–2007) and an assistant professor in the Food Research Institute and Department of Economics at Stanford University (1990–1998).

Rozelle's research focuses almost exclusively on China and is concerned with three general themes: (1) agricultural policy, including the supply, demand, and trade of agricultural projects; (2) issues involving rural resources, especially the management of water, the forests, and cultivated land; and (3) the economics of poverty, with an emphasis on the economics of education and health. He is the codirector of the Rural Education Action Project (REAP), a set of studies that seek to evaluate China's new education and health programs and to have an impact on policy. In the past several years his papers have been published in top academic journals, including *Science, Nature, American Economic Review*, and the *Journal of Economic Literature*. He is fluent in Chinese and has established a research program that has close working ties with several Chinese collaborators and policymakers. He is the chair of the International Advisory Board of the Center for Chinese Agricultural Policy.

Rozelle has received numerous honors and awards in recognition of his outstanding achievements outside and inside China. He was the 2000 Chancellor Fellow at the University of California, Davis, an award given each year to one of the university's outstanding professors. In 2007 he was made a fellow of the American Agricultural Economics Association, the highest honor in the association. During the same year, in China, Rozelle won the inaugural Chinese Academy of Science Collaboration Award for Science Research. In 2008 he became a Yangtse Scholar (Changjiang Xuezhe) in Renmin University of China (an award equivalent to that of senior Fulbright scholar). As a Changjiang Scholar, he has had the privilege of teaching and conducting research at Renmin University between 2008 and 2011. In 2008 he was awarded the Friendship Award by Chinese Premier Wen Jiabao, the highest honor that can be bestowed on a foreigner. In 2009 it was announced that Rozelle will also receive the National Science & Technology Research Collaboration Award, a prize given by the State Council to a limited number of academics for their contributions to China's science and technology research.

Rozelle is an adjunct professor at five Chinese universities (including Peking University, Renmin University, and Zhejiang University) and four universities outside of China, including the University of California, Davis.

Lily L. Tsai is associate professor of political science at MIT. Her research focuses on issues of accountability, governance, and state-society relations. She has published a book, *Accountability Without Democracy: Solidary Groups and Public Goods Provision in Rural China* (Cambridge Studies on Comparative Politics, Cambridge Univ. Press, 2007), as well as articles in the *American Political Science Review*, the *China Quarterly*, and the *China Journal*.

Andrew G. Walder is the Denise O'Leary and Kent Thiry Professor, School of Humanities and Sciences, Stanford University, where he teaches in the department of sociology. He is also a senior fellow in the Freeman Spogli Institute of International Studies and an associate of the Walter H. Shorenstein Asia-

Pacific Research Center. Among other publications, he is the author of *Fractured Rebellion: The Beijing Red Guard Movement* (Harvard Univ. Press, 2009).

Andrew Wedeman is associate professor of political science at the University of Nebraska, Lincoln, where he is also the director of Asian studies. From 2006 to 2008, he taught at the Hopkins Nanjing Center for Sino-American Studies. His research focuses on the political economy of reform in China and he is currently finishing a book examining the "double paradox" of rapid growth and intensifying corruption in post-Mao China. His recent publications include *From Mao to Market: Rent Seeking, Local Protectionism, and Marketization in China* (Cambridge Univ. Press, 2003) as well as articles in the *China Quarterly*, the *Journal of Contemporary China*, and *China Review*.

Martin K. Whyte received his B.A. from Cornell University and M.A. and Ph.D. degrees from Harvard University. He taught at the University of Michigan from 1970 to 1994, at George Washington University from 1994 to 2000, and returned to Harvard as a faculty member in 2000. He specializes in the study of grassroots social organization and social change in the People's Republic of China and has two books forthcoming reflecting his recent work on inequality there: *One Country, Two Societies: Rural-Urban Inequality in China* (editor, Harvard Univ. Press) and *Myth of the Social Volcano: Perceptions of Inequality and Distributive Injustice in Contemporary China* (Stanford Univ. Press).

Linxiu Zhang is a professor and deputy director at the Center for Chinese Agricultural Policy, Institute of Geographical Sciences and Natural Resources Research, Chinese Academy of Sciences. She obtained her Ph.D. from Reading University (UK). Her research interests include rural poverty, rural labor-market development, community governance, public investments, and the economics of rural education and health care.

Xueguang Zhou is a professor of sociology and a senior fellow at the Freeman Spogli Institute for International Studies at Stanford University. For the past five years, he has been working on an ethnographic study of rural governance in China, in which he adopts a microscopic approach to understand how peasants, village cadres, and local governments interact and search for solutions to emerging problems and challenges in their everyday lives, and how institutions are created, reinforced, altered, and recombined in response to these problems. He is now working on a series of papers that summarize findings from this project. He is also involved in a research project that examines bureaucratic behaviors in policy implementation, incentive design, and the rise of the bureaucratic state in China.

Recent and Forthcoming Publications of the Walter H. Shorenstein Asia-Pacific Research Center

Books (distributed by the Brookings Institution Press)

Rafiq Dossani, Daniel C. Sneider, and Vikram Sood. *Does South Asia Exist? Prospects for Regional Integration in South Asia.* Stanford, CA: Walter H. Shorenstein Asia-Pacific Research Center, forthcoming 2010.

Karen Eggleston, ed. *Prescribing Cultures and Pharmaceutical Policy in the Asia-Pacific.* Stanford, CA: Walter H. Shorenstein Asia-Pacific Research Center, 2009.

Donald A. L. Macintyre, Daniel C. Sneider, and Gi-Wook Shin, eds. *First Drafts of Korea: The U.S. Media and Perceptions of the Last Cold War Frontier.* Stanford, CA: Walter H. Shorenstein Asia-Pacific Research Center, 2009.

Steven Reed, Kenneth Mori McElwain, and Kay Shimizu, eds. *Political Change in Japan: Electoral Behavior, Party Realignment, and the Koizumi Reforms.* Stanford, CA: Walter H. Shorenstein Asia-Pacific Research Center, 2009.

Donald K. Emmerson. *Hard Choices: Security, Democracy, and Regionalism in Southeast Asia.* Stanford, CA: Walter H. Shorenstein Asia-Pacific Research Center, 2008.

Henry S. Rowen, Marguerite Gong Hancock, and William F. Miller, eds. *Greater China's Quest for Innovation.* Stanford, CA: Walter H. Shorenstein Asia-Pacific Research Center, 2008.

Gi-Wook Shin and Daniel C. Sneider, eds. *Cross Currents: Regionalism and Nationalism in Northeast Asia.* Stanford, CA: Walter H. Shorenstein Asia-Pacific Research Center, 2007.

Stella R. Quah, ed. *Crisis Preparedness: Asia and the Global Governance of Epidemics.* Stanford, CA: Walter H. Shorenstein Asia-Pacific Research Center, 2007.

Philip W. Yun and Gi-Wook Shin, eds. *North Korea: 2005 and Beyond*. Stanford, CA:Walter H. Shorenstein Asia-Pacific Research Center, 2006.

Jongryn Mo and Daniel I. Okimoto, eds. *From Crisis to Opportunity: Financial Globalization and East Asian Capitalism*. Stanford, CA: Walter H. Shorenstein Asia-Pacific Research Center, 2006.

Michael H. Armacost and Daniel I. Okimoto, eds. *The Future of America's Alliances in Northeast Asia*. Stanford, CA: Walter H. Shorenstein Asia-Pacific Research Center, 2004.

Henry S. Rowen and Sangmok Suh, eds. *To the Brink of Peace: New Challenges in Inter-Korean Economic Cooperation and Integration*. Stanford, CA: Walter H. Shorenstein Asia-Pacific Research Center, 2001.

Studies of the Walter H. Shorenstein Asia-Pacific Research Center
(published with Stanford University Press)

Jean Oi and Nara Dillon, eds. *At the Crossroads of Empires: Middlemen, Social Networks, and State-building in Republican Shanghai*. Stanford, CA: Stanford University Press, 2007.

Henry S. Rowen, Marguerite Gong Hancock, and William F. Miller, eds. *Making IT: The Rise of Asia in High Tech*. Stanford, CA: Stanford University Press, 2006.

Gi-Wook Shin. *Ethnic Nationalism in Korea: Genealogy, Politics, and Legacy*. Stanford, CA:Stanford University Press, 2006.

Andrew Walder, Joseph Esherick, and Paul Pickowicz, eds. *The Chinese Cultural Revolution as History*. Stanford, CA: Stanford University Press, 2006.

Rafiq Dossani and Henry S. Rowen, eds. *Prospects for Peace in South Asia*. Stanford, CA: Stanford University Press, 2005.

DATE DUE

FEB 1 0 2011	
FEB 1 0 2012	
OCT 1 0 2014	